# LONGMAN
# KEYSTONE
## E

**Anna Uhl Chamot**

**John De Mado**

**Sharroky Hollie**

PEARSON
Longman

Pearson Education, 10 Bank Street, White Plains, NY 10606

**Staff credits:** The people who made up the Longman Keystone team, representing editorial, production, design, manufacturing, and marketing, are John Ade, Rhea Banker, Liz Barker, Danielle Belfiore, Don Bensey, Virginia Bernard, Kenna Bourke, Brandon Carda, Johnnie Farmer, Maryann Finocchi, Patrice Fraccio, Geraldine Geniusas, Charles Green, Zach Halper, Henry Hild, David L. Jones, Ed Lamprich, Jamie Lawrence, Emily Lippincott, Maria Pia Marrella, Linda Moser, Laurie Neaman, Sherri Pemberton, Liza Pleva, Joan Poole, Edie Pullman, Monica Rodriguez, Tara Rose, Tania Saiz-Sousa, Donna Schaffer, Chris Siley, Lynn Sobotta, Heather St. Clair, Jennifer Stem, Siobhan Sullivan, Jane Townsend, Heather Vomero, Marian Wassner, Lauren Weidenman, Matthew Williams, and Adina Zoltan.

**Smithsonian American Art Museum contributors:** Project director and writer: Elizabeth K. Eder, Ph.D.; Writer: Mary Collins; Image research assistants: Laurel Fehrenbach, Katherine G. Stilwill, and Sally Otis; Rights and reproductions: Richard H. Sorensen and Leslie G. Green; Building photograph by Tim Hursley.

**Text design and composition:** Kirchoff/Wohlberg, Inc.

**Text font:** 11.5/14 Minion
**Acknowledgments:** See page 478.
**Illustration and Photo Credits:** See page 480.

**Library of Congress Cataloging-in-Publication Data**
Chamot, Anna Uhl.
    Longman keystone / Anna Uhl Chamot, John De Mado, Sharroky Hollie.
       p. cm. -- (Longman keystone ; E)
    Includes index.
    ISBN 0-13-158257-7 (v. E)
    1. Language arts (Middle school)--United States. 2. Language arts (Middle school)--Activity programs. 3. Language arts (Secondary)--United States. 4. English language--Study and teaching. I. Demado, John II. Hollie, Sharroky III. Title.
    LB1631.C4466 2008
    428.0071'2--dc22

                        2007049279

ISBN-13: 978-0-13-158257-6
ISBN-10: 0-13-158257-7

**PEARSON LONGMAN** ON THE WEB

**Pearsonlongman.com** offers online resources for teachers and students. Access our Companion Websites, our online catalog, and our local offices around the world.

Visit us at **www.pearsonlongman.com.**

Printed in the United States of America
2 3 4 5 6 7 8 9 10—DWL—12 11 10 09 08

# About the Authors

**Anna Uhl Chamot** is a professor of secondary education and a faculty advisor for ESL in George Washington University's Department of Teacher Preparation. She has been a researcher and teacher trainer in content-based second-language learning and language-learning strategies. She co-designed and has written extensively about the Cognitive Academic Language Learning Approach (CALLA) and spent seven years implementing the CALLA model in the Arlington Public Schools in Virginia.

**John De Mado** has been an energetic force in the field of Language Acquisition for several years. He is founder and president of John De Mado Language Seminars, Inc., an educational consulting firm devoted exclusively to language acquisition and literacy issues. John, who speaks a variety of languages, has authored several textbook programs and produced a series of music CD/DVDs designed to help students acquire other languages. John is recognized nationally, as well as internationally, for his insightful workshops, motivating keynote addresses, and humor-filled delivery style.

**Sharroky Hollie** is an assistant professor in teacher education at California State University, Dominguez Hills. His expertise is in the field of professional development, African-American education, and second-language methodology. He is an urban literacy visiting professor at Webster University, St. Louis. Sharroky is the Executive Director of the Center for Culturally Responsive Teaching and Learning (CCRTL) and the co-founding director of the nationally acclaimed Culture and Language Academy of Success (CLAS).

# Reviewers

**Sharena Adebiyi**
Fulton County Schools
Stone City, GA

**Jennifer Benavides**
Garland ISD
Garland, TX

**Tracy Bunker**
Shearer Charter School
Napa, CA

**Dan Fichtner**
UCLA Ed. Ext. TESOL Program
Redondo Beach, CA

**Trudy Freer-Alvarez**
Houston ISD
Houston, TX

**Helena K. Gandell**
Duval County
Jacksonville, FL

**Glenda Harrell**
Johnston County School Dist.
Smithfield, NC

**Michelle Land**
Randolph Middle School
Randolph, NJ

**Joseph E. Leaf**
Norristown Area High School
Norristown, PA

**Ilona Olancin**
Collier County Schools
Naples, FL

**Jeanne Perrin**
Boston Unified School Dist.
Boston, MA

**Cheryl Quadrelli-Jones**
Anaheim Union High School Dist.
Fullerton, CA

**Mary Schmidt**
Riverwood High School
Atlanta, GA

**Daniel Thatcher**
Garland ISD
Garland, TX

**Denise Tiffany**
West High School
Iowa City, IA

**Lisa Troute**
Palm Beach County School Dist.
West Palm, FL

# Dear Student,

## *Welcome to* LONGMAN KEYSTONE

*Longman Keystone* has been specially designed to help you succeed in all areas of your school studies. This program will help you develop the English language skills you need for language arts, social studies, math, and science. You will discover new ways to use and build upon your language skills through your interactions with classmates, friends, teachers, and family members.

*Keystone* includes a mix of many subjects. Each unit has four different reading selections that include literary excerpts, poems, and nonfiction articles about science, math, and social studies. These selections will help you understand the vocabulary and organization of different types of texts. They will also give you the tools you need to approach the content of the different subjects you take in school.

As you use this program, you will discover new words, use your background knowledge of the subjects presented, relate your knowledge to the new information, and take part in creative activities. You will learn strategies to help you understand readings better. You will work on activities that help you improve your English skills in grammar, word study, and spelling. Finally, you will be asked to demonstrate the listening, speaking, and writing skills you have learned through fun projects that are incorporated throughout the program.

Learning a language takes time, but just like learning to skateboard or learning to swim, it is fun! Whether you are learning English for the first time, or increasing your knowledge of English by adding academic or literary language to your vocabulary, you are giving yourself new choices for the future, and a better chance of succeeding in both your studies and in everyday life.

We hope you enjoy *Longman Keystone* as much as we enjoyed writing it for you!

Good luck!

> Anna Uhl Chamot
> John De Mado
> Sharroky Hollie

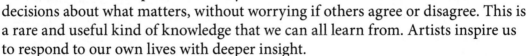

# Learn about *Art* with the
# Smithsonian American Art Museum

## *Dear Student,*

At the end of each unit in this book, you will learn about some artists and artworks that relate to the theme you have just read about. These artworks are all in the Smithsonian American Art Museum in Washington, D.C. That means they belong to you, because the Smithsonian is America's collection. The artworks were created over a period of 300 years by artists who responded to their experiences in personal ways. Their world lives on through their artworks and, as viewers, we can understand them and ourselves in new ways. We discover that many of the things that concerned these artists still engage us today.

Looking at an artwork is different from reading a written history. Artists present few facts or dates. Instead, they offer emotional insights that come from their own lives and experiences. They make their own decisions about what matters, without worrying if others agree or disagree. This is a rare and useful kind of knowledge that we can all learn from. Artists inspire us to respond to our own lives with deeper insight.

There are two ways to approach art. One way is through the mind—studying the artist, learning about the subject, exploring the context in which the artwork was made, and forming a personal view. This way is deeply rewarding and expands your understanding of the world. The second way is through the senses—letting your imagination roam as you look at an artwork, losing yourself in colors and shapes, absorbing the meaning through your eyes. This way is called "aesthetic." The great thing about art is that an artwork may have many different meanings. You can decide what it means to you.

This brief introduction to American art will, I hope, lead to a lifetime of enjoyment and appreciation of art.

**Elizabeth Broun**
The Margaret and Terry Stent Director
Smithsonian American Art Museum

# Glossary of Terms

You will find the following words useful when reading, writing, and talking about art.

**abstract**  a style of art that does not represent things, animals, or people realistically

**acrylic**  a type of paint that is made from ground pigments and certain chemicals

**background**  part of the artwork that looks furthest away from the viewer

**brushstroke**  the paint or ink left on the surface of an artwork by the paintbrush

**canvas**  a type of heavy woven fabric used as a support for painting; another word for a painting

**composition**  the way in which the different parts of an artwork are arranged

**detail**  a small part of an artwork

**evoke**  to produce a strong feeling or memory

**figure**  the representation of a person or animal in an artwork

**foreground**  part of the artwork that looks closest to the viewer

**geometric**  a type of pattern that has straight lines or shapes such as squares, circles, etc.

**mixed media**  different kinds of materials such as paint, fabric, objects, etc. that are used in a single artwork

**oil**  a type of paint that is made from ground pigments and linseed oil

**paintbrush**  a special brush used for painting

**perception**  the way you understand something you see

**pigment**  a finely powdered material (natural or man-made) that gives color to paint, ink, or dye

**portrait**  an artwork that shows a specific person, group of people, or animal

**print**  an artwork that has been made from a sheet of metal or a block of wood covered with a wet color and then pressed onto a flat surface like paper. Types of prints include lithographs, etchings, aquatints, etc.

**symbol**  an image, shape, or object in an artwork that represents an idea

**texture**  the way that a surface or material feels and how smooth or rough it looks

**tone**  the shade of a particular color; the effect of light and shade with color

**watercolor**  a type of paint that is made from ground pigments, gum, and glycerin and/or honey; another word for a painting done with this medium

# UNIT 1

# **Contents**

# UNIT 2

# Contents

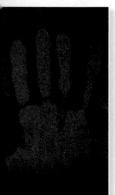

x

# Contents

# When should you take a stand?

# UNIT 4

# Contents

# Contents

UNIT 5

# Contents

THE BIG **Q** QUESTION

# **W**hy should we reach out to others?

T his unit is about reaching out. Why do people reach out to others? Sometimes it's to offer help or to receive it. Sometimes it's to make a new friend. Reading, writing, and talking about these ideas will give you practice using academic language and help you become a better student.

## READING 1: Novel Excerpt and Poetry

- From *Criss Cross* by Lynn Rae Perkins
- "Oranges" by Gary Soto

## READING 2: Science Article

- "Managing Stress" by Sarah Lennard-Brown

## READING 3: Novel Excerpt and Poetry

- From *The Phantom Tollbooth* by Norton Juster
- From "Grandma Ling" by Amy Ling

## READING 4: Science Article

- "Your Brain and Nervous System"

### Listening and Speaking

At the end of this unit, you will make a **group presentation**. In your presentation you will describe a person, place, event, or object.

### Writing

In this unit you will practice **descriptive writing**. This type of writing describes the way things look, sound, feel, smell, or taste. After each reading you'll learn a skill to help you write a descriptive paragraph. At the end of this unit, you'll use those skills to write a descriptive essay.

### QuickWrite

List ways people can reach out, such as volunteering at a local hospital.

Visit *LongmanKeystone.com*

3

## What You Will Learn

**Reading**
- Vocabulary building: *Literary terms, word study*
- Reading strategy: *Visualize*
- Text type: *Literature (novel excerpt, poetry)*

**Grammar, Usage, and Mechanics**
Compound and complex sentences

**Writing**
Describe a place

 **THE BIG QUESTION**

**Why should we reach out to others?** Think about older people you know. How are they treated? Are they respected? What problems do they have? Who helps them with their problems? In your notebook, draw a chart like the one below. Compare your chart with a partner's.

| Older People I Know | How They're Treated | Problems | Where They Live |
|---|---|---|---|
| my grandmother | with love | trouble walking | in a house with her sister |
| my neighbor | with respect | no close family | in the apartment next door |

**BUILD BACKGROUND**

In the excerpt from the novel **Criss Cross**, you will read about a teenager who meets an elderly woman with health problems. This lady lives alone. In the United States, the number of elderly—persons sixty-five years or older—is increasing. By 2030, there will be more than double the elderly population of 2000. As more people live longer, there will be more who face chronic illnesses and diseases.

Very often the elderly and the sick need assistance—they need people who are willing to reach out to them and offer them help. Look at the bar graph below. What conclusions can you draw about the elderly's need for assistance today?

**Population Aged 65 and Over, 2000 to 2050 (in millions)**

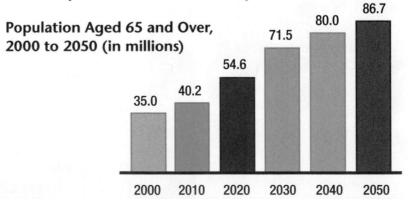

| 2000 | 2010 | 2020 | 2030 | 2040 | 2050 |
|---|---|---|---|---|---|
| 35.0 | 40.2 | 54.6 | 71.5 | 80.0 | 86.7 |

## Learn Literary Words

**Characterization** refers to the author's attempt to create or develop a character. We learn about a character from what the character says, thinks, and does, and from what other characters say and think about him or her. In *Criss Cross*, Debbie overhears her mother talking to a friend. They are talking about Debbie and Mrs. Bruning, a woman she has been helping on Saturdays. Debbie thinks her mother is exaggerating and making her sound like "a heroine" when really she is helping Mrs. Bruning because they are friends. The author is telling us, through Debbie's thoughts, that Debbie is a humble, kind, and realistic person.

The **setting** is the time and place of a story's action. The setting can tell you a lot about a character. Debbie describes Mrs. Bruning's house as "castle-y" and says that it "has an elegance and a personality." Through this description of Mrs. Bruning's house, we get the impression that Mrs. Bruning may be elegant, too.

**Figurative language** is writing that the reader isn't supposed to take literally. Authors use it to help readers visualize. One form of figurative language is personification—giving a nonhuman subject human characteristics. The author of *Criss Cross* uses personification when she compares the house to someone who has prostheses, or artificial limbs. This language makes us picture a house that needs support in order to stand. Another form of figurative language is the metaphor—describing a person or thing as though it were something else. For example, Debbie describes Mrs. Bruning as "a bottle of vinegar . . . with legs."

| Literary Words |
| --- |
| characterization |
| setting |
| figurative language |

**Practice**  Workbook Page 1

You will read about a unique house and its equally unique owner, Mrs. Bruning. As you read, note words that help you visualize the house. After reading, write what the details reveal about Mrs. Bruning's character.

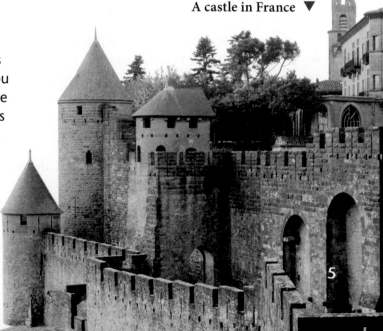

A castle in France ▼

## Learn Academic Words

Study the **red** words and their meanings. You will find these words useful when talking and writing about literature. Write each word and its meaning in your notebook. After you read the excerpt from *Criss Cross* and "Oranges," try to use these words to respond to the text.

**Academic Words**

external
interact
perspective
project
visualize

| | | |
|---|---|---|
| **external** = on the outside | ➡ | The **external** appearance of the house showed that it needed repairs. |
| **interact** = talk to other people and work together with them | ➡ | My teacher wants me to **interact** with my classmates, not work alone. |
| **perspective** = a way of thinking about something | ➡ | She thought about health from a new **perspective** after being sick. |
| **project** = a carefully planned piece of work | ➡ | For our final **project** we have to do research on castles—and try building one. |
| **visualize** = form a picture of someone or something in your mind | ➡ | Before I run, I **visualize** myself winning so I'll run faster. |

## Practice

**Workbook Page 2**

Work with a partner to answer these questions. Try to include the **red** word in your answer. Write the sentences in your notebook.

1. What buildings have **external** appearances that provide clues about the kind of activities or work that goes on inside?

2. Do you find it hard to **interact** with someone you're meeting for the first time? Why or why not?

3. Why might two people each have a different **perspective** of the same situation?

4. Do you always finish a **project** you start? If so, why? If not, why not?

5. When you're about to go to a new place, do you first try to **visualize** it? Why or why not?

▲ Starting a project

## Word Study: Double *l*s and *r*s

Double *l*s and double *r*s can occur in the middle and at the end of a word. They are never found at the beginning of a word, as is possible in some other languages. For example, the word *challenging* has a double *l* in the middle, while the word *scroll* has a double *l* at the end.

| Double *l* | | Double *r* | |
|---|---|---|---|
| Middle of Word | End of Word | Middle of Word | End of Word |
| yellow | smell | carrot | purr |
| follow | fall | porridge | err |
| hello | seagull | ferry | |
| parallel | basketball | marry | |

**Practice**

Look through the reading for other words that fit these patterns and write the words in your notebook.

▲ Our cat purrs when he sleeps.

## READING STRATEGY | VISUALIZE

Visualizing helps you understand what the author wants you to see. When you visualize, you make pictures in your mind of what you are reading. To visualize, follow these steps:

- As you read, think about what the author wants you to see in your mind.
- Pay special attention to descriptive words and figurative language.
- Stop from time to time and visualize the characters, places, and events.

As you read the excerpt from *Criss Cross*, notice the words the author uses to describe Mrs. Bruning's house. How does visualizing her house help you understand Mrs. Bruning better?

**Set a purpose for reading** In the following novel excerpt, how does Mrs. Bruning let Debbie know she needs help without actually asking her for it?

In the poem "Oranges," how does the shopkeeper reach out and help the boy although the boy says nothing?

*from*

# Criss Cross

*Lynne Rae Perkins*

*It's summer in the small town of Seldem. And it's that time of year when teenagers get to know each other better, make new friends, get summer jobs, and enjoy some free time.*

"By the way," Helen was saying. "Did I tell you that Debbie is going to go down to old Mrs. Bruning's house on Saturdays, to help her out with housework? I guess she's getting very arthritic."

Debbie's ears pricked up when she heard her name and she half-listened to her mother's version of the story. She usually sounded pretty good in her mother's stories, though not quite like herself. The stories themselves were that way, too; more entertaining than what really happened, though close enough that you could think, oh, so that's how it was, even if you had been there and it hadn't seemed that way at all. You could find out in this way that something you thought had been a disaster had actually come out quite well.

In her mother's version of the Mrs. Bruning story, Debbie was a take-charge kind of girl who saw a frail old woman in distress and went right to the rescue.

She didn't mind being cast by her mother as a heroine. But the way it happened was more accidental. And it was more equal.

Mrs. Bruning lived in one of the older houses near the bottom of Prospect Hill Road. Her house was on a corner lot, facing the side street. As you walked past it, up or down the hill, you could see into the backyard. The yard slanted up steeply away from a concrete patio, which was shaded by a corrugated fiberglass awning of faded yellow, held up by metal bars

---

**heroine**, someone who does something brave or good
**corrugated**, in rows that look like waves
**fiberglass**, a light material made from small glass threads pressed together
**awning**, a sheet of material that protects a house from sun and rain

that enclosed ornamental scrolls, painted black, barnacled with scabs of rust. The house was built of gray stone and had a castle-y appearance, if you could sift it out from the awning, and the big doorway that had been fitted with plywood to accommodate a small modern door with a crescent-shaped window, the bent and cockeyed Venetian blinds hanging behind the leaded and stained glass windows, and the sunporch tacked onto one side, shingled up to the windows with roofing shingles in variegated shades of purple, brown, and green.

Despite all of its prostheses, Debbie thought that the ivy climbing up the stone, and the stained glass, and the small porchlike recess on the second floor with the crenellated half-wall gave the house an elegance and a personality. She had always wondered what it was like inside.

She saw Mrs. Bruning out in her backyard and waved. Mrs. Bruning waved back. Then she held her hand up, as if to say "Wait a minute," and started making her way purposefully across the grass. She was short and solid, bottle-shaped. A bottle of vinegar . . . with legs. She was one of those elderly women whose chest starts about two inches below her collarbone and your main response to it is an intellectual curiosity about how that can even physically work.

barnacled, encrusted
plywood, thin sheets of wood stuck together to form a hard board
cockeyed, not straight or level
Venetian blinds, a window shade made of long flat bars
prostheses, artificial devices used to replace limbs or body parts
recess, a space in a wall
crenellated, having spaces to shoot guns and arrows through

✔ **LITERARY CHECK**

*What details does the author use to describe the setting of the story?*

**BEFORE YOU GO ON**

**1** How would you describe Mrs. Bruning?

**2** How would you describe her house?

💡**On Your Own**
Have you ever wondered what a certain house or building looked like inside?

9

She moved toward Debbie with determination, but her steps were small, baby steps, and effortful, as if each one was costing her. It was a big yard, so Debbie stepped into it and walked over to meet her, to save time. Not that she was saving it for anything in particular.

Debbie knew two things about Mrs. Bruning. One was that she had never cut her hair. At least that's what people said. It may or may not have been true, but her hair seemed as if it might be pretty long. She wore it in a heavy braid arranged around her head in a complicated way, held in place with bobby pins. The hair closest to her scalp was white and fluffy, but as the braid narrowed, it became carrot colored, then dwindled into a faded russet wisp weaving in and out of the pin-prickled coronet. It wouldn't have been that surprising to see baby birds peeping out over the top of it.

The other thing Debbie knew was that when Mrs. Bruning's husband was still alive, the two of them had owned and operated the Idle Hour Restaurant. They were German. From Germany German. Although they had been in America for a long time.

"It's going to rain," said Mrs. Bruning as they met. She was short. She only came up to Debbie's shoulder. It was an odd sensation, looking down at someone you felt you ought to be looking up to. Debbie was fairly certain Mrs. Bruning had been larger, in the past.

She looked at the sky, a dropped ceiling of soft gray wool. The air had a pre-rain stillness to it.

"Yeah," she said. She said it pleasantly, but immediately wished she had said, "Yes," or even "Yes, ma'am." Mrs. Bruning had that effect.

"Yes," she corrected herself. "I think it is. Going to rain."

"I can't get my laundry down from the clothesline," said Mrs. Bruning.

"Oh?" said Debbie. She still thought they were just making conversation.

**LITERARY CHECK**
*What form of figurative language does the author use here?*

russet, reddish-brown
coronet, a small crown

10

"Why not?" she asked. It seemed like the logical next line in the conversation.

"My hands," said Mrs. Bruning. "And my shoulders. Arthritis. For some reason they were working better this morning, I was able to hang it all up. But now they are so stiffened up on me, I can't do it. I can't get the laundry down. And it's going to rain."

She looked at Debbie expectantly. She demonstrated how her arms would only go so high, how her hands would not do what she needed them to do. "You see what I'm saying?" she said. She had bright brown eyes, like a bird's eyes.

She didn't actually ask for help, but Debbie finally realized what she was supposed to do here. She glanced at the lowered sky, the waiting laundry, and Mrs. Bruning's knotted hands.

"Oh," she said. "Let me help you."

The first cold heavy drops of rain fell on Debbie's shoulders as she carried Mrs. Bruning's laundry into the house, where it was dark. Gray light hovered outside the windows, but it couldn't penetrate the ivy. Debbie bent awkwardly over her burden, the big basket, piled high.

"Where should I put this?" she asked. "I mean, where would you like it?"

"Just in here," said Mrs. Bruning. She made her bulky way past the hall-filling obstacle of Debbie and the laundry and, a few seconds later, a switch clicked and a light came on over a kitchen sink.

---

**knotted**, lumpy

**BEFORE YOU GO ON**

1 What problem does Mrs. Bruning have?

2 How does Debbie help?

**On Your Own**
Has anyone ever reached out to you for help? What did you do?

11

"The overhead bulb is burnt out," she explained. "I can't reach it without climbing up on a chair, and then I'm afraid of falling. Just put it in the corner, on the floor. I will take care of it later."

Debbie nudged aside a small stack of newspapers with her foot and set the basket down. She stood up and turned around. The dimly lit kitchen seemed at first to be a cluttered, disorganized mess. But as her eyes adjusted, she saw spotlessly clean surfaces. Polished fixtures. The impression of disorder came from a variety of projects that Mrs. Bruning had not managed to complete. A bag of groceries sitting on one of the chairs was only half unloaded, and what had been removed from it had only made it as far as the tabletop. Next to the cans of soup, standing in tidy rows along with a box of cereal and a loaf of bread, an old typewriter held a letter in progress. Just beyond that, a neatly folded pile of bathroom towels, pink with roses, waited to be delivered to a closet somewhere in the murky house. A glass of milk and a plate with a partially eaten jelly sandwich sat nearby with a folded paper napkin tucked under its edge like a still life. On the counter by the wall were two boxes that had been neatly labeled "Christmas Ornaments: Attic." The room was full of efforts abandoned in midstream. Mrs. Bruning caught Debbie's gaze and laughed. She picked up the glass and the dish with the jelly sandwich and carried them to the sink.

"And then again," she said. "Maybe I won't." Over her shoulder, she added, "I'm going to have to think about it."

---

**murky**, dark and difficult to see through
**still life**, painting of motionless objects

Rain pelted the windows; the kitchen felt cozy. Yellow light from the shaded lamp illuminated a calendar printed on a dishtowel hanging on the wall. The months, and the verse above them, were in German. Debbie was in her second year of German, and she could tell that the rhyme was about baking a cake, though she didn't know all of the words.

" '*Schieb, schieb in Ofen nein*,' " she read aloud. "Why does it say not to put it in the oven?"

Mrs. Bruning looked at the dishtowel, then back at Debbie.

"It's not *nein* as in 'no,' " she said. "It's a shortened way of saying *hinein*, which means 'in there.' As in, 'shove it in there.' A colloquialism. A slang word."

"I didn't think German would have slang words," said Debbie. "It always sounds so precise. Except for the *schl* and *ch* sounds."

Mrs. Bruning chuckled. "I can guarantee you," she said, "we are as lazy as anyone else. Just take a look around you."

Debbie did.

"I can change your lightbulb for you," she said.

And while she did that, Mrs. Bruning put the kettle on the stove to make tea, and fished a package of vanilla sandwich cremes out of the grocery bag on the chair. That's how it had started: They liked each other.

*Before the summer was over, Debbie had cut Mrs. Bruning's long hair, met her family, and convinced her son that Mrs. Bruning should remain in her house (with some help, of course) and not be made to live in a senior citizens' home. And, as if that weren't enough, Debbie acted quickly in an emergency and saved Mrs. Bruning's life.*

---

**vanilla sandwich cremes**, cookies with filling between

✔ **LITERARY CHECK**
*Think about* **characterization**. *Read what Debbie says on this page. What kind of person is she?*

## ABOUT THE **AUTHOR**

**Lynn Rae Perkins** is an illustrator and writer who started out creating children's picture books because she loved to draw. She soon discovered that she also loved to write stories. In 2006 her novel *Criss Cross* won the Newbery Medal, an annual award for the most distinguished contribution to literature for young people. Perkins lives with her husband, her two teenaged children, and the family dog in Suttons Bay, Michigan, where she grows Christmas trees.

**BEFORE YOU GO ON**

1. Why does Mrs. Bruning laugh?

2. What do Mrs. Bruning and Debbie have in common?

**On Your Own**
Do you have any elderly friends or neighbors that you get along well with?

# Oranges

The first time I walked
With a girl, I was twelve,
Cold, and weighted down
With two oranges in my jacket.
December. Frost cracking
Beneath my steps, my breath
Before me, then gone,
As I walked toward
Her house, the one whose
Porch light burned yellow
Night and day, in any weather.
A dog barked at me, until
She came out pulling
At her gloves, face bright
With rouge. I smiled,
Touched her shoulder, and led
Her down the street, across
A used car lot and a line
Of newly planted trees,
Until we were breathing
Before a drugstore. We
Entered, the tiny bell
Bringing a saleslady
Down a narrow aisle of goods.
I turned to the candies
Tiered like bleachers,
And asked what she wanted—
Light in her eyes, a smile
Starting at the corners
Of her mouth. I fingered
A nickel in my pocket,

---

**tiered**, arranged in rows one
    above another
**bleachers**, rows of seats

14

And when she lifted a chocolate
That cost a dime,
I didn't say anything.
I took the nickel from
My pocket, then an orange,
And set them quietly on
The counter. When I looked up,
The lady's eyes met mine,
And held them, knowing
Very well what it was all
About.

       Outside,
A few cars hissing past,
Fog hanging like old
Coats between the trees.
I took my girl's hand
In mine for two blocks,
Then released it to let
Her unwrap the chocolate.
I peeled my orange
That was so bright against
The gray of December
That, from some distance,
Someone might have thought
I was making a fire in my hands.

          —*Gary Soto*

*Chocolate*

### BEFORE YOU GO ON

**1** What does the boy do on his first date?

**2** What did the boy offer for the chocolate that cost a dime?

 **On Your Own**
Have you ever had to be creative to get what you wanted?

## READER'S THEATER

Act out the following conversation.

*[Debbie hears her mother, Helen, talking to a friend.]*

**Helen:** Did you know Debbie is going to Mrs. Bruning's house on Saturdays?

**Friend:** No, why is she doing that?

**Helen:** She's going to help with chores. Mrs. Bruning has bad arthritis in her hands.

**Friend:** Oh, dear. Good for Debbie! How did that start?

**Helen:** She realized Mrs. Bruning needed help just before that rainstorm. So, of course, she rushed right over to help.

*[Debbie enters.]*

**Debbie:** Mom, that's not exactly what happened.

**Helen:** No? What happened then?

**Debbie:** Mrs. Bruning waved to me and started walking toward me, so I walked over to meet her.

**Helen:** And then she asked you for help?

**Debbie:** No, not exactly. She just mentioned that her clothes were on the line, and it was going to rain.

**Friend:** And then what happened?

**Debbie:** It took me a while to figure out what she wanted, really. And when I brought the clothes inside, I . . .

**Friend:** What's the inside like? It always looked a bit like a castle to me.

**Debbie:** Um, it was kind of dark because there was a lightbulb burned out. And there were lots of unfinished projects, like groceries that needed to be put away.

**Friend:** Sounds like a mess!

**Debbie:** No, underneath it's spotless. Mrs. Bruning just has to stop whenever her hands hurt too badly.

**Helen:** Which is exactly why Debbie volunteered to go back and help her. I don't know what she'd do without you!

**Debbie:** It's really not like that. I like Mrs. Bruning. We just get along.

▲ A clothesline

> **🔊 Speaking TIP**
>
> Use facial expressions, gestures, and other body language to show your character's feelings.

16

## COMPREHENSION

**Workbook Page 5**

Workbook Page 5

**Listening TIP**

Listen carefully to other students' ideas.

### Right There

1. What two things does Debbie know about Mrs. Bruning before she meets her?

2. Why does Mrs. Bruning say she can't get her clothes off the line?

### Think and Search

3. How is Mrs. Bruning's life changing?

4. How does Mrs. Bruning feel about Debbie? How do you know?

### Author and You

5. Would the author agree with this statement: *Sometimes when people reach out, each one of them benefits*? Explain.

6. What clues does the author give you to indicate that Debbie and Mrs. Bruning have a lot to offer each other?

### On Your Own

7. What do you think Debbie means when she says, "It was more equal"? Do you think Mrs. Bruning also reached out to Debbie? If so, how?

8. In your opinion, why might it be difficult to ask for help?

## DISCUSSION

Discuss in pairs or small groups.

- Imagine that the boy's reaching out to the saleslady in "Oranges" didn't work. How else could he have solved his problem?

- **Why should we reach out to others?** Is it sometimes difficult to reach out to someone? Why or why not?

## RESPONSE TO LITERATURE

Workbook Page 5

Imagine you are Mrs. Bruning or Debbie. Write a "Help Wanted" ad posted by Mrs. Bruning or a "Job Wanted" ad by Debbie. Or you can write a response from Debbie to an ad Mrs. Bruning posts. Be sure to use details from the selection. Look at the example.

### HELP WANTED

Handy person needed for small jobs and some cleaning in large older home. Must like working around older people. Send letter of application to the *Seldem News*—job #3.

# Grammar and Writing

## Compound and Complex Sentences

Compound sentences that show contrast use the conjunctions *yet* or *but*. Use a comma before the conjunction. Complex sentences that show contrast use *even though, although,* or *though*. Use a comma after the dependent clause when it begins the sentence.

| Compound Sentence |
| --- |
| independent clause · · · · · · · · · · independent clause |
| The house had a lot of repairs, **but** it still looked like a castle. |

| Complex Sentences |
| --- |
| dependent clause · · · · · · · · · · independent clause |
| **Although** the house had a lot of repairs, it looked like a castle. |
| independent clause · · · · · · · · · · dependent clause |
| It looked like a castle **even though** the house had a lot of repairs. |

**Practice**
**Workbook Page 6**

Work with a partner. Use the pairs of clauses and the transition words to form compound and complex sentences. Write the sentences in your notebook.

| Transition Word | Pairs of Clauses |
| --- | --- |
| 1. but | The awning was ugly. <br> The ivy gave the house elegance. |
| 2. although | The house had a tacked-on sunporch. <br> Its gray stone walls made it look solid and sturdy. |
| 3. even though | The stained glass windows were pretty. <br> The crooked Venetian blinds were visible behind them. |
| 4. but | She moved toward Debbie with determination. <br> Her steps were small, baby steps, and effortful. |
| 5. though | She could tell the rhyme was about baking a cake. <br> She didn't know all the words. |

## WRITING A DESCRIPTIVE PARAGRAPH

### Describe a Place

When you describe something, you can use **sensory details**. Often when you describe a place, you use details that appeal to the reader's sense of sight. Sensory details can also help the reader hear, feel, touch, smell, or taste what you are describing. They appeal to the reader's five senses.

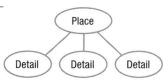

Here is a model of a descriptive paragraph that describes a place—Mrs. Bruning's house. The writer described the house from Debbie's perspective. Notice the sensory details that the writer included. He used a word web to help organize the details.

*Andrew Gerhardt*

### Mrs. Bruning's House

When Debbie first saw the house from the outside, she thought it was just an old, run-down stone house. But, as she actually looked more carefully at the details of the house that day, she realized it looked like a castle. The first thing that made her think so was the ivy-covered half-wall in the front of the house. It had crenellations, like castles have. The large arched doorway looked like it belonged in a castle, too, even though it had a modern door. Although the inside of the house was less impressive, she could see that Mrs. Bruning was trying to keep it up. And it had a warm feeling to it. Even the half-finished sandwich she had fixed for herself looked like a piece of artwork. It was so neatly arranged, Debbie thought. There were half-completed projects scattered all around the kitchen, but together they could clean it up and make it look nicer.

### Practice

Workbook Page 7

Write a paragraph describing Mrs. Bruning's place (inside and out) from the perspective of her son. He thinks the house is too much for his mother to handle—too many things to fix. Use sensory details to describe the house in a more negative light. Use one word web for the inside of the house and another for the outside of the house. Be sure to use compound and complex sentences correctly.

**Writing Checklist**

**ORGANIZATION:**
☑ I used a clear topic sentence.

**WORD CHOICE:**
☑ I chose sensory details that support the topic sentence.

## What You Will Learn

**Reading**
- Vocabulary building: *Context, dictionary skills, word study*
- Reading strategy: *Preview*
- Text type: *Informational text (science)*

**Grammar, Usage, and Mechanics**
*Can/can't* + verb for ability or possibility

**Writing**
Describe a person

### THE BIG QUESTION

**Why should we reach out to others?** Do you ever feel stressed? What sorts of things cause stress? Do you think reaching out to help someone can reduce stress? If so, how? Discuss with a partner.

In your notebook, make a chart like the one below. Then list things that make you stressed at school, at home, and with friends.

| At School | At Home | With Friends |
|---|---|---|
| Taking a test | My sister's music when I'm studying | Waiting for a friend who's late |
| | | |

### BUILD BACKGROUND

In the article **"Managing Stress,"** you will read about stress and learn how to best deal with it. Look at your list of things that stress you out. Did you include any life events such as moving or gaining a new family member?

Experts have studied and ranked life events that cause some of the most stress:

- Vacation
- Outstanding personal achievement
- Change in sleeping habits
- Moving house
- Change in personal habits

Have you experienced any of these events? If so, did you feel stressed?

▲ Moving causes stress.

## VOCABULARY

### Learn Key Words

Read these sentences. Use the context to figure out the meaning of the **red** words. Use a dictionary to check your answers. Then write each word and its meaning in your notebook.

**Key Words**

maximize
moderation
stressful
stressors
systematic
threshold

1. Eating healthy food and exercising can **maximize** your ability to manage stress.

2. Eating junk food only once in a while, in **moderation**, is a better idea than eating it all the time.

3. Moving to a new neighborhood is **stressful** because changes make some people feel nervous and uncomfortable.

4. Not everyone responds to **stressors**, or things that cause stress, in the same way.

5. Considering all possible solutions is a **systematic** approach to solving the problem.

6. Since each person has his or her own stress **threshold**, one person might be able to handle much more stress than another one can.

### Practice

**Workbook Page 8**

Write the sentences in your notebook. Choose a **red** word from the box above to complete each sentence. Then take turns reading the sentences aloud with a partner.

1. Candy and sweets are not healthy foods; you should eat them only in _____.

2. Trying out for a play or a sports team can be _____.

3. He couldn't handle one more problem that day; he had reached his stress _____.

4. They went to bed early and ate a healthy breakfast to _____ their chances of passing the science test.

5. She planned her project in a _____ way, and thought through all of her options before deciding what to do first.

6. Changes like going to a new school or starting a new job are examples of _____.

Wear comfortable sneakers when you exercise. ▼

21

## Learn Academic Words

Study the **red** words and their meanings. You will find these words useful when talking and writing about informational texts. Write each word and its meaning in your notebook. After you read "Managing Stress," try to use these words to respond to the text.

| | | |
|---|---|---|
| **environment** = the situations, things, and people that affect the way in which people live | → | A change in your **environment**, such as the birth of a baby in your family, can be stressful. |
| **factors** = one of several things that cause or influence a situation | → | Personality type is one of the **factors** that affect how people respond to stress. |
| **individual** = one person separate from others | → | The way stress affects one **individual** is different from the way it affects someone else. |
| **respond** = react or answer | → | She can **respond** to stress by taking a few deep breaths. |
| **unique** = different from all others | → | Each individual manages stress in a **unique** way. |

## Practice  Workbook Page 9

Write the sentences in your notebook. Choose a **red** word from the box above to complete each sentence. Then take turns reading the sentences aloud with a partner.

1. In our school you will be treated as an _____, not just as part of the crowd.

2. Your idea is _____. No one else in the class thought of it.

3. A change in my _____, like starting a new school, would cause me stress.

4. She didn't _____ to my question. I think she didn't hear me.

5. The schools in my city are good. That was one of the _____ that made my family decide to move here.

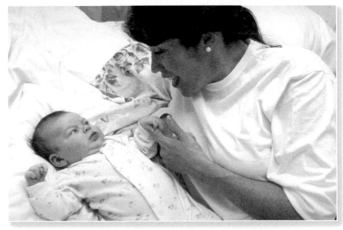

▲ A new baby in the family can be stressful.

## Word Study: Related Words

Related words are formed by adding prefixes or suffixes to a root word, or by combining a root word with another word. Knowing the meaning of a root word plus the meaning of common prefixes and suffixes can help you figure out word meanings. For example, the word *stress* means "feeling worried because of difficulties in your life." What do you think these words mean: *stressful, stressor, stress-induced*? These definitions will help you:

| | |
|---|---|
| -or: | the person or thing doing or causing an action |
| -ful: | having a particular quality |
| induce: | cause a particular physical condition, feeling, or change |

### Practice  Workbook Page 10

Work with a partner. Define the root word in each group of words below. Look up the meanings of the prefixes, suffixes, and other words to define each word or phrase.

| | |
|---|---|
| achieve | achiever, achievement |
| appropriate | inappropriate |
| fit | fitness, unfit |
| problem | problem solve |
| relax | relaxation |

## READING STRATEGY   PREVIEW

Previewing a text helps you understand the content more quickly. It also helps you establish a purpose for reading. To preview, follow these steps:

- Look at the title and headings.
- Look at the visuals and read the captions or labels.
- Read the first and last sections of each paragraph.
- What do you think you will learn? Make notes in your notebook.
- Think about what you know about the subject.

Before you read "Managing Stress," look at the title, visuals, and captions. Work with a partner. Discuss what you think you will learn in the article. Later, check to see if you were right.

 Workbook Page 11

**Set a purpose for reading** How can you reduce your stress by reaching out to other people?

# Managing Stress

*Sarah Lennard-Brown*

Stress means different things to different people. Everyone has a personal view of stress, even the experts. The most commonly accepted view of stress was developed by Richard Lazarus, an American psychologist, in 1966. He felt that stress was all about change and that each individual responds to changes (he called changes "stressors") in a unique way. This means that any change in your life, your mind, your friends and family, your body, or your environment is, to some extent, stressful. Arguing with your friends or even catching a cold involves change and therefore is stressful.

The important thing to remember is that any change is stressful—good changes as well as bad ones. A surprise birthday party and passing exams are examples of pleasurable things that can cause stress. Going to a party or passing exams can cause excitement and worry.

---

commonly accepted, agreed
  with by most people

## Examples of Things That Cause Stress

| Good Things | Bad Things |
|---|---|
| • Surprise birthday party<br>• Scoring the winning goal<br>• Passing exams<br>• Holidays<br>• Moving to a new home | • Being ill<br>• Missing the goal<br>• Failing exams<br>• Traffic delays<br>• Moving to a new home |

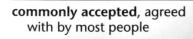

Even imagining change can be stressful. For example, thinking about what life would be like if someone you love fell ill, or what you would do if you became very poor or even rich, all involve worrying. Worrying about changes, whether they are good or bad, is stressful.

Different people respond to stressful situations in different ways. Changes that result in too much stress in one person may not affect another person. According to some researchers, approximately one person out of ten has a very low stress threshold (tolerance level) and will feel overwhelmed and distressed by normal everyday life.

# Too Much Stress Can Cause . . .

| Physical Problems | Psychological Problems | Social Problems |
|---|---|---|
| • Tiredness during the day<br>• Difficulty going to sleep<br>• Frequent waking at night<br>• Aches and pains<br>• Increased number of infections<br>• Palpitations (heart racing)<br>• High blood pressure<br>• Heart attacks<br>• Stomach cramps or ulcers<br>• Dental problems (due to excessive teeth grinding)<br>• Skin problems | • Vivid dreams<br>• Lack of interest in the world<br>• Lack of motivation<br>• Irritability<br>• Tearfulness<br>• Anxiety<br>• Poor performance at school<br>• Eating problems (too much or too little) | • Increasing arguments at home<br>• Tendency to avoid people<br>• Increased aggression (particularly in young men)<br>• Inappropriate behavior<br>• Overreaction to problems<br>• Ignoring problems |

**tolerance level,** the degree to which someone can suffer
**motivation,** desire to do something
**irritability,** state of being easily annoyed
**aggression,** angry or threatening behavior

Too much stress can cause listlessness. ▶

**BEFORE YOU GO ON**

**1** What causes stress?

**2** What are the three kinds of problems too much stress can cause?

**On Your Own**
What causes *you* stress?

25

Many factors affect the way you respond to stress as an individual. These include your genetic makeup, personality type, culture, religion, family and social background, health, environment, and life events.

## Is Your Personality . . .

| Type A | Type B |
| --- | --- |
| • Never late | • Relaxed about time keeping |
| • Competitive | • Not competitive |
| • Anticipate what others are going to say | • Good listener |
| • High achiever | • Balanced approach to achievement |
| • Impatient | • Good at waiting in line |
| • Tense | • Relaxed |
| • Tackle more than one task at a time | • Taking one step at a time |
| • Emphatic in speech | • Slow deliberate speech |
| • Care about others' opinions | • Self-reliant |
| • Quick | • Slow-moving |
| • Driven | • Easy-going |

**genetic**, relating to genes
**anticipate**, expect something to happen
**emphatic**, said in a way that shows something is important
**self-reliant**, able to act and make decisions by yourself

It is well known that some changes in your life are more stressful than others. Events such as the death of a close friend or relative, being suspended from school, or moving to a new place can be particularly challenging. Major changes like these have long-term effects on your life.

Sometimes, no matter how carefully you try to stay healthy and manage stress, things can become overwhelming. If that happens it is important to get help. Go and see your family doctor or other healthcare professional and ask for advice. However, there are many simple ways to prevent and manage stress. Taking time to take care of yourself can prevent stress from becoming a problem in your life.

## Stress Scores of Life Events *

| | |
| --- | --- |
| • Divorce | 73 |
| • Death of a close family member | 63 |
| • Personal injury or illness | 53 |
| • Expelled from school | 47 |
| • Change in health of a family member | 44 |
| • Gain of a new family member | 39 |
| • Death of a close friend | 37 |
| • Outstanding personal achievement | 28 |
| • Beginning or end of school | 26 |
| • Change in living conditions | 25 |
| • Change in personal habits | 24 |
| • Change in residence | 20 |
| • Change in school | 20 |
| • Change in recreation | 19 |
| • Change in social activities | 18 |
| • Change in sleeping habits | 16 |
| • Change in number of family get-togethers | 15 |
| • Change in eating habits | 15 |
| • Vacation | 13 |

\* on a scale of 1 to 100

## Healthy Eating

Being fit and healthy is a sure way to maximize your ability to manage stress. Healthy eating is vital to staying fit and healthy. A healthy diet includes

- plenty of fresh fruit and vegetables;
- lots of complex carbohydrates, such as whole-wheat bread, potatoes, pasta, and rice;
- moderate amounts of protein-rich foods, such as fish, chicken, soy, nuts, eggs, or red meat;
- and some fat, as in butter, margarine, oil, milk, and cheese, but in much smaller amounts.

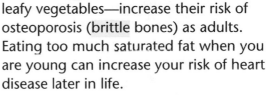

Eating five servings of fruit or vegetables per day is recommended to ensure an adequate daily vitamin intake. Vitamins are important since they help our bodies grow and function properly and fight off infections.

What you eat now will affect your health and therefore the amount of stress in your life as you grow older. Teenagers who get too little calcium—present in milk, cheese, bread, and green,

leafy vegetables—increase their risk of osteoporosis (brittle bones) as adults. Eating too much saturated fat when you are young can increase your risk of heart disease later in life.

As with most things in life, healthy eating involves moderation. Too much food or too little will cause your body chemistry to change and will therefore be a source of stress. If you feel that you weigh too much or too little, then talk to a doctor or healthcare professional.

---

**vital**, extremely important or necessary

---

**brittle**, easily broken

**BEFORE YOU GO ON**

1  What factors affect the way individuals respond to stress?

2  What is healthy eating?

**On Your Own**
What can you do to control stress in your life?

27

◀ Exercise three times a week to stay healthy.

## Exercise

Exercise is a vital part of fitness. The fitter you are, the better able you will be to manage the stresses of life. Exercise is also an excellent way to relax and "turn off" for a while. Most experts feel that you need to get 20 to 30 minutes of exercise three times a week to stay healthy. However, if you have a health problem or if you are very unfit, it is best to consult your doctor before you start a new exercise program.

Some people find it better to incorporate exercise into their daily lives rather than going to special exercise classes. This can involve sports activities such as brisk walking or bicycling rather than taking the car or bus, and using the stairs rather than the elevator.

## Rest and Relaxation

Learning how to relax is a very good way of managing stress. It can help to reduce anxiety and combat the physical effects of too much stress such as chest pain and sleep problems. There are many different ways of relaxing. Some forms of exercise, such as swimming, are very good for leaving your body relaxed. Massage and hydrotherapy have a similar effect.

**incorporate**, include
**hydrotherapy**, the medical use of water to treat injuries or diseases

## Relaxation Technique

1. Curl up your toes and tense your left foot. Let your foot relax. Think about it feeling warm and heavy and floppy. Repeat this twice.

2. Repeat this procedure with your left calf muscle, your left thigh, then with your right foot, calf, and thigh.

3. Now move slowly up your body, tensing and relaxing and thinking about each individual area—your bottom, stomach, back, chest, right shoulder, left shoulder, right hand, right forearm, right upper arm, then your left hand, forearm, and upper arm. Then slowly tense and relax your neck, then your jaw. Scrunch your face and let it relax a few times.

4. Now that you are fully relaxed, think about your breathing. Try to empty your mind of everything except breathing in and out. If other thoughts intrude, notice them, then put them away and think about your breathing again. Breathe slowly in through your nose, then out through your mouth. Repeat this for a few minutes as long as it feels comfortable.

5. Relax, and return to your normal activities.

## Role Playing

Role play involves imagining a situation—for example, trying to resist friends who are trying to get you to do something you think is wrong—and then figuring out how you could manage it. What could you say? How might people react?

## Assertiveness

Assertiveness is an important skill that can help you manage stress. When you are being assertive, you stand up for yourself and express your point of view in a manner that is direct, honest, appropriate to your situation, and respectful of the needs of the people you are dealing with.

## Being a Friend

We all need to help each other to manage stress. There are various ways you can do this. The most obvious way is by listening. It is a common saying that a problem shared is a problem halved, but it is not just problems we have to listen to. In order to have healthy, supportive relationships, you need to be able to share joys and sorrows.

Often, when people experience too much stress, they feel sad and negative. It can help them to know that you love and value them. Tell them the things that you like about them. If someone does something you like or admire, tell him or her.

It is important to share joys and sorrows. ▶

## How to Problem Solve

Problem solving is a useful strategy for managing stressful situations.

1. Sit with a piece of paper and figure out exactly what the problem is. You may find that there is more than one problem, or that some of your problems are really worries. Make a list of your problems.

2. Make a list of different ways of dealing with each problem. Brainstorm: Write down anything you can think of that might help the situation.

3. Think carefully about the different strategies you have come up with: What would happen if you tried each one? Pick a strategy that you think will be safe and effective. It can be helpful to talk through options with a friend. Make sure you think about how your strategy will affect other people.

4. Try out the strategy.

5. Evaluate how effective it was. Did it work? Did it help a little? How can you improve on the strategy?

### BEFORE YOU GO ON

**1** What are some simple ways to manage stress?

**2** What steps should you follow in order to problem solve?

**On Your Own**
How much do you exercise every week?

29

## COMPREHENSION

Workbook
Page 12

### Right There

1. What is the most commonly accepted view of stress?
2. What are some physical problems that too much stress can cause?

### Think and Search

3. How are Type A and Type B personalities different?
4. Why do different people respond differently to stress?

### Author and You

5. How important does the author believe your eating habits as a teenager are? Why?
6. According to the author, is any one method of reducing stress more helpful than the others? Why or why not?

### On Your Own

7. Do you agree that some "good" things, such as family celebrations and vacations, can cause stress? Explain.
8. Why do you think it's important to know which life events cause more stress and to know your own stress threshold?

## IN YOUR OWN WORDS

Work with a partner. Use the chart below to summarize ways to prevent and manage stress. Try to include the words in your summary.

| Subject Heading | Words to Use |
|---|---|
| Healthy Eating | moderation, maximize |
| Exercise | fitness, experts |
| Rest and Relaxation | technique, stress |
| Role Playing | imagine, resist |
| Assertiveness | point of view, respectful |
| Being a Friend | stress, listening |

### 🔊 Speaking TIPS

Be sure to use your own words so you'll be comfortable as you summarize.

Speak slowly and clearly when presenting your main points.

## DISCUSSION

Discuss in pairs or small groups.

1. What are some common sources of stress for people your age?
2. Do you agree that people with Type B personalities have less stress than Type A personalities? Why or why not?
3. Which is the most effective way to manage stress? Support your answer with examples.

**Q** **Why should we reach out to others?** How can reaching out to friends help with stress?

)) *Listening* TIP

Listen carefully to what others are saying. Don't jump ahead to the points you want to make.

## READ FOR FLUENCY

It is often easier to read a text if you understand the difficult words and phrases. Work with a partner. Choose a paragraph from the reading. Identify the words and phrases you do not know or have trouble pronouncing. Look up the difficult words in a dictionary.

Take turns pronouncing the words and phrases with your partner. If necessary, ask your teacher to model the correct pronunciation. Then take turns reading the paragraph aloud. Give each other feedback on your reading.

▲ Good friends can help you manage stress.

## EXTENSION

**Workbook Page 12**

Keep a Stress Journal for one week. Make a chart like the one below to record your observations.

| Stress Journal |
| --- |
| Day and time: |
| Stressor: |
| What you did: |
| Did it help? |
| What would you do differently? |

31

# Grammar and Writing

## GRAMMAR, USAGE, AND MECHANICS

### *Can/Can't* + Verb for Ability or Possibility

*Can* is a modal auxiliary (or helping verb). It is used in conjunction with other verbs. When writing descriptions about people, use *can* to tell what a person is good at (ability). You can also use *can* when you want to describe what a person can do to overcome his or her shortcomings (possibility). *Can* is followed by a verb in its base form.

| | |
|---|---|
| **Ability:** | She is Type B and a good listener who **can** <u>remember</u> what she's told. |
| **Possibility:** | He cares too much about what others think but **can** <u>learn</u> to be more self-reliant. |

**Practice**  **Workbook Page 13**

Work with a partner. Read the descriptions of Valerie and Tony.

| Valerie | Tony |
|---|---|
| • She lists ways to deal with a difficult situation.<br>• She is fit and has a healthy diet.<br>• She is easy going and a good listener. | • He gets confused easily when he has a problem.<br>• He is anxious and in a hurry most of the time.<br>• He is depressed and needs to lose some weight. |

Take turns making sentences with *can/can't* + the base form of the verb (or verb phrase) to describe Valerie's and Tony's abilities.

| Ability |
|---|
| problem solve |
| moderate what (she/he) eats |
| manage stress |

Take turns making sentences with *can* + the base form of the verb to describe how Tony can overcome his shortcomings.

| Possibility |
|---|
| learn techniques for coping with problems |
| learn relaxation techniques to help with the stress |
| consult a professional to talk about the causes of his weight problem |

Write the sentences in your notebook.

32

## WRITING A DESCRIPTIVE PARAGRAPH

### Describe a Person

You've learned some techniques for describing a place. Now, you'll learn some techniques for describing a person. Read the paragraph below about a person who manages stress well. Notice that in addition to describing the person's **physical and character traits**, the writer lists the things that the person does to help her manage stress well. Also, notice that he begins with an interesting first sentence and ends with a sentence that relates to the main idea. The writer uses *can* and *can't* for ability and possibility correctly. He used a word web to help him organize his ideas.

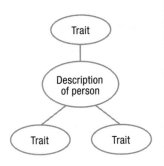

*Michael Ruiz*

### My Stress-Free Friend

I have a friend who is completely stress-free— yes, completely. She is in great shape and runs the Boston Marathon every year. She can problem-solve her way out of any conflict she has. An easygoing person, she can manage any stress in her life. Her secret is not to worry about things that are out of her hands and deal right away with things she can control. Another thing she does to manage stress is to practice yoga. This way, she can forget about her problems for a little while. Can she improve in any way? There's only one thing I can think of. She can eat more healthy foods, but she says that you have to enjoy life a little. My friend is a great role model for those who are stressed out. It may surprise you to know that my stress-free friend is sixty-five years old and doesn't have a single wrinkle on her face!

**Practice**

Workbook Page 14

Write a paragraph describing a stressed-out person. You can write about someone you know or a fictional person so you can make the person as stressed-out as you wish. Look back over the reading for information and details to help you. Use a word web to list what the person can or can't do, as well as the person's physical and character traits. Be sure to use *can/can't* + verb correctly.

**Writing Checklist**

**IDEAS:**
- ☑ My first sentence is interesting.

**ORGANIZATION:**
- ☑ The ending sentence relates to my main point.

**33**

# Prepare to Read

## What You Will Learn

**Reading**
- Vocabulary building: *Literary terms, word study*
- Reading strategy: *Identify problems and solutions*
- Text type: Literature (*novel excerpt and poetry*)

**Grammar, Usage, and Mechanics**
Simple present for habitual actions or routines

**Writing**
Describe an event

## THE BIG QUESTION

**Why should we reach out to others?** Do you ever feel sad or bored? If so, what do you do about it? Do you reach out to anyone for help? Is that person a friend? A stranger? A family member? Discuss with a partner.

## BUILD BACKGROUND

The novel ***The Phantom Tollbooth*** is a fantasy. Fantasy is a work of literature about imaginary characters living in a place that is not real. The story takes place in a land called the Doldrums with inhabitants called Lethargarians, who are small creatures that take on the color of whatever they happen to be near. Then you will read a poem called **"Grandma Ling"** by Amy Ling, about the poet's first meeting with her grandmother in Taiwan. The poem is a realistic narrative poem, based on personal experiences in the poet's own life.

▲ Novels and poems can take you to fantastic or realistic places.

## VOCABULARY

### Learn Literary Words

An **allegory** is a story or tale with two or more levels of meaning—a literal level and one or more symbolic levels. The events, setting, and characters in an allegory are symbols for ideas and qualities. For example, Milo, the main character of *The Phantom Tollbooth*, travels to the Doldrums, a place where thinking is not allowed. In English we use the term "the doldrums" to describe a state of mind of being bored and depressed, of not being able to move forward in life. So the author uses the Doldrums as an allegory for his characters' state of mind.

A **narrative poem** tells a story. The poet narrates a story much like an author of a novel or short story would. Like stories, narrative poems often include characters and a setting. Sometimes a narrative poem is very long, but sometimes it is short like the poem you will read: "Grandma Ling."

An author can use **irony**, that is, include a surprise ending or use words to suggest something quite different from their usual meanings. For example, when Milo asks the people in the Doldrums about what they do, they tell him: "It's really quite strenuous doing nothing all day, so once a week we take a holiday and go nowhere." This statement is ironic because it is unexpected. We don't expect people to take a holiday and go *nowhere*; we expect them to take a holiday and go *somewhere*.

### Practice  **Workbook** Page 15

Work with a partner. Read the sentences below. Decide whether they are examples of an allegory, irony, or a moral.

1. Fair weather friends are not worth much.
2. Milo's next stop: "Dictionopolis, a happy kingdom, located in the Foothills of Confusion and caressed by gentle breezes from the Sea of Knowledge."
3. There's lots to do; we have a very busy schedule—
   At 8 o'clock we get up, and then we spend
   From 8 to 9 daydreaming.
   From 9 to 9:30 we take our early midmorning nap. . . .

## Learn Academic Words

Study the **red** words and their meanings. You will find these words useful when talking and writing about literature. Write each word and its meaning in your notebook. After you read the excerpts from *The Phantom Tollbooth* and "Grandma Ling," try to use these words to respond to the text.

| | | |
|---|---|---|
| **analyze** = examine something in detail in order to understand it | ➡ | Please don't **analyze** every word in the article. Just try to get the main idea. |
| **concept** = an idea or thought | ➡ | When you understand the **concept** of irony, you appreciate the humor. |
| **conclude** = reach a decision based on facts or logic | ➡ | Based on the final sentence, you can **conclude** that the moral of the story is "There's wisdom in age." |
| **occur** = happen; take place | ➡ | If events **occur** that could not happen in real life, then the story is a fantasy. |
| **precisely** = exactly | ➡ | I know **precisely** what time it is: it's six minutes after one. |
| **schedule** = plan; list of times and events | ➡ | If you make a **schedule** that shows your plans for the week, you won't forget your music lessons. |

## Practice

**Workbook Page 16**

Write the sentences in your notebook. Choose a **red** word from the box above to complete each sentence. Then take turns reading the sentences aloud with a partner.

1. The test starts at _____ ten o'clock.

2. My _____ is different every day because I always do a different activity after school.

3. Before Einstein explained the _____ of gravity, people had other ideas about why objects fall to the ground.

4. If I _____ a word problem carefully, and I still don't understand it, I ask the teacher for help.

5. I read the newspaper to find out about things that _____ in my country every day.

6. The game started at 10:00, and it's 11:00 now, so it's safe to _____ that he's not coming to the game.

▲ When will she find time to make a schedule?

## Word Study: Synonyms

Synonyms are two or more words that have the same or similar meanings. Sometimes synonyms have slightly different shades of meaning. A thesaurus is a book of synonyms that can help you find the word that means exactly what you want to say. Using different words to express a thought can make your writing more interesting. Look at the following synonyms.

| Words | Synonyms |
|---|---|
| **waste time** | dawdle, lag, linger, loaf, loiter |
| **procrastinate** | delay, put off |
| **watch** | care for, look after, look at, mind, tend |
| **think** | consider, imagine, mull over, reason, work things out |

**Practice**  Workbook Page 17

Work with a partner. Draw a chart like the one above in your notebook. Add the words below to the left column of the chart. Use a thesaurus or a dictionary to find at least two synonyms for each.

| | | |
|---|---|---|
| be idle | guard | protect |
| concentrate | postpone | stall |

## READING STRATEGY | IDENTIFY PROBLEMS AND SOLUTIONS

Identifying problems and solutions in a story helps you understand the text better. To identify problems and solutions, follow these steps:

- What problem does the person have? Who helps find a solution?
- What clues in the text tell you what the problem is?
- Think about your own experience. What would you do?
- Remember that the person may try a solution that doesn't work. There may be more than one possible solution to a problem.

As you read the excerpt from *The Phantom Tollbooth,* ask yourself what problems Milo has. How does Milo try to solve his problems?

 Workbook Page 18

**Set a purpose for reading** Why does Milo want to get out of the Doldrums quickly, and how does he reach out for help? How does the grandmother in the poem reach out to her granddaughter?

*from*

# The Phantom Tollbooth

*Norton Juster*

*Milo isn't interested in much until he receives a mysterious package with an easy-to-assemble tollbooth. A map and directions come with it, along with three precautionary signs. He must slow down when approaching the tollbooth, have his fare ready, and his destination in mind. Milo randomly chooses Dictionopolis as his destination since he doesn't think any of the places on the map are real anyway. The only trouble is that he takes a wrong turn and ends up in the Doldrums with the Lethargarians.*

"Well, if you can't laugh or think, what can you do?" asked Milo.

"Anything as long as it's nothing, and everything as long as it isn't anything," explained another. There's lots to do; we have a very busy schedule—

"At 8 o'clock we get up, and then we spend

"From 8 to 9 daydreaming.

"From 9 to 9:30 we take our early midmorning nap.

"From 9:30 to 10:30 we dawdle and delay.

"From 10:30 to 11:30 we take our late early morning nap.

"From 11:30 to 12:00 we bide our time and then eat lunch.

"From 1:00 to 2:00 we linger and loiter.

"From 2:00 to 2:30 we take our early afternoon nap.

"From 2:30 to 3:30 we put off for tomorrow what we could have done today.

"From 3:30 to 4:00 we take our early late afternoon nap.

"From 4:00 to 5:00 we loaf and lounge until dinner.

"From 6:00 to 7:00 we dillydally.

"From 7:00 to 8:00 we take our early evening nap, and then for an hour before we go to bed at 9:00 we waste time.

"As you can see, that leaves almost no time for brooding, lagging, plodding, or procrastinating, and if we stopped to think or laugh, we'd never get nothing done."

"You mean you'd never get anything done," corrected Milo.

"We don't want to get anything done," snapped another angrily; "we want to get nothing done, and we can do that without your help."

---

**bide our time**, wait until the right time to do something
**dillydally**, waste time by delaying
**brooding**, thinking for a long time about something you are worried about
**lagging**, moving more slowly than other things or people
**plodding**, doing something very slowly
**procrastinating**, delaying doing something

✔ **LITERARY CHECK**
*What **irony** do you see in the Lethargarians "busy schedule"?*

**BEFORE YOU GO ON**

**1** Besides eating and sleeping, what do the Lethargarians do all day?

**2** Why can't they stop to laugh or think?

💡**On Your Own**
Do you ever dillydally or procrastinate? Explain.

"You see," continued another in a more conciliatory tone, "it's really quite strenuous doing nothing all day, so once a week we take a holiday and go nowhere, which was just where we were going when you came along. Would you care to join us?"

"I might as well," thought Milo; "that's where I seem to be going anyway."

"Tell me," he yawned, for he felt ready for a nap now himself, "does everyone here do nothing?"

"Everyone but the terrible watchdog," said two of them, shuddering in chorus. "He's always sniffing around to see that nobody wastes time. A most unpleasant character."

"The watchdog?" said Milo quizzically.

"THE WATCHDOG," shouted another, fainting from fright, for racing down the road barking furiously and kicking up a great cloud of dust was the very dog of whom they had been speaking.

"RUN!"

"WAKE UP!"

"RUN!"

"HERE HE COMES!"

"THE WATCHDOG!"

Great shouts filled the air as the Lethargarians scattered in all directions and soon disappeared entirely.

"R-R-R-G-H-R-O-R-R-H-F-F," exclaimed the watchdog as he dashed up to the car, loudly puffing and panting.

---

**conciliatory**, intended to make someone stop being angry
**strenuous**, using a lot of effort, strength, or determination
**shuddering**, shaking with fear

40

Milo's eyes opened wide, for there in front of him was a large dog with a perfectly normal head, four feet, and a tail—and the body of a loudly ticking alarm clock.

"What are you doing here?" growled the watchdog.

"Just killing time," replied Milo apologetically. "You see—"

"KILLING TIME!" roared the dog—so furiously that his alarm went off. "It's bad enough wasting time without killing it." And he shuddered at the thought. "Why are you in the Doldrums anyway—don't you have anywhere to go?"

"I was on my way to Dictionopolis when I got stuck here," explained Milo. "Can you help me?"

"Help you! You must help yourself," the dog replied, carefully winding himself with his left hind leg. "I suppose you know why you got stuck."

"I guess I just wasn't thinking," said Milo.

"PRECISELY," shouted the dog as his alarm went off again. "Now you know what you must do."

"I'm afraid I don't," admitted Milo, feeling quite stupid.

"Well," continued the watchdog impatiently, "since you got here by not thinking, it seems reasonable to expect that, in order to get out, you must start thinking." And with that he hopped into the car.

"Do you mind if I get in? I love automobile rides."

Milo began to think as hard as he could (which was very difficult, since he wasn't used to it). He thought of birds that swim and fish that fly. He thought of yesterday's lunch and tomorrow's dinner. He thought of words that began with J and numbers that end in 3. And, as he thought, the wheels began to turn.

"We're moving, we're moving," he shouted happily.

"Keep thinking," scolded the watchdog.

The little car started to go faster and faster as Milo's brain whirled with activity, and down the road they went. In a few moments they were out of the Doldrums and back on the main highway. All the colors had returned to their original brightness, and as they raced along the road Milo continued to think of all sorts of things; of the many detours and wrong turns that were so easy to take, of how fine it was to be moving along, and, most of all, of how much could be accomplished with just a little thought. And the dog, his nose in the wind, just sat back, watchfully ticking.

---

**killing time,** doing something while waiting for something else to happen
**scolded,** said angrily
**whirled,** went around and around
**detours,** longer ways of getting to a place

## ABOUT THE AUTHOR

**Norton Juster** is an architect and designer as well as an author and former professor at Hampshire College. Two of Juster's books have become films: *The Dot and the Line* and *The Phantom Tollbooth.* Inspired by his granddaughter, his next book will be for very young children. He lives in Amherst, Massachusetts.

✔ **LITERARY CHECK**

*In this **allegory**, Milo finally gets out of the Doldrums. How is this symbolic of what happens in real life?*

**BEFORE YOU GO ON**

**1** How does Milo explain what he is doing in the Doldrums?

**2** How does Milo get out of the Doldrums?

💡**On Your Own**
What will you do the next time you get stuck in the doldrums?

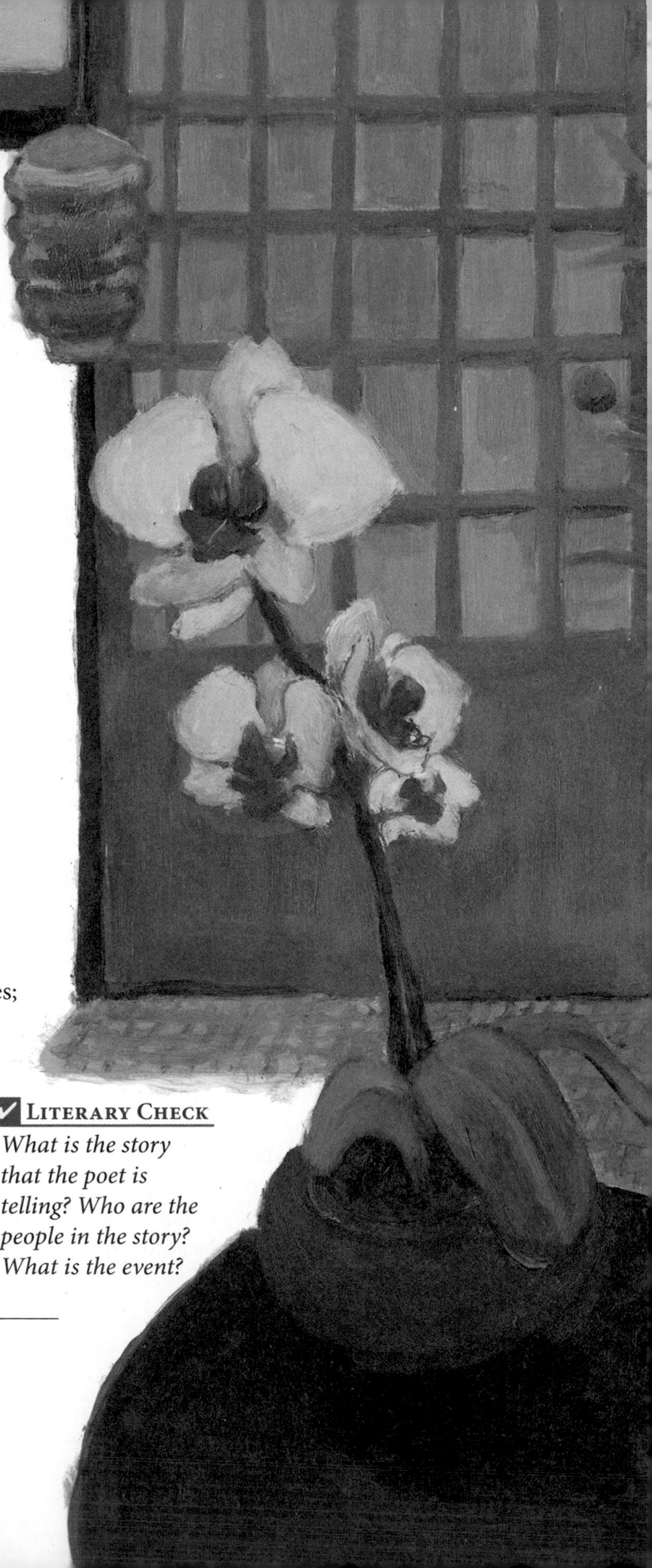

# Grandma Ling

***Amy Ling***

If you dig that hole deep enough
you'll reach China, they used to tell me,
a child in a backyard in Pennsylvania.
Not strong enough to dig that hole,
I waited twenty years,
then sailed back, half way around the world.

In Taiwan I first met Grandma.
Before she came to view, I heard
her slippered feet softly measure
the **tatami** floor with even step;
the aqua paper-covered door slid open
and there I faced
my five foot height, **sturdy** legs and feet,
square forehead, high cheeks, and wide-set eyes;
my image stood before me,
**acted on** by fifty years.

She smiled, stretched her arms
to take to heart the eldest daughter
of her youngest son a quarter century away.
She spoke a **tongue** I knew no word of,
and I was sad I could not understand,
but I could hug her.

**✔ LITERARY CHECK**

*What is the story that the poet is telling? Who are the people in the story? What is the event?*

---

**tatami**, woven of rice straw
**sturdy**, strong
**acted on**, showing the effects
**tongue**, language

## ABOUT THE **POET**

**Amy Ling** (1939–1999) was born in China and moved to the United States with her family when she was six years old. In addition to writing poetry, Ling worked as an editor of American literature anthologies. She also worked hard to create a wider audience for Asian-American writers. In the 1960s, Ling visited her grandmother in Taiwan and wrote about their first meeting in this poem.

## BEFORE YOU GO ON

**1** The first line of the poem is a common expression. Why do you think the poet begins the poem with this image?

**2** Do you think the poet resembles, or looks like, her grandmother? What evidence can you find in the poem?

**On Your Own**
Do you have grandparents? Do they live near you or far away?

43

# Review and Practice

## DRAMATIC READING

Work in groups of five or six to reread, discuss, and analyze the excerpt from *The Phantom Tollbooth*. Describe the problem that Milo encounters in the Doldrums and discuss how he finally gets out. Remember that *The Phantom Tollbooth* is an allegory: It has a deeper meaning than just a story about a boy who gets stuck in an imaginary land with strange creatures called Lethargarians. How do people in real life get stuck in the doldrums? Understanding the underlying meanings of a text will improve your dramatic reading.

After your group has reread and examined the reading carefully, read it as a play, leaving out everything but the dialogue. Assign group members to be Milo, the watchdog, and the Lethargarians. Practice acting out the dialogue. Comment on one another's oral reading and make helpful suggestions for improvements. Then present your play to the class. Use sound effects for the ticking alarm clock, if you wish.

▶)) *Speaking* TIP

Practice until you can read without looking at the dialogue so you can make eye contact with your audience.

## COMPREHENSION

Workbook
Page 19

### Right There

1. What do the Lethargarians do in the Doldrums?
2. How old is the poet when she first meets her grandmother?

### Think and Search

3. Why don't the Lethargarians like the watchdog?
4. Where does the poet live? Where does her grandmother live?

### Author and You

5. What is humorous about the watchdog? What other examples of humor can you find in this reading?
6. Do you think the poet was glad to see her grandmother? How do they reach out to each other?

### On Your Own

7. How would you advise a friend who gets stuck in the doldrums?
8. What's your relationship like with your grandparents?

## DISCUSSION

Discuss in pairs or small groups.

* The Lethargarians waste time, dawdle, delay, procrastinate, and do nothing all day. The watchdog sniffs around making sure nobody wastes time. Is the watchdog right, or is he being too strict? Should people be busy all the time? Explain.

* **Why should we reach out to others?** Both Milo in the novel excerpt and the young woman in the poem are in unfamiliar places meeting people for the first time. Do you think people in that situation might feel nervous about reaching out to someone they don't know? How would you feel in that situation?

## Listening TIP

Listen carefully to find out if you agree or disagree with others.

## RESPONSE TO LITERATURE

**Workbook**
**Page 19**

Imagine you are Milo and write a thank-you note to the watchdog. Include details about your ordeal in the Doldrums. List specific reasons why you are so grateful to him.

Dear Watchdog,
How can I ever thank you for helping me out of the Doldrums? I don't know what I would have done if you hadn't come along.

# Grammar and Writing

## Simple Present for Habitual Actions or Routines

The simple present can be used to talk about routines or things that happen regularly. You can use words like *always, never, every day,* and *once, twice, three times a day* to tell how often they occur. Notice how the simple present is used to describe the Lethargarians' schedule for one morning.

| Lethargarians' Morning Schedule | |
|---|---|
| 8:00 | We get up. |
| 8:00 to 9:00 | We daydream. |
| 9:00 to 9:30 | We take our early midmorning nap. |
| 9:30 to 10:30 | We dawdle and delay. |
| 10:30 to 11:30 | We take our late early morning nap. |
| 11:30 to 12:00 | We bide our time and then eat lunch. |

The Lethargarians get up at 8:00 **every day**.
They take naps **twice** every morning.
They **always** daydream between 8:00 and 9:00.
They dawdle and delay **every day**, and **never** hurry or rush.

**Practice**  **Workbook Page 20**

Copy the chart below into your notebook. List things you do *always, never, every day,* and *once, twice, three times* (or more often) *a day.* With a partner, use the simple present to talk about your charts.

| Frequency | Activity/Routine |
|---|---|
| always | |
| never | |
| every day | |
| _____ a day | |

# WRITING A DESCRIPTIVE PARAGRAPH

## Describe an Event

You have learned how to describe a place and a person. Now you will learn how to describe an event.

Read the paragraph below and notice how the writer uses **chronological order** to relate what happens to Milo in the Doldrums. The words *first, next, then,* and *finally* help you follow what happens.

First

↓

Next

↓

Then

↓

Finally

*Chas Robinson*

### A Day in the Life of Milo

On his way to Dictionopolis, Milo makes a wrong turn and finds himself in the Doldrums. First, he notices some strange creatures that are sitting around and looking very bored. They explain their schedule to him, which consists of dawdling and lingering. Next, Milo asks if everybody does nothing in the Doldrums. Their response is, "Everyone but the terrible watchdog. He's always sniffing around to see that nobody wastes time." Then, suddenly, the Lethargarians begin to sprint down the road screaming that the watchdog is coming. Milo approaches the watchdog and tells him how he arrived in the Doldrums in the first place. The watchdog tells Milo that if he got there by not thinking, he could leave by thinking. As Milo starts thinking, the car begins to move, the watchdog jumps in, and they are off on their way. Finally, Milo is out of the Doldrums.

## Practice

Workbook Page 21

Write a paragraph describing something you do every day. You might title it "A Day in the Life of _____." Use a sequence chart to help you organize your paragraph. Be sure to use sequence words to make your paragraph easy to follow and to use the simple present correctly.

**Writing Checklist**

**SENTENCE FLUENCY:**

☑ My sentences begin in different ways.

**CONVENTIONS:**

☑ I used the present tense for habitual action.

# Prepare to Read

## What You Will Learn

**Reading**

- Vocabulary building: *Context, dictionary skills, word study*

- Reading strategy: *Use visuals*

- Text type: *Informational text (science)*

**Grammar, Usage, and Mechanics**
Complex and compound-complex sentences

**Writing**
Describe an object

## THE BIG QUESTION

**Why should we reach out to others?** Humans are social beings. We need to be with other people, to love and be loved. Brain scans of depressed, or sad, people show areas of low activity. Do you think your brain controls your emotions? Do you think reaching out and being with other people makes you happier? Discuss with a partner.

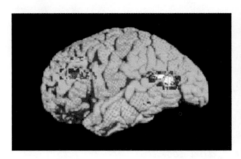

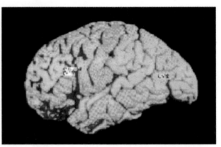

▲ A depressed brain (the red/yellow areas represent low brain activity)

▲ A normal brain

## BUILD BACKGROUND

You're going to read a science article called **"Your Brain and Nervous System."** Look at this diagram of the front of the brain and read the labels. Many parts of the anatomy have Latin names. Latin is the language of the ancient Romans. Scientists have continued to use Latin terms to name body parts since Claudius Galen (c. 130–c. 200 C.E.), the greatest surgeon of ancient times, began to classify them.

Cross section of the brain
▼ from the front

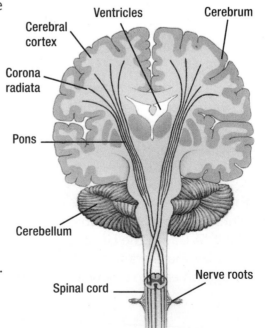

Cerebral cortex

Ventricles

Cerebrum

Corona radiata

Pons

Cerebellum

Spinal cord

Nerve roots

## Learn Key Words

Read these sentences. Use the context to figure out the meaning of the **red** words. Use a dictionary to check your answers. Then write each word and its meaning in your notebook.

1. It's difficult to tell what a young child will do. His **behavior** is impossible to guess.
2. **Nerves** connect the brain with all parts of the body.
3. The brain contains billions of cells, or **neurons**, that receive and send messages.
4. Each **organ**, or part of the body, has a function.
5. Your nervous system **relays** messages from your sense organs to your brain.
6. The brain, spinal cord, and nerves make up a **system** of the body. They work together to perform a group of functions.

### Key Words

behavior
nerves
neurons
organ
relays
system

**Practice**  Workbook Page 22

Write the sentences in your notebook. Choose a **red** word from the box above to complete each sentence. Then take turns reading the sentences aloud with a partner.

1. A group of organs that work together to perform a body function is a _____.
2. The brain is the _____ that controls the beating of your heart.
3. When you touch something hot, your nervous system _____ a message to your brain.
4. Some patterns of _____ , like lying or procrastinating, are difficult to change—but not impossible.
5. Your brain is connected to every part of your body by _____.
6. _____ are cells that create pathways in the brain.

▲ Your brain does more than give you bright ideas. It also controls your behavior.

## Learn Academic Words

Study the **red** words and their meanings. You will find these words useful when talking and writing about informational texts. Write each word and its meaning in your notebook. After you read "Your Brain and Nervous System," try to use these words to respond to the text.

| | | |
|---|---|---|
| **adaptable** = able to adjust | | My plant died when I put it outside. It wasn't **adaptable** to the cold weather. |
| **analytical** = able to use logic | | If you want to become a scientist, it helps to be **analytical**. |
| **function** = purpose; action that a thing performs | | Taking oxygen into the body is a **function** of the lungs. |
| **logical** = able to use reason | | A **logical** person is usually a good problem solver. |
| **process** = a series of actions | | The digestion **process** begins in your mouth. |
| **react** = change in response to a message or stimulus | | The brain tells your body how to **react** to what's happening around you. |

## Practice  Workbook Page 23

Work with a partner to answer these questions. Try to include the **red** word in your answer. Write the sentences in your notebook.

1. Why is it important for animals and plants to be **adaptable** to their environments?
2. Are you more **analytical** or more creative?
3. What is one **function** of your brain?
4. In what subjects do you need to use **logical** thinking?
5. Which organ is involved in the respiratory **process**?
6. How will your brain tell your body to **react** if you touch a hot stove?

▲ If you're good at chess, you're probably more analytical.

## Word Study: Roots

The root is the part of a word that contains the basic meaning of the word. English words that come from Latin—including many words used in biology—have Latin roots. The chart below shows some roots, their meanings, and some English words that contain them.

| Root | Meaning | English Word(s) |
|------|---------|-----------------|
| cerebr | cerebr | cerebrum<br>cerebellum<br>cerebral |
| corpus | main part | corpus |
| hemi | half | hemisphere |
| lobus | curved or round | lobe |
| sphaira | ball | hemisphere |

**Practice**

With a partner, look through "Your Brain and Nervous System" to find each of the English words in the chart above. Make sure you understand the meaning of each word. Check a dictionary, if necessary.

▲ North America is in Earth's northern hemisphere.

## READING STRATEGY    USE VISUALS

Using visuals helps you understand the text better. Visuals include art, photographs, diagrams, charts, maps, etc. Many informational texts include visuals. To use visuals, follow these steps:

- Look at the visuals. What type are they? What do they show?
- Pay attention to any text associated with visuals, such as captions.
- Use the visuals to help you understand difficult words in the reading.

As you read "Your Brain and Nervous System," look at the diagrams. What do they tell you about the brain and central nervous system?

**Set a purpose for reading** What part of the brain controls the emotions?

# Your Brain and Nervous System

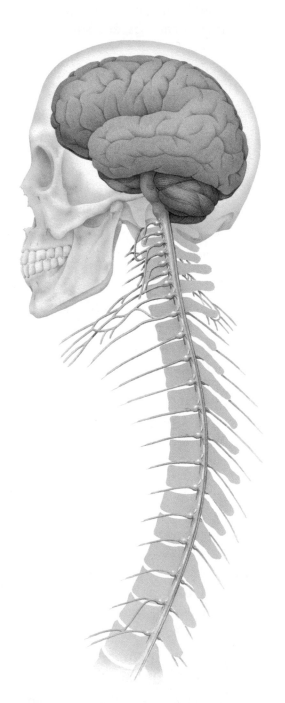

When you're taking a big math test, you know that your brain is hard at work. But your brain is doing a lot more than just remembering formulas. Those sweaty palms you get as the test starts? That's your brain at work. The relief you feel when you know an answer's right? That's your brain too.

The brain may simply be the bossiest part of the body: It tells virtually every other part of your body what to do, all the time. It not only controls what you think and feel, how you learn and remember, and the way you move your body, but also things such as the beating of your heart and whether you feel sleepy or awake.

## Why Are the Brain and Nervous System Important in Everyday Life?

You can think of the brain as a central computer that controls all the functions of your body. Then think of the **nervous system** as a network that relays messages back and forth from the brain to different parts of the body. The nervous system does this via the **spinal cord**. It runs from the brain down through the back and contains thread-like nerves that branch out to every organ and body part.

---

**formulas,** sets of principles you use to solve problems
**bossiest,** always telling someone what to do

When a message comes into the brain from anywhere in the body, the brain tells the body how to react. For example, if you accidentally touch a hot stove, the nerves in your skin shoot a message of pain to your brain. The brain then sends a message back telling the muscles in your hand to pull away.

## How the Brain Works

Considering everything it does, the human brain is incredibly compact, weighing just 3 pounds [1.3 kg.]. Its many folds and grooves, though, provide it with the additional surface area necessary for storing all of the body's important information.

The spinal cord, on the other hand, is a long bundle of nerve tissue about 18 inches [45 cm.] long and ¾ inch [2 cm.] thick. It extends from the lower part of the brain down through the spine. Along the way, various nerves branch out to the entire body. These are called the **peripheral nervous system**.

## How the Nervous System Works

The basic functioning of the nervous system depends a lot on tiny cells called **neurons**. The brain has billions of them. All neurons relay information to each other through a complex electrochemical process, making connections that affect the way we think, learn, move and, behave.

## Intelligence, Learning, and Memory

At birth, your nervous system contains all the neurons you will ever have, but many of them are not connected to each other. As you grow and learn, messages travel from one neuron to another over and over, creating connections, or pathways, in the brain. It's why riding a bike or driving a car seems to take so much concentration when you first learn but later on becomes second nature: The pathway is established.

In young children, the brain is highly adaptable. But as we age, the brain has to work harder to make new neural pathways, making it more difficult to master new tasks or change established behavior patterns. That's why many scientists believe it's important to keep challenging your brain to learn new things and make new connections.

---

compact, small but arranged so that everything fits neatly into the available space
folds and grooves, areas that rise and fall like waves
bundle, small group
second nature, a well-learned skill that becomes easy to do

▲ An octopus brain has 300 billion neurons, 200 billion more than the human brain. If you lined up all the neurons in the human brain, they would stretch about 965 kilometers (600 mi.)!

**BEFORE YOU GO ON**

1 What controls all the body's functions? What do neurons do?

2 What is memory?

💡**On Your Own**
Were you surprised at how much your brain controls? Explain.

53

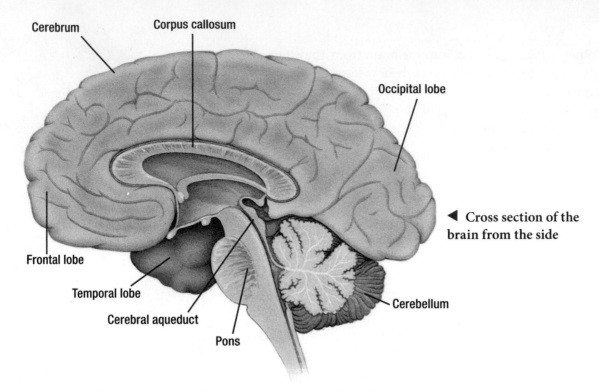

Cerebrum

Corpus callosum

Occipital lobe

◀ Cross section of the brain from the side

Frontal lobe

Temporal lobe

Cerebral aqueduct

Pons

Cerebellum

Memory is another complex function of the brain. The things we've done, learned and seen are first processed in the cortex. Then, if we sense that this information is important enough to remember permanently, it's passed inward to other regions of the brain for long-term storage and retrieval. As these messages travel through the brain, they create pathways that serve as the basis of our memory.

The brain is made up of three main sections: the forebrain, the midbrain, and the hindbrain.

## The Forebrain

The forebrain is the largest and most complex part of the brain. It consists of the **cerebrum**. This is the area with all the folds and grooves typically seen in pictures of the brain.

The cerebrum contains the information that essentially makes us who we are: our intelligence, memory, personality, emotion, speech, and ability to feel and move. Specific areas of the cerebrum are in charge of processing these different types of information. These are called **lobes**, and there are four of them: the frontal, parietal, temporal, and occipital.

The cerebrum has right and left halves, called **hemispheres**. These are connected in the middle by a band of nerve fibers (the **corpus callosum**). These fibers enable the two sides to communicate.

---

**permanently**, forever
**retrieval**, process of regaining, restoring, or remembering

Although these halves may look like mirror images of each other, many scientists believe they have different functions. The left side is considered the logical, analytical, objective side. The right side is thought to be more intuitive, creative, and subjective. So when you're doing a math problem, you're using the left side. When you're listening to music, you're using the right side. Scientists think that some people are more "right-brained" or "left-brained" while others are more "whole-brained," meaning they use both halves of their brain to the same degree.

The outer layer of the cerebrum is called the **cortex** (also known as "gray matter"). Information collected by the five senses comes into the brain from the spinal cord to the cortex. This information is then directed to other parts of the nervous system for further processing. For example, when you touch the hot stove, not only does a message go out to move your hand, but one also goes to another part of the brain to help you remember not to do that again.

In the inner part of the forebrain sit the **thalamus**, **hypothalamus,** and **pituitary gland**. The thalamus carries messages from the sensory organs like the eyes, ears, nose, and fingers to the cortex. The hypothalamus controls the pulse, thirst, appetite, sleep patterns, and other processes in our bodies that happen automatically. It also controls the pituitary gland. This gland makes the hormones that control our growth, metabolism, digestion, sexual maturity, and how we respond to stress.

## The Midbrain

The midbrain, located underneath the middle of the forebrain, acts as a master coordinator for all the messages going in and out of the brain to the spinal cord.

## The Hindbrain

The hindbrain sits underneath the back end of the cerebrum. It consists of the cerebellum, pons, and medulla. The **cerebellum** is also called the "little brain" because it looks like a small version of the cerebrum. It is responsible for balance, movement, and coordination. The **pons** and the **medulla**, along with the midbrain, are often called the **brainstem**. The brainstem takes in, sends out, and coordinates all of the brain's messages. It also controls many of the body's automatic functions, like breathing, heart rate, blood pressure, swallowing, digestion, and blinking.

---

**objective**, not influenced by your own feelings, beliefs, or ideas
**intuitive**, based on feelings rather than facts
**subjective**, influenced by personal opinion or feelings rather than fact
**coordinator**, one who organizes activities
**coordination**, the way the parts of your body work together to do something

**BEFORE YOU GO ON**

1 What part of the brain makes us who we are? Explain.

2 What are the functions of each part of the brain?

**On Your Own**
Do you think that you are more "right-brained," "left-brained," or "whole-brained"? Explain.

# Review and Practice

## COMPREHENSION  Workbook Page 26

### Right There

1. What is the peripheral nervous system?
2. What are the three main sections of the brain?

### Think and Search

3. Why is it helpful to compare the brain to a central computer?
4. Why is it amazing that the brain is so compact?

### Author and You

5. Why do you think the author describes the brain as "the bossiest part of the body"?
6. What point does the author make about challenging your brain to learn new things and make new connections?

### On Your Own

7. Why is it important to know how vital parts of the body work?
8. In your opinion, is it better to be more logical, analytical, and objective or more intuitive, creative, and subjective? Explain.

## IN YOUR OWN WORDS

Work with a partner. Copy the chart below into your notebook. Use the words in the second column to help you summarize the text.

> **Speaking TIPS**
>
> Practice until you feel confident presenting your summary.
>
> Pause after each main point and make eye contact with your partner.

| Heading | Words to Use |
|---|---|
| Why the Brain and Nervous System Are Important in Everyday Life | nervous system, spinal cord |
| How the Brain Works | compact, spinal cord, peripheral nervous system |
| How the Nervous System Works | neurons |
| Intelligence, Learning, and Memory | neurons, pathway, adaptable, memory |
| The Forebrain | cerebrum, hemispheres, right-brained, left-brained |
| The Midbrain | coordination |
| The Hindbrain | "little brain," functions |

## DISCUSSION

Discuss in pairs or small groups.

1. Do you think brain research is important? Why or why not?
2. In which professions or careers would a person have to be logical and analytical? In which ones would it be better to be intuitive or creative? Explain.

Q **Why should we reach out to others?** Which part of the brain do you think you use when you reach out to someone? Explain your answer.

**»)) Listening TIP**

If you don't understand something a speaker says, you can say, "Could you repeat that, please?"

## READ FOR FLUENCY

When we read aloud to communicate meaning, we group words into phrases, pause or slow down to make important points, and emphasize important words. Pause for a short time when you reach a comma and for a longer time when you reach a period. Pay attention to rising and falling intonation at the end of sentences.

Work with a partner. Choose a paragraph from the reading. Discuss which words seem important for communicating meaning. Practice pronouncing difficult words. Take turns reading the paragraph aloud and give each other feedback.

## EXTENSION

**Workbook
Page 26**

Use online or print resources to find out more about the brain and the nervous system, such as the autonomic nervous system, the sympathetic nervous system, and the parasympathetic nervous system. Which one prepares you for sudden stress, like seeing an accident happening? Which one prepares your body for rest? Which one controls sweating and shivering? Which part of the brain controls movements of the left and right sides of the body? Discuss what you learned with a partner.

▲ What side of the brain controls movement, such as throwing a baseball?

# Grammar and Writing

## Complex and Compound-Complex Sentences

Complex sentences have one independent clause and one or more dependent clauses.

---

**Complex Sentence**

| dependent clause | independent clause |
|---|---|

**Because** the brain is a complicated organ, scientists do not understand everything about it.

---

Compound-complex sentences have more than one independent clause, as well as one or more dependent clauses.

---

**Compound-Complex Sentence**

| dependent clause | independent clause |
|---|---|

**Because** the brain is a complicated organ, scientists do not understand everything about it,

independent clause

**but** they are discovering more information all the time.

---

Some words used to begin dependent clauses include *because, since, although, even though, when, while,* and *as;* some words used to join independent clauses include *but, and, yet, or,* and *so.*

**Practice**  **Workbook Page 27**

Work with a partner. Use the following sentence starters to form complex and compound-complex sentences about the brain. Write the sentences in your notebook.

1. Although the brain weighs only 1.3 kilograms (3 lb.), _____.

2. While the hemispheres look like mirror images of each other, _____.

3. The cerebellum is called the "little brain" _____.

4. As people age, _____.

## WRITING A DESCRIPTIVE PARAGRAPH

### Describe an Object

You have learned how to describe a place, a person, and an event. Now you will learn how to describe an object like the human brain. Then, at the end of this unit, you'll use the skills and techniques you've learned to write a longer descriptive essay.

Read the paragraph below and notice how the writer uses **spatial organization**—that is, she presents the details in an order that makes sense for the object she is describing. In this case, the writer describes the brain from front to back. She used a graphic organizer to help organize her spatial details.

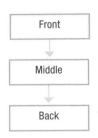

Front

↓

Middle

↓

Back

*Ashley Nicole Smith*

*Sections of the Brain*

The human brain has three main sections: the forebrain, the midbrain, and the hindbrain. Each performs different functions. The forebrain is at the very front of the brain. It contains the cerebrum, which holds the information that makes us unique, like our memory, intelligence, and speech. The cerebrum has two halves called hemispheres. The left side is the logical, analytical, and objective side, while the right side is the intuitive, creative, and subjective side. The outer layer of the forebrain is the cortex. Information from the five senses comes into the brain here. Under the middle of the forebrain is the midbrain. It controls all the messages going in and out of the brain to the spinal cord. The hindbrain is found underneath the back end of the cerebrum. It contains the cerebellum, which controls balance, movement, and coordination—important for activities such as walking and dancing.

### Practice

**Workbook Page 28**

Write a paragraph about another part of the body or any object that can be described using spatial organization. Use words like *at the top, in the middle, on the right side, on the left side,* and *at the bottom.* Use a graphic organizer to help you organize your spatial details. Be sure to use a clear topic sentence and details that support it. Use complex and compound-complex sentences correctly.

**Writing Checklist**

**ORGANIZATION:**

☑ I used a clear topic sentence.

**WORD CHOICE:**

☑ I provided descriptive details that support my topic sentence.

59

# Link the Readings

## Critical Thinking

Look back at the readings in this unit. Think about what they have in common. They all tell about reaching out. Yet they do not all have the same purpose. The purpose of one reading might be to inform, while the purpose of another might be to entertain or persuade. In addition, the content of each reading relates to the theme of reaching out differently. Now copy the chart below into your notebook and complete it.

| Title of Reading | Purpose | Big Question Link |
|---|---|---|
| From *Criss Cross* | | |
| "Oranges" | | |
| "Managing Stress" | | *You can reach out silently.* |
| From *The Phantom Tollbooth* | *to entertain* | |
| "Grandma Ling" | | |
| "Your Brain and Nervous System" | | |

## Discussion

Discuss in pairs or small groups.

- Think about the readings. Why do you think it was difficult for Debbie to reach out to Mrs. Bruning at first? Is it easy to help others who are stressed? Why or why not? The watchdog told Milo he had to help himself. Is it easier to help others or yourself? Explain your answers.

- **Q** **Why should we reach out to others?** Are some people are born with an ability to reach out more than others, or is this something a person can learn?

## Fluency Check

Work with a partner. Choose a paragraph from one of the readings. Take turns reading it for one minute. Count the total number of words you read. Practice saying the words you had trouble reading. Take turns reading the paragraph three more times. Did you read more words each time? Copy the chart below into your notebook and record your speeds.

| | 1st Speed | 2nd Speed | 3rd Speed | 4th Speed |
|---|---|---|---|---|
| Words Per Minutes | | | | |

# Projects

Work in pairs or small groups. Choose one of these projects.

**1** Look through magazines to find photos, illustrations, cartoons, and articles that show people helping others. Create a collage and give it a title that tells why reaching out is important.

**2** Each day for a week, practice the relaxation technique in the article "Managing Stress." Did the technique work? Can it help people manage stress? Write a review for a health magazine.

**3** Have a talk show about managing stress. Decide who will be the talk-show host, an expert, and the guests. List stressful situations that guests need help with and the advice the expert will offer. Practice your show and present it to the class.

**4** Make a travel brochure for a trip to the Doldrums. Answer travelers' questions. How do you get there? What do you need? What do people do there?

# Further Reading

To find out more about the theme of this unit, choose from these reading suggestions.

**Teacher Man,** Frank McCourt
This Penguin Reader® adaptation is the story of Frank McCourt, who left Ireland as a young man to live in New York. He became a teacher in a school where the students had little interest in learning.

**Getting Near to Bab,** Audrey Couloumbis
When their baby sister dies and their mother slips into a depression, Willa Jo and Little Sister are sent to bossy but good-hearted Aunt Patty. Willa Jo finds a unique way to take control of the situation in this Newbery Honor book.

**Me, Stressed Out? (Peanut's Wisdom),** Charles M. Schultz
Schultz's fascination with comic strips began when he read the Sunday comics with his father. "As a youngster, I didn't realize how many Charlie Browns there were in the world," Schulz said. "I thought I was the only one. Now I realize that Charlie Brown's goofs are familiar to everybody, adults and children alike."

# Put It All Together

## LISTENING & SPEAKING WORKSHOP
### Group Presentation

You will give a group presentation describing a person, place, event, or object that needs or provides special help.

**1** **THINK ABOUT IT** In this unit, you've learned about the importance of reaching out to others. You've also learned techniques for describing a person, place, event, and object. People in service groups often make oral presentations to ask for others' help. Their presentations must include clear and vivid decriptions.

Work in small groups. Choose one of these topics:

Why _____ should receive an award for helping _____ (Describe the person.)

Why _____ should receive disaster relief to help _____ (Describe the place.)

Why _____ is the best way to raise funds to help _____ (Describe the event.)

Why _____ should be donated to help _____ (Describe the object[s].)

▲ A speaker talks to a crowd at a fund raiser

**2** **GATHER AND ORGANIZE INFORMATION**
As a group, decide how to fill in the blanks for your topic. Then prepare your presentation. To decribe a person, include character traits and qualities. For a place, use sensory details. For an event, use sequence words. For an object, use spatial order.

**Research** Use online news links to find information. Who has done the most to help cancer research or homelessness? What areas of the world need disaster relief? Which fund-raising events have been most effective? What objects are best to donate in a disaster?

**Order Your Notes** As you research, list descriptive details and then circle the ones that best support your main idea. Organize your main points and descriptive details into an outline.

**Use Visuals** Look online and download any photos you can use.

**3** **PRACTICE AND PRESENT** Use your outline to help you with your presentation. Assign parts of the outline to each group member. Decide when to use your visuals, and make note of this in your outline. Practice your presentation as a group. As each of you presents, offer suggestions for improvement. Keep practicing until all group members know their parts well.

**Deliver Your Group Presentation** Look at your audience as you speak. Emphasize key descriptive details and remember to show your visuals. Slow down when you come to the most important points, or have a group member restate them at the end of the presentation. Make sure all group members have participated. Give members of the audience a chance to ask questions.

**4** **EVALUATE THE PRESENTATION**
You can improve your skills as a speaker and a listener by evaluating each presentation you give and hear. Use this checklist to help you judge your group's presentation and the presentations of the other groups.

☑ Was the group's message clear?

☑ Were descriptive details vivid and presented clearly?

☑ Did any speaker speak too quickly or too slowly, too loudly or too softly?

☑ Were the transitions between speakers smooth and logical?

☑ What suggestions do you have for improving the presentation?

 *Speaking* TIPS

Plan the order in which group members will speak ahead of time. This will make transitions from one person to the next go smoothly.

Be sure you are speaking slowly and clearly. Ask your listeners for feedback: *Can you hear me all right? Is this better?*

 *Listening* TIPS

Try to visualize the people, places, events or objects that are described.

Think about the group's message. Do you have any questions? Write them down, and ask them at the end of the presentation.

# WRITING WORKSHOP
## Descriptive Essay

You have learned how to write a variety of descriptive paragraphs and some techniques to develop them. Now, you will write a descriptive essay. An essay is a piece of writing that develops a specific idea. Most essays begin with an introductory paragraph that presents the writer's main idea. The writer also includes several body paragraphs that support the main idea. A good essay ends with a paragraph that restates the main idea in a new and interesting way. In a descriptive essay, the writer uses language that appeals to a reader's senses to create a vivid image of whatever is being described.

   Your writing assignment for this workshop is to write a five-paragraph descriptive essay about a person, place, event, or object.

**1 PREWRITE** Choose a topic from the Listening and Speaking Workshop that you did not already present and that has not already been described by another group. Select a topic that interests you.

**List and Organize Ideas and Details** After you choose a topic, brainstorm ideas for your essay on a descriptive details web. Be sure to include sensory details if you're planning to describe a place and to list physical and character traits for a person. Include details that tell chronological order for an event and details that show spatial organization for an object. A student named Chas wrote his essay about a place. Notice how he wrote his main idea in the center of his web and then listed descriptive details.

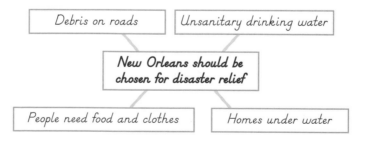

**2 DRAFT** Use the model on page 67 and your descriptive details web to help you write your first draft. Remember to include an introductory paragraph, three body paragraphs, and a concluding paragraph.

**3** **REVISE** Read over your draft. As you do so, ask yourself the questions in the writing checklist. Use the questions to help you revise your essay.

> ## SIX TRAITS OF WRITING CHECKLIST
>
> ☑ **IDEAS:** Is my main idea clear?
> ☑ **ORGANIZATION:** Are my details presented in an order that makes sense?
> ☑ **VOICE:** Does my writing express who I am?
> ☑ **WORD CHOICE:** Do I include a variety of describing words?
> ☑ **SENTENCE FLUENCY:** Do my sentences flow smoothly?
> ☑ **CONVENTIONS:** Does my writing follow the rules of grammar, usage, and mechanics?

Here are the changes Chas plans to make when he revises his first draft:

The city of New Orleans, Louisiana, was once a ~~beautiful~~ dazzling city where millions of people lived and millions more vacationed. That was before hurricane Katrina devastated the region. After Katrina, the scene in New Orleans was very different: businesses had collapsed; thousands of people were homeless; and disease was rampant. Many of the problems created by Katrina continued to exist. New Orleans should be chosen for disaster relief. because This horrible event changed the city's appearance and structure forever.

No one was prepared for the force of the storm. It struck the city with wind speeds of more than one hundred miles per hour. Pieces of *shattered* glass and splinters of wood whirled in the air. People ran, screaming, *as* to escape the water that was rapidly rising up into their houses. Much of the city was under water.

*Once the storm was over,* People faced the difficult task of figuring out what was still standing and what was destroyed. The levee system and sewage pipes had burst, creating unsanitary drinking water and spreading debris-laden muck through every street and building. Thousands of people were left without a home, food, water, or clean clothing.

Help was slow in coming. Supplies had to be flown in by helicopter and were scarce. Finally, after a few weeks, the National Guard and other groups were able to airlift people to shelters. *but* Many people remained in the ~~wreckage~~ *rubble* left by Hurricane Katrina.

Hurricane Katrina was one of the worst natural disaster in the history of the United States. New Orleans is in desperate need of disaster relief to fix the problems associated with this example of nature's fury. Help is needed to repair damaged levees, to feed hungry men, women, and children, and to restore the feelings of peace and security that existed before the storm.

## 4 EDIT AND PROOFREAD

Workbook
Page 29

Copy your revised draft onto a clean sheet of paper. Read your essay again. Correct any errors in grammar, word usage, mechanics, and spelling. Here are the additional changes Chas plans to make when he prepares his final draft.

Chas Robinson

### Help for New Orleans

The city of New Orleans, Louisiana, was once a dazzling ~~city~~ metropolis where millions of people lived and millions more vacationed. That was before hurricane Katrina devastated the region. After Katrina, the scene in New Orleans was very different: businesses had collapsed; thousands of people were homeless; and disease was rampant. Many of the problems created by Katrina continue to exist. New Orleans should be chosen for disaster relief because this horrible event changed the city's appearance and structure forever.

No one was prepared for the force of the storm. It struck the city with wind speeds of more than one hundred miles per hour. Pieces of shattered glass and splinters of wood whirled in the air as people ran, screaming, to escape the water that was rapidly rising up into their houses. Much of the city was under water.

Once the storm was over, people faced the difficult task of figuring out what was still standing and what was destroyed. The levee system and sewage pipes had burst, creating unsanitary drinking water and spreading debris-laden muck through every street and building. Thousands of people were left without a home, food, water, or clean clothing.

Help was slow in coming. Supplies had to be flown in by helicopter and were scarce. Finally, after a few weeks, the National Guard and other groups were able to airlift people to shelters, but many people remained in the rubble left by Hurricane Katrina.

Hurricane Katrina was one of the worst natural disasters in the history of the United States. New Orleans is in desperate need of disaster relief to fix the problems associated with this example of nature's fury. Help is needed to repair damaged levees, to feed hungry men, women, and children, and to restore the feelings of peace and security that existed before the storm.

**5** **PUBLISH** Prepare your final draft. Share your essay with your teacher and classmates.

Workbook
Page 30

# Bridging the Distance

*S*ome people reach out to others to help them. Others reach out because *they need help themselves. Most people realize that anyone can be in either position at any time. Many American artists have explored these changes in power and need, and how suddenly they can take place.*

### Philip Evergood, *Dowager in a Wheelchair* (1952)

"She wanted still to be young," Philip Evergood said of an old woman he saw being wheeled along Madison Avenue in New York City. She looked "alive in spirit" even though her body was only half functioning. This brief meeting was the idea, or inspiration, behind Evergood's painting *Dowager in a Wheelchair*.

The painting shows many stages of a woman's life. A young lady pushes a baby stroller in the background. A daughter pushes her aging mother in a wheelchair. An eager face appears in a taxicab window, headed somewhere in the big city. But it's the dowager, or aging woman, that takes center stage. Her stylish hat and veil are in harsh contrast to her swollen legs and claw-like hand in a black glove. The daughter clearly doesn't mind taking her mother on an outing. She wears a happy expression. All of the important figures in the picture are either being helped or helping others.

Philip Evergood, *Dowager in a Wheelchair*
(detail), 1952, oil, 47⅞ x 36 in.,
Smithsonian American Art Museum ▶

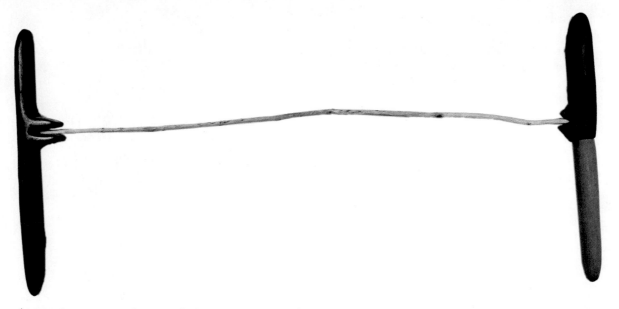

▲ Yuriko Yamaguchi, *Reach Out #3*, 1989, wood, 34 x 72½ x 3 in., Smithsonian American Art Museum

### Yuriko Yamaguchi, *Reach Out #3* (1989)

Yuriko Yamaguchi uses a different approach in this three-dimensional work to capture the things that bind people together. In *Reach Out #3,* the artist unites two figures with a stick, which reflects their conversation. It looks so fragile, like a thin string across a large space. Of course, the conversations that we all use to build our social lives are equally fragile as we work to build bonds of friendship with others.

The figures in the sculpture are made of stained and painted wood, but Yamaguchi found the stick in the woods. By using the two types of wood in her sculpture, the artist also captured the connection between man-made things and the natural world. This hanging wall structure is about "bridging a distance or void," the artist said, which is what each of us does when we reach out to another person.

Yamaguchi grew up in Japan. Even though she lives in the United States now, she often returns to her homeland for artistic inspiration.

The best artists rarely hide in their studios, but reach out into their community for ideas and connections that will give strength, depth, and beauty to their work.

## Apply What You Learned

**1** In what way does each of these two artworks "bridge the distance" between people?

**2** Do you think it is a good idea for artists to reach out into their communities for ideas? Why or why not?

 **Big Question**
Which of these artworks do you think best captures the theme of reaching out to others? Explain your answer.

 **Workbook**
Pages 31–32

# UNIT 2

## THE BIG QUESTION

# What shapes our identity?

**T**his unit is about identity. What is identity? It is as simple as what makes us unique (DNA, fingerprints) and as complex as what shapes who we are (culture, traditions, past) and what drives us (traits, styles, interests).

## READING 1: Novel Excerpt and Interview

- From *Finding Miracles* by Julia Alvarez
- "A Conversation with Julia Alvarez"

## READING 2: Social Studies Article

- From *What Do You Stand For? For Teens: A Guide to Building Character* by Barbara A. Lewis

## READING 3: Interview, Novel Excerpt, and Poetry

- "An Interview with An Na"
- From *A Step from Heaven* by An Na
- "Learning English" by Luis Alberto Ambroggio

## READING 4: Science Article

- From *Crime Scene: How Investigators Use Science to Track Down the Bad Guys* by Vivien Bowers

### Listening and Speaking

At the end of this unit, you will present a **panel discussion**.

### Writing

In this unit you will practice **expository writing**. Expository writing explains or describes something. After each reading you'll learn a skill to help you write an expository paragraph. Then, at the end of this unit, you'll use the skills to write an expository essay.

### QuickWrite

What is identity? Write three sentences about this topic.

## What You Will Learn

**Reading**

- Vocabulary building: *Literary terms, word study*

- Reading strategy: *Recognize cause and effect*

- Text type: *Literature (novel excerpt, interview)*

**Grammar, Usage, and Mechanics**

Modals: regular and irregular

**Writing**

Explain the steps in a process

### THE BIG QUESTION

**What shapes our identity?** What role do the following things play in defining who a person is? Do some have more influence than others? If so, which ones, and why?

- Background and culture
- Family and friends
- DNA and genes
- Beliefs and traditions
- Life experiences
- Likes and dislikes

Discuss your answers with a partner.

### BUILD BACKGROUND

You're going to read an excerpt from the novel **Finding Miracles** about Milly, a teenager who lives in Vermont but was adopted from Latin America when she was a baby. Milly doesn't know much about her past, including her native country. The author does not name the country, but she lets readers know that it is a Latin-American country. You will also read an interview with the author, entitled **"A Conversation with Julia Alvarez."**

Look at the map below. Do you know about any of these countries?

### Learn Literary Words

A **conflict** is a struggle or a problem, usually involving the main character or characters. The conflict may be internal (inside) the character, or external (outside) the character. The problem is usually resolved during the story. The conflict and how it is resolved help make the story interesting. Read about this character's inner conflict.

Milly's past is haunting her, and she thinks about it all the time. Who were her birth parents? What is her native country like? Can she even talk about it with others? Milly knows she must resolve her inner conflict to make sense of her life.

| Literary Words |
| --- |
| conflict |
| point of view |

A story is usually told from either the first-person or the third-person **point of view**. If the story is told from the first-person point of view, the author uses words like *I, me,* and *mine*. If the story is told from the third-person point of view, the author uses words like *she, he, her,* and *his,* and the name of the character.

**First-Person Point of View**
And though *my* hands kept breaking out in rashes, trying to tell *me* . . . *I* wasn't ready yet to open *my* box of secrets.

**Third-Person Point of View**
And though *Milly's* hands kept breaking out in rashes, trying to tell *her* . . . *she* wasn't ready yet to open *her* box of secrets.

**Practice**  **Workbook Page 33**

Work with a partner. Read the following quotes and decide if the point of view is first-person or third-person. Copy the sentences into your notebook and underline the words that helped you decide. Then rewrite the sentences using the other point of view.

I took my girl's hand
In mine for two blocks.       *(Gary Soto)*

She spoke a tongue I knew no word of,
and I was sad I could not understand,
but I could hug her.       *(Amy Ling)*

73

## Learn Academic Words

Study the **red** words and their meanings. You will find these words useful when talking and writing about literature. Write each word and its meaning in your notebook. After you read the excerpt from *Finding Miracles* and the interview with the author, try to use these words to respond to the text.

| | | |
|---|---|---|
| **adapt** = adjust to a new environment | ➡ | After we moved, it took time to **adapt** to our new home. |
| **conflict** = a situation of having to choose between opposing things | ➡ | Her **conflict** was that she wasn't sure if she wanted to share her secret or keep it hidden. |
| **identity** = who someone is | ➡ | Being Latin American is a large part of her **identity**. |
| **interpret** = clarify the meaning of something | ➡ | It is easier to **interpret** a character's actions when you understand his or her conflict. |
| **issue** = a subject or problem that people discuss | ➡ | They couldn't agree on the **issue** and agreed to research it further. |
| **reveal** = make something known that was previously secret | ➡ | She didn't want to **reveal** her secret, so she didn't tell anyone. |

## Practice  **Workbook Page 34**

Work with a partner to answer these questions. Try to include the **red** word in your answer. Write the sentences in your notebook.

1. What are some things people can do to **adapt** to a new school?
2. What is one way to deal with an inner **conflict**?
3. What does a passport reveal about your **identity**?
4. What are some things you can do to **interpret** a difficult concept?
5. What is one important **issue** you care about?
6. What do people's interests and hobbies **reveal** about them?

▲ A passport

74

## Word Study: Diphthongs /ou/ and /oi/

Say the word *cow* aloud. Notice how your mouth position changes as you say the vowel sound /ou/. The vowel sound in *cow* is called a diphthong. This sound can be spelled *ow* or *ou*. Another common diphthong in English is the sound /oi/ as in *coin*, which is spelled with the letters *oi* or *oy*. Read the chart.

| /ou/ spelled *ow, ou* | /oi/ spelled *oi, oy* |
|---|---|
| down | join |
| now | point |
| house | boy |
| found | joyful |

**Practice**
Workbook Page 35

Work with a partner. Your partner must close his or her book. Then read aloud the words in the first box below. Your partner will listen and write down the words as you say them. Check your partner's spelling. Then switch roles and repeat the activity using the words in the second box.

| brown | crowd | loudspeaker | playground | proud | without |
|---|---|---|---|---|---|

| broil | join | noise | soil | soybean | toy |
|---|---|---|---|---|---|

◀ A loudspeaker

---

**READING STRATEGY**    **RECOGNIZE CAUSE AND EFFECT**

Recognizing cause and effect helps you understand explanations in texts. To recognize cause and effect, follow these steps:

- As you read, look for events or actions in the text (the effects) and for reasons for what happened (the causes).
- Look for words and phrases such as *because, since, so that, therefore, as a result of, therefore.*
- Make sure you understand the relationship between each cause and effect.

As you read the excerpt from *Finding Miracles,* look for cause and effect. Why can't Milly write about her own life? How does she react to a new student?

Workbook Page 36

**Set a purpose for reading** How does Pablo's arrival force Milly to face her own identity?

# *from* Finding Miracles

### *Julia Alvarez*

*Milly Kaufman seems to be just another teenager living in Vermont until a new student named Pablo arrives. Meeting Pablo makes her confront her identity. She knows she is adopted but has many questions about her past and her native country—which happens to be Pablo's, too.*

I took the class where we wrote stories with Ms. Morris. It was a three-week elective we could do on the side with regular English class. I did it because, to be truthful, I needed the extra credit. I've always had big problems with writing, which I'm not going to go into here. I knew my English grade, a C, was rapidly gyrating into a D. So I signed up.

"Stories are how we put the pieces of our lives together," Ms. Morris told us that first class. The way she talked, it was like stories could save your life. She was like a fanatic of literature, Ms. Morris. A lot of kids didn't like her for that. But secretly, I admired her. She had something worth giving her life to. Except for saving my mom and dad and sister, Kate, and brother, Nate, and best friend, Em, and a few other people from a burning building, I didn't have anything I could get that worked up about.

---

**gyrating**, turning around fast in circles
**fanatic**, someone who likes something
   very much

*Today's Written Exercise*

"Unless we put the pieces together we can get lost." Ms. Morris sighed like she'd been there, done that. Ms. Morris wasn't exactly old, maybe about Mom and Dad's age. But with her wild, frizzy hair and her scarves and eye makeup, she seemed younger. She lived an hour away near the state university and drove a red pickup. Occasionally, she referred to her partner, and sometimes to her kid, and once to an ex-husband. It was hard to put all the pieces of her life together.

Ms. Morris had this exercise where we had to jot down a couple of details about ourselves. Then we had to write a story based on them.

"Nothing big," she said to encourage us. "But they do have to be details that reveal something about your real self."

"Huh?" a bunch of the guys in the back row grunted.

"Here's what I mean," Ms. Morris said, reading from her list. She always tried out the exercises she gave us. "The morning I was born, I had to be turned around three times. Headed in the wrong direction, I guess." She looked up and grinned, sort of proud of herself. "Okay, here's another one. When I was twelve, an X-ray discovered that I had extra 'wing bones' on my shoulders." Ms. Morris spread her arms as if she was ready to fly away.

The *huh* guys all shot a glance at each other like here we are in the Twilight Zone.

"So, class, a detail or two to convey the real you! Actually, this is a great exercise in self-knowledge!"

We all groaned. It was kind of mandatory when a teacher was this kindergarten-perky about an assignment.

I sat at my desk wondering what to write. My hands were itching already with this rash I always get. Since nothing else was coming, I decided to jot that down. But what came out was, "I have this allergy where my hands get red and itchy when my real self's trying to tell me something." For my second detail, I found myself writing, "My parents have a box in their bedroom we've only opened once. I think of it as The Box."

---

**Twilight Zone**, area of uncertainty
**convey**, show
**mandatory**, necessary; required
**kindergarten-perky**, confident, happy, and full of interest
**allergy**, bodily reaction

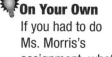 **LITERARY CHECK**

*What clues are you given about Milly's inner **conflict**?*

**BEFORE YOU GO ON**

1 How would you describe Ms. Morris?

2 How would you describe Milly?

**On Your Own**
If you had to do Ms. Morris's assignment, what would you write?

77

Ms. Morris was coming down the rows, checking on our progress. "That's great!" she whispered when she read over my paper. Now my face, along with my hands, turned red. "You could tell an interesting story with just those two facts!"

"I made them up," I said a little too quickly. Oh yeah? All she had to do was look at my hands.

"Then write a story about a character for whom those two facts are true," Ms. Morris shot back. You couldn't get around her enthusiasm, no way.

I felt relieved when music sounded over the loudspeaker for the end of the period. That's a telling detail about our school. Instead of bells, we get music, anything from classical to "Rock-a-bye, Baby" to rock. I guess we're free spirits in Vermont. Bells are too uptight for us.

I ended up writing some lame, futuristic story about this girl alien whose memory chips are kept in a box that she can't open because her hands need rebooting. Some idea from a late-night movie Em and I had seen on TV at her house, where her parents have a dish and get all the weird channels.

I could tell Ms. Morris was disappointed that I didn't write about my own life. And though my hands kept breaking out in rashes, trying to tell me *Milly! It's time!*, I wasn't ready yet to open my box of secrets.

But sometimes, like with my allergies, it takes an outside irritant to make you react. My outside "irritant" showed up the next day in Mr. Barstow's class.

He stood in front of us, head bowed, so you couldn't really see his face. His skin was golden brown like mine gets in the summer after a few weeks in the sun.

Mr. Barstow, our homeroom/history teacher, was introducing him: Pablo something something something—he must have had about four names. "Let's give our classmate a warm welcome!"

*Warm* welcome was right. It was one of those freezer-compartment January days when even people who love winter have to ask themselves, Am I out of my mind? I wasn't one of those people, winter lovers I mean. But from time to time, I had my own reasons to ask myself, Milly, are you out of your mind? Loving winter was not one of them.

---

**get around**, avoid
**free spirits**, people who live by their own rules
**dish**, kind of antenna
**irritant**, something that causes discomfort
**out of my mind**, losing my sanity

> **✔ LITERARY CHECK**
> *How does first-person point of view help you better understand what's going on with Milly?*

"Hey, class, come on. You can do better than that!" When he wasn't teaching World History or being our homeroom teacher, Mr. Barstow was the football-basketball-baseball coach. He could work up a crowd. He had less luck with ninth-grade homeroom in the middle of winter.

We managed a lukewarm applause.

Pablo wasn't dressed for cold weather at all. He had on a short-sleeve, khaki-colored shirt and a pair of new jeans that looked like they'd been ironed. Nobody at Ralston High wore jeans that were one, new; two, without a rip or tear; three, ironed. He looked so awkward up there. My heart just automatically went out to him.

---

**lukewarm**, half-hearted
**awkward**, not comfortable
**automatically**, without thinking

**BEFORE YOU GO ON**

**1** What new information do you get about Milly?

**2** How would you describe Pablo? Mr. Barstow?

**On Your Own**
Do you find it hard to write about yourself? Why or why not?

79

Mr. Barstow was going on about Pablo, how he had two older brothers, how his parents were refugees. . . . I shifted into classroom 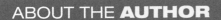cruise control . . . coasting along . . . not paying attention. . . . But then Mr. Barstow said something that made my hands begin to itch and my face darken with self-consciousness.

Em, my best friend, sits one row over and three seats in front of me. I could see her shoulders tense up. She was going to turn around any moment. *Please, Em*, I thought, *please don't!* I just couldn't stand her drawing any attention to me.

But if Em looked my way, I never knew. I stared down at the graffiti on my desk until it began to swim under my eyes, reorganizing into the shape of the country where Mr. Barstow had mentioned Pablo was from.

Besides Em, I hadn't told anyone in this room that it was the place where I came from, too.

*Later in the novel, Milly opens The Box again and also opens up to Em about her past. Then, with Pablo's help, Milly gets to find out about her native country in Latin America and her past.*

---

**cruise control**, constant speed

## ABOUT THE **AUTHOR**

**Julia Alvarez** is an award-winning Hispanic author. She read *The Arabian Nights* as a ten-year-old living in the Dominican Republic. After reading this collection of tales, she became aware of the power of stories, and of storytelling. Lying in her bed at night, she began to make up stories or repeat those she had heard in her neighborhood. Now the author of many books for young readers and adults, Alvarez is writer-in-residence at Middlebury College. She lives with her husband in Vermont.

# A Conversation with

# Julia Alvarez

**Q** Throughout the book, Milly feels simultaneously detached from and drawn to her birth country. Having left the Dominican Republic for the northeastern United States at a young age, did you experience a similar sense of conflict over which place was your "real" home?

**A** I certainly did experience very strong homesickness when I arrived in the United States at the age of ten. Although I had been born in the United States, my parents had returned to their birth country when I was three months old, so the Dominican Republic was my home; my extended *familia* were all there; Spanish was my native tongue. That first year in New York, I couldn't get used to the cold, the English language, the prejudice of some of my classmates at school who chased my sisters and me around in the playground, calling us names and telling us to go back to where we came from.

What happened, though, was that slowly I began to adapt to my new country. I learned English. I became a reader. I dreamed of writing my own stories down. When I went back "home" to the Dominican Republic for vacations, I no longer totally belonged there anymore. I had changed, become Americanized. But then, once I was back on USA soil, I also didn't feel like I was totally American. In a sense, I was a person without a country, which made me seek the company and community of books. Every writer, I believe, feels that through story we are all connected, all one human family.

Milly's case is a little different from my own experience. She wants desperately to feel 100 percent U.S. American so as not to be different from her brother and sister, Kate and Nate, who are biological siblings and children of Milly's parents. But she feels the absence of a part of her story that she has kept locked in her heart and that keeps tugging at the edges of her consciousness and prickling her skin in rashes! Like me, Milly is a hybrid, and she needs to include both parts of her story in order to be fully herself. But unlike me, Milly does not have a full-blown childhood experience of her birth country to give her a sense of what she is missing. Hers is a bigger blank than mine ever was.

---

**simultaneously**, at the same time
**detached**, removed
**biological siblings**, brothers and/or sisters who have the same parents
**tugging at**, pulling something suddenly and hard
**consciousness**, understanding what's happening
**hybrid**, a mixture of two or more things

## BEFORE YOU GO ON

**1** What does Milly have in common with Pablo?

**2** How is Milly's situation similar to and yet different from the author's?

**On Your Own**
Why is identity such an important issue and a real problem for Milly?

81

# Review and Practice

## READER'S THEATER

Act out the interview between Milly and her guidance counselor.

**Q:** Hi there, Milly. I see you signed up for Ms. Morris's class. Why?

**A:** Yeah. Between you and me, I needed the credit. I'm not a very good writer, and my grade was slipping.

**Q:** What was your first assignment?

**A:** Ms. Morris had us write down a few facts about ourselves, and then write a story about them. She gave us a couple of weird examples about herself. She's a little out there, Ms. Morris.

**Q:** So, what facts did you write about yourself?

**A:** I have this thing where my hands get all itchy, so I wrote about it. And I wrote about The Box—the one in my parents' bedroom.

**Q:** You never really told me about that. What's in The Box anyway?

**A:** We've only opened it once. Deep down I know it's time to face what's in it. But I'm not sure I'm ready. I ended up writing a science fiction story. I think Ms. Morris was upset. She wanted me to reveal the real "me."

**Q:** Are you ever going to face your box of secrets?

**A:** I don't know. But I do know that the day Pablo showed up, everything changed and I thought more about who I really am.

### 🔊 *Speaking* TIPS

Use the appropriate tone of voice, gestures, and body language for the story character you're playing.

Wait until the other speaker finishes before speaking your lines.

## COMPREHENSION

**Workbook**
**Page 37**

### Right There

1. What does Ms. Morris say about stories?
2. What two examples from her own life does Ms. Morris give?

### Think and Search

3. How does the class react to Ms. Morris's assignment?
4. Why is Ms. Morris disappointed about what Milly writes?

### Author and You

5. Would the author agree with Ms. Morris's position about stories?

6. How is the author's life similar to and different from Milly's?

### On Your Own

7. Is it important for people to know about their heritage? Explain.

8. How does your writing help you with your identity? Explain.

## DISCUSSION

Discuss in pairs or small groups.

1. Do you agree with Milly about her admiration for Ms. Morris? Would you admire her and enjoy her class? Why or why not?

2. Milly says her heart went out to Pablo, who seems not to "fit in" right away to his new school. How would you have reacted if Pablo had just entered your school? Would your heart have gone out to him? Explain.

3. Do you agree with Ms. Morris that stories help us make sense of our lives? Why or why not?

**Q** **What shapes our identity?** Do you agree that it's sometimes hard to face your identity? Why or why not?

### »)) Listening TIPS

If another person states something you were going to say, don't interrupt. Instead, listen carefully until he or she is finished—the point may not be *exactly* what you were going to say! Then make your contribution.

Listen for new ideas and perspectives. Take note of any you'd like to remember.

## RESPONSE TO LITERATURE

**Workbook Page 37**

Write a list of tips for students new to the school Milly attends. For example, how will new students know when to change classes? Why aren't there any bells? Should they sign up for Ms. Morris's writing class? Would they like Mr. Barstow's homeroom? Is there a dress code? What suggestions can you give about how to dress at the school? What's the weather like in Vermont? Who could they turn to for help getting adjusted? Milly? Em? The *huh* guys? Ms. Morris or Mr. Barstow?

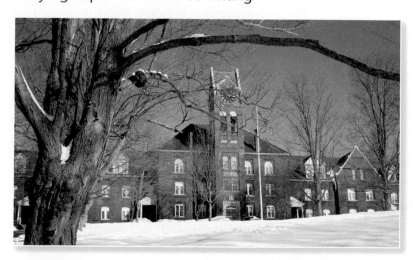

A school in Vermont ▶

# Grammar and Writing

## Modals: Regular and Irregular

Modals are helping verbs that can mean different things. Use the modals *can* and *could* to express ability in the sense of *able to*. Use *could* to express possibility, to tell about something you *might* do. Use *has to* or *have to* or *had to* to express necessity, to tell about something you *must* do.

| Express Ability | Express Possibility | Express Necessity |
|---|---|---|
| Milly **can** write about a futuristic story. Milly **could** write about the aliens, so that's what she chose. | Milly **could** write about The Box, or she **could** write about the aliens. | Milly **has to** write an assignment for her writing class. |

| Regular | | Irregular | | Irregular | |
|---|---|---|---|---|---|
| present | past | present | past | present | past |
| could | could | can | could | have *or* has (to) | had (to) |

Notice that when you use *can* or *could*, you use the base form of the verb (*write*) after the helping verb. When you use *has to* (or *have to* or *had to*), you also use the base form of the verb (*write*).

## Practice  **Workbook Page 38**

Copy the sentences below into your notebook. Use the correct form of the modal from the box and the verb (in parentheses).

| can / cannot    could / could not    has to    have to    had to |
|---|

1. The class _____ two details. (*write*—necessity)
2. The students _____ about anything as long as the details revealed something about themselves. (*write*—possibility)
3. Milly _____ about her inner conflict. (*write*—ability)
4. Someday Milly will _____ the box. (*deal with*—necessity)
5. Milly _____ that Ms. Morris was upset. (*admit*—necessity)

## WRITING AN EXPOSITORY PARAGRAPH

### Explain the Steps in a Process

At the end of this unit, you'll write an expository essay. To help you do this, you'll learn some skills to use for this type of writing. First, you'll write a paragraph that explains the steps in a process. The model below will help you write your own paragraph.

Notice how the writer uses sequence words for transitions and words that show cause-and-effect relationships. She used a sequence chart to help organize her ideas. She tells what students new to Milly's school in Vermont could do. The writer also tells why the advice could be helpful and uses words like *since* and *because*.

| First |
|---|
| ↓ |
| Next |
| ↓ |
| Last |

> Karimah McCarthy
>
> ### Starting a New School
>
> Moving to Vermont as a teenager, like Pablo, means you have to go to a new high school. Because things will probably be different from your old school, you may feel shy and scared at first. Here are some things you can do. First, ask to meet with a guidance counselor or a teacher before you start school, since they can give you some tips and offer advice. Second, be confident and don't look nervous as you meet new classmates. You can look relaxed as easily as scared, with practice! Finally, you could try asking other students questions about the school. Doing this can give you information and maybe even help you make a new friend. By following this advice, you, like Pablo, could find out, for example, how kids dress at the new school and be more comfortable on the first day.

### Practice
Workbook Page 39

Write a paragraph explaining the steps in a process. How would you advise a new student coming to your school? What are some things he or she could do to be more comfortable there? Remember to organize your paragraph using sequence words. Use words like *because* and *since* to show cause-and-effect relationships. List your steps in a sequence chart.

**Writing Checklist**

**ORGANIZATION:**
☑ The steps I used are in a logical, sequential order.

**VOICE:**
☑ You can tell I was thinking about my audience.

85

# Prepare to Read

## What You Will Learn

**Reading**

- Vocabulary building: *Context, dictionary skills, word study*

- Reading strategy: *Classify*

- Text type: *Informational text (social studies)*

**Grammar, Usage, and Mechanics**

Preference with *would + rather +* verb and unreal conditional

**Writing**

Explain how something is classified

### THE BIG QUESTION

**What shapes our identity?** How well do you know yourself? Answer these questions on your own or discuss them with a partner.

- What three words best describe you?
- What are your favorite things to do in your free time?
- How do you get along with the people in your life?
- What are your favorite things to do in the classroom: discussions? experiments? research? working with others?

Write your answers in your notebook.

### BUILD BACKGROUND

The excerpt from ***What Do You Stand For?*** is an informational text. It will help you find out about how you learn, what your interests are, what your character traits are or could be, and how you relate to other people. You'll fill out four surveys, or learning inventories, about yourself. Experts agree that we can learn in any of these eight ways:

- Words
- Numbers
- Pictures
- Music
- Self-reflection
- Physical experience
- Social experience
- Experience in the natural world

Which helps you learn best?

▲ Quiet self-reflection helps some people learn best.

### Learn Key Words

Read these sentences. Use the context to figure out the meaning of the **red** words. Use a dictionary to check your answers. Then write each word and its meaning in your notebook.

1. The **character traits** people admired most in her were her honesty and her friendliness.

2. Even though they didn't talk about it, he understood how his brother was feeling because he had **empathy** for him.

3. His friends are major **influences** in his decisions; he listens to them before making any decision.

4. She took an **inventory** about her relationships, looked at what she had checked, and realized she wanted to make new friends.

5. He had strong **relationships** with both of his parents and could talk with them about anything that was bothering him.

6. She was **tolerant** of others and respected any views and beliefs that were different from her own.

**Practice**  **Workbook Page 40**

Write the sentences in your notebook. Choose a **red** word from the box above to complete each sentence. Then take turns reading the sentences aloud with a partner.

1. Respecting the beliefs of others is one way to be _____.

2. Love and trust are part of good _____ with others.

3. A type of checklist that reveals your personality, interests, and relationships is an _____.

4. You have _____ when you have a deep understanding of how someone is feeling.

5. Qualities that describe a person are called _____.

6. Family and friends are strong _____ because they affect your decisions.

## Learn Academic Words

Study the **red** words and their meanings. You will find these words useful when talking and writing about informational texts. Write each word and its meaning in your notebook. After you read the excerpt from *What Do You Stand For?* try to use these words to respond to the text.

| | | |
|---|---|---|
| **adult** = a grown-up person | ➡ | The only **adult** he normally talked to was his teacher. |
| **attitude** = opinions and feelings | ➡ | Generally, she had a good **attitude** and didn't let things upset her. |
| **categories** = groups or divisions of things | ➡ | The inventory is divided into four **categories**. |
| **communication** = process of speaking, writing, etc. | ➡ | Good **communication** is an important part of building healthy relationships. |
| **manipulating** = making someone do what you want by deceiving or influencing him or her | ➡ | **Manipulating** friends is not a good idea, as you may end up losing their friendships. |
| **response** = something said, written, or done as a reaction to something else | ➡ | There is no right or wrong **response** to the question. |

**Practice**
**Workbook**
**Page 41**

Work with a partner to answer these questions. Try to include the **red** word in your answer. Write the sentences in your notebook.

1. Who is an **adult** that you trust? Why?
2. How would you describe your **attitude** about school?
3. How could you group all the people you know in **categories**?
4. What are some skills for good **communication** with others?
5. Why is **manipulating** your friends not recommended?
6. What kinds of questions might have more than one **response**?

Good communication builds healthy relationships.▼

88

## Word Study: Collocations with *make* and *take*

Collocations are words that are traditionally used together in English. Some collocations are formed with a verb like *make* or *take* and another word or words. Read the chart.

| make | make a decision, make (someone) laugh, make (things) work |
|------|-----------------------------------------------------------|
| take | take a look, take a (computer course), take care |

**Practice**

Work with a partner. Write the following sentences in your notebook. Fill in the blanks with *make* or *take*. Check a dictionary if you're not sure.

1. We have to _____ a choice; will we _____ a bus or walk?

2. You can _____ a break, but please watch the clock. _____ sure you're back in ten minutes.

3. _____ time in your schedule for your friends. If you _____ care of your relationships, they can last a long time.

4. When you blow out the candles, _____ a deep breath and _____ a wish.

▲ He's making a wish.

## READING STRATEGY  CLASSIFY

Classifying information helps you organize new ideas and facts. To classify, follow these steps:

- As you read, make a list of new information that you've learned.
- Review your list. Which facts are most important?
- Think about how the ideas or facts are similar and different.
- Group the facts and ideas according to their subject.

As you read "What Do You Stand For?" classify the information by category. Think about character traits, interests, relationships, and learning styles.

**89**

**Set a purpose for reading** Think about the questions you answered on page 86. After you finish the reading, answer the questions again. Did your answers change or stay the same?

*from*
# What Do You Stand For?
## FOR TEENS: A GUIDE TO BUILDING CHARACTER

*Barbara A. Lewis*

## Learning Styles Inventory

Read the following descriptions. Check the ONE that sounds most like you.

**1.** __ I like to know *why* things happen. I like to consider many different ideas. I have a good imagination, and I usually come up with good ideas. I like to find solutions to problems and issues. I like practical solutions. I don't like to set schedules; I'm very flexible.

**2.** __ I like to think about concepts. I enjoy listening to guest speakers. I love theories about *what* makes things work. I like to work hard and prefer following definite steps to find solutions. I enjoy studying principles and details, and I like columns and figures.

**3.** __ I like to know *how* things work. I enjoy lectures and abstract ideas. I like to experiment, solve problems, and make decisions. I enjoy technical tasks more than "people problems." I like to tinker, and I like schedules.

**4.** __ I like to talk about "what if" situations. I enjoy real, concrete experiences. I like to apply what I learn. I rely on my gut feelings more than on logic. I love taking risks, and I enjoy helping other people to be creative. I bring action to ideas.

---

**tinker,** fix things

# Character Traits Inventory

Read each pair of sentences. Check the ONE from each pair that describes you.
Or check BOTH sentences if you believe that you already have a particular trait
or quality but would like to develop it further.

| | | |
|---|---|---|
| 1 | ❏ I have positive attitudes. | ❏ I'd like to have better attitudes. |
| 2 | ❏ I'm kind and I care about helping others. | ❏ I need to be kinder and more caring. |
| 3 | ❏ I accept responsibility for the choices I make. | ❏ I want to learn how to accept responsibility for my choices. |
| 4 | ❏ I'm a good citizen and an involved member of my community. | ❏ I want to be a better citizen and more involved in my community. |
| 5 | ❏ I keep my body clean. | ❏ I need to work on my personal hygiene. |
| 6 | ❏ I have clean habits and a clean mind. | ❏ I'd like to have more positive habits, thoughts, and influences. |
| 7 | ❏ I communicate well with others. | ❏ I'd like to be a better communicator. |
| 8 | ❏ I work to conserve things and resources, and I'm thrifty. | ❏ I need to conserve and save better than I do. |
| 9 | ❏ I have the courage to do and become what I want to be. | ❏ I'd like to be more courageous. |
| 10 | ❏ I have empathy (deep understanding) for others. | ❏ I need to be more empathetic. |
| 11 | ❏ I have endurance and patience, even in tough times. | ❏ I need more endurance and patience. |
| 12 | ❏ I'm able to forgive others and myself. | ❏ I want to learn how to forgive more easily. |
| 13 | ❏ I'm physically, mentally, and emotionally healthy. | ❏ I want to be more physically, mentally, and emotionally healthy. |
| 14 | ❏ I'm honest and trustworthy. | ❏ I need to be more honest and trustworthy. |
| 15 | ❏ I'm a risk taker, and I have good imagination skills. | ❏ I'd like to take positive risks more easily or improve my imagination skills. |
| 16 | ❏ I have integrity. I "walk as I talk." | ❏ I want to develop my integrity. |
| 17 | ❏ I'm tolerant and fair with others. | ❏ I need to be more tolerant and fair. |
| 18 | ❏ I'm a good leader. | ❏ I'd like to be a better leader. |
| 19 | ❏ I'm a good follower. | ❏ I need to be a better follower. |
| 20 | ❏ I know when to be loyal and/or obedient. | ❏ I'd like to be more loyal and/or obedient. |
| 21 | ❏ I'm a calm and peaceful person. | ❏ I need to become more calm and/or peaceful. |
| 22 | ❏ I'm a good problem solver. | ❏ I want to be a better problem solver. |
| 23 | ❏ I have direction and purpose in my life. | ❏ I'd like to have more direction or purpose in my life. |
| 24 | ❏ I'm friendly and have healthy, positive relationships with others. | ❏ I'd like to be more friendly and to have better relationships with others. |
| 25 | ❏ I treat others with respect and courtesy. | ❏ I need to be more respectful and courteous. |
| 26 | ❏ I'm responsible and hard-working. | ❏ I want to develop my sense of responsibility and my work ethic. |
| 27 | ❏ I practice safety measures in my life. | ❏ I'd like to be more cautious and safety-conscious. |
| 28 | ❏ I'm self-disciplined. | ❏ I want to be more self-disciplined. |
| 29 | ❏ I have wisdom. | ❏ I want to develop my wisdom. |

---

**conserve**, use as little as possible so as not to waste
**thrifty**, careful with money
**endurance**, ability to withstand hardship or stress
**measures**, actions; steps

**work ethic**, belief in the moral value and importance of hard work

# Interests Inventory

For each "Would you rather . . ." list, put a 1 by the thing you like to do most, a 2 by your second choice, a 3 by your third choice, and a 4 by your fourth choice.

## I. Would you rather . . .

a. _____ paint a landscape?
b. _____ write in your journal?
c. _____ be in a play?
d. _____ surf the Internet?
e. _____ take care of your neighbor's dog?
f. _____ bandage someone's cut?
g. _____ make math flash cards for a younger kid?
h. _____ rock a baby?
i. _____ plant flowers?
j. _____ repair a light switch?
k. _____ bake cookies?
l. _____ organize your friends in a walk-a-thon?
m. _____ patrol your school halls to stop kids from running?
n. _____ play catch?
o. _____ help put a roof on a house?

## II. Would you rather . . .

a. _____ hear a symphony?
b. _____ tell a story?
c. _____ demonstrate how to do a new dance?
d. _____ work on a computer?
e. _____ go to the zoo?
f. _____ listen to someone's heartbeat?
g. _____ give a report on the weather?
h. _____ teach a younger kid how to play ball?
i. _____ learn how to raise chickens?
j. _____ put a new wheel on a bike?
k. _____ make a cake for a friend?
l. _____ make bumper stickers and sell them?
m. _____ help with a neighborhood watch?
n. _____ go swimming?
o. _____ build a playhouse for the kids in your neighborhood?

## III. Would you rather . . .

a. _____ decorate a mural?
b. _____ read a book?
c. _____ be on the program for a school assembly?
d. _____ take apart a telephone?
e. _____ find homes for abandoned animals?
f. _____ help people find jobs?
g. _____ give an inspiring speech?
h. _____ comfort a sick child?
i. _____ be a guide for hikers?
j. _____ work with hand tools (squares, saws, rules, plumb lines)?
k. _____ plan a menu?
l. _____ start a landscaping business with friends?
m. _____ start a Youth Crime Watch at your school?
n. _____ compete in sports?
o. _____ paint, plaster, or hang wallpaper?

## IV. Would you rather . . .

a. _____ play a musical instrument?
b. _____ write a poem or limerick?
c. _____ make people laugh with your jokes?
d. _____ put together a kid's toy wagon?
e. _____ watch a video on the habits of gorillas?
f. _____ counsel people who are troubled?
g. _____ research a topic you'd like to learn more about?
h. _____ play games with children?
i. _____ landscape a barren hill?
j. _____ follow directions to put a machine together?
k. _____ learn about how to season foods?
l. _____ start a recycling program at your school?
m. _____ patrol a neighborhood to keep it safe?
n. _____ watch football on TV?
o. _____ build cupboards?

---

**SCORING:** Each response begins with a letter of the alphabet. For each response you marked with a 1, 2, 3, or 4, write its letter here. (Example: 1: a, a, b, c)

**Your scores:**

1: _____, _____, _____, _____
2: _____, _____, _____, _____
3: _____, _____, _____, _____
4: _____, _____, _____, _____

guide, leader
**Youth Crime Watch,** organized group of young people who work to keep schools and communities safe
**barren,** unable to grow trees

# Relationships Inventory

For each statement in this inventory, check the box that comes closest to describing how you feel about your relationships.

| | | Most of the time | Some of the time | Seldom or never |
|---|---|:---:|:---:|:---:|
| 1. | Most of my friends seem to like me. | ❏ | ❏ | ❏ |
| 2. | My parent(s) or guardian(s) respect(s) my opinions. | ❏ | ❏ | ❏ |
| 3. | My friends seem to have a good time with me. | ❏ | ❏ | ❏ |
| 4. | My brother(s), sister(s), or parent(s) or guardian(s) seem(s) to enjoy my company. | ❏ | ❏ | ❏ |
| 5. | My peers admire me or look up to me. | ❏ | ❏ | ❏ |
| 6. | I enjoy hanging out with my friends. | ❏ | ❏ | ❏ |
| 7. | I like my teachers. | ❏ | ❏ | ❏ |
| 8. | I feel accepted by my parent(s) or guardian(s). | ❏ | ❏ | ❏ |
| 9. | My family doesn't get on my nerves. | ❏ | ❏ | ❏ |
| 10. | I'm able to talk with my parent(s) or guardian(s). | ❏ | ❏ | ❏ |
| 11. | I don't feel left out of activities with friends | ❏ | ❏ | ❏ |
| 12. | I'm satisfied with the friend(s) I have. | ❏ | ❏ | ❏ |
| 13. | My family and I share responsibilities. | ❏ | ❏ | ❏ |
| 14. | I'm confident when I am around people my own age. | ❏ | ❏ | ❏ |
| 15. | I can share my opinions with my peers. | ❏ | ❏ | ❏ |
| 16. | I don't look down on others. | ❏ | ❏ | ❏ |
| 17. | I like to talk with older people. | ❏ | ❏ | ❏ |
| 18. | I can talk easily with younger children. | ❏ | ❏ | ❏ |
| 19. | My parent(s) or guardian(s) seem(s) to understand me. | ❏ | ❏ | ❏ |
| 20. | I'm on friendly terms with most people I know in my neighborhood and community. | ❏ | ❏ | ❏ |

**SCORING:** Give yourself 1 point for every check mark in the "Most of the time" column, 2 points for every check mark in the "Some of the time" column, and 3 points for every check mark in the "Seldom or never " column.

Number of "Most of the time" responses:
_____ x 1 = _____
Number of "Some of the time" responses:
_____ x 2 = _____
Number of "Seldom or never" responses:
_____ x 3 = _____
TOTAL _____

Now turn to page 404 to interpret your scores.

## BEFORE YOU GO ON

**1** What qualities do you like in a friend? Use the inventories to help you.

**2** Are you surprised by any of your results? Why?

**On Your Own**
How do the inventories help you understand your own identity better?

## COMPREHENSION

Workbook
Page 44

### Right There

1. Why is there no right or wrong answer to the Learning Styles Inventory?

2. How is the Character Traits Inventory interpreted?

### Think and Search

3. How does the scoring work for the Interests Inventory?

4. Why is a low score good in the Relationships Inventory?

### Author and You

5. The author states that the inventories are meant to help you understand yourself, not to label you. How can labels be limiting?

6. The author suggests talking to an adult if you scored high on the Relationships Inventory. Why are healthy relationships important? How might it be helpful to talk to someone you trust?

### On Your Own

7. How can knowing how you learn best help you in school?

8. How can finding out more about your interests, character traits, learning style, and the way you relate to others help you know what you stand for?

## IN YOUR OWN WORDS

Review your results for the inventories. Copy the chart below into your notebook. Write down what you learned about yourself from each inventory.

| Inventory Name | What I Learned |
|---|---|
| Learning Styles | |
| Character Traits | |
| Interests | |
| Relationships | |

## DISCUSSION

Discuss in pairs or small groups.

1. What did you think about the Learning Styles Inventory? Was it helpful or do you think you fit more than one category? Explain.

2. People don't always agree on the six or ten character traits that everyone needs to have. What do you think they are?

3. Look back at your answers to the Interests Inventory. Which letters didn't you list? Do you think it's because you have less or no interest in these areas or because you haven't had much experience in them?

**What shapes our identity?** If you were to take these inventories again in one year, what do you think would change? What wouldn't? What do you think influences the development of a person's identity?

## READ FOR FLUENCY

It is often easier to read a text if you understand the difficult words and phrases. Work with a partner. Choose a section from the reading. Identify the words and phrases you do not know or have trouble pronouncing. Look up the difficult words in a dictionary.

Take turns pronouncing the words and phrases with your partner. If necessary, ask your teacher to model the correct pronunciation. Then take turns reading the section aloud. Give each other feedback on your reading.

## EXTENSION
**Workbook**
**Page 44**

Learning about yourself can motivate you to make changes in your life, like trying a new hobby or making positive changes in your relationships. Setting a goal is a great way to make change happen. Complete the chart below to identify the steps you will follow to meet your goal.

| My goal: |
| --- |
| What I will do: |
| How I'll know that I've accomplished my goal: |
| My reward: |

 *Speaking* TIPS

If someone indicates that he or she doesn't understand your point, try restating it in other words.

Think before you speak. Then speak slowly and clearly.

*Listening* TIPS

If you don't know how to respond to a question, try listening to others first. They may give you some ideas.

Listen carefully so you don't repeat the exact same point someone else made—unless you want to emphasize it or add to it.

# Grammar and Writing

### Preference with *would + rather* + Verb and Unreal Conditional

Questions that begin "Would you rather . . ." ask you to state a preference, for example: *Would you rather paint a landscape or plant flowers?* In your answer, use *would rather* or the contraction *'d rather* + the base form of the verb: *I'd rather paint a landscape* or *I'd rather paint a landscape than plant flowers.*

> **Would** you **rather go** swimming or go to the zoo? I**'d rather go** swimming.
> She **would rather take care of** the neighbor's dog than **repair** a light switch.
> He**'d rather be** a firefighter than a police officer.

Use the unreal conditional to describe what you're not doing now but would like to do. Unreal conditional sentences have an *if* clause and a result clause, for example: *If he studied harder, he'd get better grades.*

Use the simple past form of the verb in the *if* clause. (If the verb is *be*, use *were* for all persons.) Use *would* or *might* + the base form of the verb in the result clause.

> *if* clause           result clause
> **If** I **were** more patient, my family **would** not **get** on my nerves.
>
> *if* clause           result clause
> **If** I **had** more positive influences, I might **have** better friends.

## Practice

Workbook Page 45

Complete the sentences with the correct form of the verb in parentheses.

1. She'd rather _____ (be) a leader than a follower.
2. I would talk more with them if they _____ (be) more open.
3. I might take more risks if I _____ (have) more confidence.
4. She'd rather _____ (listen) to music than to someone's heartbeat.
5. He'd rather _____ (tell) a story than give a report on the weather.

96

## WRITING AN EXPOSITORY PARAGRAPH

### Explain How Something Is Classified

At the end of this unit, you'll write an expository essay. To help you do this, you'll write another kind of expository paragraph and learn some skills to use for explaining how something is classified. The model below about the Character Traits Inventory will help you write your own paragraph. The writer used a word web to help organize her traits.

Notice that the writer explains how the results of the Character Traits Inventory can be classified. What categories does the writer use? What details does she give about herself?

> Chelsea A. Hamlet
>
> ### My First Lesson in Building Character
>
> Here's how I grouped the results of the Character Traits Inventory: (1) What traits I would like to have or strengthen and (2) Which trait I'd like to work on first. I realized that overall I am a considerate, hardworking, and fair person. However, there are some traits that I need to strengthen and develop. These are developing better attitudes, being more positive and courageous, and being a better citizen and communicator. I would also like to develop my integrity, be friendlier, and have better relationships. Usually, I talk more than listen. And usually, I am more friendly with the most popular kids than with people who might be better friends. So I'm going to work first on being friendlier with all of my classmates so I can have better relationships. If I were a better listener, I'd probably find out who I have more in common with. Taking this inventory was a wake-up call for me!

### Practice

**Workbook Page 46**

Write a paragraph explaining how the Learning Styles Inventory, Relationships Inventory, or Interests Inventory can be interpreted using classification. Use a word web to help organize your ideas. Be sure to use *would + rather + verb* and unreal conditionals correctly as you talk about your learning style, relationship style, and interests.

**Writing Checklist**

**IDEAS:**
- [x] My message is focused and clear.

**ORGANIZATION:**
- [x] I included important details related to my topic.

97

## What You Will Learn

**Reading**

- Vocabulary building: *Literary terms, word study*

- Reading strategy: *Identify author's purpose*

- Text type: *Literature (interview, novel excerpt, poetry)*

**Grammar, Usage, and Mechanics**

*Have to* + verb for necessity and *supposed to* (*be*) + verb (*-ing*) for expectation

**Writing**

Write a cause-and-effect paragraph

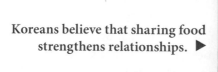

▲ These are the Korean characters for "love."

### THE BIG QUESTION

**What shapes our identity?** Do you or someone you know speak more than one language? If so, do you use one language more at home? At school? Do you have problems switching back and forth? What are the advantages of speaking more than one language? Are there any problems? Does language express who you really are? Discuss with a partner.

### BUILD BACKGROUND

You will read an excerpt from a novel called *A Step from Heaven*, about a Korean-American family living in southern California. You'll also read an interview with its author, entitled "**An Interview with An Na.**" Here are some facts about Korean culture:

- The family is a very important part of Korean life.
- Traditionally, the father is the head of the family.
- Traditionally, the first son is responsible for staying with his parents and caring for them for the rest of their lives.
- Korean women keep their surnames after they get married, but their children usually take the surname of their father.
- When entering a Korean home, people should remove their shoes.

Do you know any other facts about Korean culture?

Finally, you will read a poem, "Learning English," by Luis Alberto Ambroggio.

Koreans believe that sharing food strengthens relationships. ▶

## VOCABULARY

### Learn Literary Words

The **theme** is the central message or insight into life that you get from a work of literature. Usually, the theme comes from the conflict.

Read this summary of the story "The Emperor's New Clothes."

**Literary Words**

theme
suspense

---

An emperor loved clothes. Knowing this, two sly men promised to make him a suit out of cloth so special that only intelligent people could see it. Soon all the townspeople knew about the cloth. They were curious to find out who was intelligent and who was stupid. Although the emperor couldn't see the cloth, he didn't want people to think he was stupid. So he said nothing. When it came time for a procession into town, the emperor wore the suit. People cheered as he paraded by. A young voice piped, "But he has nothing on!" People began saying that the emperor was naked. The emperor knew they were right, but held his head high and proceeded on.

---

The theme of this story is that it takes the innocence of a child to see people and things as they really are.

**Suspense** is a feeling of uncertainty about the outcome of events in a literary work. Writers often create suspense by keeping readers wondering how a problem or conflict is going to be resolved.

Read this excerpt from *The Hound of the Baskervilles* by Sir Arthur Conan Doyle.

---

I was at Holmes's elbow, and I glanced for an instant at his face. It was pale and exultant, his eyes shining brightly in the moonlight. But suddenly they started forward in a rigid, fixed stare, and his lips parted in amazement. At the same instant Lestrade gave a yell of terror and threw himself face downward upon the ground. I sprang to my feet, ... my mind paralyzed by the dreadful shape which had sprung out upon us from the shadows of the fog. A hound it was, an enormous coal-black hound, but not such a hound as mortal eyes have ever seen.

---

The author uses suspense by making the reader wonder what will happen next.

**Practice**  **Workbook** Page 47

In small groups, discuss themes of movies or TV shows you've seen or books you've read. Write one example each for theme and for suspense, and explain why they are good examples.

## Learn Academic Words

Study the red words and their meanings. You will find these words useful when talking and writing about literature. Write each word and its meaning in your notebook. After you read "An Interview with An Na," the excerpt from *A Step from Heaven*, and "Learning English," try to use these words to respond to the text.

### Academic Words

achieve
adequate
construct
culture
emphasis
perception

| | | |
|---|---|---|
| **achieve** = succeed in getting a good result | ➡ | She was determined to **achieve** good grades in high school and go on to college. |
| **adequate** = enough; satisfactory but not excellent | ➡ | Her grades were **adequate**, but not high enough to get into college. |
| **construct** = make by placing parts together | ➡ | She had to **construct** a story to hide her lie. |
| **culture** = type of civilization; art, food, social norms of a civilization | ➡ | He learned that the Korean **culture** has different traditions and values from his. |
| **emphasis** = special importance | ➡ | In their family, **emphasis** was put on the boy. |
| **perception** = seeing or noticing; ability to perceive | ➡ | Her **perception** was that he was lying, and soon she caught him in a lie. |

## Practice  **Workbook** Page 48

Work with a partner to answer these questions. Try to include the red word in your answer. Write the sentences in your notebook.

1. Why is it so important to **achieve** success in school?
2. How would you advise someone who doesn't feel **adequate** at playing sports or a musical instrument?
3. Why do you think it's hard to successfully **construct** a lie?
4. How might one **culture** be different from another?
5. What qualities in a friend do you put **emphasis** on? Why?
6. Why might one person have a different **perception** of a situation or event than another person?

## Word Study: Spelling Long *a*

The letter *a* stands for different sounds. Short *a* is usually spelled *a*.
Long *a* has several different spellings: *a_e*, *ay*, and *ai*. Read the
examples of each long *a* sound-spelling in the chart below.

| a_e | ay | ai |
|------|------|---------|
| grade | day | raise |
| face | play | rainbow |

### Practice

Work with a partner. Take turns reading the sentences below.
Then write the sentences in your notebook and circle each
word that has long *a* sound-spelling.

1. What's the name of the play you saw last night?
2. Mrs. Diaz made cakes and lemonade for the party.
3. Which way will the wind blow today? I'd like to go sailing.
4. Have you taken the team to the game before?
5. Jane and Kate are hanging wallpaper instead of painting
   the bathroom.

▲ They prefer wallpaper
to paint.

## READING STRATEGY | IDENTIFY AUTHOR'S PURPOSE

Identifying an author's purpose (or reason for writing) can help you
analyze information better. To identify an author's purpose, ask yourself
these questions as you read:

- Am I learning new information? Is this entertaining? Is the author
  trying to persuade me about something?
- Is there more than one reason the author wrote this? If so, what are
  the reasons?

As you read the excerpt from *A Step from Heaven,* try to identify what
the author's purpose is. What message is An Na sending about identity?

**Set a purpose for reading** Why was there a conflict between An Na's own culture and her new culture when she was growing up? What are Young Ju Park's conflicts about her identity? In the poem, how is the young man caught between two cultures and languages?

# An Interview —with— An Na

Q *Like Young Ju [the main character] in* A Step from Heaven, *you are an American-raised child of Korean immigrants. Did you get the idea for her story from your own experiences growing up?*

A The initial stirrings for the story stemmed from one of my memories. For example, I remember getting my hair permed, and being told that all Americans have curly hair. But as the novel grew, it became Young Ju's story.

Q *Did you ever feel like Young Ju, caught between your Korean heritage and your desire to be "American"?*

A That was really a conflict when I was growing up. At church with my Korean friends, I was outgoing and gregarious, and I wasn't ashamed of my family or my house. But I went to a pretty affluent high school, and it was difficult being in honors classes, feeling kind of poor and out of place because I was Korean American. But I was different from Young Ju, much more outspoken. I really fought hard for the things I believed in.

Q A Step from Heaven *covers so much ground. It begins when Young Ju is four and ends when she is about to go off to college. Was the scope of the narrative a conscious decision on your part?*

A I wanted readers to feel like they were reliving Young Ju's childhood with her. Memory doesn't come as a complete story with a beginning, middle, and end, but rather lives in moments that focus on a smell or a touch or a feeling. This was what I wanted to convey when I began to construct Young Ju's life from a very young age to her years as a teenager. Hopefully, readers will leave the novel understanding how bits and pieces of Young Ju's childhood shaped who she became as an adult.

---

**stirrings**, first ideas; inspiration
**stemmed**, developed
**permed**, put curls in straight hair
**gregarious**, friendly
**affluent**, having plenty of money

---

**conscious**, intentionally done

# from

# A Step from Heaven

### An Na

*When Young Ju Park is just four years old, she first hears the words
Mi Gook—Korean for "America." She is certain the words mean "heaven."
But when the Parks—Young Ju; her mother and father, Uhmma and Apa;
and her brother Joon Ho—move to America to join her aunt and uncle,
Gomo and Uncle Tim a year later, life is far from easy. They all struggle to
adjust to a new language and a new culture—and to finding jobs and going
to school in southern California.*

## Burying Lies

In second grade you have to do a lot of talking. Not as much coloring.
Not as much play time. Just a lot of talking and listening and reading. So
in Mrs. Sheldon's class, if you do not have anything to show when it is your
turn to share, you can talk about important news. I have nothing to show,
but I want to say something important. Something I have been thinking
about for a long time.

Finally, when it is my turn to share, I run up to the front of the
classroom. I put my hands behind my back, cross my fingers, and tell
everyone, "My brother. He die."

"Oh, my. Oh, I'm sorry," Mrs. Sheldon says, then hurries over to hug me.
She pulls me close.

"I the only Park now. I keep name like boy."

---

**cross my fingers**, put one finger over another (because you are telling a lie)

### BEFORE YOU GO ON

1. What memory gave An Na the idea to write the novel?

2. What does *Mi Gook* mean? What does Young Ju think it means?

**On Your Own**
What aspects of An Na's life do you think helped shape her identity?

**103**

Her forehead bunches up like crinkled paper and her eyes squeeze shut in the corners. She does not understand the English that sounds perfect in my head and then comes out messy as the can of spaghetti Uhmma lets me eat on Saturdays if I help with the laundry.

John Chuchurelli, who always has to sit on the Time-Out rug, raises his hand and asks, "How did he die?"

"John," Mrs. Sheldon shouts, "what a thing to ask! Do you want to sit on the rug?"

John looks like he is thinking maybe this is a good idea. The rug is far from the blackboard and that means he does not have to pay attention. But then he shakes his head no. Mrs. Sheldon blows out her breath. I run back to my desk while Mrs. Sheldon stands in front of the class plucking at the skin of her neck. She always does that when she is thinking.

"You know what, class? I know it's not a Friday, but I think this is a good time to make Young a warm fuzzy. Don't you think that will make Young and her family feel better?"

"Yes!" everybody cheers because warm fuzzies are only for Fridays after the spelling test and today is Wednesday. Warm fuzzies take half a day to make and half a day to clean up. Yarn puddles all over the floor until all that is left are a few round, fuzzy balls with strange names like Pluto, Strawberry, and Bluebeard.

For the whole morning everyone makes fuzzies. Then one by one they bring their fuzzies over to my desk. They put the fuzzy down and tell me its name.

"Please take care of Sunshine."

"I hope Melonhead makes you feel better."

Soon I have a million fuzzies covering my desk. I circle them with my arms and rub my cheeks against their soft yarn fur.

At lunch, Amanda says I can have her last piece of candy because her grandma died last year and she knows what it is like to be sad. After P.E., Mrs. Sheldon gives me a special card with lots of scratch-and-sniff stickers she hands out only for perfect papers in spelling. My spelling is never perfect. But today I am special. I play with my fuzzies, scratch and sniff my stickers, and think about how nice it is that my brother is dead.

✔ **LITERARY CHECK**
*How does John's question help the* **suspense** *begin to build?*

---

**Time-Out rug,** place where young people are asked to stay until they can behave
**plucking,** pulling quickly
**warm fuzzy,** something soft
**P.E.,** physical education class

When I get home from school, Gomo, who comes over to watch us during the day so Uhmma can sew clothes at the factory, is playing with Joon Ho. Gomo points to the kitchen table.

Young Ju, look at those pretty flowers. Your school sent them, Gomo says.

My eyes blink twice. Hard. Like they cannot believe those white and yellow flowers are sitting on the table. I take off my shoes and try to walk to my room.

Come here, Gomo says. She goes over to the flowers. I am so scared my toes curl into the carpet.

What does this mean? Gomo asks, waving a small white card. Why are they sorry about our loss? Even though Gomo has been here for a long time, her English is not that good.

I look down at the orange carpet and stare at all the shaggy strands between my toes. Think. Think. I look up at Gomo and something flies out of my mouth. "I loss spelling contest my school. I come in second."

Speak Korean, Gomo says. She likes to talk Korean at our house because in her house Uncle Tim wants only English. He wants Gomo to learn how to talk nice to his family. Gomo says speaking English all the time makes her head hurt.

I lost the spelling contest at school. I came in second, I say.

Second place. That is good news, not a loss. Your Uhmma and Apa will be so happy. Flowers for second place are very nice, Gomo says.

I hold my book bag with all the fuzzies and the special Mrs. Sheldon card close to my stomach and slowly back up toward the door. My feet feel around for my shoes. When I find them, I yell out to Gomo, I am going outside to play.

I do not want to answer any more questions. I have to hide the fuzzies and the card or else I will be in big trouble for lying.

Along the side of the house, where Mr. Owner keeps all the broken things like smashed windows and a tired chair with a missing seat, there is an old tree stump. The dirt around the stump is soft and crumbly. I pick up a stick and start to dig. Both hands work fast. Both ears listen for any Gomo footsteps. Soon a hole the size of a small pot grows down. I make sure no one is watching and open my school bag. I kiss each fuzzy good-bye.

### BEFORE YOU GO ON

1 How does Young Ju feel at school?

2 How does this change when she gets home?

**On Your Own**
How would you feel? Why?

**105**

"Sorry, Roly-Poly. Bye, Melonhead," I say and drop them into the hole. I sniff Mrs. Sheldon's pretty card with all the rainbow smells one more time and pat it down next to the fuzzies. I cover my lies with dirt.

I am in the bathroom washing my face and hands with soap three times when Uhmma gets home. Uhmma always says lies smell worse than dead fish. I can hear Gomo telling her about the flowers. I walk out of the bathroom. Uhmma stands by the kitchen table sniffing the flowers. Her eyes are closed.

Young Ju, come here, Gomo says, waving me to hurry up. I walk over to the couch and wonder if Uhmma can smell the lie in the flowers. Uhmma opens her eyes and holds out her arm for me. I take baby steps. Stop far away so she cannot smell me. But then Uhmma reaches out and pulls me close to her side.

I am proud of you, Young Ju, Uhmma says, looking down into my eyes. You are a smart girl and someday you will be a smart woman.

After Gomo leaves, Uhmma does not sit too tired to talk on the couch with Joon Ho sleeping in her arms. Tonight she makes me sit next to her and talk about what I would like to be someday. Maybe I can be a doctor or a lawyer, or maybe a professor like some other important Parks. Uhmma tells me stories about the great Parks of our past while Joon Ho sleeps. I listen to Uhmma and think, I cannot be the great son, but I can do important things. Then I will be the famous Park in the family. Maybe even better than first son.

Even though I am supposed to be sleeping, my eyes are still open when Apa comes home from his night job cleaning the lawyers' offices. From my bed I can only hear Uhmma and Apa, murr, murr, murr talking in the living room. Does Apa think I can be an important Park like our past grandfathers?

When Uhmma and Apa's bedroom door closes, I jump out of bed and run to the kitchen. I open the stuck drawer. It screams skeeee! It is hurt. My heart booms louder than the drums on the radio, but Uhmma and Apa do not open their bedroom door. I carefully pick out the flashlight Uncle Tim gave Apa for our first Mi Gook Christmas and slide in the drawer slow slow so it will not scream.

I run back to my room. Before I get back into bed, I say a quick prayer like I promised, Thank you, God, for not telling Uhmma about the lie. Then all night, until my eyes do not want to stay open, I study for the Friday spelling test.

✔ **LITERARY CHECK**

*How does this conversation with her mother help you understand Young Ju's conflict and the theme better?*

---

**first son**, first-born son in a family

# Learning English

Life
to understand me
you have to know Spanish
feel it in the blood of your soul.

If I speak another language
and use different words
for feelings that will always stay the same
I don't know
if I'll continue being
the same person.

—*Luis Alberto Ambroggio*
*translated from Spanish by Lori M. Carlson*

## ABOUT THE **POET**

**Luis Alberto Ambroggio** is a Hispanic-American poet who was born in Córdoba, Argentina, but has lived in the United States since 1967. He is also an aircraft pilot. Ambroggio has published nine collections of poetry. His poems appear widely in anthologies in Latin America, Europe, and the United States. He currently lives in McLean, Virginia.

## BEFORE YOU GO ON

1 Why does Young Ju take the flashlight from the kitchen drawer?

2 What is the problem expressed in the poem?

**On Your Own**
Have you ever done something wrong? What were the consequences?

# Review and Practice

## DRAMATIC READING

One of the best ways to understand a poem is to memorize it, or learn it by heart. Work with a partner. Reread "Learning English." Take turns using your own words to interpret the poem. What do you think the poet means by "you have to know Spanish / feel it in the blood of your soul," by "feelings that will always stay the same," and by "I don't know if I'll continue being the same person"? Reread the poem until you can both memorize it. Then recite the poem. Comment on each other's oral reading and make suggestions for improvements. Then recite the poem to the whole class.

## COMPREHENSION

Workbook
Page 51

### Right There

1. What was the important news that Young Ju told the class?
2. What did John Chuchurelli ask?

### Think and Search

3. How was the author's life similar to and different from Young Ju's?
4. Can Young Ju finally bury the lie when she gets home? Why or why not?

### Author and You

5. Why do you think the author titled the book *A Step from Heaven*?
6. How important do you think culture and family is to the author? Why?

### On Your Own

7. If you don't speak the same native language as someone, can you really know and understand that person? Why or why not?
8. How would you advise someone who feels pressured to lie or be deceitful?

## DISCUSSION

Discuss in pairs or small groups.

1. Do you agree with An Na that "Memory doesn't come as a complete story with a beginning, middle, and end, but rather lives in moments that focus on a smell or a touch or a feeling"? How might this apply to your life or the life of someone you know? What moments help define you? How might this quote help you better understand the author's purpose?

2. Why did Young Ju tell the lie she told? What pressures do you think she felt? How else might she have handled how she was feeling?

3. How would you rate this story? Would you recommend it? To whom? Why? Would you like to read the rest of the book? What else would you like to know about Young Ju's life? Why?

**Q** **What shapes our identity?** Do you think speaking a second language influences a person's identity? Why or why not?

## RESPONSE TO LITERATURE

**Workbook**
**Page 51**

Imagine you are an older, teenage Young Ju and in high school. Your writing teacher has given you an assignment to write about something that happened to you as a child, something that has helped shape the person you've become. Write about the day you shared your "important news." How did you feel about lying to your class? About the flowers the class sent? About how the lie you told kept growing? About your mother's talk with you that night? About the pressures you felt? To help you get started, brainstorm your ideas in a word web like the one below. Write "Lie" in the center and include details to show what happened as a result of the lie.

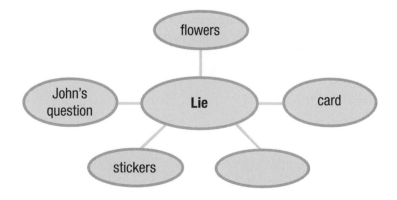

# Grammar and Writing

### *Have to* + Verb for Necessity and *supposed to (be)* + Verb *(-ing)* for Expectation

To express a necessity to do something, use the modal *have to* with the base form of the verb.

> In second grade, you **have to do** a lot of talking.
> To understand me, you **have to know** Spanish.
> I **have to hide** the fuzzies and the card or else I will be in trouble for lying.

To express something you're expected to do but either you don't do it or are not obligated to do it, you can use *supposed to be* + the *-ing* form of the verb. Use the present form of *be* for present or future expectations.

> Even though I **am supposed to be sleeping**, my eyes are still open when Apa comes home from his night job cleaning the lawyers' offices.

To express expectation, you can also simply use *supposed to* + the base form of the verb.

> Young Ju is **supposed to succeed** in school.

**Practice**  **Workbook Page 52**

Work with a partner. Write sentences in your notebook about things you have to do at school and then things you're supposed to do or be doing. Be sure to use *have to* and *supposed to* and the correct form of the verb.

## Write a Cause-and-Effect Paragraph

You've already learned about two kinds of expository writing—steps in a process and classifying. Now, you'll write a paragraph that shows cause-and-effect relationships, and learn some skills to use. The model below will help you write your own cause-and-effect paragraph.

| Cause |
|-------|
| ↓ |
| Effects |

Notice that the writer shows cause-and-effect relationships by using words like *since, because, so, therefore, if/then,* and *as a result.* He used a cause-and-effect chart to organize his ideas. Notice, too, that the writer begins sentences in different ways.

*Will Trigg*

*When the Pressure Is On, Lying Is Not an Option*
Everyone wants their parents to be proud of them. We also enjoy receiving gifts and having everyone's attention. In this story, Young Ju is hoping for all of these things, however, she does not realize the consequences of telling the class that her brother died. Her lie leads to her classmates making warm fuzzies for her, Mrs. Sheldon giving her a card of scratch-and sniff stickers, and flowers being sent to her house, since everyone feels sorry for her. When Gomo asks where the flowers came from, Young Ju has to make up another lie to keep her secret hidden. She says that she came second in the spelling test, and as a result she must study hard for the next test so she does well. Because of this, she has brought herself into even greater risk of being caught by her parents and her teacher. Therefore, she feels more and more scared and guilty. If she hadn't told a lie in the first place, then she wouldn't be in this situation.

### Practice

Workbook
Page 53

Write a cause-and-effect paragraph about someone who did something wrong, and the effects of his or her actions. It could be someone you read about in the newspaper or saw on TV or in a movie. What did the person do, and why? What were the consequences? List your ideas in a cause-and-effect chart. Use cause-and-effect words to make relationships between your ideas clear. Be sure to correctly use *have to* and *supposed to* for obligations.

**Writing Checklist**

**ORGANIZATION:**
☑ My main idea is clearly stated.

**SENTENCE FLUENCY:**
☑ My sentences begin in different ways.

111

# Prepare to Read

## What You Will Learn

**Reading**

■ Vocabulary building: *Context, dictionary skills, word study*

■ Reading strategy: *Connect ideas*

■ Text type: *Informational text (science)*

**Grammar, Usage, and Mechanics**
Factual conditionals: present and future

**Writing**
Write instructions

 **THE BIG QUESTION**

**What shapes our identity?** What do you know about how crimes are solved? How do detectives and investigators find out the identity of a criminal? What role does science play? Work with a partner. Copy the word web into your notebook and fill in your ideas.

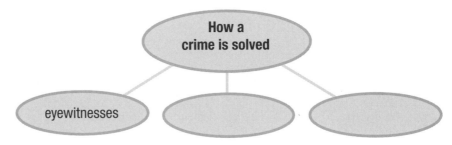

How a crime is solved

eyewitnesses

**BUILD BACKGROUND**

In the science article from ***Crime Scene: How Investigators Use Science to Track Down the Bad Guys***, you'll discover what makes a person unique and how this helps investigators solve crimes. Two things that make each person unique are fingerprints and DNA. DNA is **d**eoxyribo**n**ucleic **a**cid—it is found in the body's cells. Only identical twins have the same DNA. Here are some facts about fingerprints and DNA.

- Fingerprinting has helped police solve crimes since the late nineteenth century.
- There are three different patterns of fingerprints: loops, whorls, and arches.
- Police use a fine powder to lift fingerprints.
- Birds have DNA, too.
- Scientists have DNA specimens dating back 120 million years.

Your fingerprint is unique. ▶

## VOCABULARY

### Learn Key Words

Read these sentences. Use the context to figure out the meaning of the **red** words. Use a dictionary to check your answers. Then write each word and its meaning in your notebook.

**Key Words**

authorized
biometric
captivity
data bank
genetic
laser
technologies

1. You need permission before you are **authorized** to be at a crime scene.

2. **Biometric** computer technology scanned, measured, and recorded the size and shape of his hand.

3. Animals in **captivity** are no longer free to live in their natural environment.

4. Fingerprints are stored in a large computer **data bank**, which can be used to make a match with a crime scene fingerprint.

5. DNA is the **genetic** information that you inherited from your biological parents.

6. The police used a **laser** so they could see the fingerprints better.

7. New **technologies**, like computers and lasers, have changed how police solve crimes.

**Practice**  Workbook Page 54

Write the sentences in your notebook. Choose a **red** word from the box above to complete each sentence. Then take turns reading the sentences aloud with a partner.

1. They found a match to the criminal's fingerprints in the _____.

2. Computer technology that records body measurements is called _____ technology.

3. He lied about the birds he sold, saying that he had not found them in the wild but in _____.

4. You must be _____ or have written permission to enter.

5. Police can use a _____ to find and see fingerprints.

6. _____ information is found in DNA.

7. Data banks and lasers are examples of _____ that help police catch criminals.

## Learn Academic Words

Study the **red** words and their meanings. You will find these words useful when talking and writing about informational texts. Write each word and its meaning in your notebook. After you read the excerpt from *Crime Scene*, try to use these words to respond to the text.

**Academic Words**

distinctive
evidence
identical
identification
invisible
visible

| | | |
|---|---|---|
| **distinctive** = clearly marking a person or thing as different from others | ➡ | I knew it was Juan from across the room. He has a very **distinctive** laugh. |
| **evidence** = facts, objects, or signs that show something exists or is true | ➡ | The jury believed the **evidence** against him, and found him guilty. |
| **identical** = exactly the same | ➡ | The twins are **identical**, so it is hard to tell them apart. |
| **identification** = official documents that prove who you are | ➡ | He used his passport for **identification**. |
| **invisible** = not able to be seen | ➡ | Though fingerprints are usually **invisible**, they are left on everything you touch. |
| **visible** = clear; able to be seen | ➡ | When the police shone the laser on the doorknob, the fingerprints became **visible**. |

## Practice  **Workbook Page 55**

Work with a partner to answer these questions. Try to include the **red** word in your answer. Write the sentences in your notebook.

1. What are some of your **distinctive** physical features?
2. Why is **evidence** important in criminal court cases?
3. Do you think two people can be **identical** in every way?
4. When do you need **identification**?
5. Why do you think fingerprints are usually **invisible**?
6. What aspects of a person's identity are **visible**?

▲ Identical twins

## Word Study: Compound Words

Compound words can be formed in different ways. Look at the chart below. Notice how defining each word clarifies the meaning of the compound word.

| Compound Word | Type | Each Word Defined |
|---|---|---|
| ink pad | two separate words | ink (colored liquid used for writing) + pad (cushion for stamping) |
| fingertip | two words joined together | finger + tip (end) |
| light-colored | hyphenated combination | light + colored |

**Practice**  **Workbook** Page 56

Work in pairs. Copy the chart above into your notebook. Add the words below to the left column of your chart. Then complete the chart. Use a dictionary to help you.

| | | | |
|---|---|---|---|
| bank account | eyewitness | identical twins | password |
| blue-green | farmhouse | magnifying glass | plastic bag |

## READING STRATEGY   CONNECT IDEAS

When you connect ideas, you look for the most important idea in each paragraph and think about how it fits with the other ideas in the text. To connect ideas, follow these steps:

- Read the section headings (if there are any). Do they give you clues about the main ideas in the text?
- Read each paragraph and make note of the main ideas.
- Review your notes. How are the ideas similar? What connects them to each other?

As you read the excerpt from *Crime Scene,* look for ideas that are similar. Think about what connects each idea to the next.

 **Workbook** Page 57

**Set a purpose for reading** How does science define someone's identity?

# *from* Crime Scene:
## How investigators use science to track down the bad guys

*Vivien Bowers*

## Fingerprints

There's no one just like you, or just like anyone else. Look carefully at your fingers. Notice the pattern of lines on the pads of your fingertips that give your fingers extra grip. They also serve as a tool for identifying people. Nobody else has a fingerprint exactly the same as yours, not even your identical twin. And fingerprints don't change from birth to death.

### Oops! And Oops Again!

It was a case of mistaken identity that happened not once, but twice, in the years before police started using fingerprint identification.

In 1897 an innocent man, Adolph Beck, was arrested for cheating women of their money. Actually another man, William Thomas, was the crook, but Beck looked so much like Thomas that the women swore Beck was the one who had tricked them. After five years in jail Beck was released, but he was almost immediately arrested again for more crimes that Thomas had committed. Fortunately, before Beck could go to jail again, a police officer on the case saw Thomas in another

**William Thomas and Adolph Beck**

jail (he had been arrested for trying to sell stolen goods). Beck was released.

Would you be able to tell one man from the other? Several eyewitnesses couldn't. But before fingerprinting was used to identify criminals, eyewitness testimony might have often convicted the wrong person.

---

**crook**, dishonest person or criminal
**swore**, promised truthfully

**testimony**, formal statement that something is true

## Print Patterns

All fingerprints can be divided into three pattern classes: loops, whorls, and arches.

**LOOPS** (60–65 percent of people have this kind) can start from left or right. Two loops (one right and one left) can curl around each other.

**WHORLS** (30–35 percent) have a full circle at the center.

**ARCHES** (5 percent) have a clear arch shape around the center, with other lines arching around.

## Fingerprinting the Culprit

At the scene of the crime, police investigators search for fingerprints. Fingers get sweaty and oily, so everyone who touches an object leaves behind their very own "stamp"—a pattern of little ridges. Some prints are visible, like a sooty or bloody handprint left on a wall. Most are latent, which means they are invisible to the human eye.

## Lifting Prints

Police use fine powders that stick to faint, oily prints and make them more visible. Dark powders show up on light-colored surfaces; white or gray powder is used for dark surfaces. Police can use chemicals that react with oil and make the prints visible. Or they use ultraviolet and laser lights. Under the blue-green light of the laser, prints that were invisible actually glow.

In seconds, police can take a digital photo of a print and send it by photophone to a computerized fingerprint data bank to check for a match.

To see fingerprints on something like a plastic bag, police use a particular kind of glue. In an airtight container with the plastic bag, the glue gives off fumes that cause chemicals to build up on the oily surface of the print. The print is then treated with a special dye to make it visible.

---

**sooty**, black and powdery
**ultraviolet**, light that is beyond the range people can see

## Foiled by Fingerprints

In 1963, thirty men jumped a train traveling from Glasgow, Scotland, to London, England. They made off with mailbags containing more than 2,500,000 pounds (that's worth about U.S. $43 million today). The Great Train Robbery was one of the best-organized robberies ever—almost!

After the robbery, the thieves hid out at a farmhouse where they divided up the money. Someone was supposed to wipe away the fingerprints, but no cleaning up was done. Police found fingerprints all over the place.

Within days, most of the robbers were arrested.

---

### BEFORE YOU GO ON

1. Before fingerprinting was used, how were cases often solved?

2. Why do police use different methods to lift fingerprints?

**On Your Own**
What kind of fingerprint pattern do you have?

# Clue In

Become a fingerprint expert. First make a fingerprint, then lift and dust one. It takes practice to get it right.

1. Rub a pencil on a sheet of white paper. Then rub the tip of your index finger on the pencil mark until it is covered with pencil lead.

2. Put the sticky side of a piece of clear tape over the finger, and carefully peel the tape off. Stick the tape to a sheet of yellow or white paper. Wash your finger.

3. Examine your fingerprint (a magnifying glass is helpful) and decide what pattern class it is. Do all your fingers have the same print pattern?

Have a member of your family or a friend make a mystery print. It will be more fun if you don't know for sure who made the print. The person making the mystery print should first make his or her fingertips oily by rubbing them with some vegetable oil. Then they should press a finger on a smooth, flat surface (like a shiny tabletop).

1. Choose contrasting powder to dust the print—white talcum powder for a dark surface; black pencil powder (made by rubbing a pencil tip with fine sandpaper) or cocoa powder for a light surface. You won't need much.

2. Brush the powder very lightly over the print using a soft feather or soft paintbrush. Gently! When the print starts to appear, stroke in the direction of the ridges.

3. When the fingerprint is fully developed, press a piece of clear sticky tape on the print. Press down hard on the tape and rub it well with your fingernail.

4. Peel off the tape carefully and stick it onto a piece of paper that contrasts in color with the powder.

5. Take fingerprints from your family and friends (press their fingers on a washable ink pad and then paper, or use the method above). Label each one. Now check the mystery print against the prints you have labeled. Can you identify the mystery print?

## DNA—It's in the Genes

What's DNA? It's the greatest breakthrough in forensic science since the discovery of fingerprints. DNA, short for deoxyribonucleic acid, is found in cells of a living body. Each of your DNA molecules contains genetic information that makes you look like you, and not like a turtle or a cat or your brother. Only identical twins have identical DNA.

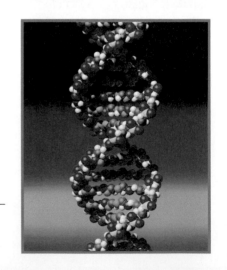

---

**forensic science**, the branch of science involved in solving crimes

**molecules**, smallest units of a substance

## Autorad-ical Proof

Comparing DNA is a complicated process. Tests are done at different points along a strand or molecule of DNA. The results, one row, or *lane*, with dark bands for each test, are placed side by side and compared in an autoradiogram (autorad for short).

DNA samples from different people give different patterns. If two lanes show the same pattern, the DNA samples probably come from the same person. To make sure, scientists will compare more fragments of the two DNA molecules to see if they, too, create identical autorad patterns.

---

**fragments**, small pieces

▲ A geneticist examines a DNA autoradiogram.

# More DNA Evidence

Don't sneeze! You'll leave DNA on this book! Super sleuths today can even get a DNA sample from a smudged fingerprint. One time, the police solved a burglary using DNA evidence found on the doorknob of the house. It came from invisible skin cells that flaked off the burglar's hand when he turned the knob.

---

**sleuths**, people who try to find out information about a crime

## DNA Data

A single DNA molecule consists of two spiral strands linked in what is known as a double-helix formation. If you stretched all the DNA from a single cell end to end, it would be more than 6 feet (2 meters) long.

---

**spiral**, curved

A sneeze ▶

**BEFORE YOU GO ON**

**1** How can scientists be sure they have a DNA match?

**2** How can a person leave DNA behind at a crime scene?

💡**On Your Own**
Would you like to be a forensics expert? Why or why not?

119

## All A-Clone

Remember the book and movie *Jurassic Park*? DNA extracted from dinosaur blood inside a mosquito preserved in amber for millions of years was used to make dinosaurs. It was just a story, right? Well, scientists actually do have DNA from specimens in amber—a 30-million-year-old bee and a 120-million-year-old weevil. And in February 1997, a whole sheep was cloned from the DNA of another sheep. The future is bright for DNA evidence. Imagine if police could take a single hair from a crime scene and use the information in it to work up a physical description of the person it came from!

---

**amber**, yellowish-brown substance
**weevil**, small insect
**cloned**, copied from a single cell

## Generating a "Hit" (Ouch!)

Police have access to two DNA data banks. One contains DNA profiles from criminals convicted of serious crimes. The other contains DNA from crime scenes. Here's how it works. If police are investigating a new crime, they can submit a profile of DNA found at the crime scene. Maybe they'll get a hit—the DNA will match DNA found at a previous crime scene. It looks like the same criminal was involved in both crimes! Or perhaps the DNA will match a previously convicted offender already listed in the data bank, who is now back in the community. Time to pay him or her a visit!

Anytime DNA from a newly convicted criminal is added to the data bank, it may show a match with a "cold case"—a previously unsolved crime. Bingo!

---

**profiles**, short descriptions

# DNA for the Birds

All living things—including birds—have DNA. Police in Britain used DNA tests to prove that a man was illegally selling wild peregrine falcons. Peregrine falcons are endangered so, to protect their numbers in the wild, only falcons bred in captivity can be legally sold. A dealer claimed that the 20 young birds he had for sale were all the chicks of the three pairs of adult birds he owned. DNA tests proved otherwise. They showed that the birds had come from six sets of parents. The birds must have been captured from the wild. The dealer was sentenced to 18 months in jail.

# Authorized Personnel Only!

"Photo identification card, please. What's your password?"

Only authorized people can access private bank accounts, log onto company computers or enter nuclear power facilities. They use secret passwords, photo identification or plastic identity cards that allow them to pass through the security gate. Trouble is, passwords can be forgotten or overheard. Identity cards can be stolen or faked.

One thing that can't be easily stolen or faked is you! There's nobody else exactly the same as you. Today, using biometric technologies, a computer can scan you and transform you into a set of measurements, creating a unique "mathematical description" that can be stored in the computer. So if someone comes along pretending to be you, even if they look a lot like you and are carrying your identification, the computer will know better.

## Voice
The distinctive tone and sound pattern of your voice can be captured by a computer.

## Fingerprint
Your fingerprint pattern can be scanned and stored digitally. No more inky prints on paper.

## Eyes
The colored part of the eye, the iris, has a beautiful pattern of colors and shapes that's unique to each person and can be recorded.

## Hand
A 3-D imaging device scans your hand and fingers, creating a digital description of its size and shape.

## Face
A computer scans your face, measuring how the parts fit together such as the distance between the eyes, ears and nose.

## ABOUT THE **AUTHOR**

**Vivien Bowers**, a Canadian writer, was born in Vancouver, British Columbia. After graduating from the University of British Columbia and earning a teaching certificate, she taught fifth grade for several years. Then she turned to freelance writing. She has since produced many books and articles, many of them about science subjects. Bowen's *Crime Scene* won an award from the American Association for the Advancement of Science.

## BEFORE YOU GO ON

**1** Why does the author say that the future is bright for DNA evidence?

**2** Why is the use of biometric technologies preferred over other methods of identification?

**On Your Own**
How would science identify you?

## COMPREHENSION

**Workbook Page 58**

### Right There

1. What three patterns can fingerprints be divided into?
2. What is DNA?

### Think and Search

3. How do data banks help investigators identify criminals?
4. How did the peregrine falcon dealer get caught?

### Author and You

5. Would the author agree that forensic science is developing and improving every day? What makes you think so?
6. The author implies that biometric technologies are becoming more common. What are some pros and cons of this technology?

### On Your Own

7. Do you agree that DNA is the greatest breakthrough in forensic science since the discovery of fingerprints? Explain.
8. Would crime investigation be an interesting career? Explain.

## IN YOUR OWN WORDS

Work with a partner. Look at the headings below from *Crime Scene*. Review the text under each heading. What is the main idea? Write a short summary. Think about how the ideas are connected.

| Headings | |
|---|---|
| Fingerprints | DNA—It's in the Genes |
| Oops! And Oops Again! | Autorad-ical Proof |
| Print Patterns | More DNA Evidence |
| Foiled by Fingerprints | All A-Clone |
| Fingerprinting the Culprit | Generating a "Hit" (Ouch!) |
| Lifting Prints | DNA for the Birds |
| Clue In | Authorized Personnel Only! |

**Speaking TIPS**

As you summarize, emphasize major points. Ask if there are any questions.

Pause after each main point before going on to the next one.

## DISCUSSION

Discuss in pairs or small groups.

1. Many people are against fingerprinting and the use of biometric technologies in schools. How do you feel about this issue? What do you think the profiles might be used for? Is this a good idea? Explain.

2. How do you think biometric technologies might be used in the future? Do you think they'll change the way we live our daily lives? How?

**Q** **What shapes our identity?** Do you think there are any problems with using scientific methods to define someone's identity? Why or why not?

**»)⌓ Listening TIPS**

If you strongly agree or disagree with others, listen carefully and take notes. Use your notes to repeat key points as you wrap up.

Listen for viewpoints you hadn't considered. Ask questions if you want to know more.

## READ for FLUENCY

When we read aloud to communicate meaning, we group words into phrases, pause or slow down to make important points, and emphasize important words. Pause for a short time when you reach a comma and for a longer time when you reach a period. Pay attention to rising and falling intonation at the end of sentences.

Work with a partner. Choose a paragraph from the reading. Discuss which words seem important for communicating meaning. Practice pronouncing difficult words. Take turns reading the paragraph aloud and give each other feedback.

## EXTENSION

**Workbook Page 58**

Do some research to find out more about one of the following issues:

- Cloning
- Biometric technologies in schools

Are there any benefits? What are the drawbacks? Then choose one of these issues and write a letter to the editor of a magazine or newspaper stating why you are for or against the issue. What is your position on this issue? Use facts and examples from your research to support it.

▲ Dolly, the cloned sheep

# Grammar and Writing

## GRAMMAR, USAGE, AND MECHANICS

### Factual Conditionals: Present and Future

A conditional sentence includes an *if* clause and a main clause. The *if* clause describes a condition, and the main clause describes the result or possible result of it. Use a comma when the *if* clause comes before the main clause.

The factual conditional in the present is used to describe a fact that is always true. Use the simple present for both the *if* clause and the main clause.

> **If** two lanes **show** the same pattern, the DNA samples probably **come** from the same person.
>
> The DNA samples probably **come** from the same person **if** two lanes **show** the same pattern.

The factual conditional in the future is used to describe future situations that have a real possibility of happening. Use the simple present for the *if* clause and the simple future (*will* + base verb) in the main clause.

> Scientists **will compare** more fragments of the two DNA molecules to see **if** they, too, **create** identical autorad patterns.
>
> To see **if** they, too, **create** identical autorad patterns, scientists **will compare** more fragments of the two DNA molecules.

## Practice

**Workbook Page 59**

Copy the sentences into your notebook. Decide if the sentence is a factual conditional in the present or in the future, and then write the correct forms of the verbs.

1. They _____ (convict) her if there _____ (be) a DNA match.

2. Fingerprinting _____ (be) more fun if you _____ (be) unaware of who made the prints.

3. If you _____ (stretch) all the DNA from a single cell end to end, it _____ (be) almost 2 meters (6 ft.) long.

4. If you _____ (have) an identical twin, your DNA _____ (be) the same.

124

# WRITING AN EXPOSITORY PARAGRAPH

## Write Instructions

At the end of this unit, you'll write an expository essay. To help you do this, you'll write a how-to paragraph—one that gives instructions about how to do something—and you'll learn some skills to use. The model below will help you write your own how-to paragraph.

Notice that the writer begins her paragraph with an interesting sentence that gets the reader's attention. She uses sequence words such as *first*, *second*, and *next*, to make the order of the instructions clear. The writer also uses directions that are easy to follow. She used a sequence chart to help organize her ideas.

First
↓
Second
↓
Next
↓
Then
↓
Finally

*Kate Munz*

### How to Catch a Crooked Bird Dealer

Selling endangered birds is a risky business. If you don't follow the rules, you can get in a lot of trouble. Some bird dealers will do anything to make a profit, even selling birds from the wild. That's illegal. Only birds born from parents in captivity may be sold. There are steps that can be taken to prove the birds being sold are from captivity or from the wild. First, samples of DNA are taken from each of the chicks. Second, a sample of each parent's DNA is taken. Next, the samples are compared. If there is a DNA match with the parents (in captivity), then the chicks are legal. If there is no DNA match between the chicks and their parents, this proves that the chicks are from the wild. Following these steps will uncover a crooked bird dealer.

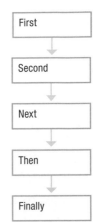

## Practice

**Workbook**
Page 60

Write a paragraph that explains, step by step, how to identify who made a mystery print. You can use information from the article (see "Clue In" on page 118). List the steps in a sequence chart. Be sure to use sequence words to make your instructions clear and easy to follow. Use factual conditionals correctly.

**Writing Checklist**

**ORGANIZATION:**
☑ My writing is interesting and easy to follow and understand.

**IDEAS:**
☑ My beginning catches the interest of my readers.

# Link the Readings

## Critical Thinking

Look back at the readings in this unit. Think about what they have in common. They all tell about identity. Yet they do not all have the same purpose. The purpose of one reading might be to inform, while the purpose of another might be to entertain or persuade. In addition, the content of each reading relates to identity differently. Now copy the chart below into your notebook and complete it.

| Title of Reading | Purpose | Big Question Link |
|---|---|---|
| From *Finding Miracles* | | |
| From *"What Do You Stand For?"* | | |
| *"An Interview with An Na"* | | *Childhood experiences shape identity.* |
| From *A Step from Heaven* | | |
| "Learning English" | | |
| From *Crime Scene* | *to inform* | |

## Discussion

Discuss in pairs or small groups.

**Q** **What shapes our identity?** Think about the readings. How much does a person's background shape his or her identity? Do you think a person's identity changes over time? Can a person have identity problems when he or she is part of two cultures? Do you think your identity is defined by your DNA or your culture and background or both?

## Fluency Check

Work with a partner. Choose a paragraph from one of the readings. Take turns reading it for one minute. Count the total number of words you read. Practice saying the words you had trouble reading. Take turns reading the paragraph three more times. Did you read more words each time? Copy the chart below into your notebook and record your speeds.

| | 1st Speed | 2nd Speed | 3rd Speed | 4th Speed |
|---|---|---|---|---|
| Words Per Minute | | | | |

# Projects

Work in pairs or small groups. Choose one of these projects.

**1** Make a collage of pictures, quotes, and objects that reveals aspects of your identity. Share with the class.

**2** In a small group, do the "Clue In" activity on page 118. To make it more fun, have a "secret" volunteer from a small group of possible "suspects" make the print. Fingerprint each of the suspects and lift the mystery print. Who is the "culprit"? Share the steps you took to solve the "case" with the class.

**3** Work in groups of three to conduct a TV talk show about the pros and cons of using biometric technologies in schools or of cloning. Decide who will be the host and who will take the pro and the con sides. Prepare questions for the host and answers for the "experts."

**4** Write a poem that begins "Life / to understand me / you have to . . ." Take turns reading each other's poems and guessing the identity of the poet!

# Further Reading

To find out more about the theme of this unit, choose from these reading suggestions.

**The Prisoner of Zenda,** Anthony Hope
This Penguin Reader® is an adaptation of a classic story of mistaken identity. The day before his coronation, a king meets a man who looks exactly like him. Through a trick, they switch places.

**My Name Is Asher Lev,** Chaim Potok
Asher Lev wants to draw and paint the world he knows and the pain he feels. He must learn to master his extraordinary gift without giving up any part of his deeply felt Judaism.

**Blood and DNA Evidence: Crime-Solving Science Experiments,** Kenneth G. Rainis
Each chapter begins with the tale of an actual murder. Then the reader is guided through simulated experiments and examination of clues that will lead to the murderer. The experiments are challenging and fun for all.

# Put It All Together

### Panel Discussion

You will take part in a panel discussion about identity.

**1** **THINK ABOUT IT** Work in small groups. Choose an identity issue from one of the readings in this unit, such as:

- Being adopted by parents from a different culture can present challenges.
- Taking inventories can help us better shape who we are and become.
- Identifying with more than one culture sometimes causes confusion.
- Using biometric technologies is controversial to many people.

Assign a role to each group member. One person should be the moderator, or leader, of the panel. Choose from this list for the other panel members: parent or guardian, author, psychologist, forensic scientist, teenager, sociologist, teacher.

**2** **GATHER AND ORGANIZE INFORMATION** Decide how to organize your panel discussion. What aspects of the topic will you discuss?

**Research** Do some research about the issue and your role. What ideas should you get across to the audience? If you are the moderator, create a list of questions to ask the panelists. If you are a panelist, write a brief description of your role. For example: *I'm Sophie. I speak English and French.* Give it to the moderator.

**Order Your Notes** Make a list of important points that are key to your role. Think about the positions others might make, and how you'll respond.

**Use Visuals** Find some visuals such as charts, tables, and graphs to help illustrate your postion on the issue.

▲ A U.S. Customs officer views biometrics data.

**3** **PRACTICE AND PRESENT** Practice as a group. Have the moderator introduce the issue and the panelists, then ask questions for the panel members to answer. Use your notes to help you act out your role during the discussion. Keep your notes nearby, but practice discussing the topic until you don't have to depend on them.

**Deliver Your Presentation** Stand in a semicircle at the front of the room. Face the audience as you speak. Remember to stay in character, and make sure each panelist participates.

**4** **EVALUATE THE PRESENTATION**
You can improve your skills as a speaker and a listener by evaluating each presentation you give and hear. Use this checklist to help you judge your panel discussion and those given by your classmates.

- ☑ Were the panelists convincing in their roles?
- ☑ Can you clearly state each panelist's position?
- ☑ Did each panelist really listen to what others said and respond appropriately?
- ☑ Did the moderator give a clear introduction and ask good questions?
- ☑ What suggestions do you have for improving the panel discussion?

**Speaking TIPS**

Ask questions if you don't understand a point under discussion.

Remember to be polite and respectful, even when others disagree with you.

**Listening TIPS**

Be a good listener. Let other panelists finish speaking before you make your next point.

Take notes as other people talk. Write down what you'd like to add in response. This way you'll remember what you wanted to say when it's your turn to speak.

# WRITING WORKSHOP
## Expository Essay

You have learned how to write a variety of expository paragraphs and some techniques to develop them. Now you will put together what you've learned to write an expository essay in the form of an informational report. An informational report explains and provides facts about a topic. Like other expository essays, an informational report begins with a paragraph that presents the writer's main idea. The report includes several body paragraphs that support the main idea and ends with a paragraph that restates the main idea in a new and interesting way.

   Your writing assignment for this workshop is to write a five-paragraph informational report about identity.

**1** **PREWRITE** Before you choose a topic, brainstorm facts that you already know about identity and list them in your notebook. Then, use your list to help you focus on a topic. For example, if your list includes many scientific facts, you might want to write a report about how science defines identity. Other topics to consider include how culture affects identity, or how either language or the environment shapes who we are.

**List and Organize Ideas and Details** After choosing a topic, use a graphic organizer like the idea web below to list and connect important ideas that you plan to write about. A student named Ashley decided to write an informational report explaining how science defines identity. Here is the idea web she prepared.

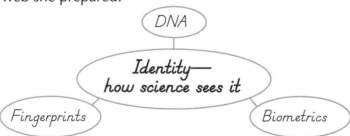

**2** **DRAFT** Use the model on page 133 and your idea web to help you write a first draft. Remember to include an introductory paragraph, three body paragraphs, and a concluding paragraph.

**3** **REVISE** Read over your draft. As you do so, ask yourself the questions in the writing checklist. Use the questions to help you revise your essay.

## SIX TRAITS OF WRITING CHECKLIST

☑ **IDEAS:** Is my main idea clear?

☑ **ORGANIZATION:** Are my ideas presented in an order that makes sense?

☑ **VOICE:** Is my voice lively and informative?

☑ **WORD CHOICE:** Did I use transition and sequence words to show how my ideas are connected?

☑ **SENTENCE FLUENCY:** Do my sentences flow smoothly?

☑ **CONVENTIONS:** Does my writing follow the rules of grammar, usage, and mechanics?

Here are the changes Ashley plans to make when she revises her first draft:

Science and Identity

What makes you a special person? In many ways, you are different from everyone else in the world. All the traits that make you *you* are called your *identity*. Culture and environment influence our identity. Science, however, also plays an important part in shaping who we are. DNA is contained in every cell of our body. DNA stands for deoxyribonucleic acid. It create many of our physical and behavioral traits. It has an impact on us. *how we look, walk, talk, and act.* Interestingly, every individual's DNA is unique. Although identical twins start out with the same DNA, changes happen that make their DNA a little different even before the twins are born.

Scientists started to understand DNA only recently. *Since then,* It has become a major tool used by government and business. Police can use DNA to identify criminals, for example *because* Everyone's DNA is different. Even if there is no eye witness to a murder, DNA may be present in clues left at the scene of a crime. *In the past,* Fingerprints often helped to identify suspects, since fingerprints have unique patterns. *Now,* Even if a fingerprint is badly smudged, the DNA in a drop of blood or a strand of hair can help police identify someone.

A new technology, called biometrics, is being used to identify ordinary people in everyday life. Biometrics is the automated recognition of people. *Because* Everyone has unique physical traits, Biometrics machines can identify you by scanning your face, fingers, or eyes. Biometrics machines are already in use at some airports. Today, most people ~~has~~ *have* to use a passport to fly many places. One day, biometrics machines may completely replace the need for things such *as* credit cards and passports.

Identity is special and unique. It is made up of many different characteristics. Science helps to create identity, and today the individual can be identified in new ways.

**4 EDIT AND PROOFREAD**  Workbook Page 61

Copy your revised draft onto a clean sheet of paper. Read it again. Correct any errors in grammar, word usage, mechanics, and spelling. Here are the additional changes Ashley plans to make when she prepares her final draft.

Ashley Nicole Smith

Science and Identity

What makes you a special person? In many ways, you are different from everyone else in the world. All the traits that make you *you* are called your *identity*. Culture and environment influence our identity. Science, however, also plays an important part in shaping who we are.

DNA stands for deoxyribonucleic acid. It create~s~ many of our physical and behavioral traits. DNA is contained in every cell of our body. It has an impact on how we look, walk, talk, and act. Interestingly, every individual's DNA is unique. Although identical twins start out with the same DNA, changes happen that make their DNA a little different even before the twins are born.

Scientists started to understand DNA only recently. Since then, it has become a major tool used by government and business. Police can use DNA to identify criminals, for example, because everyone's DNA is different. Even if there is no eye witness to a murder, DNA may be present in clues left at the scene of a crime. In the past, fingerprints often helped to identify suspects, since fingerprints have unique patterns. Now, even if a fingerprint is badly smudged, the DNA in a drop of blood or a strand of hair can help police identify someone.

A new technology, called biometrics, is being used to identify ordinary people in everyday life. Biometrics is the automated recognition of people. Because everyone has unique physical traits, biometrics machines can identify you by scanning your face, fingers, or eyes. Biometrics machines are already in use at some airports. Today, most people have to use a passport to fly many places. One day, biometrics machines may completely replace the need for things such as credit cards and passports.

Identity is special and unique. It is made up of many different characteristics. Science helps to create identity, and today the individual can be identified in new ways. ⌐and scientific

**5** **PUBLISH**  Prepare your final draft. Share your essay with your teacher and classmates.

Workbook
Page 62

# Exploring Mixed Identity in America

*P*robably more than any other country in the world, the United States is a "melting pot" of people who come from somewhere else. For these people, figuring out what to keep from the "old" world and what to embrace in the "new" often leads to some difficult decisions about what food to eat, clothes to wear, and language to speak. American art is rich with examples of artists trying to capture this tension in their own lives and in the lives of others.

### Maria Castagliola, *A Matter of Trust* (1994)

When Maria Castagliola turned fourteen, her parents sent her from their home in Cuba to live with relatives in Florida. Even though her parents joined her several months later, Maria never forgot the sense of fear she felt when she had to move to the United States.

As an adult, Castagliola began to explore her art. She remembered that during her childhood her mother sewed secondhand clothes and miraculously transformed them into "new" clothes with her needle and thread. She decided to make her own quilt, *A Matter of Trust*. Castagliola collected secrets from family and friends which they sealed in envelopes. She then sewed them into a quilt between layers of fiberglass window screens. The frightened fourteen-year-old Cuban girl had matured into an American adult who continued to explore her personal identity while building a new sense of community through her art.

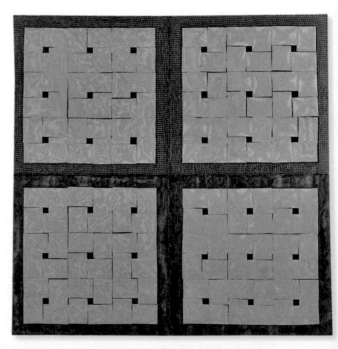

▲ Maria Castagliola, *A Matter of Trust*, 1994, paper and fiberglass, 72 × 72 × ⅛ in., Smithsonian American Art Museum

134

◀ Pepón Osorio, *El Chandelier*, 1988, chandelier with objects, 60⅞ × 42 in. diam., Smithsonian American Art Museum

## Pepón Osorio, *El Chandelier* (1988)

Artist Pepón Osorio celebrates his Puerto Rican culture in *El Chandelier*. He wanted to imitate the type of chandelier often found in the apartments of Puerto Ricans living in New York. In Osorio's piece, all sorts of brightly colored, inexpensive decorations such as baby dolls and sculptures of saints hang side by side. As an artist, he admired the spirit of these chandeliers. He saw them as symbols of hope and good humor in the face of hardship. They also reminded him of the elaborate cakes his mother used to decorate when he was a boy growing up in Puerto Rico. She worked as a baker and often made wedding cakes. "They were incredible productions," he says. "Fountains, sugar, dolls, oceans!" Both the cakes and the chandeliers celebrate togetherness.

If most Americans traced their family history back far enough, they would find that their ancestors came from other countries and had to learn how to adjust to life in a new country.

### Apply What You Learned

**1** In what ways are these artworks concerned with the experience of immigrants in America?

**2** What kind of painting or other artwork would you create to explore the idea of identity in America?

**Big Question**
Why do you think exploring identity in America is a popular subject for so many artists?

**Workbook**
Pages 63–64

# When should you take a stand?

THE BIG
QUESTION

SAVE YOUR
EARTH
YOU CAN'T
GET OFF

This unit is about taking a stand. Taking a stand helps us find out what is important to us in our families, our communities, our country, and ourselves. Reading, writing, and talking about these ideas will give you practice using academic language and help you become a better student.

### READING 1: Novel Excerpt
- From *going going* by Naomi Shihab Nye

### READING 2: Social Studies Article
- From *Freedom Walkers: The Story of the Montgomery Bus Boycott* by Russell Freedman

### READING 3: Short Story
- "The Ravine" by Graham Salisbury

### READING 4: Social Studies Article
- "Speak Your Mind" by Charlotte Steinecke and Emily Cutler

## Listening and Speaking

At the end of this unit, you will host and put on a **TV news show**.

## Writing

At the end of this unit, you will write a **persuasive essay**. Persuasive writing attempts to convince readers to adopt an opinion or take a course of action.

### QuickWrite

What are some issues that people in your community or country feel strongly about? List as many ideas as you can. Then share your ideas with a partner.

## What You Will Learn

**Reading**

- Vocabulary building: *Literary terms, word study*

- Reading strategy: *Distinguish fact from opinion*

- Text type: *Literature (novel excerpt)*

**Grammar, Usage, and Mechanics**

*Used to* + verb and *would* + verb for habit in the past

**Writing**

Write an advertisement

###  THE BIG QUESTION

**When should you take a stand?** To take a stand on an issue is to say in front of others that you are strongly in support of something, or strongly against it. For example, some people feel strongly that there is too much violence on TV. They take a stand on this issue by writing to the television companies and insisting that they reduce the amount of violence in their programs. What are some other examples of issues that people take a stand on? Have you ever taken a stand on an issue? Discuss with a partner.

### BUILD BACKGROUND

In the excerpt from the novel ***going going***, Florrie is upset about all the new franchises and chain stores going up in her hometown of San Antonio, Texas. On her sixteenth birthday, she announces her plan to boycott all chains and to support local businesses only.

What do you know about San Antonio? Look at a few of its landmarks. Why do you think Florrie wants to preserve these and other landmarks in her city?

▲ Tower of the Americas

▲ The Alamo

River Walk ▶

## VOCABULARY

### Learn Literary Words

When you read *going going*, you'll see that Florrie is so driven to achieve her goal that she exaggerates a lot. The author uses **hyperbole** to develop Florrie's character. Hyperbole is a deliberate exaggeration or overstatement. Read to see how Florrie uses hyperbole to convince her family to join her.

> "No chains! Take off your chains! We'll learn a little more about what it felt like to be alive a hundred years ago."

Will her family really find out what life was like a hundred years ago by supporting local shops? The author also uses hyperbole in the title, *going going*. This phrase is used at an auction when an item is sold to the highest bidder. The auctioneer calls out "going, going, gone!" Without her boycott, will San Antonio's character be completely "gone"?

When a story is told from the third person, an author can also show you what a character thinks and feels by using **dialogue**. A dialogue is a conversation between characters. In poems, novels, and short stories, dialogue is usually shown by quotation marks (" ") to indicate a speaker's exact words. In a play, dialogue follows the names of characters, and no quotation marks are used.

Literature that contains well-written dialogue is often more enjoyable to read. It helps us understand the characters' thoughts and opinions. Dialogue provides interaction between the characters. As you read the dialogue in *going going*, notice if the dialogue helps you understand the emotions and visualize the body language of Florrie and her family.

### Practice
Workbook
Page 65

The following statements are examples of hyperbole. Read them aloud. Discuss the meaning of each with a partner.

> I almost died laughing!
> It rained cats and dogs yesterday.
> I've heard that joke a thousand times!

Create your own hyperbole and write it in your notebook. Form small groups and share your hyperboles with each other. Choose the best one in your group, and read it aloud to the class.

## Learn Academic Words

Study the **red** words and their meanings. You will find these words useful when talking and writing about literature. Write each word and its meaning in your notebook. After you read *going going,* try to use these words to respond to the text.

**Academic Words**

access
community
construction
establishment
previous
principle

| | | |
|---|---|---|
| **access** = the right to enter a place, use something, or see something | → | You can't get **access** to that building. You have to be an employee to enter it. |
| **community** = a group of people who live in the same town or area | → | Most people in the **community** were upset when their favorite downtown store closed. |
| **construction** = the process of building something, such as a house or road | → | The **construction** began, and new stores were soon built on the farmland. |
| **establishment** = an institution, especially a business, store, or hotel | → | The locally owned **establishment** had been open for years, and it was the best cheese shop in town. |
| **previous** = happening or existing before a particular event, time, or thing | → | The **previous** owner tried hard to keep his small business, but in the end, he had to sell it to someone else. |
| **principle** = a moral rule or set of ideas that makes you behave in a particular way | → | I want to boycott chain stores on **principle**; I think they are destroying the character of our town. |

## Practice

**Workbook**
Page 66

Work with a partner to answer these questions. Try to include the **red** word in your answer. Write the sentences in your notebook.

1. How would you feel if **access** to your local library was restricted?

2. How has your **community** changed over the years?

3. What happens during **construction** of a new building?

4. What is your favorite eating **establishment** in your town?

5. How can a **previous** owner of a store help a new one?

6. What is a **principle** you feel strongly about?

A site of construction in
downtown Houston ▶

## Word Study: Homophones

Some words sound alike, but they have different spellings and meanings. These words are called homophones. Recognizing homophones can help you with a word's meaning. Read the following sentences and notice the homophones *would* and *wood*. Which one is the past tense of *will*? Which one means "the material that trees are made of"?

> "Remember how sad Grandpa Hani **would** get when another little shop closed down?"
> "They were too busy, like, chopping **wood**."

Use the context of the sentence to help you with the meanings. You can also use a dictionary if you are not sure.

**Practice**  Workbook Page 67

Read the list of homophones in the box below. Look up any words you don't know. Then choose four sets of homophones and write sentences for them in your notebook. Share your sentences with a partner.

| | | | |
|---|---|---|---|
| blue / blew | knights / nights | read / red | to / too / two |
| buy / by | know / no | real / reel | weak / week |
| for / four | not / knot | right / write | where / wear |
| knew / new | one / won | see / sea | whole / hole |

## READING STRATEGY | DISTINGUISH FACT FROM OPINION

Distinguishing a fact from an opinion will help you form ideas about what you read. A fact is something that can be proved. An opinion is what someone believes or thinks. It's not right or wrong. It just cannot be proved. Texts often contain both facts and opinions. To distinguish between facts and opinions, follow these steps:

- As you read, ask yourself whether you can check what you are reading in an encyclopedia or history textbook, or by looking at other research. If you can, it's probably a fact.

- Look for phrases the author uses to give opinions, for example, *I think, I believe, I suppose, personally, We should, We have to.*

- Look for strong adjectives that signal opinions, for example, *crazy, wonderful, terrifying, horrible, bad.*

As you read the excerpt from *going going*, look for facts and opinions. How can you tell the difference between them?

 Workbook Page 68

141

**Set a purpose for reading** In the following novel excerpt, Florrie takes a very strong stand on an issue she cares about. Does Florrie convince you to take her point of view?

*from*

# going going

*Naomi Shihab Nye*

In this novel excerpt, Florrie decides—on her sixteenth birthday—to take a stand to preserve the character and charm of San Antonio by boycotting chains and supporting only local businesses. She first tries to enlist the aid of her family, which isn't easy. But for Florrie, taking this stand isn't so difficult—she's been thinking about it for a long time.

"Okay, guys, this year my wish is . . . hey *familia*, everyone listening? My *wish* is that none of you will visit or patronize any franchise establishment for the rest of this calendar year, starting today! That equals sixteen weeks, one week for each year of my life. This will be a *serious project*. We will support independent businesses for all our needs, as much as is possible. Okay? Agreed?"

Florrie took a deep breath, blew, and snuffed the little flickers out.

*If there could be silence like a pool of spilled paint. Silence strung like a clothesline with nothing on it.*

Her father got an odd grin on his face, but didn't say anything.

Her mother raised her eyebrows.

"Are you crazy?" her brother True said, raising both arms toward the ceiling. "Making a wish that intrudes on all our lives like that?"

"I've been thinking about it so much for so long! Remember how sad Grandpa Hani would get when another little shop closed down? It's an experiment! Can it even be done anymore? Downtown is turning into a bunch of hotels and nothing else! Tourist stuff! No real stuff! We have to do this: we have no choice!"

Her whole family kept staring at her so she just continued.

"Like, it might be hard if the car breaks down and we need a part or something. Gas might be hard. We can make a few exceptions if necessary. But how will we know if we don't try? Just sixteen little weeks. We're a pilot program! You can stand it!"

She was almost shouting by now.

"We sure *do* have a choice," growled True. "Whatever wild idea suits you is suddenly good for us, too? Who do you think you are? I mean, since you don't even drive, how often did you visit the gas station anyway?"

Florrie just kept right on talking. "No chains! Take off your chains! We'll learn a little more about what it felt like to be alive a hundred years ago. I also wish we would walk everywhere or ride bikes or take the trolley or bus. As much as possible."

"You only get one wish, not two," said True.

"Ruben and I got lost on an access road in Corpus Christi last weekend and it was terrifying! We could have been anywhere. There were no landmarks," said Florrie.

---

**patronize**, regularly use
**franchise establishment**, a business that has permission to sell a company's goods or services
**snuffed the little flickers out**, put out any remaining flames on the candles
**pilot program**, a test that is done to see if an idea or product will be successful
**trolley**, electric vehicle for carrying passengers

✔ **LITERARY CHECK**
*Read Florrie's description of downtown San Antonio. How is this an example of hyperbole?*

**BEFORE YOU GO ON**

**1** How long does Florrie want the boycott to last?

**2** How is Florrie's family reacting to her birthday wish?

💡**On Your Own**
How would you react to Florrie's idea?

143

Della was drumming her fingers on the table, smiling slightly. "But where will we get our groceries? And what about all my produce for the restaurant? And everything else the restaurant needs every day? I don't know about that. Come to think of it, the produce vendors I buy from are pretty independent, aren't they?"

"I think it's great," said Ruben. "Let's do it."

True said, "Mom! Dad! Are you trying to be nice to her just because it's her birthday? I don't think anyone should be allowed to make a wish that infringes on the lives of everyone else in the family. Isn't that kind of *bossy*?"

"Stop being a sheep!" said Florrie. Now she was twirling in a circle, her arms out like a propeller. "Stop following the flock! It is time to wander over the hill to find a better meadow."

"I like my meadow!" said True.

Now Ruben was striding around the dining room with his hands up in the air, looking like one of the raggedy street preachers in Travis Park. "I say, let's *all* try it, *absolutely*!" He spoke with such enthusiasm the rest of them felt surprised. He rarely got excited. "It sounds like fun. And Florrie's right. It would be a nice way to honor the past, all the small businesses and stores that are disappearing—"

"We have to save them, Dad!" yelled Florrie. She threw her arms around him.

"Well, we won't. But it's a nice idea."

"My father believed in this, too," said Della, half to herself, running her fingers along the edge of her floral place mat. "We all really believe in this . . . we just do what's easier. . . ."

True stared. Had his entire family been seized by mind control? "But the spirit of one hundred years ago was desperate, you guys! They wanted to be *us*. They wanted to press a button and have something delivered, or order food from their cars. They wanted *cars*! We should be looking forward more than looking back. Why pretend our ancestors had it so good? Who cares about them, anyway?"

Florrie felt a flame burning inside her tongue.

"True, maybe you—don't—care—about—them. They probably didn't care about you, either. They were too busy, like, chopping wood. But we are not doing this for them. *We are doing it for ourselves*. Don't you see?

✔ **LITERARY CHECK**

*How do Florrie's parents, Della and Ruben, feel about Florrie's plan? How do you know? How does the **dialogue** help you?*

---

**produce**, food that has been grown or farmed, especially fresh fruit and vegetables
**vendors**, people who sell things
**infringes**, limits someone's freedom in some way
**striding**, taking long steps while walking

144

Did you read where Ralph Nader said, 'To the youth of America . . . beware of being trivialized by the commercial culture that tempts you daily.' Did you read that?"

True said, "Gee, I did not."

Ruben said, "Ralph is right. It does. Tempt you. Commercial culture tempts adults just as much."

True said, "So now we're on a first-name basis with Nader?"

"Always have been," Ruben said. "He cares about little guys."

True said, "I care about ease and comfort."

"We could eat at El Viento every night!" Florrie said. "It would qualify."

"Wouldn't that be sweet? Then we could clean all the tables! And don't we eat there all the time already? You're so tyrannical, Florrie. I don't know why you think you have so much power."

Florrie shrugged. "I don't. But it's my *birthday*. Remember?"

Florrie insisted on long handshakes with everyone, in agreement. True held his hand behind his back, crossing his fingers, till Florrie pulled it out, pressed it to her forehead, and kissed it. He was so shocked he gripped her hand as it went up and down, shaking his head *no* the whole time.

Sixteen weeks of no franchises. As much as was possible. *Agreed.*

\* \* \*

Florrie's friends expected her to be a little different. She always had been.

In sixth grade Ms. Phillips, her Keystone English teacher, had given her students the assignment to write their life stories in the form of a children's book. Some students added stick figure drawings and some did small paintings in watercolor. Florrie wrote her life story as if it were a fairy tale.

*Once there was a girl who lived in an old neighborhood and loved old things in a way that even she could not understand. At the turn of the millennium, she kept wishing it were the* previous *millennium.*

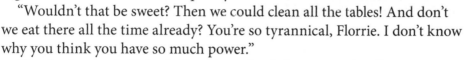

**Ralph Nader**, an American attorney who promotes consumer rights
**trivialized**, made something important seem less important than it really was
**commercial culture**, society driven by money or profits
**stick figure**, simple drawing of a person

**BEFORE YOU GO ON**

**1** Does Florrie's family go along with her plan? How do you know?

**2** What kind of children's book does Florrie choose to tell her life story?

**On Your Own**
Would you choose a fairy tale or another kind of children's book to tell your life story?

145

*She loved Old Ladies, Elderly Men, Old Houses, Old Spoons, Old Books, Old Bowls, Old Maps, Lace Curtains, Antique Bedspreads, Recipes, Remedies, Stories (but not the dumb stories about knights and battles, which did not interest her in the least), Vintage Postcards and Tintype Photographs, Doilies, Velvet Pillows, Black-and-White Movies, Rocking Chairs, and Vintage Toys, and best of all, she loved Old Buildings and Businesses run by Real People. She loved things that were Fading and Disappearing. How could she help protect them in the World?*

*The girl knew that once they were gone, it would be really hard for them ever to come back and start over again, like some species of Lost Animals. She also noticed that nobody else was talking about this enough. So, in her own mind she decided to become a Protector, a Spokesperson, for things that were being wrecked and erased in the world, by Big Business Corporations, Urban Development, and basically People with Too Many Dollar Bills.*

*It would be a Long Road. It would be more like an Endless Journey among destructionists who put up lying signs—MAKING WAY FOR PROGRESS— when they wreck wonderful buildings, as if to trick us. But we are Not Imbeciles. Once you find out what you care about in life, you have No Choice. You have to work for it.*

*What if you love a Tree? A Crane? What if you would prefer to pay close attention to Screech Owls rather than to Human Beings? What if you decide to work on behalf of all Seven-year-olds with Cancer or Attention Deficit Disorder? You have to find some Job To Connect To What You Love.*

Ms. Phillips wrote, "A little scattered" in the upper right-hand corner but read Florrie's essay out loud to the class. She always did that with at least three of her students' papers. She said Florrie's burst of passion was original and admirable and wished her luck in her mission. She also suggested Florrie consider studying German someday since she seemed to have such a strong affection for the Capital Letter, along with everything else.

A girl named Beth had passed Florrie a note. "I'll work with you" was all it said, with a lavish heart drawn on it, signed "B."

Florrie's friend Zip said her convictions made him feel a little embarrassed about his own story. He had described the life of an armadillo in the Texas hill country who decides to wear a baseball cap but can't find one small enough to fit.

---

**vintage**, old and of high quality
**tintype**, a photograph made on an iron plate
**doilies**, small decorative mats made of lace
**imbeciles**, people who are extremely stupid
**attention deficit disorder**, a developmental disorder characterized by inattention
**lavish**, very generous or complicated

One of her classmates stole a MAKING WAY FOR PROGRESS sign from a construction site (very uncharacteristic behavior for a Keystone student, said Ms. Phillips) and gave it to Florrie all wrapped up, because she hated it so much.

\* \* \*

So, years later, extending the project from her family to her classmates didn't seem like such a farfetched thing to do.

The day after her birthday, Florrie tacked up posters on the bulletin board in the lunchroom calling for a "Meeting of the Minds." Then she took them down. That sounded too much like work. School was already work. She had to make this sound like an adventure.

ARE YOU INDEPENDENT?

EXPERIMENT WITH US!

SUPPORT INDEPENDENT ENTERPRISE IN SAN ANTONIO!

MEET ON GRASS OUTSIDE THEATER AT 3:15 THURSDAY FOR 15 MINUTES THAT COULD CHANGE YOUR LIFE!!!!!!!

---

**farfetched**, unlikely to be true and so difficult to believe
**enterprise**, company, organization, or business

## ABOUT THE **AUTHOR**

**Naomi Shihab Nye** was born in St. Louis, Missouri, but spent much of her high school years in Jordan and Palestine. Her father is Palestinian, her mother American. Nye and her parents eventually moved to San Antonio, Texas, where she earned a bachelor's degree from Trinity University. This award-winning Arab-American author has also written poetry, short stories, and essays.

## BEFORE YOU GO ON

**1** What questions does Florrie ask in her fairy tale? How does she answer them?

**2** What do Florrie's sixth-grade classmates and her teacher, Ms. Phillips, think about what she wrote?

**On Your Own**
Do you think anyone will come to Florrie's meeting and join her in taking a stand? Why or why not?

147

## READER'S THEATER

🔊 *Speaking* TIP

Wait until the character before you has finished speaking before saying your lines.

Act out this interview between Florrie and a television reporter.

**Reporter:** How did your project to boycott certain businesses start?

**Florrie:** Officially, it started as my sixteenth birthday wish. That's how I got my family on board. But I had been thinking about it for a long time.

**Reporter:** When did you first start thinking about it?

**Florrie:** My grandfather used to get sad every time a small business would close down. Also, I've always loved old things. I wrote about it once in sixth grade—in a fairy tale.

**Reporter:** What gave you the idea to organize a group at school?

**Florrie:** Ms. Phillips, my sixth-grade teacher, read that fairy tale to the class. Some of my friends told me they supported me. So it made sense to start with them.

**Reporter:** Can you share the plan for anyone who might want to join you?

**Florrie:** It's simple. We rely on independent establishments for what we need—as much as possible. No franchises. With some things, like gas, it's hard. But, in general, it's easy to support locally owned businesses. I hope everyone jumps on board!

## COMPREHENSION  Workbook Page 69

**Right There**

1. What is Florrie's birthday wish?

2. How does her brother, True, react to her wish?

**Think and Search**

3. Rate the family members. Who is the easiest for Florrie to convince? Why?

4. How does her fairy tale help you better understand Florrie's motivation?

### Author and You

**5.** How do you think the author feels about Ralph Nader's message to the youth of America? Why?

**6.** The author and her main character are both from San Antonio and share a common background. Why do you think the author wrote *going going*?

### On Your Own

**7.** How important is it to feel strongly about an issue before you take a stand on it? Why?

**8.** How do you think writing can help a person take a stand?

## DISCUSSION

Discuss in pairs or small groups.

▲ A trolley

• Do you agree or disagree with Florrie's idea? Would you want to try it with your family, your classmates, and your community? For example, would you try to convince them to take a bus or a trolley everywhere? Explain.

**Q When should you take a stand?** What issues do you feel passionate about? Do you feel strongly enough to take a stand on them? Compare your ideas with those of others.

## RESPONSE to LITERATURE

**Workbook Page 69**

Decide whether you would help Florrie win over the San Antonio community or whether you would take the opposite position—that chains and franchises can actually help a community. Use a *pro/con* graphic organizer to help you decide. Divide into two groups—one *pro* and one *con*. If you're on the *pro* side, look back at pages 143–145 for ideas. If you're on the *con* side, reread True's objections to get some ideas. List your main points. Then debate the issue—to boycott or not to boycott—and take turns sharing your views with the class.

»)) *Listening* TIP

Think about the points others are making. Try to relate them to ideas you have.

| Pro | Con |
|-----|-----|
|     |     |

# Grammar and Writing

## GRAMMAR, USAGE, AND MECHANICS

### *Used to* + Verb and *Would* + Verb for Habit in the Past

A habit in the past expresses an action that was regularly repeated in the past but no longer continues. Use *used to* + base form of the verb to talk about habits in the past.

> Remember how sad Grandpa **used to get** when another little shop closed down?

You can also use *would* + base form of the verb. It has the same meaning as *used to*.

> Remember how sad Grandpa **would get** when another little shop closed down?

## Practice

**Workbook Page 70**

Imagine that Florrie's plan is successful, and she convinces her family and classmates to change their habits. Using the words in the chart, work with a partner to write sentences from the perspective of Florrie's family and friends. Describe their old and new habits. Use *used to* + base form of the verb or *would* + base form of the verb for habits in the past and simple present for new habits. Write the sentences in your notebook.

| 1. shop | Before, we used to shop for food at the big-chain supermarkets, but now we go to the local grocer. |
|---|---|
| 2. buy clothes | Before, we would always . . . |
| 3. get gas | |
| 4. go to school | |
| 5. order restaurant supplies | |

## WRITING A PERSUASIVE PARAGRAPH

### Write an Advertisement

At the end of this unit, you'll write a persuasive essay. To help you do that, you'll write a paragraph that enlists the support of others and uses some techniques found in ads or commercials.

| Used to | Now |
|---------|-----|
|         |     |

Ads get people to do something. In this case, the writer of the radio commercial below tries to convince others to join his cause— supporting local, independent businesses. Notice how the writer uses strong words and phrases like *taking over* and *tower above* and opinion phrases like *we have to*. Also, notice the effective use of *used to* and *now* to support his position. The writer used a T-chart to organize his ideas.

*Jack Kefauver*

#### Support Local Businesses

Join the effort to stop the franchises and big chain stores from taking over our San Antonio! You used to be able to go down to the corner store and someone who knew your name greeted you as you came in. Now no one knows who you are. Stores used to have food and clothing at low prices. Now if you want a cup of coffee, it's five dollars instead of one dollar. We need to buy our produce fresh from local farms instead of from big-brand stores with fruit and vegetables coated in wax. We must boycott the businesses that tower above our friendly neighborhood stores. We have to band together to stop the tide of brand names and flashing neon lights. Let's put up a dam by supporting only local businesses so that we won't ever be threatened again by the rising floodwaters of big business! Join our cause today and get back the San Antonio you remember.

### Practice
**Workbook Page 71**

Write a paragraph that advertises a cause that you believe in. Be sure to use strong words, opinion words, and *used to* and *now*. Use a T-chart and list details for *used to* and *now*.

**Writing Checklist**

**VOICE:**
- ☑ My writing shows how strongly I feel about this issue.

**IDEAS:**
- ☑ My message is focused and clear.

**151**

## What You Will Learn

**Reading**
- Vocabulary building: *Context, dictionary skills, word study*
- Reading strategy: *Recognize sequence*
- Text type: *Informational text (social studies)*

**Grammar, Usage, and Mechanics**
Simple past

**Writing**
Write a critique

## THE BIG QUESTION

**When should you take a stand?** Can you think of a time when you were treated unfairly? How did it make you feel? What did you do about it? Share your story with a partner.

## BUILD BACKGROUND

You're going to read an excerpt from **Freedom Walkers: The Story of the Montgomery Bus Boycott,** which tells about the events leading up to the boycott in Alabama. It began officially on December 5, 1955, and ended on December 20, 1956. For 381 days, African Americans boycotted and did not ride the segregated city buses.

Look at the timeline below. It lists the dates the bus boycott began and ended. It also lists the individuals who were involved and the dates of key events that led up to the boycott. Do you recognize any of the names? In this reading you will learn more about these people and the events they were involved in.

▲ A segregated trolley

▲ Walking to work

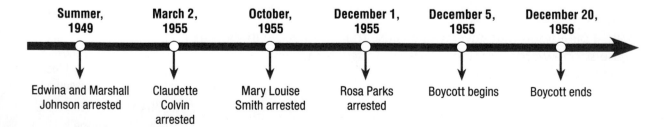

| Summer, 1949 | March 2, 1955 | October, 1955 | December 1, 1955 | December 5, 1955 | December 20, 1956 |
|---|---|---|---|---|---|
| Edwina and Marshall Johnson arrested | Claudette Colvin arrested | Mary Louise Smith arrested | Rosa Parks arrested | Boycott begins | Boycott ends |

## VOCABULARY

### Learn Key Words

Read these sentences. Use the context to figure out the meaning of the **red** words. Use a dictionary to check your answers. Then write each word and its meaning in your notebook.

| Key Words |
| --- |
| accustomed |
| entitled |
| offense |
| official |
| privilege |
| protested |
| vacated |

1. I have grown **accustomed** to the heat. It doesn't bother me anymore.

2. The bus driver claimed the girl was not **entitled** to a seat and had to give it up.

3. She parked her new car in a "no parking" zone. She had to pay a small fine for the **offense**.

4. The **official** rule was that blacks didn't have to give up their seats to whites, but very often blacks did anyway.

5. Whites had the **privilege** to choose where they sat. Blacks did not have this privilege.

6. The people didn't want the building to be taken down. They **protested** by standing in front of it day and night.

7. The man **vacated** his seat so the pregnant woman could sit down.

### Practice  Workbook Page 72

Write the sentences in your notebook. Choose a **red** word from the box above to complete each sentence. Then take turns reading the sentences aloud with a partner.

1. It is a _____ to meet the queen. Not everyone has a chance to meet her.

2. The band members' sisters thought they were _____ to free admission, so they got mad when they were told to pay twenty dollars each.

3. They were not _____ to living in the country. Before, they had always lived in cities.

4. They quickly _____ the building when the fire broke out.

5. They _____ against the construction because they didn't want any more office buildings on their street.

6. They were charged with the _____ but soon were let go when it became clear they were innocent.

7. According to the _____ rules, no one can use the pool after sunset. But in actual practice, people do.

## Learn Academic Words

Study the **red** words and their meanings. You will find these words useful when talking and writing about informational texts. Write each word and its meaning in your notebook. After you read *Freedom Walkers*, try to use these words to respond to the text.

**Academic Words**

constitutional
occupying
policy
required
restricted
violating

| | | |
|---|---|---|
| **constitutional** = officially allowed or restricted by a government's set of rules | ➡ | The United States Constitution grants everyone the **constitutional** right to free speech. |
| **occupying** = filling a particular amount of space | ➡ | Whites were accustomed to **occupying** seats at the front of the bus. |
| **policy** = a way of doing things that has been officially agreed upon and chosen by a political party, business, or organization | ➡ | Most students agreed with the school's **policy** about no cell phones in the classroom. |
| **required** = something that must be done because of a rule or law | ➡ | Passport photos are **required** and must be a certain size. |
| **restricted** = controlled or limited | ➡ | Entrance to the government building is **restricted** to employees and government officials, so the students couldn't go in. |
| **violating** = disobeying or doing something against a law, rule, agreement, etc. | ➡ | She could be arrested for **violating** the law since driving without a license is illegal. |

## Practice

**Workbook Page 73**

Work with a partner to rewrite the sentences. Use the **red** word in each new sentence. Write the sentences in your notebook.

1. Our rights, given to us by the Constitution, cannot be taken away from us. (**constitutional**)

2. Do you know who will be in your state's Senate seats next year? (**occupying**)

3. Does your school have rules about what you can wear to school? (**policy**)

4. Which courses must be taken in order to get a driver's license? (**required**)

5. Why is the entrance to some buildings limited? (**restricted**)

6. What are the penalties for disobeying international law? (**violating**)

## Word Study: Long *i*

In *Freedom Walkers*, you'll read a number of words that have the sound you hear in the words *find* and *sign*. There are several different ways that the long *i* sound can be spelled. It will help you to be aware of these spellings so that you'll know whether to use the short or long *i* sound. It will also help to notice inflections (endings). The inflections below are in parentheses to help you recognize the base word.

| Long *i* | | | | | |
|---|---|---|---|---|---|
| **i_e** | | | **ai-** | **-igh** | **-y** | **-i** |
| arrive fine ride | aside like rid(ing) | drive(r) require(d) white | aisle | high   right | by            cry(ing) my occupy(ing) why | behind |

**Practice**

Work with a partner. Divide up the words in the chart above and copy them into your notebook. Then write a sentence using each word. Take turns reading each sentence aloud and repeating the word for your partner to spell.

**Civil Rights leaders** ▶

## READING STRATEGY   RECOGNIZE SEQUENCE

Recognizing sequence will help you understand what you read. Knowing the sequence or order of events in a text is important because it helps you to understand the order in which things happened. To recognize sequence, follow these steps:

- As you read, look for words the author uses to show sequence, for example, *first*, *then*, *next*, *finally*, *last*, *while*, *during*, and *after*.
- Look for dates and times, for example, *morning*, *yesterday*, *Friday*, *in 1897*.
- Check to see if the dates are arranged from the earliest date to the latest date. If they are, the events are in chronological order.
- It may help you to draw a timeline of the events the author describes.

As you read the excerpt from *Freedom Walkers*, make a note of the sequence in which things happened. How does this help you understand the African Americans' frustrations and concerns better?

**Set a purpose for reading** The individuals described in this novel excerpt took a stand on the same issue and acted on their beliefs in a similar way. What issue did they take a stand on, and how did they do it?

*from* # Freedom Walkers

*Russell Freedman*

## "It's my constitutional right"

*—Claudette Colvin*

Two youngsters from New Jersey—sixteen-year-old Edwina Johnson and her brother Marshall, who was fifteen—arrived in Montgomery to visit relatives during the summer of 1949. No one told them about the city's segregation laws for buses, and one day they boarded a bus and sat down by a white man and boy.

The white boy told Marshall to get up from the seat beside him. Marshall refused. Then the bus driver ordered the black teenagers to move, but they continued to sit where they were. Up North, they were accustomed to riding integrated buses and trains. They didn't see now why they should give up their seats.

The driver called the police, and Edwina and Marshall were arrested. Held in jail for two days, they were convicted at a court hearing of violating the city's segregation laws. Judge Wiley C. Hill threatened to send them to reform school until they were twenty-one, but relatives managed to get them an attorney. They were fined and sent back to New Jersey.

---

**reform school**, a special school for young people who have broken the law

Claudette Colvin ▶

During the next few years, other black riders were arrested and convicted for the same offense—sitting in seats reserved for whites. They paid their fines quietly and continued to ride the public buses. It took a spunky fifteen-year-old high school student to bring matters to a head.

Claudette Colvin was an A student at all-black Booker T. Washington High. She must have been paying attention in her civics classes, for she insisted on applying the lessons she had learned after boarding a city bus on March 2, 1955.

Claudette was on her way home from school that day. She found a seat in the middle of the bus, behind the section reserved for whites. As more riders got on, the bus filled up until there were no empty seats left. The aisle was jammed with passengers standing, mostly blacks and a few whites.

The driver stopped the bus and ordered black passengers seated behind the white section to get up and move farther back, making more seats available for whites. Reluctantly, black riders gave up their seats and moved into the crowded aisle as whites took over the vacated seats.

Claudette didn't move. She knew she wasn't sitting in the restricted white section. She felt that she was far enough back to be entitled to her seat. A pregnant black woman was sitting next to her. When the driver insisted that the woman get up and stand in the aisle, a black man in the rear offered her his seat, then quickly left the bus to avoid trouble.

Claudette was now occupying a double seat alone. "Hey, get up!" the bus driver ordered. Still she refused to move. None of the white women standing would sit in the empty seat next to Claudette. It was against the law for blacks to sit in the same row as a white person.

The driver refused to move the bus. "This can't go on," he said. "I'm going to call the cops." He did, and when the police arrived, he demanded that Claudette be arrested.

"Aren't you going to get up?" one of the police officers asked.

"No," Claudette replied. "I don't have to get up. I paid my fare, so I don't have to get up." At school, Claudette had been studying the U.S. Constitution and the Bill of Rights, and she had taken those lessons to heart. "It's my constitutional right to sit here just as much as that [white] lady," she told the police. "It's my constitutional right!"

---

**spunky**, full of energy and determination
**civics**, a school subject dealing with the rights and duties of citizens and the way government works
**Bill of Rights**, a written statement of the most important rights of the citizens of the United States

**BEFORE YOU GO ON**

**1** What caused the driver to stop the bus?

**2** What wouldn't Claudette do?

**On Your Own**
What would you have done if you were Claudette? Why?

Blacks had been arrested before for talking back to white officials. Now it was Claudette's turn. She was crying and madder than ever when the police told her she was under arrest. "You have no right to do this," she protested. She struggled as they knocked her books aside, grabbed her wrists, and dragged her off the bus, and she screamed when they put on the handcuffs.

"I didn't know what was happening," she said later. "I was just angry. Like a teenager might be, I was just downright angry. It felt like I was helpless." She remained locked up at the city jail until she was bailed out later that day by the pastor of her church.

Under Montgomery's segregation laws, Claudette was in fact entitled to her seat behind the whites-only section. If no seats were available for blacks to move back to as additional white passengers boarded the bus, then they were not required to give up their seats. That was the official policy. But in actual practice, whenever a white person needed a seat, the driver would order blacks to get up and move to the back of the bus, even when they had to stand in the aisle.

Prosecutors threw the book at Claudette. She was charged not only with violating the segregation laws, but also with assault and battery for resisting arrest. "She insisted she was colored and just as good as white," the surprised arresting officer told the judge at the court hearing.

▲ "Colored Waiting Room" at a bus terminal in Mississippi

---

**threw the book at**, punished someone as severely as possible
**assault and battery**, the threat to use force on another and the carrying out of the threat

After a brief trial in juvenile court, Claudette was found guilty of assault. She was fined and placed on probation in her parents' custody. She had expected to be cleared, and when the judge announced his verdict, she broke into agonized sobs that shook everyone in the crowded courtroom.

"The verdict was a bombshell!" Jo Ann Robinson recalled. "Blacks were as near a breaking point as they had ever been."

In October 1955, several months after Claudette was convicted, Mary Louise Smith, an eighteen-year-old black girl, was arrested when she refused to move to the back of the bus so a white woman could take her seat. "[The driver] asked me to move three times," Smith recalled. "And I refused. I told him, 'I am not going to move out of my seat. I am not going to move anywhere. I got the privilege to sit here like anybody else does.'"

Smith's case did not create the furor that the Colvin case did, because Smith chose to plead guilty. She was fined five dollars.

Two months later, on December 1, 1955, another black woman boarded a city bus and found an empty seat just behind the white section. She was Rosa Parks.

▲ Mary Louise Smith today

---

**probation**, system that allows criminals to leave prison early or not go to prison at all based on good behavior
**custody**, the act or right of guarding
**agonized**, suddenly or intensely emotional
**bombshell**, a shocking piece of news
**furor**, a sudden expression of anger or excitement

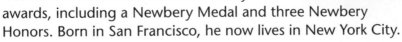

## ABOUT THE **AUTHOR**

**Russell Freedman** is a nonfiction author who writes mainly about history and the people who shape it. His subjects have included Eleanor Roosevelt, Abraham Lincoln, and Native-American chief Crazy Horse. His work has earned him many awards, including a Newbery Medal and three Newbery Honors. Born in San Francisco, he now lives in New York City.

## BEFORE YOU GO ON

**1** What was Claudette charged with? What was she found guilty of?

**2** How did Mary Louise Smith's and Claudette Colvin's cases differ? Why?

**On Your Own**
Why were the stands each individual took important?

### Right There

1. What didn't Edwina and Marshall Johnson know?
2. What was Claudette Colvin charged with?

### Think and Search

3. How were the incidents involving the Johnsons, Claudette Colvin, and Mary Louise Smith similar and yet different?
4. What was the official policy for whites and blacks riding Montgomery buses before 1956? Did Claudette violate this policy? Explain.

### Author and You

5. Why do you think the author chose the title *Freedom Walkers*?
6. The author implies that Claudette's case was very important. What clues in the text suggest this? Do you agree that her case was important?

### On Your Own

7. Do you think that young people should take a stand on important issues no matter what their age? Can young people make a difference?
8. We often associate only "big names" and not lesser-known individuals with important historical events. Why do you think this is so?

## IN YOUR OWN WORDS

Work in groups of four. Arrange yourselves in pairs. Have one pair prepare a word web with details about Edwina and Marshall Johnson. Have the other pair prepare a word web with details about Claudette Colvin. Then take turns presenting the details you listed, until you have summarized the reading.

160

## DISCUSSION

Discuss in pairs or small groups.

1. Why do you think the boycott was successful after so many years of injustice? Why was this a turning point in U.S. history?

2. Even if something is official policy, should it always be followed no matter what? Why or why not?

**Q** **When should you take a stand?** Why are boycotts effective? How can a boycott be a powerful way to take a stand?

 **Listening TIP**

Be a careful listener so you don't repeat what someone else has already contributed to the discussion.

## READ FOR FLUENCY

It is often easier to read a text if you understand the difficult words and phrases. Work with a partner. Choose a paragraph from the reading. Identify the words and phrases you do not know or have trouble pronouncing. Look up the difficult words in a dictionary.

Take turns pronouncing the words and phrases with your partner. If necessary, ask your teacher to model the correct pronunciation. Then take turns reading the paragraph aloud. Give each other feedback on your reading.

## EXTENSION

**Workbook Page 76**

Go to the library and check out the book *Freedom Walkers* or use Internet resources to research what happened after Rosa Parks boarded the bus on December 1, 1955. Copy the timeline on page 152. Add other key events and describe the key events in detail.

Discuss the events in a small group. How did the actions of Edwina and Marshall Johnson, Claudette Colvin, and Mary Louise Smith help the larger cause? How did these young people help to bring about real change? Then as a class, display and compare your timelines. Did you include the same key events? If not, which ones would you add?

▲ The Montgomery Sheriff's Department booking photo of Rosa Parks

# Grammar and Writing

## Simple Past

Use the simple past for actions that started and ended in the past. The verb form is the same for all persons.

Study the spelling patterns of the verbs in the chart below. For most verbs, add -ed. If a verb ends in -e, add -d. If a verb ends in a vowel + y, change y to i and add -d. If a verb ends in a vowel + consonant, double the consonant, then add -ed.

| Regular Verb | Spelling Pattern | Verb Used in Simple Past |
|---|---|---|
| call | add -ed | The driver **called** the police. |
| manage | add -d | Relatives **managed** to get them an attorney. |
| pay / reply | change y to i and add -d<br>change y to i and add -ed | They **paid** their fines.<br>"No," Claudette **replied**. |
| jam | double the m and then add -ed | The aisle was **jammed** with passengers. |

Many verbs are irregular. Irregular past tense verbs often look different from the base form. Here are just a few examples:

| Irregular Verb | Verb Used in Simple Past |
|---|---|
| is<br>give<br>know<br>feel<br>choose | Claudette **was** on her way home from school.<br>Black riders **gave** up their seats.<br>She **knew** she was sitting in the restricted white section.<br>I **felt** like I was helpless.<br>She **chose** to plead guilty. |

## Practice
**Workbook Page 77**

Work with a partner. In your notebook, copy and complete the following paragraph with the simple past form of the verbs in parentheses.

During the summer of 1949, Edwina and Marshall Johnson (come) to Montgomery, Alabama, to visit relatives. When they (board) a bus and (sit) next to a white man and boy, the boy (tell) Marshall to get up, but Marshall (refuse), and the driver (call) the police. The police (arrest) the two teenagers. The family (hire) an attorney. The judge (fine) them and (send) them back to New Jersey.

## WRITING A PERSUASIVE PARAGRAPH

### Write a Critique

At the end of this unit, you'll write a persuasive essay. To help you do that, you'll write a critique that reviews an excerpt or a book you've read. The model below reviews the book *Freedom Walkers* and will help you write your own critique.

In a critique, a writer recommends that others read or do *not* read the book. A critique gives reasons and examples to support the writer's main ideas. Notice how the writer effectively uses strong words and phrases like *phenomenal* and opinion phrases like *a must-read*. Notice also that he describes the important events in the book in a logical way so that the reader knows how the events are connected. Read the critique and decide if it convinces you to read the rest of the book.

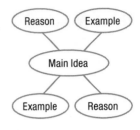

Reason   Example

Main Idea

Example   Reason

---

Chas Robinson

*Freedom Walkers*

   *Freedom Walkers* is an important book for anyone interested in the civil rights movement. This book is about frustrated teens who stood up for their rights before the Montgomery bus boycott. Claudette Colvin was an A student at her high school. One day after school, she boarded a bus home. As the bus began to fill up, she was asked to give up her seat to a white person. Having taken her studies of the Constitution and the Bill of Rights to heart, she knew she was as entitled to that seat as any white person and was willing to fight for it. Claudette was just one example of the many young people who helped in the fight for equality and should be recognized like Rosa Parks and Dr. King. *Freedom Walkers* did just that; it is a phenomenal book and a must-read for anyone interested in the subject or who wants a motivating story that they can relate to.

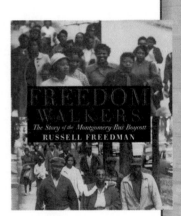

**Practice**

Write your own critique reviewing the excerpt from *Freedom Walkers* or another excerpt or book you've read. Use a word web to list your main idea and your strong phrases, opinion phrases, and supporting details. Be sure to use the simple past correctly.

### Writing Checklist

**VOICE:**
☑ My readers could tell right away how I felt about this book.

**ORGANIZATION:**
☑ I included details to support my opinion.

163

## THE BIG QUESTION

### When should you take a stand?

Peer pressure is when your peers (people your age) try to influence how you act. For example, a few kids in school might try to get you to miss class with them, or someone on your sports team might try to convince you to be mean to another player. What are some reasons why people sometimes give in to peer pressure? Discuss with a partner.

## BUILD BACKGROUND

In the short story **"The Ravine,"** you will read about four friends, three of whom apply pressure on the fourth, Vinny, to jump off a steep 50-foot ledge. What do you know about peer pressure? Read these facts about influences on teens.

▲ Ravine Waterfalls on Big Island, Hawaii

- High self-esteem and self-confidence help teenagers resist peer pressure.

- Parents who show more interest, understanding, and helpfulness have a greater influence on their children than those parents who don't.

- Teenagers choose their friends based on similar values and attitudes.

- Teenagers spend twice as much time with their friends as with their parents.

- Teenagers engage in risky behaviors because of the strong need to belong.

Can you identify with any of these statements? Discuss with a partner.

### Learn Literary Words

When you read a short story like "The Ravine," think about the main **character's motivation**. Motivation explains "why" a character did or said something. As you read, look for reasons why the character thinks, feels, acts, and behaves in a certain way. Sometimes a character's motivation will change during the course of the story. For example, in "The Ravine," an important motivating factor for Vinny is peer pressure. But other things motivate him as well. As you read, ask yourself what the motivation is behind the things Vinny says and does.

**Flashback** is a reference to something that happened earlier in the story or in the character's past. Authors sometimes use flashback to help us better understand the background to a conflict and the character's motivation. In "The Ravine," the author refers back to an accident involving a boy who was killed at the waterfall. Referring back to this incident helps us understand Vinny's feelings about his current situation.

**Plot** is the sequence of events in a literary work. The structure of a plot varies from story to story, but often a plot will have these elements:

basic situation → conflict → climax → resolution → conclusion

In many stories, the *conflict* is associated with a goal the main character is trying to achieve. Very often the character faces complications when trying to reach this goal, which increases the tension. The *climax* is the point in the story with the highest tension. The *resolution* is what happens to the character after reaching or failing to reach his or her goal.

**Practice**

Workbook Page 79

With a partner, choose a story that you both have read. Take turns describing the elements of the plot, including the basic situation, the conflict and its complications, the climax, the resolution, and the conclusion.

**Literary Words**

character motivation
flashback
plot

## Learn Academic Words

Study the **red** words and their meanings. You will find these words useful when talking and writing about literature. Write each word and its meaning in your notebook. After you read "The Ravine," try to use these words to respond to the text.

**Academic Words**

affect
circumstances
injure
internal
predict
reconstruct

| | | |
|---|---|---|
| **affect** = do something that produces a change in someone or something; influence | → | The boy's death would **affect** the way Vinny thought about the swimming hole forever. |
| **circumstances** = the facts or conditions that affect a situation, action, event, etc. | → | The boy died at the ravine fifteen days ago. Under these **circumstances**, it wasn't right to go there and have fun. |
| **injure** = hurt a person or animal | → | The boy was afraid to climb the tree because he didn't want to **injure** himself again. Last time he tried it he fell and hurt his arm. |
| **internal** = inside something, such as your body | → | Outside she looks confident, but inside she feels confused. Her feelings of confusion are **internal** only. |
| **predict** = foretell | → | There was no way to **predict** what would happen if they jumped off the cliff. |
| **reconstruct** = construct or enact again | → | It was almost impossible to **reconstruct** what had happened to him since no one was with him. |

## Practice

**Workbook Page 80**

Work with a partner to answer these questions. Try to include the **red** word in your answer. Write the sentences in your notebook.

1. Why do you think tragedies **affect** people differently?
2. What **circumstances** cause people to feel nervous?
3. How could you **injure** yourself playing sports?
4. How is an external conflict different from an **internal** one?
5. What do you **predict** the weather will be like tomorrow?
6. Why do police talk to witnesses and **reconstruct** an accident?

166

## Word Study: Inflections *-ed* and *-ing*

Sometimes you will read words that have the ending *-ed* or *-ing*. To read one of these words, look at the base word and the inflectional ending. The spelling of the word will tell you if the vowel sound is long or short.

If the word has a short vowel sound followed by a single consonant, the final consonant is doubled before the *-ed* or *-ing* is added.

If the word has a long vowel sound and ends with *e*, the *e* is dropped before the *-ed* or *-ing* is added.

|  | **Short Vowel** | **Long Vowel** |
|---|---|---|
| -ed | smell → smel**led** | wave → wav**ed** |
|  | drop → drop**ped** | roll → rol**led** |
| -ing | walk → walk**ing** | freeze → freez**ing** |
|  | swim → swim**ming** | cascade → cascad**ing** |

**Practice**
Workbook Page 81

Read aloud the following words with a partner. Write each word in your otebook with the *-ed* and *-ing* endings.

| challenge | continue | jump | laugh | open | use |
|---|---|---|---|---|---|
| climb | fake | land | mind | talk | vanish |

▲ He jumped into the water.

## READING STRATEGY | PREDICT

Predicting helps you better understand and focus on the text. Before you read, predict (or guess) what the story will be about. You can also make new predictions as you're reading. To predict, follow these steps:

- Stop reading from time to time and ask yourself, "What will happen next?"
- Look for clues in the story and illustrations. Think about what you already know. Make a prediction
- As you read, check to see if your prediction is correct. If it isn't, you can change your prediction.

As you read "The Ravine," stop from time to time and check to see if your prediction was correct. Did you learn anything new that made you want to change your prediction? Make a new prediction, if necessary.

Workbook Page 82

167

**Set a purpose for reading** How do Vinny's friends pressure him to jump? How does Vinny give in to this peer pressure, or take a stand against it?

# The Ravine *Graham Salisbury*

When Vinny and three others dropped down into the ravine, they entered a jungle thick with tangled trees and rumors of what might have happened to the dead boy's body.

The muddy trail was slick and, in places where it had fallen away, flat-out dangerous. The cool breeze that swept the Hawaiian hillside pastures above died early in the descent.

There were four of them—Vinny; his best friend, Joe-Boy; Mo, who was afraid of nothing; and Joe-Boy's haole girlfriend, Starlene— all fifteen. It was a Tuesday in July, two weeks and a day after the boy had drowned. If, in fact, that's what had happened to him.

Vinny winced. He didn't want to be here. It was too soon, way too soon. Two weeks and one day.

He saw a footprint in the mud and stepped around it.

---

**slick**, wet and slippery
**flat-out**, completely
**haole**, Hawaiian word for white person
**winced**, suddenly changed one's facial expression after
    remembering something painful

The dead boy had jumped and had never come back up. Four search and rescue divers hunted for two days straight and never found him. Not a trace. Gave Vinny the creeps. It didn't make sense. The pond wasn't that big.

He wondered why it didn't seem to bother anyone else. Maybe it did and they just didn't want to say.

Butchie was the kid's name. Only fourteen.

Fourteen.

Two weeks and one day ago he was walking down this trail. Now nobody could find him.

The jungle crushed in, reaching over the trail, and Vinny brushed leafy branches aside. The roar of the waterfall got louder, louder.

\* \* \*

Starlene said it was the goddess that took him, the one that lives in the stone down by the road. She did that every now and then, Starlene said, took somebody when she got lonely. Took him and kept him. Vinny had heard that legend before, but he'd never believed in it.

Now he didn't know what he believed.

The body had to be stuck down there. But still, four divers and they couldn't find it?

Vinny decided he'd better believe in the legend. If he didn't, the goddess might get mad and send him bad luck. Or maybe take *him*, too.

*Stopstopstop! Don't think like that.*

Starlene swam across to the waterfall on the far side of the pond and ducked under it, then climbed out and edged along the rock wall behind it, moving slowly, like a spider. Above, sun-sparkling stream water spilled over the lip of a one-hundred-foot drop.

Mo and Joe-Boy threw their towels onto the rocks and dove into the pond. Vinny watched, his muddy towel hooked around his neck. Reluctantly, he let it fall, then dove in after them.

He followed Joe-Boy and Mo to the waterfall and ducked under it. They climbed up onto the rock ledge, just as Starlene had done, then spidered their way over to where you could climb to a small ledge about fifteen feet up. They took their time because the hand and footholds were slimy with moss.

Starlene jumped first. Her shriek echoed off the rocky cliff, then died in the dense green jungle.

Mo jumped, then Joe-Boy, then Vinny.

The fifteen-foot ledge was not the problem.

---

**the creeps**, scary, uncomfortable feelings
**legend**, an old, well-known story, often about brave people or adventures
**lip**, the edge of a piece of land

**BEFORE YOU GO ON**

1 Who was the dead boy and what was done to try to find him?

2 How long has it been since the boy disappeared in the ravine?

**On Your Own**
Have you ever seen a waterfall?

**169**

It was the one above it, the one you had to work up to, the big one, where you had to take a deadly zigzag trail that climbed up and away from the waterfall, then cut back and forth to a foot-wide ledge something more like fifty feet up.

That was the problem.

Vinny swam back over to the other side of the pond, where he'd first gotten in. His mother would kill him if she ever heard about where he'd come. After the boy drowned, or was taken by the goddess, or whatever happened to him, she said never to come to this pond again. Ever. It was off-limits. Permanently.

But not his dad. He said, "You fall off a horse, you get back on, right? Or else you going to be scared of it all your life."

His mother scoffed and waved him off. "Don't listen to him, Vinny, listen to me. Don't go there. That pond is haunted." Which had made his dad laugh.

But Vinny promised he'd stay away.

But then Starlene and Joe-Boy said, "Come with us anyway. You let your mommy run your life, or what?" And Vinny said, "But what if I get caught?" And Joe-Boy said, "So?"

Vinny mashed his lips. He was so weak. Couldn't even say no. But if he'd said, "I can't go, my mother won't like it," they would have laughed him right off the island. No, he had to go. No choice.

So he'd come along, and so far it was fine. He'd even gone in the water. Everyone was happy. All he had to do now was wait it out and go home and hope his mother never heard about it.

When he looked up, Starlene was gone.

He glanced around the pond until he spotted her starting up the zigzag trail to the fifty-foot ledge. She was moving slowly, hanging on to roots and branches on the upside of the cliff. He couldn't believe she was going there. He wanted to yell, *Hey, Starlene, that's where he* died!

But she already knew that.

Mo jumped from the lower ledge, yelling, "Banzaiiii!" An explosion of coffee-colored water erupted when he hit.

Joe-Boy swam over to where Starlene had gotten out. He waved to Vinny, grinning like a fool, then followed Starlene up the zigzag trail.

Now Starlene was twenty-five, thirty feet up. Vinny watched her for a while, then lost sight of her when she slipped behind a wall of jungle that blocked his view. A few minutes later she popped back out, now almost at the top, where the trail ended, where there was nothing but mud and a few plants to grab on to if you slipped, plants that would rip right out of the

**LITERARY CHECK**

*What is the main conflict in the plot?*

---

**off-limits**, beyond the area where someone is allowed to go
**scoffed**, laughed at a person or idea
**mashed**, crushed something until it was soft

**170**

ground, plants that wouldn't stop you if you fell, nothing but your screams between you and the rocks below.

Vinny's stomach tingled just watching her. He couldn't imagine what it must feel like to be up there, especially if you were afraid of heights, like he was. *She has no fear*, Vinny thought, *no fear at all. Pleasepleaseplease, Starlene. I don't want to see you die.*

Starlene crept forward, making her way to the end of the trail, where the small ledge was.

Joe-Boy popped out of the jungle behind her. He stopped, waiting for her to jump before going on.

Vinny held his breath.

Starlene, in her cutoff jeans and soaked T-shirt, stood perfectly still, her arms at her sides. Vinny suddenly felt like hugging her. Why, he couldn't tell. *Starlene, please.*

She reached behind her and took a wide leaf from a plant, then eased down and scooped up a finger of mud. She made a brown cross on her forehead, then wiped her muddy fingers on her jeans.

She waited.

Was she thinking about the dead boy?

She stuck the stem end of the leaf in her mouth, leaving the rest of it to hang out. When she jumped, the leaf would flap up and cover her nose and keep water from rushing into it. An old island trick.

She jumped.

Down, down.

Almost in slow motion, it seemed at first, then faster and faster. She fell feetfirst, arms flapping to keep balance so she wouldn't land on her back, or stomach, which would probably almost kill her.

Just before she hit, she crossed her arms over her chest and vanished within a small explosion of rusty water.

Vinny stood, not breathing at all, praying.

Ten seconds. Twenty, thirty . . .

She came back up, laughing.

*She shouldn't make fun that way*, Vinny thought. It was dangerous, disrespectful. It was asking for it.

Vinny looked up when he heard Joe-Boy shout, "Hey, Vinny, watch how a man does it! Look!"

Joe-Boy scooped up some mud and drew a stroke of lightning across his chest. When he jumped, he threw himself out, face and body parallel to the pond, his arms and legs spread out. *He's crazy*, Vinny thought, *absolutely insane.* At the last second Joe-Boy folded into a ball and hit. *Ca-roomp!* He came up whooping and yelling, "*Wooo! So good!* Come on, Vinny, it's hot!"

**BEFORE YOU GO ON**

**1** Which ledge was the problem?

**2** What made the area where Starlene was dangerous?

**On Your Own**
Which makes more sense to you—Vinny's mother's advice or his father's advice? Why?

**171**

Vinny faked a laugh. He waved, shouting, "Naah, the water's too cold!"

Now Mo was heading up the zigzag trail—Mo, who hardly ever said a word and would do anything anyone ever challenged him to do. *Come on, Mo, not you, too.*

Vinny knew then that he would have to jump.

Jump, or never live it down.

Mo jumped in the same way Joe-Boy had, man-style, splayed out in a suicide fall. He came up grinning.

Starlene and Joe-Boy turned toward Vinny.

Vinny got up and hiked around the edge of the pond, walking in the muddy shallows, looking at a school of small brown-backed fish near a ginger patch.

Maybe they'd forget about him.

Starlene torpedoed over, swimming underwater. Her body glittered in the small amount of sunlight that penetrated the trees around the rim of the ravine. When she came up, she broke the surface smoothly, gracefully, like a swan. Her blond hair sleeked back like river grass.

She smiled a sweet smile. "Joe-Boy says you're afraid to jump. I didn't believe him. He's wrong, right?"

Vinny said quickly, "Of course he's wrong. I just don't want to, that's all. The water's cold."

"Naah, it's nice."

---

**splayed out**, having fingers, arms, or legs wide apart
**ginger**, a hot-tasting light-brown rooted plant
**torpedoed**, moved quickly and smoothly, like a torpedo
**rim**, the outside edge of something

172

Vinny looked away. On the other side of the pond Joe-Boy and Mo were on the cliff behind the waterfall.

"Joe-Boy says your mom told you not to come here. Is that true?"

Vinny nodded. "Yeah. Stupid, but she thinks it's haunted."

"She's right."

"What?"

"That boy didn't die, Vinny. The stone goddess took him. He's in a good place right now. He's her prince."

Vinny scowled. He couldn't tell if Starlene was teasing him or if she really believed that. He said, "Yeah, prob'ly."

"Are you going to jump, or is Joe-Boy right?"

"Joe-Boy's an idiot. Sure I'm going to jump."

Starlene grinned, staring at Vinny a little too long. "He is an idiot, isn't he? But I love him."

"Yeah, well . . ."

"Go to it, big boy. I'll be watching."

Starlene sank down and swam out into the pond.

*Ca-ripes.*

Vinny ripped a hank of white ginger from the ginger patch and smelled it, and prayed he'd still be alive after the sun went down.

He took his time climbing the zigzag trail. When he got to the part where the jungle hid him from view, he stopped and smelled the ginger again. So sweet and alive it made Vinny wish for all he was worth that he was climbing out of the ravine right now, heading home.

But of course, there was no way he could do that.

Not before jumping.

He tossed the ginger onto the muddy trail and continued on. He slipped once or twice, maybe three times. He didn't keep track. He was too numb now, too caught up in the insane thing he was about to do. He'd never been this far up the trail before. Once he'd tried to go all the way, but couldn't. It made him dizzy.

When he stepped out and the jungle opened into a huge bowl where he could look down, way, way down, he could see there three heads in the water, heads with arms moving slowly to keep them afloat, and a few bright rays of sunlight pouring down onto them, and when he saw this, his stomach fluttered and rose. Something sour came up and he spit it out.

It made him wobble to look down. He closed his eyes. His whole body trembled. The trail was no wider than the length of his foot. And it was wet and muddy from little rivulets of water that bled from the side of the cliff.

---

scowled, looked at someone in an angry or disapproving way
ca-ripes, an expression used to show fear or annoyance
wobble, move from side to side in an unsteady way

**BEFORE YOU GO ON**

1 What did Starlene, Joe-Boy, and Mo all do?

2 Why do you think Vinny can't tell his friends that he doesn't want to jump?

On Your Own
What do you think will happen next? Why?

**173**

The next few steps were the hardest he'd ever taken in his life. He tried not to look down, but he couldn't help it. His gaze was drawn there. He struggled to push back an urge to fly, just jump off and fly. He could almost see himself spiraling down like a glider, or a bird, or a leaf.

His hands shook as if he were freezing. He wondered, *Had the dead boy felt this way?* Or had he felt brave, like Starlene or Joe-Boy, or Mo, who seemed to feel nothing.

Somebody from below shouted, but Vinny couldn't make it out over the waterfall, roaring down just feet beyond the ledge where he would soon be standing, cascading past so close its mist dampened the air he breathed.

*The dead boy had just come to the ravine to have fun*, Vinny thought. Just a regular kid like himself, come to swim and be with his friends, then go home and eat macaroni and cheese and watch TV, maybe play with his dog or wander around after dark.

But he'd done none of that.

Where was he?

✔ **LITERARY CHECK**
*How does the **flashback** help develop the main conflict?*

Inch by inch Vinny made it to the ledge. He stood, swaying slightly, the tips of his toes one small movement from the precipice.

Far below, Joe-Boy waved his arm back and forth. It was dreamy to see—back and forth, back and forth. He looked so small down there.

For a moment Vinny's mind went blank, as if he were in some trance, some dream where he could so easily lean out and fall, and think or feel nothing.

A breeze picked up and moved the trees on the ridgeline, but not a breath of it reached the fifty-foot ledge.

Vinny thought he heard a voice, small and distant. Yes. Something inside him, a tiny voice pleading, *Don't do it. Walk away. Just turn and go and walk back down.*

". . . I can't," Vinny whispered.

*You can, you can, you can. Walk back down.*

Vinny waited.

And waited.

Joe-Boy yelled, then Starlene, both of them waving.

Then something very strange happened.

---

**glider**, engineless light airplane
**precipice**, very steep side of a mountain or cliff
**ridgeline**, top of a high place

Vinny felt at peace. Completely and totally calm and at peace. He had not made up his mind about jumping. But something else inside him had.

Thoughts and feelings swarmed, stinging him: *Jump! Jump! Jump! Jump!*

But deep inside, where the peace was, where his mind wasn't, he would not jump. He would walk back down.

*No! No, no, no!*

Vinny eased down and fingered up some mud and made a cross on his chest, big and bold. He grabbed a leaf, stuck it in his mouth. *Be calm, be calm. Don't look down.*

After a long pause he spit the leaf out and rubbed the cross to a blur.

They walked out of the ravine in silence, Starlene, Joe-Boy, and Mo far ahead of him. They hadn't said a word since he'd come down off the trail. He knew what they were thinking. He knew, he knew, he knew.

At the same time the peace was still there. He had no idea what it was. But he prayed it wouldn't leave him now, prayed it wouldn't go away, would never go away, because in there, in that place where the peace was, it didn't matter what they thought.

Vinny emerged from the ravine into a brilliance that surprised him. Joe-Boy, Starlene, and Mo were now almost down to the road.

Vinny breathed deeply, and looked up and out over the island. He saw, from there, a land that rolled away like honey, easing down a descent of rich Kikuyu grass pastureland, flowing from there over vast highlands of brown and green, then, finally, falling massively to the coast and flat blue sea.

He'd never seen anything like it.

Had it always been here? This view of the island?

He stared and stared, then sat, taking it in.

He'd never seen anything so beautiful in all his life.

## ABOUT THE **AUTHOR**

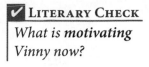

**Graham Salisbury** was born and raised in Hawaii. He wore no shoes until the sixth grade and didn't see snow until he was nineteen. His many books for young readers include *Eyes of the Emperor* and *Blue Skin of the Sea*. Before becoming an author, Salisbury skippered a glass-bottomed tourist boat and worked as a deckhand on deep-sea fishing boats. An avid surfer, he also once formed a rock-and-roll band. He now lives with his family in Portland, Oregon.

**BEFORE YOU GO ON**

1. What thoughts does Vinny have about the dead boy?

2. What does the tiny voice inside of Vinny tell him?

**On Your Own**
How would you feel standing on the ledge?

175

# Review and Practice

## READER'S THEATER

Speaking TIP

Use the appropriate tone of voice for your character.

Act out the following conversation between Vinny and his mother.

**Vinny's mother:**  What did you do today?

**Vinny:**  Don't get mad, okay?

**Vinny's mother:**  Why? What did you do?

**Vinny:**  I know you told me not to go, but I went down to the ravine. Joe-Boy, Mo, and Starlene were . . .

**Vinny's mother:**  Vinny, that place is haunted! It's only been a couple of weeks since that boy died down there! They haven't even found his body. His poor mother!

**Vinny:**  Relax, Mom. It's okay. I didn't jump.

**Vinny's mother:**  Really? None of you jumped?

**Vinny:**  No, they all jumped, Mom. It just didn't seem right after that boy and all. It was like they were tempting fate, or the stone goddess, or something.

**Vinny's mother:**  Listen to me, Vinny. Don't ever go there again!

**Vinny:**  Okay, Mom. I won't. It wasn't any fun, anyway.

## COMPREHENSION

Workbook
Page 83

**Right There**

1. Where and when does the story take place?

2. Who are the main characters in this short story?

**Think and Search**

3. Why didn't Vinny want to go to the ravine? Why did he go?

4. What theories did people have about what happened to the boy? Which one seems most probable?

**Author and You**

5. Why do you think the author wrote this story?

6. Why do you think the author created the characters of Starlene, Joe-Boy, and Mo, and portrayed them as he did?

7. How about you? Would you take a risk that is life threatening because your friends expected you to? Why or why not?

8. What qualities help a young person do what is right?

## DISCUSSION

»)⃝ *Listening* TIP

Be a critical listener. Listen for key words and details. Take notes about points you agree and disagree with.

Discuss in pairs or small groups.

1. What factors influenced Vinny's decision not to jump? The dead boy? Vinny's parents? Seeing his friends do something "insane"? Rank the influences on him.

2. Look back at the list of influences on teenagers on page 164. Relate the facts to Vinny's situation. Does he seem like the kind of person who could overcome such pressure? Why?

**Q When should you take a stand?** What would you have done? Would you have been able to take a stand against peer pressure, as Vinny did? Have you ever done so?

## RESPONSE TO LITERATURE

Workbook
Page 83

Imagine you are a crime scene reporter. It's been fifteen days since the boy disappeared—or went missing in the ravine. Bring the public up to date. What are the theories? Do young kids still go to the ravine to tempt fate—despite the dangers? Describe the area. Will you mention the legend about the goddess? Will you interview Starlene, Mo, Joe-Boy, Vinny? How about Vinny's parents? Work in small groups to discuss your ideas. Then either write your ideas for a feature story for the newspaper or create an oral report for the TV evening news. Take turns reading or presenting to the class.

▲ The evening news

# Grammar and Writing

## Reported Speech

Reported speech is used to tell another person what someone said. The pronoun and verb usually change in reported speech. Use *told* when you mention the listener(s); use *said* when you don't. Here are some examples:

| Rules | Example Sentences |
|---|---|
| If the verb in the quoted speech is an imperative, it usually changes to an infinitive. | *Quoted:* His mom told him, "**Listen** to me." <br> *Reported:* His mom told him **to listen** to her. |
| If the verb in the quoted speech is in the present, it usually changes to the past. | *Quoted:* Vinny said, "The water **is** too cold." <br> *Reported:* Vinny said (that) the water **was** too cold. |
| If the verb in the quoted speech is in the past, it usually changes to the past perfect. | *Quoted:* Joe-Boy said, "Vinny's mom **told** him not to come here." <br> *Reported:* Joe-Boy said (that) Vinny's mom **had told** him not to come here. |
| If the verb in the quoted speech is in the present perfect, it usually changes to the past perfect. | *Quoted:* Vinny said, "**I've heard** that legend before." <br> *Reported:* Vinny said (that) he **had heard** that legend before. |
| If the verb in the quoted speech is in the present continuous, it usually changes to the past continuous. | *Quoted:* Starlene said, "**I'm watching** you." <br> *Reported:* Starlene said that she **was watching** him. |

**Practice**  **Workbook Page 84**

Work with a partner. Rewrite the quoted speech below in your notebook, putting it in reported speech. Make necessary verb and pronoun changes.

1. Vinny said, "My friends are putting pressure on me to jump."
2. Joe-Boy said, "Watch how a man does it."
3. Vinny said, "I've never seen anything like this."
4. Vinny told Starlene, "Joe-Boy's an idiot."

## WRITING A PERSUASIVE LETTER

### Write a Personal Letter

You are going to write a short, persuasive letter. In the model, written by a student named Nola Smith, the writer is taking on the role of Vinny. In the letter, Vinny is trying to persuade his mother to understand why he had to go against her advice and accompany his friends to the ravine. Notice the structure of the letter: It has a date; salutation or greeting; body; closing; and signature. The writer used a graphic organizer to put her letter into the correct format. Also, observe how the writer effectively uses reported speech.

*July 25, 2009*

Dear Mom,

    Can you ever forgive me? I know you're upset that I went to the ravine and almost jumped off the ledge. But I had to go up there and see the danger for myself. Now I understand why you told me not to. It was so dangerous. But Joe-Boy, Mo, and Starlene had all jumped, and told me to do it, too. They pressured me into going there in the first place. I thought that I had to jump to prove myself to them even though I was scared. But when I got up to the top, I remembered what you had said. You had told me that the pond was off limits and that you didn't want me to go there ever. I realized that even though everyone else had jumped, I didn't have to jump, too, just to fit in. And I had the courage not to jump, Mom. I learned a good lesson—to always do what I feel is right deep down.

                       Love,
                       Vinny

### Practice  Workbook Page 85

Imagine you are Vinny and write a letter to one of his friends. What will your position be and how will you persuade the friend to understand why you did not jump? Use a graphic organizer to put your letter into the correct format. Be sure to use reported speech correctly.

**Writing Checklist**

**VOICE:**
☑ My reader will understand my position and feel sympathetic toward me.

**ORGANIZATION:**
☑ I included reasons and examples that supported my opinion.

179

# Prepare to Read

## What You Will Learn

**Reading**
- Vocabulary building: *Context, dictionary skills, word study*
- Reading strategy: *Evaluate new information*
- Text type: *Informational text (social studies)*

**Grammar, Usage, and Mechanics**
Passive form of modals: *should + be + past participle*

**Writing**
Write a letter to the editor

---

### THE BIG QUESTION

**When should you take a stand?** With a partner, look at national news magazines and newspapers with state and national news. Make a list of issues you each feel strongly about. Are there issues you would take a stand for or against?

### BUILD BACKGROUND

In the next reading, **"Speak Your Mind!"** student writers Charlotte Steinecke and Emily Cutler give practical advice on how you can take a stand on issues you believe in. Do you think taking a stand can make a difference? Consider this: Many Americans protested against the Vietnam War in the 1960s, saying the United States shouldn't be involved in it. The lack of support by American citizens eventually led to complete U.S. withdrawal from Vietnam in 1975.

Read about some opinions held by many Americans, and the historical events that resulted from people taking a stand on these issues.

▲ Anti-Vietnam War protesters march with signs

| Opinions of Many Americans | ⟹ | Historical Events |
|---|---|---|
| Workers should receive good pay, reasonable hours, and a safe working environment. | ⟹ | **1886** Skilled workers unite to form the American Federation of Labor (A.F. of L.). |
| At least a portion of our natural landscape should never be destroyed. | ⟹ | **1890** Yosemite Valley and other areas become federally protected national parks. |
| African Americans should be given the right to vote. | ⟹ | **1965** The Voting Rights Act is passed. |
| Students and teachers should be allowed to freely express their opinions. | ⟹ | **1969** The U.S. Supreme Court decides in favor of allowing freedom of speech in schools. |

## Learn Key Words

Read these sentences. Use the context to figure out the meaning of the **red** words. Use a dictionary to check your answers. Then write each word and its meaning in your notebook.

**Key Words**

apathy
blog
Congress
petition
protest

1. Her friends didn't care about the election. Their **apathy** upset her, so she wrote an article in the student newspaper about it.

2. My father always writes in his **blog** about the day's news events. A lot of our relatives go online to read it because his commentary is interesting.

3. Representatives and senators in the U.S. **Congress** decide what our national laws should be.

4. If you don't want bus fares to increase, sign this **petition**. We plan to send it to our local politician so she knows how we feel about the issue.

5. In 1965, thousands of Americans marched through Washington, D.C., to **protest** the lack of jobs and freedom for African Americans.

**Practice**  **Workbook Page 86**

Write the sentences in your notebook. Choose a **red** word from the box above to complete each sentence. Then take turns reading the sentences aloud with a partner.

1. The members of _____ are elected to represent the people in their state.

2. Marching in front of the White House is one way to _____ against something you want to see changed.

3. I read a _____ every day to get up-to-date information about important news in my country.

4. There is a lot of _____ about issues that affect our town. That's why not very many people attend the town meetings.

5. Instead of signing a _____ with everyone else, you can write a letter expressing your personal opinion and send it to your congressperson.

▲ The U.S. Capitol Building, where members of Congress meet

181

## Learn Academic Words

Study the **red** words and their meanings. You will find these words useful when talking and writing about informational texts. Write each word and its meaning in your notebook. After you read the two features in "Speak Your Mind!" try to use these words to respond to the text.

| | | |
|---|---|---|
| **activist** = a person who performs some kind of action in an effort to gain social or political change | ➡ | The great leader and social **activist** Mohandas Gandhi used peaceful efforts to gain civil rights and freedom for his people. |
| **communicate** = exchange information | ➡ | Newspaper reporters should **communicate** the facts about a news event, not their personal opinions. |
| **elections** = a process by which people decide who will represent them in government | ➡ | Every two years we hold **elections** to replace representatives in Congress. |
| **public awareness** = common knowledge about a social or political issue | ➡ | Media such as TV and newspapers help raise **public awareness** of issues around the world. |
| **publication** = a book, magazine, etc. | ➡ | The school started a **publication** that included student essays and poems. |

## Practice

**Workbook** Page 87

Write the sentences in your notebook. Choose a **red** word from the box above to complete each sentence. Then take turns reading the sentences aloud with a partner.

1. Over the years, celebrities like Bono and Sting have contributed to _____ of poverty in Africa.

2. Martin Luther King Jr. was a very famous social _____.

3. Our teacher wants us to participate in class discussions and _____ our ideas.

4. _____ are important in a democratic government. They allow people to choose leaders that represent their points of view.

5. Our school's nature club creates a _____ every year. It includes articles written by students about issues affecting our environment.

▲ Singer Bono, of the band U2, speaks to the U.S. Senate about AIDS research.

## Word Study: Long /oo/

Listen to the vowel sound you hear in the word *news*. The vowel sound you hear in this word is spelled *ew*. The sound can be spelled in other ways, too. Since some words have the same spelling yet are pronounced differently, you may need to learn how to pronounce a few common words.

The chart below has examples of words pronounced like *news*. It also shows you some words that have similar spellings but different pronunciations.

| o | u_e | ue | ough | oo | ou |
|---|-----|-----|------|-----|-----|
| d**o** | r**u**de**ne**ss | gl**ue** | thr**ough**(out) | ch**oo**se | gr**ou**p |
| **BUT** | | | | | |
| g**o** | ens**u**re | arg**ue** | th**ough** | l**oo**k | ab**ou**t |

**Practice**

Work with a partner. Divide up the words in the box below and copy them into your notebook. Take turns reading each word aloud for your partner to spell.

| | | | | |
|---|---|---|---|---|
| count | look | proud | to | too |
| country | newspaper | school | today | you |

---

**READING STRATEGY** | **EVALUATE NEW INFORMATION**

Evaluating new information helps you connect new information to information you already know. It also helps you understand the content of a text more easily. To evaluate new information, follow these steps:

- Before you read, ask yourself, "What do I know about this subject?"
- As you read, make a note of the new information you find.
- Compare the new information to what you already know. Is it similar or different from what you know?
- Does the new information help you understand the subject better?

Before you read "Speak Your Mind!" think about what you know about the role of politicians and what people can do to change laws. As you read, make a note of new and interesting information. Use a T-chart to list what you knew already and what you learn.

**Set a purpose for reading** Which of the ways described in the reading would you choose to speak your mind? Would voting at an early age be a good way to take a stand on important issues?

# Speak Your Mind!

## How to Get a Voice in Government and Make Yourself Heard!

### Charlotte Steinecke

A politician's job is to represent the people—that's you and me!—so what do you do when a politician is on the other side of an issue you feel strongly about? Don't worry, there are several ways to speak up—some you can do on your own and some take the effort of many people working together.

▲ A student speaks his mind while others listen.

## 1 Communicate
### *with your politician directly.*

Many websites feature senators' contact information—a good place to look is www.congress.org, a site containing a directory of every member of Congress. If you're going to write to or e-mail your politicians, remember to be polite, explain your views, and thank them for their time. Rudeness or "you're wrong" statements won't convince your congressperson. Politicians are more likely to notice you if you prove to be a respectful and intelligent individual who has a clear view of the world around you! They're also more likely to notice you if you write a personal letter instead of using a form letter.

---

**contact information,** ways to reach someone: phone, e-mail, address, etc.
**form letter,** standard letter sent to many people and not personalized

Form letters are still OK, though, especially if you're not sure how to start. Many websites have draft letters that you can send as is, add to, or change. You can find websites by typing your topic into a search engine and seeing what comes up!

▲ Signing a petition

**❷ Petitions** *are a good way to circulate ideas in your school and community.*

People often use petitions to raise public awareness. Although they don't always result in immediate action, they get people thinking about an issue, which can bring about change.

---

**search engine**, a computer program to find information on the Internet

▲ Making posters is a good way to communicate your message.

**❸ If you want** *to get your message out in print, start an alternative newspaper or magazine with like-minded friends.*

You don't need a publisher for this—just a computer, copy machine, and people to give it to. Be sure to back up opinions with facts. Pay attention to the layout— pictures can help catch readers' eyes. Choose a name for your paper, plan out publication dates, and create article lists. Don't fret about size: one front-and-back page makes a great weekly paper. If you don't want to create a print newspaper, you can write about your opinions on a blog or personal website and hand out the web address to friends and family.

---

**layout**, the way in which writing and pictures are arranged on a page
**web address**, the URL (Uniform Resource Locator) of a page on the Internet

**BEFORE YOU GO ON**

**1** What kind of attitude should you have when you write to your politicians?

**2** Which is better to send to a politician—a personal letter or a form letter?

**On Your Own**
Have you ever read an alternative newspaper or a blog? If so, what's your opinion about it?

## ④ Protest!

The written word can be very powerful, but a group of people protesting together in a public space can communicate in a way that one person cannot. Sometimes, when politicians won't listen to one person, they'll listen to a lot of people talking about the same thing. If you feel ambitious, organize your own protest. Hand out fliers and get your friends and family involved. You can march in your local park or hold a letter-writing party where everyone composes a letter to your senator or representative.

Picketing is a specific kind of protesting that happens when people form a line, usually in front of a building so that people can't get past without noticing them. Picketers carry signs, hand out literature, and protest the actions of an organization. You can get creative with picketing—create signs with slogans that support your view and make up chants to recite on the picket line. Getting involved with a picket line really makes people take notice.

You also can use silence to protest, and sometimes it's more effective than yelling.

---

**fliers,** sheets of paper advertising something
**slogans,** easy-to-remember short phrases used by politicians and advertising companies

## Voice Box

*Welcome to Voice Box, where we discuss hot topics. This time, we're talking about lowering the voting age.*

*Emily Cutler*

Not long ago, several groups in the U.S. fought for the right to vote. Women couldn't vote until 1920. Native Americans couldn't vote until 1924, and then only in some states. And until Congress passed the Voting Rights Act in 1965, many African Americans couldn't vote because they couldn't pass the required literacy tests (which were often rigged) or pay poll taxes. During the Vietnam War, 18-year-olds claimed they were old enough to vote if they were old enough to fight. Congress agreed, and in 1971, they changed the legal voting age from 21 to 18.

Some people think the voting age should be lowered again. They argue that letting young people vote will decrease voter apathy.

---

**rigged,** arranged or influenced in a dishonest way to get a certain result
**poll taxes,** taxes required for voting

California Senator John Vasconcellos recently proposed an amendment that would give 16-year-olds a half vote and 14-year-olds a quarter vote in California elections. Iowa, Washington, Maine, Texas, and Minnesota also have considered lowering the voting age.

Opponents of the change say 16-year-olds aren't mature enough to vote. They point out that teenagers' judgment hasn't fully developed yet and they might be too easily persuaded by political candidates, parents, and teachers. But those in favor of lowering the voting age say that because teenagers study current events, politics, and government in school, they know just as much as most adults.

Some people also say that since teenagers often hold jobs and pay taxes, they should be allowed to vote.

---

**amendment**, a change, especially in the words of a law

## What Do You Think?

1. At what age should people be allowed to vote? Why?
2. Should kids' votes count as full votes or partial votes?
3. Would you vote in national elections if you could? Why or why not?
4. Do you think politicians would treat young people differently if teenagers could vote?

Vote yes on March 8th for Better Schools and Jobs

## BEFORE YOU GO ON

1. What do picketers do?
2. What are four ways that voting rights changed in the United States?

**On Your Own**
Do you think lowering the voting age is an important topic? Why or why not?

READING
4

## COMPREHENSION  Workbook Page 90

### Right There

1. Where can you find contact information for members of Congress?

2. What is a good way to circulate ideas in your school and community?

### Think and Search

3. What are the four different ways of speaking up that are mentioned in the first article? What are the advantages of each?

4. Why is it sometimes more effective when people take a stand together than when one person does it alone?

### Author and You

5. Do you think Charlotte Steinecke is herself an activist? Why or why not?

6. Why do you think Emily Cutler writes about lowering the voting age for Voice Box? What do you think her position is on this issue?

### On Your Own

7. Where do you stand on lowering the voting age? Why?

8. What is the most effective way to bring about real change? Why?

## IN YOUR OWN WORDS

Work with a partner. Copy the chart below into your notebook. Discuss the purpose and main idea of each selection. Then, in your own words, take turns summarizing each one.

| Title of Selection | Purpose | Main Idea |
|---|---|---|
| "How to Get a Voice in Government and Make Yourself Heard!" | | |
| "Voice Box" | | |

## DISCUSSION

»))) *Listening* TIP

Ask the speaker questions if you want to know more about his or her views.

Discuss in pairs or small groups.

1. Which magazine article was more interesting to you? The first one or the second one? Why?

2. Would you vote in national elections if the voting age were lowered and you could? Why? How might voting benefit younger voters?

**Q When should you take a stand?** Discuss some issues you feel strongly about. Choose one. How would you take a stand on it? Would you write a letter, circulate a petition, form a picket line, start an alternative newspaper or magazine, or use silence? Why?

## READ FOR FLUENCY

When we read aloud to communicate meaning, we group words into phrases, pause or slow down to make important points, and emphasize important words. Pause for a short time when you reach a comma and for a longer time when you reach a period. Pay attention to rising and falling intonation at the end of sentences.

Work with a partner. Choose a paragraph from the reading. Discuss which words seem important for communicating meaning. Practice pronouncing difficult words. Take turns reading the paragraph aloud and give each other feedback.

## EXTENSION

**Workbook**
Page 90

Every minute in every nation around the world, you can find people who are taking a stand on issues they care about. Work in small groups to learn about the people listed here and what they stand for (or stood for when they were living): Cesar Chavez, Ralph Waldo Emerson, Mohandas Gandhi, Aung San Suu Kyi, Wangari Maathai, Anwar Al Sadat, and Elie Wiesel. Choose one person from the list to research. Then share your research findings with the other members of your group.

▲ Aung San Suu Kyi (center)

# Grammar and Writing

### Passive Form of Modals: *should* + *be* + Past Participle

Use the passive when the focus is on the action and not the performer. When talking about issues we feel strongly about, we can use *should* with the passive voice because we want to stress the action.

In the following example, the writer wants to emphasize *what* the students should be allowed to do, not *who* should allow the students to do it.

> Students **should be allowed** to voice their opinions in school.

To form the passive, use the simple present or simple past of *be* plus the past participle of the verb. Remember that regular past participles are formed with + *-d* or *-ed*. For example, *lower* + *-ed* = *lowered*.

> The voting age **should be lowered**.

There are often spelling changes when you add *-ed* to the verb. For example, stop + *-ed* = stopped.

> Voter apathy **should be stopped**.

There are many irregular past participles. For example, *write* → *written*.

> You opinions **should be written** on a blog.

## Practice  Workbook Page 91

Copy the paragraph below into your notebook. Use the verbs in parentheses to complete the paragraph. Use *should* + *be* + past participle. Compare your answers with a partner.

> In my opinion, the voting age (not lower). Before teenagers are allowed to vote, I believe they (educate) for many years, and they (well-inform) about history and contemporary politics. Even though teenagers (not allow) to vote until they are eighteen, they (give) the chance to get involved in the political process. For example, they (allow) to attend protests or sign petitions.

# WRITING A PERSUASIVE LETTER

## Write a Letter to the Editor

At the end of this unit, you will write a persuasive essay. To help you do this, you will write a short persuasive letter to the editor of a newspaper or magazine. Look at the model below and notice the structure of the letter. It has a date, salutation or greeting, body, closing, and signature.

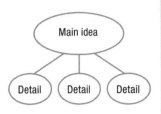

Notice that the writer clearly states his opinion and supports it with details. He used a main idea and a details web to organize his ideas. Notice that the writer uses *should be* + the past participle to introduce his opinion. How does he appeal to your emotions? Are you convinced that the voting age should be lowered?

May 16, 2009

To the Editor:

    I think that the voting age should not be lowered. Teenagers are not mature enough to vote. Most of us are too easily persuaded by other people's opinions. Because of this fact, most of us would be easily manipulated by political campaigns. In addition, I think most teenagers don't care enough about the issues to vote. A lot of people I know don't read the newspaper or Internet blogs because they are not interested in the news. On the other hand, by the time we are 18 years old, we will know more about what is going on in our city, state, and country, and we will know what our own opinions are. Therefore, we will be able to choose who we want to represent us. That is my view on lowering the voting age.

                Sincerely,
                Andrew Gerhardt

## Practice

**Workbook Page 92**

Write a letter to the editor stating your position on this issue. Should the voting age be lowered? If so, to what age? Should the vote be a full or a partial vote? Why? What details will you use to support your position? Use a main ideas and detail web to organize your ideas. How will you appeal to your readers' emotions? Be sure to use *should + be + past participle* correctly.

**Writing Checklist**

**WORD CHOICE:**
☑ I chose words carefully to create emotional appeal.

**ORGANIZATION:**
☑ I included facts and examples to support my opinion.

# Link the Readings

## Critical Thinking

Look back at the readings in this unit. Think about what they have in common. They all tell about taking a stand. Yet they do not all have the same purpose. The purpose of one reading might be to inform, while the purpose of another might be to entertain or persuade. In addition, the content of each reading relates to taking a stand differently. Now copy the chart below into your notebook and complete it.

| Title of Reading or Selection | Purpose | Big Question Link |
|---|---|---|
| From *going going* | | |
| From *Freedom Walkers* | | |
| "The Ravine" | | *A teen stands up to peer pressure.* |
| "Speak Your Mind!" | *to persuade* | |

## Discussion

Discuss in pairs or small groups.

- Which reading broadened your understanding of ways to bring about change? Would you like to read more from the book or magazine it's from? Why?

- **Q When should you take a stand?** According to the readings, what are different ways to bring about change? How do the readings show what it means to take a stand?

## Fluency Check

Work with a partner. Choose a paragraph from one of the readings. Take turns reading it for one minute. Count the total number of words you read. Practice saying the words you had trouble reading. Take turns reading the paragraph three more times. Did you read more words each time? Copy the chart below into your notebook and record your speeds.

| | 1st Time | 2nd Time | 3rd Time | 4th Time |
|---|---|---|---|---|
| Words Per Minute | | | | |

# Projects

Work in pairs or small groups. Choose one of these projects.

**1** Look through magazines and newspapers to find photos, illustrations, and articles that show or tell about people taking a stand. Create a collage and give it a title that tells why taking a stand is important.

**2** Create an alternative newspaper for your school or community. Choose a main topic for your issue—one that relates to taking a stand. Decide which features you'll have. Will you include a Voice Box, letters to the editor, informative articles, an interview, a biographical feature? Write your features and create a layout for your issue. Include photographs and drawings. Share your newspaper with your school or with people in your community.

**3** Make a travel brochure for a trip to San Antonio, Texas. Answer travelers' questions. How can travelers best experience its charm? Include information about landmarks and local, independently owned restaurants and shops—be creative and make some up.

# Further Reading

To find out more about the theme of this unit, choose from these reading suggestions.

**The Rainmaker,** John Grisham
This Penguin Reader® adaptation tells the story of a young lawyer's first important case. He's up against the best attorneys money can buy.

**A Dream of Freedom,** Diane McWhorter
A Pulitzer Prize-winning author gives an overview of the civil rights movement. She places her readers in the middle of the bus boycotts, the demonstrations, and the brave acts that eventually led to a new America.

**The Kid Who Ran for President,** Dan Gutman
With his friend as campaign manager and his former babysitter as running mate, twelve-year-old Judson Moon runs for President of the United States on the Lemonade Party. Judd promises to abolish homework if kids can get their parents to vote him in.

# Put It All Together

## LISTENING & SPEAKING WORKSHOP

### TV News Show

With a group, you will present a TV news show about taking a stand. Your show will feature stories and people from the readings in this unit.

**1** **THINK ABOUT IT** Work in small groups. Review the unit readings and think about how you can turn them into segments (individual stories) on your TV news show. Plan a segment for each person in your group. Choose from these ideas or develop your own.

- The day's top news story: Report on a situation such as Florrie's or Vinny's. Put a news spin on what Florrie is doing in San Antonio or on what happened fifteen days ago in the ravine.
- A "Look Back" segment: Pick a topic such as the Montgomery bus boycott.
- A "Focus on Youth" segment: Interview teenagers about their opinions on an issue such as lowering the voting age.
- Teaser for a future program: Describe an upcoming show on taking a stand that will highlight one of the issues discussed in this unit.

**2** **GATHER AND ORGANIZE INFORMATION** Decide who will present each segment. Discuss and plan the overall structure of your show. If possible, watch a TV news show to get ideas.

**Research** Search the appropriate unit reading(s) for details to use in your segment. Take notes on what you find. Check the short bios you wrote for the Extension activity on page 189 for other information you can use.

**Order Your Notes** Make a list of important points that are key to your segment. Think about the best order for telling your story, and make an outline showing your main points in order.

**Use Visuals** Look for photos and other visuals that will help viewers understand your news story. Think about how and when you will show each visual, and mark those places in your outline.

**Prepare a Script** Use your outline and notes to write a script for your story. Start by introducing yourself and your segment: for example, "Hi, I'm Breanna Barker from the Channel 5 Evening News. Tonight's Look Back segment features Claudette Colvin."

**3** **PRACTICE AND PRESENT** Read your script over and over again until you know it well. As a group, practice presenting your TV news show until all members can deliver their segments confidently, glancing at their scripts only occasionally. Work on making smooth transitions between segments.

**Deliver Your TV News Show** Speak loudly enough so that everyone in the class can hear you. Say each word carefully so that it is clear. Emphasize key ideas by pausing, slowing down, speaking more loudly, or restating them at the end of your segment.

**4** **EVALUATE THE PRESENTATION**
You can improve your skills as a speaker and a listener by evaluating each presentation you give and hear. Use this checklist to help you judge your group's TV news show and the news shows of your classmates.

- ☑ Was each segment interesting, brief, and clear?
- ☑ Was the news show presented in a professional way? Was the reporting accurate?
- ☑ Did the show inform you about the unit topic—taking a stand?
- ☑ Could you hear and understand each speaker easily?
- ☑ What suggestions do you have for improving the show?

# WRITING WORKSHOP
## Persuasive Essay

You have learned how to write a variety of persuasive paragraphs and some techniques to develop them. In this workshop you will write a persuasive essay. In a persuasive essay, the writer tries to convince readers to agree with a specific opinion or to take a specific action. A good persuasive essay begins with a paragraph that clearly states the writer's opinion. Clearly organized facts, examples, and details support the writer's opinion. Opposing arguments are identified and answered. Strong words and opinion phrases appeal to readers' emotions. The essay ends with a paragraph that restates the writer's opinion in a new and memorable way.

Your assignment for this workshop is to write a five-paragraph persuasive essay about an issue that you care about in your school or community.

**1** **PREWRITE** Brainstorm a list of topics for your essay in your notebook. Choose an issue that you can write about with knowledge and enthusiasm. What is your stand on this issue? Brainstorm a list of strong, persuasive words that will convince readers to agree with your opinion.

**List and Organize Ideas and Details** To organize ideas for your essay, create a T-chart. A student named Jack wanted to persuade readers to join in a protest to keep a skateboard park open. Here is his T-chart.

| FOR Keeping Park Open | AGAINST Keeping Park Open |
|---|---|
| skateboarding is popular<br>park is very safe place to skateboard<br>parents and kids created park together<br>skateboarding is great exercise | skateboarding can be dangerous<br>park is expensive to maintain |

**2** **DRAFT** Use the model on page 199 and your T-chart to help you write a first draft. Remember to state your opinion clearly and to organize your supporting facts, details, and examples in a logical sequence. Be sure to include both sides of the argument in order to refute opposing opinions.

**3** **REVISE** Read over your draft. As you do so, ask yourself the questions in the writing checklist. Use the questions to help you revise your essay.

### SIX TRAITS OF WRITING CHECKLIST

☑ **IDEAS:** Do I state my opinion in my first paragraph?

☑ **ORGANIZATION:** Do I present both sides of the argument?

☑ **VOICE:** Does my writing show my feelings about the issue?

☑ **WORD CHOICE:** Do I include strong words and opinion phrases?

☑ **SENTENCE FLUENCY:** Do my sentences begin in different ways?

☑ **CONVENTIONS:** Does my writing follow the rules of grammar, usage, and mechanics?

Here are the changes Jack plans to make when he revises his first draft:

---

Keep Our Park Open!

For a long time the skateboard park in town has been a place to have fun. However, the town thinks that the park should be ~~close~~ closed down. I strongly disagree with this decision. I believe we need to keep the park open, and that a protest should be ~~hold~~ held to show our support for it

In this town, skateboarding is a very popular activity. Town representatives worry about the dangers of skateboarding. Before the park was opened, kids ~~sometimes~~ though, used to practiced in unsupervised areas where There was a much greater chance that they would get hurt. Also when kids did have accidents, no one would be around to help them. Many parents and kids worked hours to get the park up-and-running. They will be

---

upset to know that their work is like dust in the wind.

In addition,
The park should be ~~keep~~ kept open because skateboarding is terrific

exercise. the town representatives say that the park is expensive to

maintain, but what could be a better facility for kids? The surgeon

general recently advised kids to get exercise If we remove the park,

skateboarders will get less exercise. because They will have nowhere to go for

their favorite activity.

How can we
~~We should~~ change the town's decision. ? An effective and efficient way to protest

the closing would be to hold a skateboard marathon at the park. If

we put the word out, kids who enjoy skateboarding will come to the

gathering to help out the cause. If we advertise the protest with flyers

pamphlets, and posters, people who don't even ~~no~~ know about the park will

be encouraged to show up, support the effort, and enjoy themselves.

If we can inspire enough people we can keep the park open.

Skateboarding is fun, great exercise, and—in the proper

environment—safe. Generations to come should be able to enjoy what

we are enjoying right now. That is why the park should stay open.

**4 EDIT AND PROOFREAD**  Workbook Page 93

Copy your revised draft onto a clean sheet of paper. Read it again. Correct
any errors in grammar, word usage, mechanics, and spelling. Here are the
additional changes Jack plans to make when he prepares his final draft.

Jack Kefauver

Keep Our Park Open!

For a long time, the skateboard park in town has been a place to have fun. However, the town thinks that the park should be closed down. I strongly disagree with this decision. In this town, skateboarding is a very popular activity. I believe we need to keep the park open, and that a protest should be held to show our support for it.

Town representatives worry about the dangers of skateboarding. Before the park was opened, though, kids used to practice in unsupervised areas where there was a much greater chance that they would get hurt. Also, when kids did have accidents, no one would be around to help them. Many parents and kids worked hours to get the park up-and-running. They will be upset to know that their work is like dust in the wind.

In addition, the park should be kept open because skateboarding is terrific exercise. the town representatives say that the park is expensive to maintain, but what could be a better facility for kids? The surgeon general recently advised kids to get exercise. If we remove the park, skateboarders will get less exercise because they will have nowhere to go for their favorite activity.

How can we change the town's decision? An effective and efficient way to protest the closing would be to hold a skateboard marathon at the park. If we put the word out, kids who enjoy skateboarding will come to the gathering to help out the cause. If we advertise the protest with flyers, pamphlets, and posters, people who don't even know about the park will be encouraged to show up, support the effort, and enjoy themselves.

If we can inspire enough people, we can keep the park open. Skateboarding is fun, great exercise, and—in the proper environment—safe. Generations to come should be able to enjoy what we are enjoying right now. That is why the park should stay open.

**5** **PUBLISH** Prepare your final draft. Share your essay with your teacher and classmates.

Workbook
Page 94

# Battling Inequality

*T*he people of the United States don't always feel united. During the 1960s and 1970s, for example, African Americans staged protests to draw attention to unequal treatment. At the same time, many women wrote books and articles challenging the idea that all women should stay at home and be housewives. Today, different racial, ethnic, and gender groups continue to struggle with inequality in American society. Artists often use their art to express their frustration and anger nonviolently.

## William H. Johnson, *Three Great Abolitionists: A. Lincoln, F. Douglass, J. Brown* (about 1945)

In *Three Great Abolitionists: A. Lincoln, F. Douglass, J. Brown*, painter William H. Johnson, an African-American artist, celebrates three important figures involved in freeing blacks from slavery.

Frederick Douglass, a former slave and a great orator and writer, stands at the center of the group, with President Abraham Lincoln to the right of the painting. On the left is John Brown, who also played an important role in the fight against slavery. All three men have joined their hands over a piece of paper, a government document that was signed by Lincoln and that called for an end to slavery in America.

▲ William H. Johnson, *Three Great Abolitionists: A. Lincoln, F. Douglass, J. Brown*, about 1945, oil, 37⅜ × 34¼ in., Smithsonian American Art Museum

▲ Miriam Schapiro and Sherry Brody, *Dollhouse*, 1972, mixed media, 79¾ x 82 x 8½ in., Smithsonian American Art Museum

## Miriam Schapiro and Sherry Brody, *Dollhouse* (1972)

In *Dollhouse*, artists Miriam Schapiro and Sherry Brody used a traditional girl's toy to explore the pros and cons of domestic life for some women. They mixed comforting objects with scary objects in each of the rooms. Notice the huge spider in the baby's room on the top left. A bear looks through the window at the baby. Even the fanciest room seems a bit suffocating. It has no windows. With these small gestures, these two women artists question the stereotype that all women are happy to have no life other than that of wife and mother. In the top right room, they created an artist's studio, to show that the lady who lives in *their* house takes her own work seriously.

**Workbook**
Pages 95–96

201

THE BIG QUESTION

# What does it take to beat the odds?

This unit is about people who face challenging obstacles in their lives and beat the odds. What makes this theme so compelling? When we read about things that seem impossible to do, it gives us hope and vision.

### READING 1: Oral Narrative and Novel Excerpt

- "The Great Circle" by Hehaka Sapa
- From *Touching Spirit Bear* by Ben Mikaelsen

### READING 2: Math and Science Articles

- "Take a Chance" by Johnny Ball
- "A Survival Mini-Manual" from *Time for Kids Almanac*

### READING 3: Tall Tale and Song

- "John Henry" by Adrien Stoutenburg
- "John Henry" by Pete Seeger

### READING 4: Social Studies Articles

- From *Franklin Delano Roosevelt: The New Deal President* by Brenda Haugen
- *"Eleanor Roosevelt"* by Catherine Thimmesh

## Listening and Speaking

At the end of this unit, you will conduct an **interview**.

## Writing

In this unit you'll practice **narrative writing**. Narrative writing tells a story. After each reading you'll learn a skill that will help you write a narrative paragraph. At the end of the unit, you will use these skills to write a narrative essay.

## QuickWrite

Make a list of people who do things that seem impossible to do.

## What You Will Learn

**Reading**
- Vocabulary building: *Literary terms, word study*
- Reading strategy: *Read for enjoyment*
- Text type: *Literature (oral narrative and novel excerpt)*

**Grammar, Usage, and Mechanics**
Transitions and transitional expressions

**Writing**
Write a narrative paragraph

 **THE BIG QUESTION**

**What does it take to beat the odds?** Why do you think some teenagers feel that nobody understands them? What are some challenges that teenagers face today? Why is it harder for some teenagers to beat the odds than for others?

## BUILD BACKGROUND

Many Native American cultures believe that the circle is an important symbol, representing everything around us. Hahaka Sapa, a Native American holy man, said, "The seasons form a great circle in their changing, and always come back again to where they were. The life of a man is a circle from childhood to childhood, and so it is in everything where power moves." The reading **"The Great Circle"** further explains the importance of this symbol in Native American cultures.

Because of the significance of the circle, Native Americans developed an alternative approach to dealing with lawbreakers called *circle justice.* Circle justice was introduced in the United States by Native American cultures. In circle justice the focus is more on rehabilitation and responsibility than on punishment. The hope is that the lawbreaker will begin to realize the effect his or her actions are having on community, peers, and family, as well as, of course, the victim and the victim's family. This is usually done with the help of a mediator, or another person who helps the lawbreaker and victim work things out.

In ***Touching Spirit Bear***, you will read about an angry and troubled teenager named Cole. Cole intentionally and seriously injures a classmate, so he must face the justice of the court system. That is, until a member of his community offers Cole an alternative—circle justice.

◀ A mediator helps two people work things out.

## VOCABULARY

### Learn Literary Words

When you read an adventure story like the one in the excerpt from *Touching Spirit Bear*—a story with one main **character**—it is helpful to notice the character's motivation and to look for any changes. Ask yourself: How does Cole change from the beginning of the story to the end? Read how Cole answers a question at the beginning of the story. What does this tell you about Cole?

> "How would you feel if a bear made its den beside the stream?"
> Cole shrugged. "I'd kill it."

For most of the excerpt, Cole lies injured after a bear attack. Since the story is told from the third person limited **point of view**, you know that the narrator sees the world through only one character's eyes— Cole's —and reveals only his thoughts. What do you think will happen in a story with only one main character who is lying alone injured? Think about the title and what you know about conflict in stories. Will the conflict be external or internal? Why? Read how the narrator reveals Cole's thoughts:

> What did it matter anymore if he died? Nobody else cared about him, so why should he care about himself?

### Practice
Workbook Page 97

Work with a partner. Discuss the following:

- Think of a story you have read in which characterization is more important than plot. Describe the main character and how he or she changes.
- Do you prefer reading stories written in first- or third-person point of view? Why? Use selections you have read to support your position.

## Learn Academic Words

Study the **red** words and their meanings. You will find these words useful when talking and writing about literature. Write each word and its meaning in your notebook. After you read "The Great Circle" and the excerpt from *Touching Spirit Bear,* try to use these words to respond to the text.

| | | |
|---|---|---|
| **cycle** = related events that happen again and again in the same order | → | The seasons of the year repeat in a **cycle:** winter, spring, summer, and fall. |
| **generations** = time periods in which people of about the same age lived and died | → | My family has been living in the United States for several **generations.** My first relatives came in 1770. |
| **ignore** = not pay any attention to someone or something | → | He hoped the bear would **ignore** him and continue on its way. |
| **injuries** = physical harm or damages caused by an accident or attack | → | Some of his **injuries** from the bear attack were scratches, bruises, and broken bones. |
| **symbol** = picture, person, or object that represents something else | → | An eagle is a **symbol** of the United States of America. |

## Practice  Workbook Page 98

Work with a partner to complete these sentences using the sentence starters. Include the **red** word in your sentence. Then write the sentences in your notebook.

1. The life **cycle** of a . . .
2. For **generations,** her family has . . .
3. She could no longer **ignore** the . . .
4. His **injuries** were caused by . . .
5. A **symbol** of . . .

▲ A symbol of justice

206

## Word Study: Suffix

A suffix is a group of letters added to the end of a word to form a new word. When you add a suffix to a word, the meaning changes. Read the chart below. Notice how the suffix changes the meaning of the base word.

| Suffix | Meaning | Examples |
|--------|---------|----------|
| -less | not or without | help**less**, use**less**, motion**less** |
| -ness | having a quality of | gentle**ness**, loneli**ness** |
| -able | having a quality of | miser**able**, depend**able** |
| -ment | in a state of | banish**ment**, excite**ment** |

**Practice**

Work with a partner. Read the words in the box below. Use the suffixes *-less*, *-ness*, *-able*, or *-ment* to form new words. Write the new words in your notebook. Next to each word, write the definition. Use a dictionary if you need to.

| | | | | | |
|------|----------|-------|-------|-------|------|
| care | conscious | enjoy | love | state | weak |
| clue | content | happy | rough | treat | |

## READING STRATEGY | READ FOR ENJOYMENT

Reading for enjoyment improves your ability to read for information. You may learn new words and ideas that you will see again in nonfiction texts. To read for enjoyment, follow these steps:

- As you read, pay attention to the characters, setting, and illustrations. Think about how they increase your enjoyment.
- Stop from time to time and think about the reason you enjoyed a particular passage or chapter.

As you read "The Great Circle" and the excerpt from *Touching Spirit Bear*, focus on the characters and setting. Ask yourself, "How does the author make this fun, interesting, or exciting for me to read?"

**Set a purpose for reading** As you read, notice how Cole relates to the symbolism of the circle. Will this symbolism help Cole beat the odds and survive his life-threatening situation?

# The Great Circle

*Hehaka Sapa*
*Oglala Sioux, Lakota 1931*

You have noticed that everything an Indian does is in a circle, and that is because the Power of the World always works in circles, and everything tries to be round. In the old days when we were a strong and happy people, all our power came to us from the sacred hoop of the nation, and so long as the hoop was unbroken, the people flourished. The flowering tree was the living center of the hoop, and the circle of the four quarters nourished it. The east gave peace and light, the south gave warmth, the west gave rain, and the north with its cold and mighty wind gave strength and endurance. This knowledge came to us from the outer world with our religion. Everything the Power of the World does is done in a circle. The sky is round, and I have heard that the earth is round like a ball, and so are all the stars. The wind, in its greatest power, whirls. Birds make their nests in circles, for theirs is the same religion as ours. The sun comes forth and goes down in a circle. The moon does the same, and both are round.

Even the seasons form a great circle in their changing, and always come back again to where they were. The life of a man is a circle from childhood to childhood, and so it is in everything where power moves. Our tipis were round like the nests of birds, and these were always set in a circle, the nation's hoop, a nest of many nests, where the Great Spirit meant for us to hatch our children.

## ABOUT THE AUTHOR

**Hehaka Sapa** is the Native American name for Black Elk (1863–1950), a holy man of the Oglala Lakota (Sioux). Black Elk witnessed many key events of the American Indian Wars. In 1931, he related his experiences and spiritual vision in an interview with Missouri poet John G. Neihardt. His son Ben Black Elk translated his father's words into English for Neihardt.

### BEFORE YOU GO ON

1. What examples of a circle are given in this narrative?

2. What are the four quarters of the circle? What does each do?

**On Your Own**
Do you think the circle is an important symbol? Why?

# from
# Touching Spirit Bear

### Ben Mikaelsen

*Fifteen-year-old Cole Matthews has committed a serious crime. Garvey, a Native American Tlingit elder, suggests circle justice for Cole, and banishment to a deserted island in Alaska. Cole knows it won't be easy. Almost immediately after being left on the island, he rebels by burning down the shelter that Edwin, another community member, had built for him. He attempts to escape the island, but fails. He encounters a mythical Spirit Bear and tries to kill it. The bear mauls him, and he is left wounded and alone.*

## Before the Bear Attack

"How would you feel if a bear made its den beside the stream?"

Cole shrugged. "I'd kill it."

The potbellied elder nodded with a knowing smile. "Animals feel the same way. Don't forget that." He turned to Cole and placed a hand on his shoulder. Cole tried to pull away, but Edwin gripped him like a clamp. "You aren't the only creature here. You're part of a much bigger circle. Learn your place or you'll have a rough time."

"What is there to learn?"

"Patience, gentleness, strength, honesty," Edwin said. He looked up into the trees. "Animals can teach us more about ourselves than any teacher." He stared away toward the south. "Off the coast of British Columbia, there is a special black bear called the Spirit Bear. It's pure white and has pride, dignity, and honor. More than most people."

"If I saw a Spirit Bear, I'd kill it," Cole said.

Edwin tightened his grip as if in warning. "Whatever you do to the animals, you do to yourself. Remember that."

## After the Bear Attack

A constant rain and shrouded gray sky masked the passing of hours, leaving Cole in a cruel time warp with only one possible end. He tried not to think about the end, but he could not ignore the maddening pain from his wounds.

As gusts of wind drove the chill deeper into his body, rain kept falling, penetrating his will, seeping into his consciousness, and flooding his soul. This rain fully intended to kill.

As Cole weakened, he stared up at the giant spruce tree towering above him. Desperate tears welled up inside and squeezed past his eyelids. The wind gusted harder.

What did it matter anymore if he died? Nobody else cared about him, so why should he care about himself? As Cole's gaze drifted among the branches of the tree, a small bird's nest tucked into the fork of two branches caught his attention. The nest rested near the trunk, protected from both the wind and the rain. As Cole watched, a small gray sparrow landed in the nest, twitched about with a flurry of activity, then flew off. Soon it returned again.

Each time the sparrow returned, it carried a bug or a worm in its beak and busied itself over the nest. The visits brought faint chirping sounds. Cole squinted and made out little heads jutting above the nest. This was a mother bird feeding her young. Up there on a branch, barely spitting distance away, little sparrows rested dry and warm, having food brought to them in the comfort of a nest built by their mother.

---

**shrouded**, covered with clouds
**time warp**, the feeling that you are in a different time instead of in the present
**will**, the determination to do something you have decided to do

✔ **LITERARY CHECK**

*How does the **point of view** in the excerpt help you know Cole's thoughts?*

**BEFORE YOU GO ON**

**1** What four things does Edwin tell Cole there are to learn?

**2** After the attack, where is Cole and what is going on with him?

**On Your Own**
Based on what you have read so far, what do you think the odds are that Cole will survive?

The sight of the baby birds irritated Cole. Without his injuries, he could easily have crawled up and knocked the nest down. That's what the stupid birds deserved.

After feeding, the mother flitted to a branch near the nest. She ruffled her wings and chest feathers, keeping an eye on her young. Watching the bird made Cole curse every second of his miserable and haphazard life. If he were the mother bird, he would just leave the babies to fend for themselves. She didn't owe them anything.

That's how Cole felt—he didn't owe anyone anything. Nobody had ever cared for him, so why should he care about anyone else? He wouldn't even be here on this island, injured, if it weren't for other people and their lame ideas. Nothing had been his fault. Cole's bitterness flickered to life once more. His anger helped to focus his thoughts, but it could not stop the frigid drizzle or the torturing pain that wracked his body. Nor could it ward off the loneliness.

The wind that tugged at Cole's tattered clothing seemed distant. As his attention drifted and his senses dulled, rain numbed his face. Cole stared blankly at the thin sliver of blue sky on the western horizon. Exhaustion finally dragged him into a stuporous sleep.

---

**haphazard**, not organized or planned
**lame**, too silly or stupid to be believed
**drizzle**, light rain
**stuporous**, being in a state in which you cannot think clearly

Unconscious, he dreamed of the colorful at.óow blanket. His left hand twitched and moved back and forth, pretending to pull the at.óow over his freezing body. The imaginary blanket shielded him from the cold as it had protected many generations before him. Under the imaginary blanket, he slept soundly.

A loud rumble woke Cole from his sleep. At first he thought he had gone blind. Then slowly he realized it was nighttime. The wind had let up, but the cold rain still fell relentlessly from some endless reservoir in the sky. Then a blinding flash of lightning lit the horizon. Seconds later, deep rumbling thunder rolled overhead, followed by another flash of lightning.

Before the light collapsed back into darkness, Cole realized the at.óow he had dreamed of was not covering him. And he sensed a presence. He peered wide-eyed into the black night but could see nothing. Then lightning flashed again with a sharp crack, closer this time. In that instant, Cole saw it, ghostlike. Barely fifty feet away, the giant Spirit Bear stood motionless in the rain.

---

**at.óow blanket**, a blanket that is handed down for generations in Tlingit families; one cannot own it but just be its caretaker
**relentlessly**, continuously; without stopping
**reservoir**, a large amount of something that has not yet been used

**BEFORE YOU GO ON**

**1** What does Cole think about his life?

**2** What does Cole see during the lightning flash? How far away is it?

**On Your Own**
How do you think Cole regards the at.óow blanket?

**213**

Then the night went black again.

Terrified, Cole waited, his eyes prying at the darkness. Had the bear returned to kill him? As he waited, the storm worsened. The wind picked up, gusting harder. Rain fell in torrents, and thunder rumbled across the sky like empty barrels rolling toward the horizon. When the next bolt of lightning lit the bay, Cole searched frantically.

Nothing! Gone! Again the Spirit Bear had vanished.

Cole grimaced. He hated this bear. What a coward. This creature was waiting until he grew so weak he couldn't fight back. Then it would finish him off. Cole moaned as a violent gust of wind pummeled his body. Would the bear just kill him and leave him to the seagulls, or would it eat him?

Lightning flashed closer, stabbing down with long, probing fingers. The rumbling thunder started crashing and exploding. To protect himself, Cole tried to curl into a ball but pain stung at his chest, lungs, and useless hip, and he cried out, "Help me! Somebody help me!" Then a searing light flashed, and a deafening explosion detonated beside him. He heard a cracking sound as the sky crashed to earth with a violent impact that shook the ground. Splinters of branches rained down. Then came silence and calm, as if the impact had paralyzed the sky. The rain and wind paused, and an acrid smell like burning wire filled the air.

Cole lay frozen by fear. A sobering power had attacked the earth. This power made the bear's attack seem gentle. "No more! No more!" he moaned. "Please, no more!"

But there was more. The storm raged on as Cole lay trembling, his eyes frantic. The explosion had shocked his mind awake. Never in his life had he felt so exposed, so vulnerable, so helpless. He had no control. To this storm, he was as insignificant as a leaf. Cole blinked in stunned realization. He had always been this weak. How could he have ever thought he truly controlled anything? Cole swallowed the taste of bile in his throat and listened to the rumbling overhead. Then once more he lost consciousness.

When he awoke next, the rain had stopped. Vaguely, he could make out the big spruce tree lying on the ground only feet away from where he lay. Moment by moment, he sorted out what had happened during the storm. Lightning had struck the tree. The splitting sound, the thunderous impact, the splintering and bits of branches showering him, all had happened when the huge tree crashed to earth.

Cole gazed up at the night sky. A bright full moon drifted ghostlike among the broken clouds. The tortured air had calmed but still shifted back and forth. Cole felt desperately weak. Fighting to survive, he could

---

**prying**, forcing something open
**pummeled**, hit someone many times
**sobering**, making someone or something feel more serious

214

stay here a short while longer. Giving up, he could pass quickly over the edge. Which way did he want to go? He clenched his teeth against the pain and despair. Which way did he want to go?

Cole focused his blurred vision on the full moon. It helped him to remain on this side. As he stared, he puzzled at the moon's shape. Something in that hazy shape held meaning. Edwin had said something about a circle. So had Garvey. What had they said? Cole could not remember, but he kept staring up.

Later, Cole flopped his head to the side. He could make out the bay and see moonlight reflecting against one shore. The shoreline faded into darkness in the shadow of the trees. Seeing no sign of the Spirit Bear, Cole returned his attention to the fallen tree beside him.

That was when he remembered the baby sparrows. He tried to make out where they might be now among the fallen and twisted branches. He squinted harder, but all he saw was black. What had happened to the baby birds?

Mustering all his strength, he raised his head, and with a weak and pinched voice he called into the darkened branches, "Are you okay?"

---

**hazy**, unclear
**mustering**, finding or gathering

✔ **LITERARY CHECK**

*How does Cole's puzzling over the circle symbol and the questions he asks reflect changes in his character?*

## ABOUT THE **AUTHOR**

**Ben Mikaelsen** was raised in Bolivia and moved to the United States when he was about thirteen. While still in high school, he took up skydiving and flying. His adventurous spirit is reflected in his numerous award-winning novels for teenagers, including *Touching Spirit Bear* and *Rescue Josh McGuire*. Mikaelsen and his wife, Melanie, currently live in a log cabin near Bozeman, Montana. Their twenty-year-old pet is a 700-pound black bear, Buffy, which they adopted when it was a cub.

**BEFORE YOU GO ON**

1 What realization does Cole have?

2 What happened while Cole was asleep?

**On Your Own**
In your opinion, which way does Cole decide to go? Why?

## DRAMATIC READING

"The Great Circle" is an oral narrative that was recorded in writing in 1931. One of the best ways to understand an oral narrative is to read it aloud. Work in small groups to reread, discuss, and interpret "The Great Circle." Identify different ways the great circle is symbolized. What do you visualize? Write down any images that come to mind. Work together to interpret any difficult words or phrasing. Use a dictionary and ask your teacher for help, if necessary.

After your group has reread and examined the oral narrative carefully, assign one part of it to each group member and memorize it. Then work together to recite the narrative. Comment on each other's oral reading and make helpful suggestions for improvement. Continue practicing until you each feel comfortable with your part. Then recite the entire narrative for the class.

**Speaking TIP**

Remember that this is an oral narrative. Tell your story in a way that will engage your listeners.

## COMPREHENSION

Workbook
Page 101

### Right There

1. What warning does Edwin give Cole?
2. What does Cole see up in the giant spruce tree?

### Think and Search

3. How is the weather changing? How does this affect Cole?
4. How does Cole change in this excerpt?

### Author and You

5. How do you think the author of *Touching Spirit Bear* feels about circle justice? Why?
6. How do you think the author feels about animals?

### On Your Own

7. If you could question Cole, what would you ask him about his experience during the storm?
8. Do you think you could survive alone on an island?

## DISCUSSION

Discuss in pairs or small groups.

1. From what you read, why is Cole in this situation? What do you think his main problem or issue is? Is it that he cannot take responsibility for his actions? Is it his anger? Is it his parents? Is it his values?

2. How aware are you that you are part of a larger group? Give an example of how your behavior might impact members of the larger community, not just those people who are close to you.

 **What does it take to beat the odds?** Advocates of circle justice and other mediation programs believe that justice happens when there is forgiveness and healing. Do you agree? Where would you draw the line? Can all offenses be helped with circle justice? Explain your position.

## RESPONSE TO LITERATURE

**Workbook**
Page 101

Periodically, sponsors of circle justice, like Edwin and Garvey, have to report back to the circle of community members who are overseeing the program to ensure that justice happens. Imagine that you are Edwin or Garvey and have learned how Cole changed after the storm. Write a letter stating why you think Cole is changing and why you believe circle justice will work in his case. Remember that the circle wants facts and examples. There is a lot at stake. Be convincing.

▲ A circular cross section of an acacia tree

### Listening TIP

Listen as others give their ideas. If you have something to add to what someone else has said, wait until the speaker finishes. Then, use a transition to lead into your point, such as "I agree. To me, Cole's main problem is . . ."

# Grammar and Writing

## Transitions and Transitional Expressions

In the novel excerpt *Touching Spirit Bear,* the author uses transitions and transitional expressions to narrate the story chronologically. Transitions and transitional expressions include *at first, next, before, after, by the time, as, soon, then, until, when, while, in that instant,* and *finally.* Noticing these words and expressions helps readers follow the order of events in a story.

> Exhaustion **finally** dragged him into a stuporous sleep.
> **At first** he thought he had gone blind. **Then** slowly he realized it was nighttime.
> **Then** lightning flashed again. . . . **In that instant**, Cole saw it, ghostlike.

Transitions and transitional expressions are often used in time clauses. When you use transitions, avoid sentence fragments (incomplete sentences) by connecting a time clause to a main clause.

> **Time Clause** + Main Clause
>
> **When he awoke next**, the rain had stopped.
> **As he waited**, the storm worsened.
> **After feeding**, the mother flitted to a branch near the nest.

## Practice

Work with a partner. Copy the sentences below into your notebook. Put the events in chronological order. Then, use the transition words in the box to complete the sentences.

| after | before | finally | until | when |
| --- | --- | --- | --- | --- |

1. _____ the storm, Cole saw that the spruce tree had fallen.
2. Cole was lying wounded _____ he noticed the bird's nest.
3. _____ the bear attack, Cole said he'd kill the bear.
4. _____, Cole asked the baby sparrows if they were okay.
5. Cole slept _____ the thunder awoke him.

218

# WRITING A NARRATIVE PARAGRAPH

## Write a Narrative Paragraph

At the end of this unit, you will write a narrative essay. In order to do this, you will need to learn some techniques for writing a narrative, or a description of events told as a story. You already know some characteristics of stories: setting, characterization, conflict, point of view, theme, suspense, character motivation, flashback, and plot.

Read the paragraph below about a dangerous situation revealed in the novel *Hatchet*. Notice that the writer relates the events in a logical sequence, using transitions such as time clauses to help the reader follow the order of events.

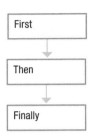

| First |
| Then |
| Finally |

*Ashley Nicole Smith*

### Hatchet

This book is about a thirteen-year-old boy named Brian Robeson. It starts with Brian heading off to spend his summer with his father (his parents are divorced). Before he left, his mother gave him a hatchet, which he put in his belt. Brian took a small plane to get to his father's house, and was the only passenger. At one point, the pilot let Brian try flying the plane. But then, suddenly, the pilot had a heart attack and died. Brian had to land the plane in the water by himself. Now, all alone, he had to learn how to survive in the Canadian wilderness. He had to deal with insects, birds, and fish. He had to find food and shelter, and make fire. It turned out to be a lucky thing that he had his hatchet with him! Was Brian ever found? Did he survive or did he die? You will have to read the book to find out!

**Practice**

Write your own narrative paragraph about a dangerous situation. It could be about you, someone you know, or someone you have read about. List the events of the ordeal in a sequence-of-events chart. Arrange the events in a logical sequence, such as chronological order. Be sure to include transition words such as *then*, *before*, *after*, *finally*, *as*, *when*, and *at first*.

**Writing Checklist**

**VOICE:**
☑ I used a strong voice to make my reader sense the danger.

**ORGANIZATION:**
☑ I organized my ideas using a logical sequence.

219

# Prepare to Read

## What You Will Learn

**Reading**

■ Vocabulary building: *Context, dictionary skills, word study*

■ Reading strategy: *Skim*

■ Text type: *Informational text (math and science)*

**Grammar, Usage, and Mechanics**

Gerunds as objects of verbs and objects of prepositions

**Writing**

Write a story with a starter

### THE BIG QUESTION

**What does it take to beat the odds?** People in dangerous or life-threatening situations have to beat the odds in order to survive. With luck you will never be in a situation where your life is in danger, but you never know.

What are some good survival skills to have? Work in small groups and discuss. List some situations in which you would need to have good survival skills in order to beat the odds.

### BUILD BACKGROUND

You are going to read two informational texts. The first one, the article **"Take a Chance,"** explains a kind of math called *probability*. Probability means how likely it is that something will happen, exist, or be true. This selection gives examples of how probability plays a role in games, science, and everyday life.

The second selection is an article called **"A Survival Mini-Manual."** It gives tips for surviving dangerous situations, such as being attacked by a bear or a shark, or being caught in a lightning storm.

▲ Students place their hands on a meteorite.

### Learn Key Words

Read these sentences. Use the context to figure out the meaning of the **red** words. Use a dictionary to check your answers. Then write each word and its meaning in your notebook.

1. Rudolph Boysen **bred** a blackberry with a raspberry and a loganberry. The result was a new berry called the boysenberry.

2. The divers **equalized** pressure in their eardrums by swallowing.

3. The probability of a coin landing heads up is **expressed** as 0.5, or 50 percent.

4 If there is a big crowd at a concert, I like to **maneuver** myself to the front so I can see better.

5. Sharks eat different types of **prey**, such as seals and smaller fish.

6. In an avalanche, try to grab onto a **stationary** object like a tree so the fast-moving snow doesn't carry you down the mountain.

**Practice**  **Workbook Page 104**

Write the sentences in your notebook. Choose a **red** word from the box above to complete each sentence. Then take turns reading the sentences aloud with a partner.

1 The sum of 12 and 7 is _____ as 12 + 7.

2. Don't move your arm when you get a shot. Keep it _____.

3. She tried to _____ the car around the giant tree in the middle of the road.

4. Many animals hunt for _____ at night.

5. Mendel discovered genes when he _____ the offspring of purple-flowered peas with white-flowered peas.

6. Chewing gum on the plane _____ the pressure in my ears.

## Learn Academic Words

Study the **red** words and their meanings. You will find these words useful when talking and writing about informational texts. Write each word and its meaning in your notebook. After you read "Take a Chance" and "A Survival Mini-Manual," try to use these words to respond to the text.

| | | |
|---|---|---|
| **conduct** = allow electricity or heat to travel along or through | ⇒ | If you are in a lightning storm, avoid touching anything that can **conduct** electricity. |
| **definitely** = certainly, without any doubt | ⇒ | I knew she would be there because she said she was **definitely** coming. |
| **encounter** = meet someone or see something without planning to | ⇒ | If you're in an area where bears live—like a wooded habitat—you might **encounter** one. |
| **estimate** = judge an approximate value, amount, cost, etc. | ⇒ | Probability can help you **estimate** your chances of winning the football game. |
| **surviving** = continuing to stay alive or exist | ⇒ | The chances of **surviving** a car accident are much better if you have a seat belt on. |

## Practice  Workbook Page 105

Work with a partner to rewrite the sentences. Use the **red** word in each new sentence. Write the sentences in your notebook.

1. Wires allow electricity to pass through them. (**conduct**)
2. For sure, I am going to take physics before I graduate. (**definitely**)
3. If you walk in the woods in the morning, you might find a herd of deer. (**encounter**)
4. Let's guess how much money we'll earn this summer. (**estimate**)
5. Your chances of living through a small earthquake are very good. (**surviving**)

The wires in a lightbulb conduct electricity. ▶

## Word Study: *r*-controlled Vowels

When the letter *r* follows a vowel, it usually changes the vowel sound. Here are some examples using the sound /ûr/. The chart shows four different spellings for this vowel sound.

| *r*-Controlled Vowel /ûr/ | | | |
|---|---|---|---|
| **er** | **ir** | **or** | **ur** |
| experts | third | word | hurt |

**Practice**

Work with a partner. Take turns reading the words in the box.

| author | dirt | first | history | mother | survival | turn | universe |
|---|---|---|---|---|---|---|---|

Copy the chart below into your notebook. List the words according to the spelling of the *r*-controlled vowel sound. Then add one word of your own to each column.

| **er** | **ir** | **or** | **ur** |
|---|---|---|---|
| | | | |
| | | | |
| | | | |

## READING STRATEGY    SKIM

Skimming a text helps you get a general understanding of what the text is about. To skim a text, follow these steps:

- Look at the title and any visuals.
- Read the first paragraph quickly. Then read the first sentence of the paragraphs that follow.
- Don't stop at any words you don't know—skip over them.
- Try to summarize what you learned.

Skim the following articles and think about the subject. What do you already know about it? What more do you think you will learn?

223

**Set a purpose for reading** Ever wonder what the odds are that you could be struck by lightning? Learn how to avoid letting this and other catastrophes happen to you.

# Take a Chance!

*Johnny Ball*

What's the chance of being struck by lightning or hit by a meteorite when you go for a walk? If you fly in a plane, what's the chance of crashing or seeing a flying pig through a window? To answer these questions precisely, you need a branch of math called probability.

## What Is Probability?

Probability is expressed by a number from zero to one. A probability of zero means something definitely won't happen, whereas a probability of one means it definitely will. Anything in between means something may happen. For instance, the chance of a coin landing heads up is a half, or 0.5.

## The Laws of Luck

Here's a handy tip. In math questions about probability, look for the words "or" and "and." When you see the word "or," chances are you'll need to **add up** probabilities to get your answer. So the chance of rolling a one *or* a two with a

cube (from one to six) would be 1/6 + 1/6 = 1/3. When you see "and," you'll probably have to **multiply**. For instance, the chance of getting a six *and* another six on two cube rolls is 1/6 X 1/6 =1/36.

## Mendel's Numbers

In the 1850s, Austrian monk Gregor Mendel made an amazing discovery thanks to probability. Mendel bred purple-flowered peas with white-flowered peas and found that all the offspring were purple. He decided these must have "white" in them, but it just wasn't showing. So he bred the offspring with each other. Now there were four possibilities. The new parents could pass on one purple each, a purple and a white, a white and a purple, or two whites. If purple was present, it would show over white, and so on average, only a quarter of the plants would be white. They were. Mendel had discovered genes.

---

**branch**, one part of a large subject of study or knowledge

**offspring**, the descendents of a person, animal, or plant
**genes**, parts of cells in living things that control how they develop

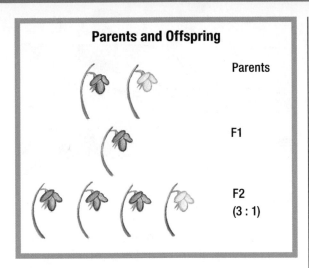

**Parents and Offspring**

Parents

F1

F2
(3 : 1)

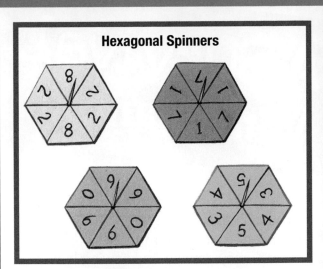

**Hexagonal Spinners**

## Sneaky Spinners

Here's a game of chance you'll keep winning at. Make four spinners like the ones here by cutting out cardboard hexagons and writing numbers on them. Push a toothpick through the center of each. Then challenge a friend to a spinner match. Point out that they can choose any spinner they want, and the numbers on each one add up to 24, so the game must be fair. Look at the highest number on their spinner, then make sure you pick the spinner with the next number up (but if your friend takes the one with an 8 on it, you take the one with the 5 on it). You'll have a two-thirds chance of winning each match!

## Risky Business

The table shows a person's chance of dying from various causes, based on death rates in Europe and North America.

| Cause of Death | Chance of Dying in a Year |
| --- | --- |
| Road accident | 1 In 4,000 |
| Flu | 1 in 5,000 |
| Falling | 1 in 16,000 |
| Playing soccer | 1 in 25,000 |
| Struck by lightning | 1 in 10 million |
| Hit by meteorite (estimate) | 1 in a trillion |

## ABOUT THE **AUTHOR**

**Johnny Ball** is a British television personality and author who specializes in presenting science and mathematics to young audiences. He has written five children's books. A former comedian, he was the host of *Play School*, the popular British children's TV series. The father of three grown children, he lives with his wife in South Bucks, United Kingdom.

**BEFORE YOU GO ON**

**1** In math questions about probability, what two words should you look for?

**2** Thanks to probability, what did Mendel discover?

**On Your Own** How can you use probability?

# A Survival Mini-Manual

You never know when disaster will strike. If it does, it's important to be prepared. Your life—or the lives of others—may depend on knowing how to get out of a jam. Here are some tricks that experts say will increase a person's chances of surviving a sticky situation.

## You are bitten by a snake

Even if you saw it done in a movie, don't try to suck the venom and spit it out. This will make you absorb even more venom. Remain calm. Most snake bites aren't fatal, and panic will only make your heart beat faster, speeding the spread of the venom through your body. Clean the wound the way you would treat any other type of cut. Then tie a band between the wound and your heart to keep the venom from spreading too quickly. Don't make the band as tight as a tourniquet. Seek medical attention right away.

## You are in water with sharks

Try to keep still, to keep the shark from noticing you. If you think it's attacking, hit it in the eyes or gills with your fists or any hard object. (Punch the nose only if you can't reach the eyes or gills.) Sharks aren't interested in going after prey that fights back, so it will probably swim away. To avoid this frightening encounter, don't swim alone far from the ocean's shore or during the twilight or evening. Stay out of water if you have an open wound, because the blood will attract sharks.

## You are attacked by a bear

Don't turn your back on the bear and run away. The bear will think you are prey and chase you. There's no way you can outrun a bear. Nor can you outclimb one. Bears will chase you up a tree, where there's no escape. Your best option is to lie down and play dead. With any luck, the bear will lose interest and leave.

## You are caught in an avalanche

Get out of its way by running from its path. Close your mouth to keep it free of snow. When the snow hits, try to stay on its surface. Do this by moving your arms as if you're swimming. If this doesn't work, try to grab a tree or some other stationary object as you move by. If you get buried, create an air pocket around your nose or mouth by cupping your hands. It will allow you to breathe until you are rescued.

## You are stuck in quicksand

Just remember: don't struggle wildly. Thrashing around will make you sink faster. Quicksand is sand saturated with underground water. Like regular water, you float on its surface. Try shifting your body until you're lying on your back. Now you can float on the quicksand as if you were in a swimming pool. Maneuver yourself to the edge of the quicksand and escape.

## You are in a lightning storm

It's not what you do—it's what you shouldn't do. Don't stay in high places or on open ground. Don't stand under a tree or a flagpole or in a picnic area, baseball dugout or bleachers. Don't go near metal fences or any body of water. It's better to stand inside a large building than a small one. Once inside, don't touch anything leading to the outside that conducts electricity, such as metal window frames, showers or pipes. Don't use a telephone, computer or TV. If you're inside a car, roll up the windows and try not to touch anything that can conduct electricity.

## Your car is sinking

First, open the car windows. You want water to fill the car so the pressure on the inside and outside of the car is equal. Now you will be able to open the doors. Get out of the car as quickly as possible. If you can't open the windows, try to break them. If that doesn't work, wait as water coming through the trunk and engine slowly fills the car. Once the water has reached your head, the water pressure should be equalized. Hold your breath, open the door and swim out.

## Your tongue is stuck to a cold pole

This isn't life-threatening, but it is painful and embarrassing. The best advice is to not put your tongue on a freezing pole in the first place. But if you do, don't try to quickly pull your tongue off the pole—you may rip it! Instead, move your hands (they should be in gloves!) over the pole near your tongue. This should warm the pole enough to let you slowly pull your tongue off. If warm water is nearby, splash it over your tongue to thaw it. Don't put cool water or your saliva over the area: they will both freeze, making the situation even stickier.

### BEFORE YOU GO ON

**1** What shouldn't you do if you are bitten by a snake?

**2** If you encounter a bear, what should you do?

**On Your Own**
Which survival tip surprised you the most?

227

# Review and Practice

## COMPREHENSION  Workbook Page 108

### Right There

1. What does a probability of 0 mean? How about a probability of 1?

2. What should you *not* do if you are stuck in quicksand?

### Think and Search

3. Which dangerous situation is mentioned in both articles? How likely is this to happen? What survival skills can help?

4. What are three pieces of advice for getting out of a sticky situation?

### Author and You

5. Do you think it is effective to write about possible disasters or dangerous situations in a lighthearted and entertaining way? Does the message still get across? Why?

6. Johnny Ball is a former comedian and was the host of a British children's TV series. From what you read, how do you think his background helped him write "Take a Chance!"?

### On Your Own

7. How important do you think it is to have survival skills for certain disasters or dangerous situations? Explain.

8. What dangerous situations do you think people fear the most? Why?

## IN YOUR OWN WORDS

Work with a partner. Take turns summarizing the articles. To do this, use the headings you listed when you applied the reading strategy on page 223. You can use a chart like this one:

|  | Headings | Main Ideas |
|---|---|---|
| "Take a Chance!" |  |  |
| "A Survival Mini-Manual" |  |  |

🔊 *Speaking* TIP

Knowing what a word means and how to pronounce it will help you as you give your summary. If you don't know, check with your partner or look it up in a dictionary.

## DISCUSSION

Discuss in pairs or small groups.

1. What is the most important piece of information about survival that you gained from reading the two articles? Why?

2. Which dangers do you think everyone should be prepared to deal with? Which ones do you think most people will never have to deal with?

3. How do you think a basic knowledge of probability can help you in your life? Give an example.

 **What does it take to beat the odds?** What movies, books, or TV shows that you are familiar with develop the theme "beating the odds" or deal with survival? What makes these movies or shows compelling?

**Listening TIP**

If you don't understand a point that's being made, ask the person to repeat it and listen carefully. If the point is still unclear, ask questions.

## READ FOR FLUENCY

It is often easier to read a text if you understand the difficult words and phrases. Work with a partner. Choose a paragraph from the reading. Identify the words and phrases you do not know or have trouble pronouncing. Look up the difficult words in a dictionary.

Take turns pronouncing the words and phrases with your partner. If necessary, ask your teacher to model the correct pronunciation. Then take turns reading the paragraph aloud. Give each other feedback on your reading.

## EXTENSION

**Workbook Page 108**

In small groups, decide on some other disasters or dangerous situations you would like to know more about. Then do research to find out some survival skills people should have in those situations. Write your own "Survival Mini-Manual" with tips. Add illustrations or charts that show the probability of being in such situations. Share your manual with the class.

▲ This running track has been damaged by an earthquake.

# Grammar and Writing

## Gerunds as Objects of Verbs and Objects of Prepositions

A gerund is a verb that is used as a noun. A gerund is formed by using the base form of the verb + *-ing*. Gerunds can be objects of certain verbs.

> Here's a game of chance you'll keep **winning** at.
> Try **shifting** your body until you're lying down.
> Did you finish **playing** the game?

Gerunds can also be used as objects of prepositions. Prepositions are words such as *by, to, for, in, on, about,* and *from*.

> Make the game by **cutting out** four cardboard hexagons.
> You can increase your chance of **surviving** a snake bite by **staying** calm.
> Keep the venom from **spreading** too quickly.

The chart below shows some of the verbs that can be followed by a gerund.

| | | | | | |
|---|---|---|---|---|---|
| admit | dislike | finish | miss | recommend | suggest |
| avoid | enjoy | give up | practice | report | support |
| consider | explain | imagine | prevent | resist | try |
| deny | feel like | keep | quit | risk | understand |

## Practice

Work with a partner. Talk about one of the disaster situations in the reading. Write sentences about the disaster in your notebook. Use gerunds with the sentence starters below.

| | |
|---|---|
| Would you risk . . . ? | How can you avoid . . . ? |
| How can you prevent . . . ? | Do you ever worry about . . . ? |
| What is the chance of . . . ? | Are you afraid of . . . ? |

## WRITING A NARRATIVE PARAGRAPH

### Write a Story with a Starter

To help you write a narrative composition at the end of this unit, read the model narrative paragraph below. The writer used this story starter to write a paragraph about a lightning storm: *It was a dark and stormy night.* . . . The story tells how a dangerous situation was avoided by using some effective survival skills. Notice how the story starter sets the scene and then how the setting is developed. The writer used a word web to list these details. As you read the model, look for gerunds as objects of verbs and as objects of prepositions.

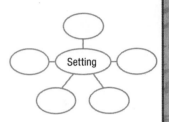

*Will Trigg*

### A Stormy Night

It was a dark and stormy night when I suddenly found myself in a field with trees all around me. Since I knew that lightning usually strikes the tallest object, I avoided being near the trees. I tried lying down as close to the ground as possible. It was then that I saw a small shack. As I was deciding whether I should take cover in the shack, I noticed that it had a metal roof. I remembered how metal conducts electricity, so I resisted going in there. A little further away, I saw a large building. I knew that was the safest place to be because of its size and because I would be indoors. Luckily, it was open. When I got inside, I kept from touching anything electrical. Although I was very wet, I was safe because I knew where the safest place was and also where I could have been in the most danger.

### Practice

**Workbook**
**Page 110**

Look back at the selection "A Survival Mini-Manual." In small groups, make up story starters for each disaster. Then choose one of the story starters and write a story. Use a setting word web to list details. Then use the model to help you write your narrative paragraph. Remember to use elements of a story, such as plot, character, and conflict. Be sure to use gerunds as objects of verbs and as objects of prepositions correctly.

**Writing Checklist**

**SENTENCE FLUENCY:**
☑ My sentences begin in different ways.

**ORGANIZATION:**
☑ My story is told in a way that helps my reader follow the events.

## What You Will Learn

**Reading**

■ Vocabulary building: *Literary terms, word study*

■ Reading strategy: *Draw conclusions*

■ Text type: *Literature (tall tale and song)*

**Grammar, Usage, and Mechanics**
Agreement with generic nouns and indefinite pronouns

**Writing**
Rewrite a familiar story

 **THE BIG QUESTION**

**What does it take to beat the odds?** Have you ever read a story or seen a movie about a person who faced a difficult physical challenge? What did he or she have to do in order to beat the odds and win? Discuss with a partner.

**BUILD BACKGROUND**

You will read a tall tale called **"John Henry."** Some historians think a person named John Henry actually existed. They believe he was a former slave who lived during the late 1800s. This was a period of time in which the United States was undergoing many changes, and people told tall tales to try to make sense of these changes. These tales changed many times over and then were related by others, such as author Adrien Stoutenburg, through the years. What do you know about this period of time? In small groups, look at the timeline below and discuss the events.

| California gold rush begins | American Civil War begins | American Civil War ends | First continental railroad is completed | First commercial telephone exchange opens | American Indian Wars end |
|---|---|---|---|---|---|
| **1848** | **1861** | **1865** | **1869** | **1878** | **1890** |

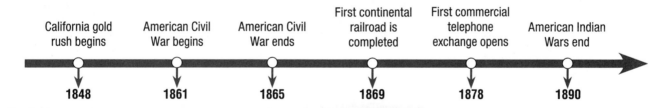

## VOCABULARY

### Learn Literary Words

Tall tales and songs are part of oral tradition and are passed along by word of mouth. Literary devices make the tales and songs easy to remember. Here are some literary devices used in the selections you are about to read:

**Hyperbole** is a deliberate exaggeration often used in tall tales, saying that something is much bigger, smaller, faster, etc., than it really is.

> People down South still tell stories about John Henry . . . how he could whirl a big sledge so lightning-fast you could hear thunder behind it.

**Imagery** is figurative language used to create word pictures. These pictures, or images, appeal to the senses—sight, sound, taste, touch, smell—or to movement. Which sense does this example of imagery appeal to?

> John Henry's heart beat in rhythm with the falling hammers.

**Repetition** is often used in tall tales and songs. It takes many different forms:

- The repetition of initial consonant sounds (**alliteration**): "I **h**ad a mighty **h**ammer in my **h**and."

- The repetition of vowel sounds (**assonance**): "**I** can dr**i**ve one of those sp**i**kes all b**y** m**y**self."

- The repetition of sounds at the end of words (**rhyme**): "You **beat** that steam engine by four **feet**."

- A pattern of beats or stresses (**rhythm**). Here the rhythm imitates the sounds of a hammer: "Hammer's gonna be the death of me, Lord. Lord. Hammer's gonna be the death of me."

### Practice
**Workbook Page 111**

With a partner, read the definitions and examples above. Find the lyrics to a favorite song or the words to a favorite poem. Look for any examples of the literary devices above. Then use these devices to help you interpret the song or poem and read or sing it aloud for the class.

## Learn Academic Words

Study the **red** words and their meanings. You will find these words useful when talking and writing about literature. Write each word and its meaning in your notebook. After you read the tall tale "John Henry" and listen to the song, try to use these words to respond to the text.

**Academic Words**

challenge
labor
methods
period
physical
technology

| | | |
|---|---|---|
| **challenge** = something that tests one's skill or ability | → | John Henry was ready for the **challenge** of testing his skill against the power of the steam drill. |
| **labor** = work, especially work using a lot of physical effort | → | It took the **labor** of many to build the railroad. |
| **methods** = planned ways of doing something | → | The **methods** used to build the railroad changed with the invention of the steam drill. |
| **period** = length of time | → | Tall tales helped people understand the changes taking place during the **period** of westward expansion. |
| **physical** = relating to someone's body | → | His **physical** strength was exceptional; it was said that he could lift 1,000 pounds! |
| **technology** = the use of scientific or industrial methods | → | Because of new **technology**, fewer people were needed to complete the job. |

## Practice
**Workbook Page 112**

Write the sentences in your notebook. Choose a **red** word from the box above to complete each sentence. Then take turns reading the sentences aloud with a partner.

1. Improvements in _____ have made cars more energy efficient.

2. The transcontinental railroad was built by manual _____. Over ten thousand workers were used on the project.

3. It took about six years to build the railroad—a relatively short _____ of time.

4. Her teacher has taught her some special _____ to improve her skills on the violin.

5. In tall tales, it is common for _____ characteristics of people to be exaggerated.

6. Chemistry is a _____ for me because I'm not good at math.

▼ An early locomotive

234

## Word Study: Long e

The letter *e* stands for different sounds. Short *e* is usually spelled *e*. Long *e* has several different spellings: *ee, ea, e, ie, ey,* and *y*. Read the examples of each long *e* sound-spelling in the chart below.

| ea | ee | e | ie | y / ey |
|---|---|---|---|---|
| steam | steel | he | believe | city |
| dream | feeling | even | Willie | honey |

Remember that some of these spellings can stand for different sounds, such as the *y* in *sky*.

## Practice
### Workbook Page 113

Work with a partner. Your partner must close his or her book. Then choose four of the words listed in the chart below and read them aloud to your partner. Your partner will listen and dictate the words as you say them. Once you've read the four words, check your partner's spelling. Then switch roles.

| | | | | | |
|---|---|---|---|---|---|
| beat | feel | heated | mean | reach | squarely |
| cheer | free | honey | need | seems | we |
| everything | greenhorn | lean | piece | she | worried |

## READING STRATEGY | DRAW CONCLUSIONS

Drawing conclusions helps you figure out the meanings of clues and events in a text. Good readers are like detectives. They put together the clues until they can draw a conclusion. To draw a conclusion, follow these steps:

- Look for clues in the text. Use a graphic organizer to list the clues.
- Think about what you already know from similar situations that you have read about or experienced.
- Draw a conclusion about what is happening in the text by considering the clues you've discovered and what you already know about the subject.

As you read "John Henry," ask yourself what conclusions you can draw about this tall tale.

### Workbook Page 114

**Set a purpose for reading** The task that John Henry faced was nearly impossible to accomplish. What kind of character traits did he have to demonstrate in order to successfully beat the odds?

# John Henry

*A tall tale retold by Adrien Stoutenburg*

*In the days of the frontier and westward expansion in the United States, the country was changing fast. Tall tales began to be told in the 1800s as a way of understanding all that was going on. The tales developed amazing heroes. One timeless figure was the legendary railroad wonder John Henry. It was said that he did the impossible—he won a steel-driving contest against a steam engine.*

▲ A U.S. postal stamp portraying John Henry, July 11, 1996

People down South still tell stories about John Henry, how strong he was, and how he could whirl a big sledge so lightning-fast you could hear thunder behind it. They even say he was born with a hammer in his hand. John Henry himself said it, but he probably didn't mean it exactly as it sounded.

The story seems to be that when John Henry was a baby, the first thing he reached out for was a hammer which was hung nearby on the cabin wall.

John Henry's father put his arm around his wife's shoulder. "He's going to grow up to be a steel-driving man. I can see it plain as rows of cotton running uphill."

One night, John Henry told his folks about a dream he had had.

"I dreamed I was working on a railroad somewhere," he said, "a big, new railroad called the C. & O., and I had a mighty hammer in my hand. Every time I swung it, it made a whirling flash around my shoulder. And every time my hammer hit a spike, the sky lit up from the sparks."

"I believe it," his father said. "You were born to drive steel."

"That ain't all of the dream," John Henry said. "I dreamed that the railroad was going to be the end of me and I'd die with the hammer in my hand."

---

**whirl**, spin around quickly
**sledge**, a large, heavy hammer

The next morning, John Henry bundled up some food in a red bandanna handkerchief, told his parents good-by, and set off into the world. He walked until he heard the clang-clang of hammers in the distance. He followed the sound to a place where gangs of men were building a railroad. John Henry watched the men driving steel spikes down into the crossties to hold the rails in place. Three men would stand around a spike, then each, in turn, would swing a long hammer.

▲ A steam locomotive

John Henry's heart beat in rhythm with the falling hammers. His fingers ached for the feel of a hammer in his own hands. He walked over to the foreman.

"I'm a natural steel-driving man," he said. "And I'm looking for a job."

"How much steel-driving have you done?" the foreman asked.

"I was born knowing how," John Henry said.

The foreman shook his head. "That ain't good enough. I can't take any chances. Steel-driving's dangerous work, and you might hit somebody."

"I wouldn't hit anybody," John Henry said, "because I can drive one of those spikes all by myself."

The foreman said sharply, "The one kind of man I don't need in this outfit is a bragger. Stop wasting my time."

John Henry didn't move. He got a stubborn look around his jaw. "You loan me a hammer, boss mister, and if somebody will hold the spike for me, I'll prove what I can do."

The three men who had just finished driving in a spike looked toward him and laughed. One of them said, "Anybody who would hold a spike for a greenhorn don't want to live long."

"I'll hold it," a fourth man said.

John Henry saw that the speaker was a small, dark-skinned fellow about his own age.

---

**bandanna**, a square piece of colored cloth worn around the head or neck
**spikes**, things that are long and thin with sharp points, especially metal
**crossties**, beams that connect and support the rails of a railroad
**foreman**, someone in charge of a group of workers
**greenhorn**, someone who lacks experience in a job

✔ **LITERARY CHECK**
*Was John Henry really born knowing how to drive steel? How is this use of* **hyperbole** *effective in developing the superhuman hero John Henry?*

**BEFORE YOU GO ON**

1 What did John Henry dream?

2 After he left home, where did John Henry go?

**On Your Own**
Do you think John Henry will get the job? Why or why not?

**237**

The foreman asked the small man, "D'you aim to get yourself killed, Li'l Willie?"

"Tap it down gentle, first," said Li'l Willie.

But John Henry had already started to swing. He brought the hammer flashing down, banging the spike squarely on the head. Before the other men could draw a breath of surprise, the hammer flashed again, whirring through the air like a giant hummingbird. One more swing, and the spike was down, its steel head smoking from the force of the blow.

The foreman blinked, swallowed, and blinked again. "Man," he told John Henry, "you're hired!"

That's the way John Henry started steel-driving.

\* \* \*

One day the tunnel boss Cap'n Tommy Walters of the C. & O. Railroad was standing watching John Henry, when a stranger in city clothes walked up to him.

"Howdy, Cap'n Tommy," said the stranger. "I'd like to talk to you about a steam engine I've got for sale. My engine can drive a drill through rock so fast that not even a crew of your best men can keep up with it."

"I don't need any machine," Cap'n Tommy said proudly. "My man John Henry can out-drill any machine ever built."

"I'll place a bet with you, Cap'n," said the salesman. "You race your man against my machine for a full day. If he wins, I'll give you the steam engine free."

Cap'n Tommy thought it over. "That sounds fair enough, but I'll have to talk to John Henry first." He told John Henry what the stranger had said. "Are you willing to race a steam drill?" Cap'n Tommy asked.

John Henry ran his big hands over the handle of his hammer, feeling the strength in the wood and in his own great muscles.

"A man's a man," he said, "but a machine ain't nothing but a machine. I'll beat that steam drill, or I'll die with my hammer in my hand!"

"All right, then," said Cap'n Tommy. "We'll set a day for the contest."

Polly Ann [John Henry's wife] looked worried when John Henry told her what he had promised to do.

---

**hummingbird**, A very small bird, with wings capable
   of beating very rapidly
**steam engine**, an engine that converts the heat energy
   of pressurized steam into mechanical energy
**drill**, a tool or machine used for making holes in
   something hard

"Don't you worry, honey," John Henry said. It was the end of the workday, with the sunset burning across the mountain, and the sky shining like copper. He tapped his chest. "I've got a man's heart in here. All a machine has is a metal engine." He smiled and picked Polly Ann up in his arms, as if she were no heavier than a blade of grass.

* * *

Cap'n Tommy held up the starting gun. For a second everything was as silent as the dust in a drill hole. Then the gun barked, making a yelp that bounced against mountain and sky.

John Henry swung his hammer, and it rang against the drill.

At the same time, the steam engine gave a roar and a hiss. Steam whistled through its escape valve. Its drill crashed down, gnawing into the granite.

John Henry paid no attention to anything except his hammer, nor to any sound except the steady pumping of his heart. At the end of an hour, he paused long enough to ask, "How are we doing, Li'l Willie?"

▲ A Palmer Hayden painting of John Henry competing with a steam drill

Willie licked his lips. His face was pale with rock dust and with fear. "The machine's ahead, John Henry."

John Henry tossed his smoking hammer aside and called to another helper, "Bring me two hammers! I'm only getting warmed up."

He began swinging a hammer in each hand. Sparks flew so fast and hot they singed his face. The hammers heated up until they glowed like torches.

"How're we doing now, Li'l Willie?" John Henry asked at the end of another hour.

Li'l Willie grinned. "The machine's drill busted. They have to take time to fix up a new one. You're almost even now, John Henry! How're you feeling?"

"I'm feeling like sunrise," John Henry took time to say before he flashed one of his hammers down against the drill. "Clean out the hole, Willie, and we'll drive right down to China."

Cap'n Tommy's gun cracked. The judges ran forward to measure the depth of the holes drilled by the steam engine and by John Henry. At last, the judges came walking back and said something to Cap'n Tommy before they turned to announce their findings to the crowd.

---

**copper,** an orange-brown metal
**gnawing,** biting something, usually for a long time
**busted,** broken
**drive right down to China,** get through to the other side

**BEFORE YOU GO ON**

1 What does the salesperson claim his engine can do?

2 What is Polly Ann's reaction?

**On Your Own**
Do you think John Henry will beat the odds and win the race against the steam engine?

239

Cap'n Tommy walked over to John Henry, who stood leaning against the face of the mountain.

"John Henry," he said, "you beat that steam engine by four feet!" He held out his hand and smiled.

John Henry heard a distant cheering. He held his own hand out, and then he staggered. He fell and lay on his back, staring up at the mountain and the sky, and then he saw Polly Ann and Li'l Willie leaning over him.

"Oh, how do you feel, John Henry?" Polly Ann asked.

"I feel a bit tuckered out," said John Henry.

▲ Visitors at the site where John Henry battled the drill

"Do you want me to sing to you?" Li'l Willie asked.

"I got a song in my own heart, thank you, Li'l Willie," John Henry said. He raised up on his elbow and looked at all the people and the last sunset light gleaming like the edge of a golden trumpet. "I was a steel-driving man," he said, and lay back and closed his eyes forever.

Down South, and in the North, too, people still talk about John Henry and how he beat the steam engine at the Big Bend Tunnel. They say, if John Henry were alive today, he could beat almost every other kind of machine, too.

Maybe so. At least, John Henry would die trying.

---

**staggered**, walked in an unsteady way
**tuckered out**, wearied; exhausted

## ABOUT THE **AUTHOR**

**Adrien Stoutenburg** (1916–1982) was born in Darfur, Minnesota. An author and poet, she attended the Minneapolis School of Arts. She later served for many years as a librarian in Richfield, Minnesota. She also worked as a local political reporter and editor. Stoutenberg wrote numerous books, most notably *American Tall Tales.*

# John Henry

John Henry was about three days old,
sittin' on his papa's knee.
He picked up a hammer and a little piece of steel;
said, "Hammer's gonna be the death of me, Lord, Lord.
Hammer's gonna be the death of me."
The captain said to John Henry,
"Gonna bring that steam drill 'round.
Gonna bring that steam drill out on the job.
Gonna whop that steel on down. Down, Down.
Whop that steel on down."
John Henry told his captain,
"A man ain't nothin' but a man,
But before I let your steam drill beat me down,
I'd die with a hammer in my hand. Lord, Lord.
I'd die with a hammer in my hand."
John Henry said to his shaker,
"Shaker, why don't you sing?
I'm throwin' thirty pounds from my hips on down.
Just listen to that cold steel ring. Lord, Lord.
Listen to that cold steel ring."
The man that invented the steam drill
Thought he was mighty fine,
But John Henry made fifteen feet;
The steam drill only made nine. Lord, Lord.
The steam drill only made nine.
John Henry hammered in the mountain
His hammer was striking fire.
But he worked so hard, he broke his poor heart.
He laid down his hammer and he died. Lord, Lord.
He laid down his hammer and he died.

— *Pete Seeger*

## ABOUT THE **SONGWRITER**

**Pete Seeger** is a renowned folksinger, songwriter, social activist, author, and environmentalist. He attended Harvard College but left in his sophomore year to travel around the country collecting songs. Seeger later began a successful performance and recording career. He lives near the city of Beacon, New York.

## BEFORE YOU GO ON

**1** In the tall tale, what were John Henry's last words?

**2** According to the song, what did John Henry pick up when he was about three days old?

**On Your Own**
Which did you enjoy more—the tall tale or the song? Why?

# Review and Practice

## READER'S THEATER

In small groups, act out John Henry's job interview.

**John Henry:** I'm looking for a job. I'm a natural at driving steel.

**Foreman:** How much experience do you have?

**John Henry:** I've known how since I was a baby. My father always said I was a natural.

**Foreman:** [*shakes his head*] That's not good enough for me. It's dangerous work.

**John Henry:** Let me show you. I can drive the spikes by myself.

**Foreman:** [*sharply*] Okay, that's it. I don't need a bragger working for me.

**John Henry:** Please—I just need a hammer and I'll prove it to you.

**Onlooker:** [*laughs*] Anyone who'd hold a spike for this greenhorn isn't going to live long.

**Li'l Willie:** [*helpfully*] I'll hold the spike for you.

[*Li'l Willie holds the spike.*]

**Foreman:** You'll get yourself killed, Li'l Willie.

**Li'l Willie:** Tap it down gently, first, John Henry.

[*With just two swings, John Henry hammers the spike down, and the steel head smokes from the force of the blow.*]

**Foreman:** [*blinks, swallows, and blinks again*] I've seen enough! John Henry, you're hired!

## COMPREHENSION

**Workbook Page 115**

**Right There**

1. Why did John Henry tell Polly Ann not to worry?

2. What bet does the salesperson make with Cap'n Tommy?

**Think and Search**

3. In the tall tale, who wins and by how much?

4. How is the outcome different in the song? Why do you think the details are different?

**Author and You**

5. The author of the tall tale writes like a poet. How is this approach more effective than a simple narrative?

6. Is the song easy to remember? What techniques did the songwriter use to help you?

**On Your Own**

7. What present-day figure would be a good subject for a tall tale? Why?

8. Which exaggerates the qualities of a hero more effectively—a song or a tall tale? Why?

**»⌐ Listening TIP**

If you disagree with another student's viewpoint, wait until he or she is finished speaking to make your point. Listen carefully so that you can make your point effectively.

## DISCUSSION

Discuss in pairs or small groups.

1. Describe John Henry's character. What do you admire about him?

2. In the tale, John Henry had a wife, Polly Ann. How do you think she felt about his life's work?

**Q What does it take to beat the odds?** To overcome a physical challenge, a person needs to be strong. Are there other traits that a person needs? Explain.

## RESPONSE TO LITERATURE

**Workbook Page 115**

Write an obituary notice about John Henry's death. An obituary notice gives details about birth, accomplishments, cause of death, funeral services, and who in the family is left behind. Copy this notice into your notebook and complete it. Use your imagination. When do you think John Henry was born? Who did he leave behind?

**John Henry**, born 18 _____; died 18 _____
Henry was born with _____. He died while _____ at _____
in _____. Known for his _____, _____, and _____, Henry
worked for years as a _____. He leaves behind his wife
_____, _____, and good friend _____. Memorial services
will be held _____. In lieu of flowers, his family requests that
contributions be made to _____.

# Grammar and Writing

## Agreement with Generic Nouns and Indefinite Pronouns

Generic nouns, such as *a person, a student,* and *a woman,* are used to represent a whole group. Compare these sentences:

- A student just handed me this note. (*a student* refers to a particular student)
- A student must get good grades to enter this college. (*a student* is a generic noun; it refers to anyone who is a student)

Indefinite pronouns, such as *something, anyone,* and *no one,* are used in place of nouns. They do not refer to any particular person or thing. Indefinite pronouns and generic nouns must agree in person, number, and gender. Indefinite pronouns are always third-person singular, but generic nouns may be third-person singular or plural.

Look at the examples below from the tall tale "John Henry."

| Generic Nouns |
|---|
| **People** down South still **tell** stories about John Henry. **They** even **say** he was born with a hammer in his hand. |
| "**A man is a man**," he said, "but **a machine isn't** anything but **a machine**." |

| Indefinite Pronouns |
|---|
| **Anybody** who **would hold** a spike for a greenhorn **doesn't want** to live long. |
| If **somebody will hold** the spike for me, I'll prove what I can do. |
| For a second **everything was** as silent as the dust in a drill hole. |

**Practice**

Workbook
Page 116

Copy the sentences below into your notebook. Choose the correct verb in parentheses to complete each sentence. Compare your answers with a partner.

1. Somebody (was helping / were helping) John Henry.
2. That kind of man (is / are) a bragger.
3. No one (is able to / are able to) to stop John Henry.
4. John Henry said, "Nobody (believes / believe) that I can drive steel."
5. They (wants / want) to place a bet with John Henry.
6. People (loves / love) to tell stories about John Henry.

244

# WRITING A NARRATIVE PARAGRAPH

## Rewrite a Familiar Story

The tall tale "John Henry" is told from the omniscient, third-person point of view, which means the story is told from the narrator's point of view. You are going to shift the point of view and tell the story from one of the character's perspectives. Scan the story dialogue. Notice how it reveals the characters' thoughts and feelings. This will be useful to you as you write from one of the character's perspectives.

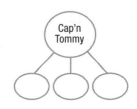

Read the model about the race with the steam engine told from Cap'n Tommy's point of view. The writer used a word web to list Cap'n Tommy's thoughts and feelings as expressed in the dialogue.

Andrew Gerhardt

### Man Against Machine

Today a man trying to sell me a steam engine approached me. I told him I didn't need a steam drill because I had John Henry and his hammer. With it, he could out-drill any machine there was. The man thought I was crazy, so we made a bet. John Henry would race the engine to see which could drill the fastest into the mountain, and if he won, the man would give me his steam drill for free. I couldn't pass up this opportunity, so I went over to John Henry to make sure it was okay with him. He said he would do it, and he sounded confident that he could win. We both had no doubt that my man would beat the machine.

### Practice

**Workbook Page 117**

Choose Polly Ann, L'il Willie, or the steam engine salesperson. Write about the incident told in the model from that character's point of view. For example, if you choose Li'l Willie, you could include details that he might know from working closely with John Henry. You could also look at the dialogue in the story for clues about his thoughts and feelings. List your ideas in a graphic organizer. Remember to make your tale true to reflect John Henry's heroic character. Be sure to use generic nouns and indefinite pronouns correctly.

### Writing Checklist

**VOICE:**
☑ My reader can tell that I care about my characters.

**ORGANIZATION:**
☑ My story has an interesting beginning and clear ending.

# Prepare to Read

## What You Will Learn

**Reading**

■ Vocabulary building: *Context, dictionary skills, word study*

■ Reading strategy: *Summarize*

■ Text type: *Informational text (social studies)*

**Grammar, Usage, and Mechanics**
Habit in the past: *would; past ability: could/couldn't*

**Writing**
Write a biographical paragraph

### THE BIG QUESTION

**What does it take to beat the odds?** When a person has health problems, simple, everyday tasks can seem much more difficult to accomplish. Chronic health problems (those that last for a long time) can be even more difficult to endure. What do you think it's like to suffer from a chronic health problem? What kinds of obstacles do you think people with chronic illnesses have to overcome?

### BUILD BACKGROUND

In this section you will read an excerpt from ***Franklin Delano Roosevelt: The New Deal President***. Roosevelt was president of the United States from 1933 to 1945. The excerpt deals with Roosevelt's beating the odds—how he developed polio, became paralyzed, and yet went on to become one of the most important presidents in American history. Then you will read **"Eleanor Roosevelt,"** an excerpt from a book about women in politics. Both selections highlight Eleanor's role in Roosevelt's life and presidency.

Roosevelt was president during times of great change in the United States and in the world. What do you know about events that happened in the United States and the world during the years Roosevelt was president? Look at the timeline below and discuss it with a partner.

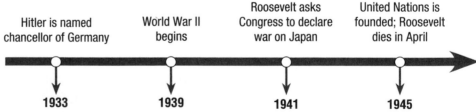

| Hitler is named chancellor of Germany | World War II begins | Roosevelt asks Congress to declare war on Japan | United Nations is founded; Roosevelt dies in April |
|---|---|---|---|
| **1933** | **1939** | **1941** | **1945** |

◀ FDR delivered his first "fireside chat" in 1933.

## VOCABULARY

### Learn Key Words

Read these sentences. Use the context to figure out the meaning of the **red** words. Use a dictionary to check your answers. Then write each word and its meaning in your notebook.

1. Eleanor Roosevelt was an **advocate** for the poor and underprivileged and fought for their rights.

2. Eleanor Roosevelt **championed** the advancement of women in politics by going to rallies and speaking out on their behalf.

3. The doctor made a surprising **diagnosis**: Franklin Roosevelt had a disease that normally affected children.

4. As a first lady, Eleanor Roosevelt **engaged** in politics and often made suggestions to her husband.

5. Franklin Roosevelt had all the **symptoms** of the flu: a headache, sore throat, and fever.

6. Franklin Roosevelt was president during some of the most difficult and **turbulent** times in history, including World War II.

**Practice**  **Workbook Page 118**

Write the sentences in your notebook. Choose a **red** word from the box above to complete each sentence. Then take turns reading the sentences aloud with a partner.

1. When his _____ became worse and his temperature rose, he went immediately to the doctor.

2. Doctors may do tests before giving their preliminary _____.

3. The period right after World War II was a very _____ one for the world.

4. Someone who speaks on behalf of others is an _____ for them and their cause.

5. They became _____ in the debate when the issue affected them personally.

6. She _____ many causes, such as helping the underprivileged.

## Learn Academic Words

Study the **red** words and their meanings. You will find these words useful when talking and writing about informational texts. Write each word and its meaning in your notebook. After you read the excerpt from *Franklin Delano Roosevelt* and "Eleanor Roosevelt" from *Madam President*, try to use these words to respond to the text.

| | | |
|---|---|---|
| **assumed** = took control, power, or a particular position | ➡ | The student **assumed** the position of team leader when no one else seemed to be in charge. |
| **contacted** = got in touch with, wrote, or telephoned someone | ➡ | She **contacted** a doctor because she was worried about her husband's illness. |
| **image** = the opinion that people have about someone or something | ➡ | The president worked hard to have a good **image** by always telling the truth and addressing the issues. |
| **intensified** = increased in strength, size, or amount | ➡ | As he got sicker, his suffering and pain **intensified**. |
| **persisted** = continued to exist or happen | ➡ | The pain **persisted** for many days. |
| **virtually** = almost completely | ➡ | The drastic change in his health seemed to happen **virtually** overnight. |

## Practice  Workbook Page 119

Write the sentences in your notebook. Choose a **red** word from the box above to complete each sentence. Then take turns reading the sentences aloud with a partner.

1. The volunteers _____ many people by telephone and by e-mail to get their support.

2. His illness _____ for the rest of his life.

3. When the discomfort _____, they knew it was something serious.

4. People may not vote for a politician with a poor public _____.

5. Many of the programs Roosevelt introduced are _____ nonexistent today, though some, like Social Security, remain.

6. She _____ the role of manager of her husband's health care.

▲ Roosevelt assumed the presidency despite having polio.

## Word Study: Long *o*

In the following readings, you'll read a number of words that have the sound you hear in the words *hope* and *shown*. Here are some different ways that the long *o* sound can be spelled:

| Long *o* | | | |
|---|---|---|---|
| **o** | **o_e** | **ow** | **oa** |
| so | spok | kno | road |
| | e | w | |

Remember that *o* can sometimes stand for other sounds, as in the words *of* and *confined*.

**Practice**  **Workbook** Page 120

Work with a partner. Your partner must close his or her book. Choose four of the words from the chart and read them aloud. Your partner will listen and dictate the words as you say them. Check your partner's spelling. Then switch roles.

| | | | | |
|---|---|---|---|---|
| chose | home | no | phone | show |
| float | known | only | post | throat |
| go | most | own | radio | those |

## READING STRATEGY　SUMMARIZE

Summarizing helps you remember the most important points in a text. To summarize, follow these steps:

- Read the text. Then reread each paragraph or section.
- Decide what the main idea is in each paragraph or section. Make notes. Leave out details such as dates and places.
- Write a few sentences that summarize the main ideas.

As you read the following articles, stop from time to time and make a note of the main ideas. Summarize the text in two or three sentences using your own words.

 **Workbook** Page 121

**Set a purpose for reading** Roosevelt faced enormous challenges physically and politically. What did it take for him to beat the odds and come out a winner?

*from*

# FRANKLIN DELANO ROOSEVELT
## The New Deal President

*Brenda Haugen*

*What are the odds that a thirty-nine-year-old just diagnosed with polio would go on to become the only president elected to more than two terms in office? It was while vacationing with his family in Canada that Roosevelt went to bed one night and awoke the next morning unable to walk.*

Eleanor contacted a country doctor to examine her husband. Dr. E. H. Bennett thought Roosevelt was just suffering from a bad cold. But when Roosevelt's health grew worse, Bennett was stumped. He couldn't explain Roosevelt's severe leg and back pain. In a couple of weeks, his suffering intensified. He couldn't move any of the muscles below his chest, though the pain there persisted. His temperature shot up to 39 degrees Celsius (102 degrees Fahrenheit). Even the weight of the bedsheets caused him terrible anguish.

A combination of pain and numbness spread throughout Roosevelt's shoulders, arms, and fingers. A specialist, Dr. William Keen, thought there might be a blood clot in Roosevelt's spine, so he prescribed massage, an order Eleanor followed faithfully.

> *Normal human body temperature is around 37 degrees Celsius (98.6 degrees Fahrenheit). When a person has a fever, it can be a signal of disease. The brain raises the body's temperature to help fight viruses and bacteria. The higher temperature makes the body a less comfortable place for the viruses to be. However, a fever higher than 39.4 C (103 F) can cause harm to a person's brain.*

---

**anguish**, suffering caused by extreme pain or worry
**blood clot**, a mass of blood that becomes almost solid
**viruses**, very small organisms that often cause infectious disease
**bacteria**, very small living organisms that sometimes cause disease

Franklin D. Roosevelt in 1918, three years before contracting polio ▶

Eleanor Roosevelt, a key figure in her husband's success in politics ▼

*Polio is caused by a virus, which affects people in different ways. Some patients feel mild symptoms such as headaches, sore throats, and fevers, which often disappear after a day. Others, like Franklin Roosevelt, suffer permanent paralysis. In the 1950s, scientist Jonas Salk developed the first vaccine to help prevent polio.*

When Roosevelt's suffering continued, another specialist, Dr. Robert Lovett, was called. Lovett gave a diagnosis that shocked everyone—infantile paralysis, also known as polio. Until Lovett arrived, no one really even thought of polio because it was considered a disease that only struck children. Roosevelt's son James remembered:

> We were all shocked. Mother's first reaction was panic. She wondered what would happen to them and their lives. Then she feared for the health of her children. However, Dr. Lovett decided that if we had not already shown symptoms of the disease and were kept in quarantine away from father, we would probably be all right.

Apparently Roosevelt had come in contact with the polio virus and, because of his recent strenuous activities, was unable to fight it off. However, Lovett believed Roosevelt would get better, though it might take months.

---

**paralysis,** loss of the ability to move or feel part of your body

**BEFORE YOU GO ON**

**1** Who did polio usually strike?

**2** What did Dr. Lovett conclude about the rest of the family?

**On Your Own**
How would you have felt if you were Roosevelt's son James?

251

Roosevelt kept up hope for at least a partial recovery, but it didn't happen. He would never walk again without leg braces and support. Eventually, he would be confined to a wheelchair.

Virtually overnight, 39-year-old Roosevelt went from being strong and athletic to paralyzed and bedridden. He could have let his disability get the better of him. He could have followed the path his mother, Sara, wanted for him. She urged him to lead a life of leisure on the family's estate in New York. Instead, Roosevelt chose to continue living a life of public service. He would serve as governor of New York and later be elected president of the United States during one of the most turbulent times in the nation's history. His determination to overcome his physical disabilities would later be reflected in his determination to overcome some of the nation's most difficult times.

Roosevelt was elected president four times and served longer than any other in history. When he first took office, the country stood in the midst of the Great Depression, the greatest economic crisis the United States had ever faced. Millions of people were unemployed. Many were homeless and starving. The situation grew worse when dust storms and drought struck the country's heartland and food supply, causing the Dust Bowl.

With his New Deal programs, Roosevelt made sweeping changes to bring immediate aid to those who were suffering. The work Roosevelt did during the Great Depression saved a desperate nation. Yet it wouldn't be the only challenge he would face. Around the same time Roosevelt was first elected president, a man named Adolf Hitler came to power in Germany. The world watched as Hitler conquered numerous countries in a quest to create a German empire across much of Europe. The September 1939 invasion of Poland marked the beginning of World War II. Though most Americans wanted to stay out of the war, Roosevelt knew it would only be a matter of time before the United States would become part of it.

▲ A rare photo of Roosevelt in his wheelchair

## ABOUT THE **AUTHOR**

**Brenda Haugen** worked in the newspaper business, becoming an award-winning journalist, before she began devoting herself to writing books. A graduate of the University of North Dakota in Grand Forks, she has written and edited many books, most of them for children. Haugen lives with her family in North Dakota.

*from*
**Madam President**

# Eleanor Roosevelt

*Catherine Thimmesh*

She put the "first" in first lady. Hold her own press conferences? She was the first. Deliver a weekly radio address? First again. Write a daily newspaper column? You guessed it—numero uno. She also delivered countless speeches, published hundreds of articles, and wrote several books. She was Eleanor Roosevelt, and in the 1930s she assumed the role of first lady as none before her had done. Eleanor was a trumpeter of just causes, a tireless advocate for the underprivileged, and undoubtedly, the most engaged and politically influential woman the United States had ever seen. Her immense popularity brought with it unheard of power for a first lady—and she wasn't shy about using it. Eleanor championed the advancement of women and made it a point to consistently bring issues of women's equality front and center—for the president and for the nation.

Her reminding apparently paid off. It was her husband, after all, who appointed the first woman to serve in a presidential cabinet. And if Mrs. R. (as she was affectionately called) ever wearied of accumulating a string of "firsts," she didn't show it. After a twelve-year stint as first lady, she was appointed the U.S. delegate, or representative, to the newly formed United Nations—an official government post. Another first.

## ABOUT THE **AUTHOR**

**Catherine Thimmesh** graduated from the University of Minnesota with a degree in art history. Besides *Madam President*, her books include *Team Moon* and *Girls Think of Everything*. When she's not writing, Thimmesh enjoys reading, playing with her two young children, and taking flying trapeze lessons every week at circus school.

## BEFORE YOU GO ON

**1** What did Roosevelt's mother, Sara, want him to do once they learned he had polio?

**2** What were some of Eleanor Roosevelt's "firsts"?

**On Your Own**
Which of Eleanor's accomplishments impresses you the most?

253

## COMPREHENSION

Workbook
Page 122

### Right There

1. At what point in Roosevelt's life was he stricken with polio?

2. After twelve years of being first lady, what government post was Eleanor Roosevelt appointed to?

### Think and Search

3. What was going on in the United States when Roosevelt first took office and what did Roosevelt do about it? Do you think he was successful? Why or why not?

4. How was Eleanor Roosevelt unlike any first lady before her?

### Author and You

5. Why do you think the author devoted a good part of her book *Franklin Delano Roosevelt* to the way Roosevelt dealt with his illness?

6. According to both authors, why was Eleanor Roosevelt an exceptional wife and first lady?

### On Your Own

7. How would you advise a close friend or family member who suddenly lost the use of his or her legs?

8. What, in your opinion, makes a president remarkable?

## IN YOUR OWN WORDS

With a partner, skim the readings and list events in Roosevelt's life in the order that they happened. Begin with his being stricken and then diagnosed with polio. Next, list offices Roosevelt held and situations he had to deal with as president. Include Eleanor Roosevelt and her role and positions. Use the list to summarize what you learned about the Roosevelts in the two readings. Be sure to include ages, time frames, and other details. Create some visuals to go with your summary. Take turns presenting your summary to the class.

 *Speaking* TIP

As you present your summary to the class, emphasize transition clauses and phrases.

## DISCUSSION

Discuss in pairs or small groups.

1. How would you rate Franklin D. Roosevelt as president? Do you consider him remarkable? Explain.

2. How would you rate Eleanor as first lady? Do you consider her remarkable? Explain.

3. Eleanor championed many causes. How important do you think it is to have individuals in high positions behind a cause? How much do you think Eleanor helped the advancement of women and women's equality? Explain.

**Q What does it take to beat the odds?** The reading suggests Roosevelt beat the odds. Do you think this is true? Use examples to explain your opinion. Can you think of other people today who have beat the odds?

**Listening TIP**

Listen carefully to the points others make. You may be able to use some of them to strengthen your own position.

## READ FOR FLUENCY

When we read aloud to communicate meaning, we group words into phrases, pause or slow down to make important points, and emphasize important words. Pause for a short time when you reach a comma and for a longer time when you reach a period. Pay attention to rising and falling intonation at the end of sentences.

Work with a partner. Choose a paragraph from the reading. Discuss which words seem important for communicating meaning. Practice pronouncing difficult words. Take turns reading the paragraph aloud and give each other feedback.

## EXTENSION  Workbook Page 122

The informational texts you read focused only on certain times and aspects of the Roosevelts' lives. Choose a part of their lives that you'd like to find out more about. For example, what accomplishments did Roosevelt make as governor of New York? How did Roosevelt and Eleanor meet and how did they go on to get married, despite his mother's view that they were too young? Why was a photograph of Roosevelt in a wheelchair rare? What books did Eleanor write? Read more from the book *Franklin Delano Roosevelt* by Brenda Haugen or find other books or sources on the Internet. Write a short report and share it with the class.

▲ Franklin Roosevelt with his wife, Eleanor, and his mother

# Grammar and Writing

## GRAMMAR, USAGE, AND MECHANICS

### Habit in the Past: *Would*; Past Ability: *Could/Couldn't*

Habit describes what a person does on a regular basis. Use *would* to express habit in the past. When you use *would* in this way, it has the same meaning as *used to*.

> When the doctors thought Roosevelt had a blood clot, Eleanor **would** massage his back every day.

Ability describes what a person can or can't do. Use *could* or *couldn't* to express past ability or inability.

> Before his illness, Roosevelt **could** walk.
> He **couldn't** move any of the muscles below his chest.

**Practice**  **Workbook** Page 123

In small groups, answer the questions below about situations from the selections. Use *would* and *could/couldn't* in your answers. Write the answers in your notebook.

1.  What would Eleanor do when a list of appointments would come out with no women's names on it?

2.  What could Roosevelt foresee about the United States' involvement in World War II?

3.  When Roosevelt was first stricken with polio, what couldn't the family—who showed no symptoms themselves—do with their father?

4.  Why couldn't the doctors make the diagnosis of polio right away?

## WRITING A NARRATIVE PARAGRAPH

### Write a Biographical Paragraph

To help you write a narrative essay at the end of this unit, you will learn how to write a biographical paragraph. The model paragraph below is about Eleanor Roosevelt.

   Notice how the writer develops Eleanor's character by telling of her lonely, sad childhood and how she went on to beat the odds. She used a word web to organize her ideas. What character traits of Eleanor Roosevelt does the writer develop? How does she do this? Notice the elements of a story in the paragraph: point of view, character development, and conflict and resolution.

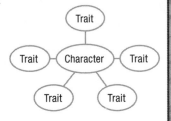

*Karimah McCarthy*

*Eleanor Roosevelt*

   Eleanor Roosevelt was a very strong woman who overcame many obstacles in her life. When she was young, Eleanor's mother used to make her feel as if she was nothing   a disappointment to the family. By the time she was ten, Eleanor had been through some pretty tough times. She had lost her mother, father, and brother. At this point, some may have thought Eleanor would never get her life together. But this was not the case, because Eleanor went on to marry the twenty-sixth president of the United States, Franklin D. Roosevelt. Unlike her own mother, Eleanor was a very supportive wife and loving parent. Even though Eleanor Roosevelt had a rough childhood, she did not show it.

**Practice**

Write a biographical paragraph about an individual that you consider to have beaten the odds. Use a word web to organize your ideas. Be sure to use *would* to express habit in the past, and *could* or *couldn't* to tell about past abilities or inabilities.

**VOICE:**
☑ My strong feelings about this individual are evident.

**ORGANIZATION:**
☑ I organized events in my narrative in a logical way.

# Link the Readings

## Critical Thinking

Look back at the readings in this unit. Think about what they have in common. They all tell about beating the odds. Yet they do not all have the same purpose. The purpose of one reading might be to inform, while the purpose of another might be to entertain or persuade. In addition, the content of each reading relates to beating the odds differently. Now copy the chart below into your notebook and complete it.

| Title of Reading | Purpose | Big Question Link |
|---|---|---|
| "The Great Circle" From *Touching Spirit Bear* | *to inform* | |
| "Take a Chance" "A Survival Mini-Manual" | | |
| "John Henry" (tall tale) "John Henry" (song) | *to entertain* | |
| From *Franklin Delano Roosevelt* "Eleanor Roosevelt" | | *It tells how he beat the odds.* |

## Discussion

Discuss in pairs or small groups.

- According to the readings, what are some ways to beat the odds? How do the readings show what it means to beat the odds?

- **What does it take to beat the odds?** Which reading broadened your understanding of beating the odds? Would you like to read more from the book or larger work it's from? Why?

## Fluency Check

Work with a partner. Choose a paragraph from one of the readings. Take turns reading it for one minute. Count the total number of words you read. Practice saying the words you had trouble reading. Take turns reading the paragraph three more times. Did you read more words each time? Copy the chart below into your notebook and record your speeds.

| | 1st Speed | 2nd Speed | 3rd Speed | 4th Speed |
|---|---|---|---|---|
| Words Per Minute | | | | |

# Projects

Work in pairs or small groups. Choose one of these projects.

**1** Put on a TV show. The guests should role-play characters from this unit using a different point of view. For example, tell Cole's story from his mother's point of view, Eleanor Roosevelt's story from a grandchild's point of view, etc.

**2** Stoutenburg's *American Tall Tales* also tells the stories of these folk heroes: Paul Bunyan, Pecos Bill, Stormalong, Mike Fink, Davy Crockett, Johnny Appleseed, and Joe Margarac. Get the book from the library or do research on the Internet. Then choose a folk hero and write your own tale or song about him or her.

**3** Choose one of these historical figures who made a difference: Abraham Lincoln, Anne Hutchinson, Bridget "Biddy" Mason, Crazy Horse, and Sam Houston. Write questions and answers for an interview with the individual. Present your interviews to the class.

# Further Reading

To find out more about the theme of this unit, choose from these reading suggestions.

**Saving Private Ryan,** Max Allan Collins
In this Penguin Reader® adaptation, Captain John Miller and his soldiers are on a mission to find a missing paratrooper whose family has already lost three sons in World War II.

**Within Reach: My Everest Story,** Mark Pfetzer and Jack Galvin
In 1996, sixteen-year-old Mark Pfetzer became Mount Everest's youngest climber. His moment-by-moment narrative takes us up the mountain, across the ice, and into the "Death Zone."

**The Wright Brothers: How They Invented the Airplane,**
Russell Freedman
Through photos and first-person accounts, Freedman relates the events that led to an invention that changed the world.

# Put It All Together

### Interview

You and a partner will role-play an interview for the class. One of you will play a TV or newspaper reporter; the other will play a person who survived a disaster.

**1** **THINK ABOUT IT** Reporters often talk to people who survive disasters or accomplish other things against the odds. In their interviews, reporters ask questions to find out how these individuals beat the odds. With a partner, prepare to role-play your own interview. Think about the disasters you read about in "A Survival Mini-Manual." Choose one of these disasters or another one that you know about, such as a tsunami, a tornado, or an earthquake.

▲ Making eye contact is important in an interview.

**2** **GATHER AND ORGANIZE INFORMATION** With your partner, decide who will be the reporter (interviewer) and who will be the survivor of the disaster. Start a list of questions and answers for your interview.

**Research** Use the library or Internet to search for information about the disaster you chose. Look for articles about survivors. Choose one situation and survivor. Take notes about what happened to that person and how he or she beat the odds and survived.

**Order Your Notes** Based on your research, complete your list of questions and answers. Write them on separate note cards and then arrange them in a logical order for your interview. Decide how you will begin and end your interview.

**Use Visuals** Find pictures of the actual disaster or a similar one. Decide how to use these with your interview. Make or find some simple props and costumes to help illustrate your roles during the interview.

**3** **PRACTICE AND PRESENT** Use your note cards to practice your interview. Try to speak naturally, using the cards as a memory aid rather than reading them. If new questions arise from your conversation, add them to your list. Omit any questions that seem unimportant or not interesting. Practice until your interview flows comfortably. Use appropriate gestures and facial expressions, along with tone of voice, and remember to show your visuals.

**Deliver Your Interview** Be convincing and stay in character as a reporter and survivor. Maintain good eye contact with each other. Emphasize key ideas by asking for a question to be repeated or by repeating an answer.

**4** **EVALUATE THE PRESENTATION** You can improve your skills as a speaker and a listener by evaluating each presentation you give and hear. Use this checklist to help you judge your interview and the interviews of your classmates.

- ☑ Did the interviewer ask interesting questions? Did the survivor give appropriate answers?
- ☑ Were the questions asked in a logical order?
- ☑ Were both speakers easy to hear and understand?
- ☑ Did you learn how the person being interviewed beat the odds?
- ☑ What suggestions do you have for improving the interview?

*Speaking* TIPS

Remember to introduce yourself at the beginning of the interview and to say thank you at the end.

Sit or stand so that your partner and the audience can see your face. Speak loudly enough for everyone to hear you.

*Listening* TIPS

When you are interviewing someone, listen carefully to his or her answers and ask appropriate follow-up questions, even if they're not on your list.

When you are being interviewed, ask to have a question repeated or rephrased if you don't understand it.

# WRITING WORKSHOP

## Narrative Essay

In this workshop, you will write a narrative essay. In a narrative essay, events are presented as a story. Narratives can be fiction, telling about characters and events created from imagination. They can also be nonfiction, telling about real people and events. Elements of a strong narrative essay include a story starter that captures readers' interest. The writer describes the setting of events, and the physical and character traits of the individuals involved. Events usually are told in sequence and focus on conflicts or problems that have to be overcome. Another important element of a narrative essay is whether the story is told from the first-person or third-person point of view.

Your assignment for this workshop is to write a narrative essay about an individual who met a challenge and beat the odds.

**1 PREWRITE** Brainstorm a list of individuals you would like to write about. For example, your list might include an individual from this unit, a folktale character, someone interviewed in the Listening and Speaking Workshop, or others. If you choose an individual or folktale hero you read about, be sure to retell that individual's story in your own words.

**List and Organize Ideas and Details** Use a story chart to organize ideas for your narrative essay. A student named Nola decided to write about the tall-tale hero Stormalong. Here is her story chart:

| Narrator | Characters | Setting | Beginning | Middle | End |
|----------|-----------|---------|-----------|--------|-----|
| third person | Stormalong Kraken Other Sailors | the sea | beats the Kraken | wins the race | sails the sky |

**2 DRAFT** Use the model on page 265 and your story chart to help you write a first draft. Remember to begin with a lively story starter and to tell events in chronological order.

**3** **REVISE** Read over your draft. As you do so, ask yourself the questions in the writing checklist. Use the questions to help you revise your narrative essay.

## SIX TRAITS OF WRITING CHECKLIST

☑ **IDEAS:** Do I include a strong story starter?

☑ **ORGANIZATION:** Does my story have a beginning, middle, and end?

☑ **VOICE:** Does my writing show energy and emotion?

☑ **WORD CHOICE:** Do I use descriptive words to show physical and character traits?

☑ **SENTENCE FLUENCY:** Do I use transitional phrases effectively to help readers follow my story?

☑ **CONVENTIONS:** Does my writing follow the rules of grammar, usage, and mechanics?

Here are the changes Nola plans to make when she revises her first draft:

The Story of Stormalong

*Do you know what ? It's , ugly*
A Kraken is a huge sea monster, with many long legs like an

*nasty*                          *would be*
octopus and claws like a crab. Most people were terrified to fight a

*tallest, biggest,*
Kraken—but not Stormalong, the bravest sailor ever to sail the seas.

As a teenager, he was hired to be a cabin boy on a boat headed

for China. Stormalong's mother didn't want him to become a sailor

*At last,*
because his father had died at sea. Stormy overcame her worry.

The voyage seemed peaceful until suddenly the boat, the Silver Maid,

*grabbed*
lurched to a stop. A Kraken had it in its arms! Young Stormy

263

volunteered to fight the Kraken so the ship could keep sailing. he

jumped overboard, wrestled the monster, and tied all its legs in a knot.

    Stormy though was too big to keep working on such small

schooners. What did he do? *He didn't give up!* He wanted to stay on the sea, so he built

his own ship. *Then,* He decided to become a whaler. The whales seemed just

about the right size for him! *Finally,* He had found his perfect job—he loved

whaling and was so good at it.

    Yet poor Stormy's troubles still weren't over because bigger, faster

st*a*eemships posed new threats to him. Now, Stormy wanted to be

the <u>best</u> seaman and to have the <u>best</u> ship in the whole world So

determined was he to out-sail one of the st*a*eemships, the *Liverpool*

*Packet*, that he raced the rival ship and won—but wrecked his own

ship and died in the process.

    Stormalong, the *tallest, biggest,* bravest sailor ever to sail the seas, was willing to

persevere until the last moment. And now, he continues to live on in

the imagination and folktales of Americans. Stormalong still sails the

sky in his great ship, hunting sky whales as he always dreamed.

## 4 EDIT AND PROOFREAD

Copy your revised draft onto a clean sheet of paper. Read it again. Correct
any errors in grammar, word usage, mechanics, and spelling. Here are the
additional changes Nola plans to make when she prepares her final draft.

Nola Smith

The Story of Stormalong

Do you know what a Kraken is? It's a huge, ugly sea monster, with many long legs like an octopus and nasty claws like a crab. Most people would be terrified to fight a Kraken—but not Stormalong, the tallest, biggest, bravest sailor ever to sail the seas.

Stormalong's mother didn't want him to become a sailor because his father had died at sea. At last, Stormy overcame her worry. As a teenager, he was hired to be a cabin boy on a boat headed for China. The voyage seemed peaceful until suddenly the boat, the Silver Maid, lurched to a stop. A Kraken had grabbed it in its arms! Young Stormy volunteered to fight the Kraken so the ship could keep sailing. he jumped overboard, wrestled the monster, and tied all its legs in a knot.

Stormy, though, was too big to keep working on such small schooners. What did he do? He didn't give up! He wanted to stay on the sea, so he built his own ship. Then, he decided to become a whaler. The whales seemed just about the right size for him! Finally, he had found his perfect job—he loved whaling and was so good at it.

Yet poor Stormy's troubles still weren't over because bigger, faster steamships posed new threats to him. Now, Stormy wanted to be the best seaman and to have the best ship in the whole world. So determined was he to out-sail one of the steamships, the *Liverpool Packet*, that he raced the rival ship and won—but wrecked his own ship and died in the process.

Stormalong, the tallest, biggest, bravest sailor ever to sail the seas, was willing to persevere until the last moment. And now, he continues to live on in the imagination and folktales of Americans. Stormalong still sails the sky in his great ship, hunting sky whales as he always dreamed.

**5** **PUBLISH** Prepare your final draft. Share your narrative essay with your teacher and classmates.

Workbook
Page 126

# Beating the Odds

*W*hat are the chances that you'll win the lottery or live to be 100? People love to guess their odds of winning, especially when it comes to money and sports. Sometimes people buy lottery tickets and hope to pick the lucky numbers. Other times they take more serious chances that involve physical or financial risks. Many American artists have explored the various ways that humans try to beat the odds.

### Carmen Lomas Garza, *Lotería-Tabla Llena* (1972)

Friends and family, both young and old, sit around a table outdoors in Carmen Lomas Garza's print. This festive night scene is framed by trees, a low stone wall, and strings of lights with decorative tissue-paper cutouts called *papel picado*. The table is filled with refreshments, toys, and pieces to play *Lotería*, a Mexican game of chance similar to Bingo. Each player has a game board, or *tabla*, that has rows of pictures called *monitos* instead of numbers and letters. The older man on the left is the announcer. He randomly chooses a picture card and calls out clues in the form of poems or riddles. The players try to guess the picture. They talk among themselves while matching the picture on their board and then cover it with a chip. The game is in full swing,

▲ Carmen Lomas Garza, *Lotería-Tabla Llena*, 1972, etching and aquatint, 16¾ × 21 in., Smithsonian American Art Museum

but some of the children are getting sleepy. It's hard to tell who will be the first to fill his or her board and win!

Garza grew up within a close-knit Mexican-American community in south Texas. Her attitudes about that community influenced her artwork. She felt that by focusing on joyful memories of her everyday life, her art could help eliminate the racism she experienced as a child. In choosing to show a scene like playing *Lotería*, Garza hoped others could beat the odds.

◀ Eric Hilton, *Storm*, 1996, crystal on granite, 9½ x 8 x 8 in., Smithsonian American Art Museum

## Eric Hilton, *Storm* (1996)

In *Storm*, Eric Hilton created a small sculpture of cut crystal to capture a disturbance. It could be the sea getting stirred up by strong winds or perhaps something whirling in outer space. Sometimes each of us feels trapped in our small personal storms, like the bubble in the glass. The world can seem cold and unyielding. We can feel boxed in, like the sharp rectangular shape of Hilton's piece.

But there's also something beautiful about the disturbance. If the crystal were completely clear, it would have no drama, no story to tell.

In the end, each of us battles the odds to create our own life stories. Sometimes these battles make us stronger and more interesting people.

## Apply What You Learned

**1** In what way does each of these artworks reflect a different aspect of beating the odds?

**2** Which of these two artworks do you feel is more universal in its appeal to all people, as opposed to just Americans? Explain your answer.

**Q Big Question**
Which of these artworks do you think best captures the idea of beating the odds? Explain your answer.

**Workbook**
Pages 127–128

THE BIG
Q
QUESTION

# How do conflicts affect us?

**T**his unit is about conflicts. How do conflicts come about and how are they resolved? Reading about different conflicts and their outcomes can help us with conflicts in our own lives.

**READING 1: Play Excerpt**

■ From *Romeo and Juliet* by William Shakespeare, adapted by Diana Stewart

**READING 2: Social Studies Article**

■ "Furious Feuds: Enemies by Association" by Alfred Meyer

**READING 3: Novel Excerpt**

■ From *Romiette and Julio* by Sharon M. Draper

**READING 4: Social Studies Article**

■ From *Conflict Resolution: The Win-Win Situation* by Carolyn Casey

## Listening and Speaking

At the end of this unit, you will choose a topic and conduct a **TV talk show**.

## Writing

At the end of this unit, you will write an **expository essay**. Expository writing in this unit includes comparing and contrasting, evaluating, presenting a problem and solution, and answering the 5W questions (*Who? Where? When? What? Why?*) in a news article format.

### QuickWrite
Write about a conflict you are familiar with.

Visit *LongmanKeystone.com*

# Prepare to Read

## What You Will Learn

**Reading**

- Vocabulary building: *Literary terms, word study*

- Reading strategy: *Monitor comprehension*

- Text type: *Literature (play excerpt)*

**Grammar, Usage, and Mechanics**
Transforming nouns into adjectives

**Writing**
Write a news article

### THE BIG QUESTION

**How do conflicts affect us?** Conflict affects everyone differently. Some people avoid conflict in their lives because it makes them feel uncomfortable; some allow conflict in their lives because it doesn't bother them; and some actually *look* for conflict. Think of a time when you had a conflict with a friend or a family member. How did it make you feel?

### BUILD BACKGROUND

You're going to read scenes from the first two acts of an adaptation of the play **Romeo and Juliet** by William Shakespeare, an English playwright who lived from 1564 to 1616. To help you understand the English spoken then, it is useful to know the sequence of events in these scenes.

- Romeo and Juliet belong to two rival families: the Capulets (Juliet) and the Montagues (Romeo).
- The Prince of Verona breaks up a fight started by servants of the Capulets and the Montagues.
- Benvolio convinces Romeo to go to a costume party at the Capulets to help him stop thinking about his girlfriend, Rosaline.
- Before the party, Paris, a nobleman and count, asks for Juliet's hand in marriage.
- Lady Capulet then asks her daughter Juliet to consider Paris's offer.
- Romeo and Juliet meet at the party and fall in love.
- Juliet reveals to her nurse that her only love is a Montague.
- Romeo and Juliet vow to marry.

▲ Romeo thinks the sleeping Juliet is dead.

270

### Learn Literary Words

**Foreshadowing** is the use of clues or symbols to show what will happen in the future. Shakespeare does not keep the end of his play a secret. In a prologue at the beginning of the play, a chorus—a group of actors who help tell the story—reveals that Romeo and Juliet will take their own lives.

**Literary Words**

foreshadowing
stage directions

This prologue is not an example of foreshadowing, because it doesn't give *clues* that the main characters will die, it *says* they will. However, throughout the rest of the play, there are many clues that foreshadow their deaths. In this scene, Juliet says that if she finds out Romeo is already married, she will live the rest of her life unmarried.

> "If he be married. / My grave is like to be my wedding bed"

Without knowing it, Juliet is foreshadowing her future, because she does actually die in her wedding bed.

**Stage directions** are notes included in a play about the staging and the performance (appearances, personalities, and actions of the characters). The directions appear in italics within brackets and are read, not spoken. How do these stage directions help you understand the story?

> [*Romeo continues to watch Juliet from across the room. Their eyes meet. Both of them are struck with love. Romeo makes his way to her side. Gladly she goes with him to dance in a quiet corner.*]

**Practice**  **Workbook Page 129**

With a partner, read how Juliet learns what family Romeo comes from. Discuss the foreshadowing and stage directions. What will happen next?

> [*The end of the party has arrived. Lord Capulet wishes his guests good night. As they leave, Juliet calls her nurse to her side and points out Romeo.*]
> **Juliet**: Come here, nurse. Who is yond gentleman?
> **Nurse**: His name is Romeo, and a Montague, the only son of your great enemy.

## Learn Academic Words

Study the **red** words and their meanings. You will find these words useful when talking and writing about literature. Write each word and its meaning in your notebook. After you read the scenes from *Romeo and Juliet,* try to use these words to respond to the text.

| | |
|---|---|
| **adaptation** = something that is changed to be used in a new or different way | The **adaptation** of this play is shorter and simpler than the original Shakespeare play. |
| **drama** = a play that is serious | The **drama** reaches a climax when Romeo thinks Juliet is dead and takes his own life. |
| **identities** = the qualities that make people recognizable | Since it was a masquerade party, Benvolio and Romeo wore masks to hide their true **identities**. |
| **outcome** = final result | The play has a tragic **outcome**. In the end, the two main characters die. |
| **presumption** = something that you think must be true | Romeo saw Juliet lying there. He didn't know for sure, but his **presumption** was that she was dead. |

## Practice

**Workbook**
**Page 130**

Write the sentences in your notebook. Choose a **red** word from the box above to complete each sentence. Then take turns reading the sentences aloud with a partner.

1. Those men are spies for the government. They can't tell anyone their true _____.

2. My school performed an _____ of the play. The original version was too long.

3. I know he usually wins at chess, but don't make a _____ that you can't beat him. You're a good player, too.

4. If you want to laugh, watch a funny movie. If you want to cry, watch a _____.

5. Both soccer teams are great, so no one knows what the _____ of the game will be.

▲ A scene from the movie adaptation of Shakespeare's *Romeo and Juliet*

## Word Study: Antonyms

Recognizing antonyms—words that are opposite in meaning—will help you understand feelings and situations in the play. Read the examples:

| Word | Antonym | Word | Antonym |
|------|---------|------|---------|
| begins | ends | long | short |
| enter | exit | sad | happy |
| foe | friend | smooth | rough |
| good morning | good night | young | old |

**Practice**

Work with a partner. Read the words in the first column of the chart below. Find the antonym for each word in the second column. Take turns using the antonym pairs in a sentence. Write the sentences in your notebook.

| | |
|---|---|
| brave | forget |
| invited | peaceful |
| remember | cowardly |
| slow | quick |
| start | satisfied |
| unsatisfied | stop |
| violent | uninvited |

## READING STRATEGY   MONITOR COMPREHENSION

As you read, look for the following features of a play and use them to help you monitor comprehension.

- The descriptions of each scene: Ask yourself, Who is in the scene? Where does it take place? When is it happening? What's happening? Why?

- The character's name, what the character says, and stage directions: To understand the English language that the characters use, think about the meaning of the words you know and what you already know about the plot.

- The end of a scene: Stop and paraphrase what happened in the scene. Make predictions about what you think will happen next.

READING 1

LITERATURE

PLAY

**Set a purpose for reading** What is the conflict that affects Romeo and Juliet? Look for dialogue that shows they are aware of the conflict and are nervous about it.

# *from* Romeo and Juliet

***William Shakespeare***

***Adapted by Diana Stewart***

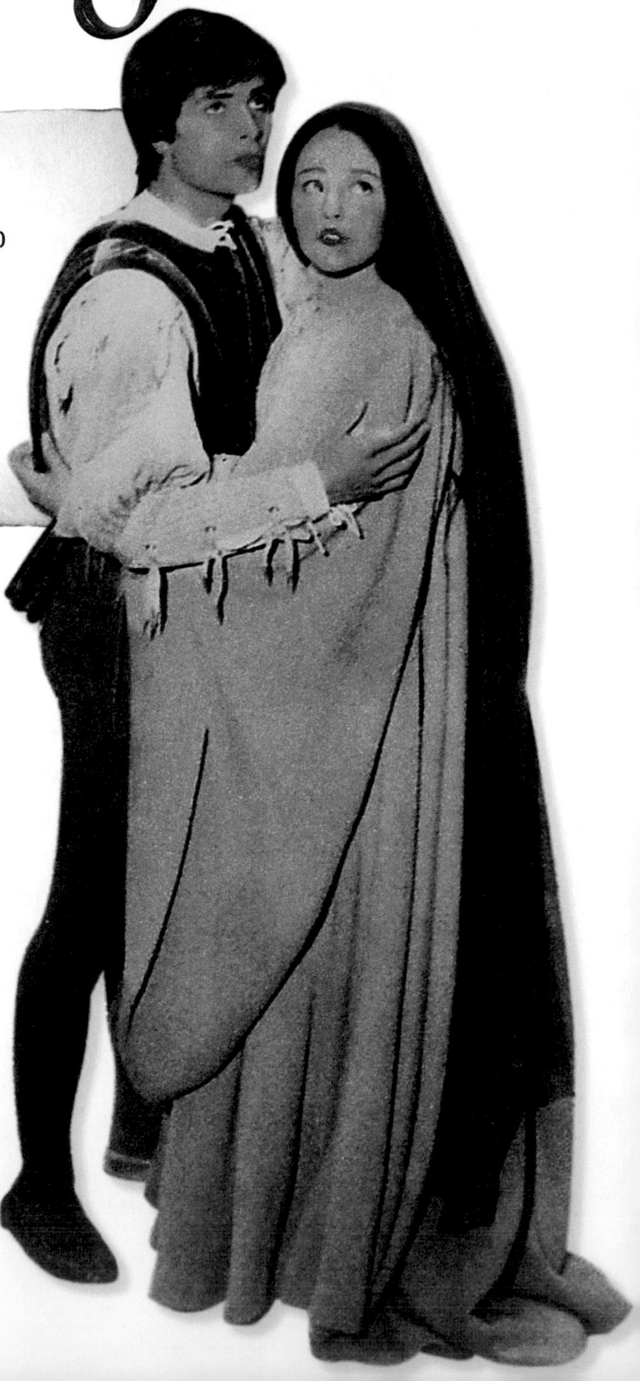

## Cast of Characters

Romeo, son of Montague
Juliet, daughter of Capulet
Nurse to Juliet
Lord Capulet
Lady Capulet
Tybalt, nephew to Lady Capulet
Benvolio, a cousin of Romeo
Paris, a suitor of Juliet
The Prince of Verona
Servants to Capulets
Servants to Montagues
Citizens of Verona

## ACT I

### *Scene 1*

*The scene is a public road in Verona, Italy, in the sixteenth century. Servants from the House of Capulet and the House of Montague have met on the street and started a fight. Benvolio, a cousin of Romeo Montague, enters. He draws his sword to stop the fighting.*

BENVOLIO: Stop, fools! Put up your swords. You don't know what you are doing!

[*Tybalt enters and draws his sword. He is a cousin of Juliet Capulet.*]

TYBALT: Turn, Benvolio; look upon thy death.

BENVOLIO: I only keep the peace. Put up thy sword.

---

**draws his sword**, takes out his weapon

**TYBALT:**   What, sword drawn and talk of peace? I hate the word peace as I hate hell, all Montagues, and thee. Fight, coward!

[*Benvolio has no choice but to fight Tybalt. A crowd gathers, including Lord and Lady Capulet and Lord and Lady Montague. As the fighting gets more violent, the Prince of Verona enters with his followers. He is furious with both the noble families.*]

**PRINCE:**   Stop, you enemies to peace!
On pain of torture, throw your weapons to the ground
And hear the sentence of your Prince.
Three fights by the Capulets and Montagues
Have broken the quiet of our streets.
If ever you disturb our streets again,
Your lives shall pay.
You, Capulet, shall go along with me;
And Montague, come to me this afternoon.
On pain of death, all men depart.

[*They all exit but Benvolio. He greets Romeo, Lord Montague's son, as he enters.*]

**BENVOLIO:**   Good morrow, cousin.

**ROMEO:**   Is the day so young?

**BENVOLIO:**   It is just nine.

**ROMEO:**   Ay me! Sad hours seem long.

**BENVOLIO:**   What sadness makes Romeo's hours long? In love?

**ROMEO:**   Out—

**BENVOLIO:**   Of love?

**ROMEO:**   Out of her favor where I am in love.

**BENVOLIO:**   Tell me, who is it that you love?

**ROMEO:**   Cousin, I do love a woman. But she hath sworn to love no man.

**BENVOLIO:**   Be ruled by me; learn to forget her.

**ROMEO:**   O, teach me how I should forget to think!

**BENVOLIO:**   Forget by letting thine eyes examine other beauties.

**ROMEO:**   He that is struck with love cannot forget the treasure of his heart. Farewell. Thou canst not teach me to forget.

[*They exit.*]

---

**furious,** extremely angry
**canst not,** cannot

✔ **LITERARY CHECK**
*How do the stage directions help you understand what's happening, and who's talking to who?*

**BEFORE YOU GO ON**

**1** Which two characters wanted the fighting to stop?

**2** Why is Romeo sad?

💡**On Your Own**
Did anyone ever try to help you forget something that made you sad? Did it help?

## Scene 2

*A street in Verona. Lord Capulet enters with Count Paris—a young nobleman of Verona who wants to marry Lord Capulet's daughter Juliet.*

**PARIS:**   But now, my lord, what say you? Will you give me the fair Juliet for my wife?

**CAPULET:**   My child hath not seen the end of fourteen years;
Let two more summers pass
Before we think her ripe to be a bride.
Woo her, gentle Paris, win her heart.
This night I hold a feast.
I have invited many a guest,
And you among them. Come, go with me.

*[Capulet calls his servant over and gives him a paper with the names of the guests to be invited to the party that evening.]*

**CAPULET:**   Go, sirrah, through fair Verona;
Find those persons whose names are written there.

*[Capulet exits with Paris. The servant looks at the paper, but he cannot read. He sees Benvolio and Romeo entering and goes to them for help. He gives Romeo the list of names and asks him to read it aloud.]*

**ROMEO:**   *[After having read the list]* A fair assembly. Where should these guests come?

**SERVANT:**   To our house.

**ROMEO:**   Whose house?

**SERVANT:**   My master's. My master is the great rich Capulet; and if you be not of the house of Montague, I pray come and drink a cup of wine tonight.

*[As the servant leaves, Benvolio has an idea. He and Romeo will go to the Capulet party. Then Romeo can compare his love with all the other beautiful girls. This should cure his lovesickness.]*

**BENVOLIO:**   *[to Romeo]* At this same feast of Capulet's
Comes the fair Rosaline whom thou so loves;
Go tonight, and compare her face with some that I shall show.

**ROMEO:**   I'll go along, no such sight to be shown,
But to rejoice in the beauty of mine own.

*[They exit.]*

---

**sirrah**, slang name for a servant

▲ Nurse watches as Lady Capulet asks Juliet to consider marrying Paris.

*Scene 3*

*The setting is a room in the Capulet house. Juliet's mother is talking to the old nurse who has raised Juliet from a baby.*

LADY CAPULET:   Nurse, where is my daughter? Call her forth to me.

NURSE:   What, Juliet!

JULIET:   [*entering*] How now? Who calls?

NURSE:   Your mother.

JULIET:   Madam, I am here. What is your wish?

LADY CAPULET:   Tell me, daughter Juliet, what think you of marriage?

JULIET:   It is an honor that I dream not of.

LADY CAPULET:   Well, think of marriage now. The brave Paris seeks you for his love. What say you? Can you love the gentleman?

[*They are interrupted by a servingman.*]

SERVANT:   Madam, the guests are come, supper served up. I beg you follow straight.

LADY CAPULET:   We follow thee. Juliet, the Count Paris awaits you.

[*They exit.*]

**BEFORE YOU GO ON**

**1** Why does Capulet's servant talk to Romeo and Benvolio?

**2** What does Lady Capulet talk to Juliet about?

**On Your Own**
How would you feel if you were Juliet?

277

*Scene 4*

*The scene is a hall in Capulet's house. Present are Lord and Lady Capulet, Juliet, Tybalt, and the guests dressed in costumes and masks. Music begins and the company dances. Romeo and Benvolio are there in disguise. Romeo is looking at the girls, trying to find his beloved Rosaline, when he sees Juliet. All thought of Rosaline goes out of his head.*

**ROMEO:**    [*to a servant*] What lady is that which doth grace the hand of yonder knight?

**SERVANT:**    I know not, sir.

**ROMEO:**    O, she teaches the torches to burn bright!
Did my heart love till now?
For I never saw true beauty till this night.

[*Tybalt is standing near with Lord Capulet. He recognizes Romeo's voice.*]

**TYBALT:**    This voice belongs to a Montague.
[*to a servant*] Get me my sword, boy.
Now, by the honor of my kin,
To strike him dead I hold it not a sin.

**CAPULET:**    Why, how now, cousin? Why do you storm so?

**TYBALT:**    Uncle, this is a Montague, our foe.

**CAPULET:**    Young Romeo is it?

**TYBALT:**    'Tis he, that villain Romeo.

**CAPULET:**    Be merry, gentle cousin, let him alone.
And, to say truth, Verona brags of him
To be a good and well-mannered youth.
Therefore be patient; take no notice of him.

**TYBALT:**    I'll not endure him!

**CAPULET:**    He shall be endured! Am I the master here, or you? Go to! Go to! You are too quick to anger.

[*Tybalt is furious that Romeo has come to the party uninvited. Too angry to stay and enjoy the dance, he leaves. Romeo continues to watch Juliet from across the room. Their eyes meet. Both of them are struck with love. Romeo makes his way to her side. Gladly she goes with him to dance in a quiet corner.*]

---

**doth grace the hand of**, is with; accompanies
**endure**, put up with

**ROMEO:** [*touching Juliet's hand*]
If I profane with my unworthy hand
This holy shrine, the fine is this:
My lips will ready stand
To smooth that rough touch with a tender kiss.

**JULIET:** Good pilgrim, you do blame your hand too much,
Which well-mannered devotion shows in this,
For saints have hands that pilgrims' hands do touch,
And palm to palm is the pilgrim's kiss.

**ROMEO:** O, then, dear saint, let lips do what hands do!
[*They kiss.*]

**NURSE:** Madam, your mother wants a word with you.

**ROMEO:** [*to the nurse after Juliet has gone*] Who is her mother?

**NURSE:** Why, sir, her mother is the lady of the house.

**ROMEO:** Is she a Capulet? Oh dear heart!

▲ Romeo touches Juliet's hand.

[*The end of the party has arrived. Lord Capulet wishes his guests good night. As they leave, Juliet calls her nurse to her side and points out Romeo.*]

**JULIET:** Come here, nurse. Who is yond gentleman?

**NURSE:** His name is Romeo, and a Montague, the only son of your great enemy.

**JULIET:** My only love! Monstrous love it is to me
That I must love an enemy.

**NURSE:** What is this? What is this?

**JULIET:** A rhyme I learnt from one I danced with.

**NURSE:** Come, let's away; the strangers all are gone.

[*They exit.*]

---

**profane**, treat something holy in a disrespectful way
**pilgrim**, someone who travels a long way to a holy place
**yond**, at a distance but in sight

**BEFORE YOU GO ON**

**1** Why does Tybalt hate Romeo, even though he doesn't know him?

**2** What do Romeo and Juliet find out about each other?

**On Your Own**
What makes this story a good drama?

# ACT II

*Scene 1*

*The scene is the orchard at the back of Capulet's house. Romeo has climbed the orchard wall in the hope of getting one more look at his beloved Juliet. His hope is rewarded when Juliet appears at the window to her room.*

**ROMEO:**   But soft! What light through yonder window breaks?
It is the East, and Juliet is the sun!
It is my lady! Oh, it is my love!
Oh, that she knew she were!
See how she leans her cheek upon her hand!
Oh, that I were a glove upon that hand,
That I might touch that cheek!

**JULIET:**   Ay me!
[*She is unhappy because Romeo is a Montague.*]

**ROMEO:**   She speaks!

**JULIET:**   O Romeo, Romeo! Wherefore art
thou Romeo?
Deny thy father and refuse thy name;
Or, if thou will not, be but sworn my love,
And I'll no longer be a Capulet.

**ROMEO:**   [*to himself*] Shall I hear more, or shall I
speak at this?

**JULIET:**   'Tis but thy name that is my enemy.
Thou art thyself, even though a Montague.
What's in a name? That which we call a rose
By any other name would smell as sweet.
Romeo, throw off thy name,
And for thy name, take all myself.

**ROMEO:**   I take thee at thy word.
Call me but love, and I'll be new named;
Henceforth I never will be Romeo.

**JULIET:**   What man art thou, thus hidden in the night?

**ROMEO:**   By a name
I know not how to tell thee who I am.
My name, dear love, is hateful to myself
Because it is an enemy to thee.

**JULIET:**   Art thou not Romeo, and a Montague?

**ROMEO:**   Neither, fair maid, if either thee dislike.

▲ Juliet appears outside her room.

---

**wherefore,** why

280

**JULIET:** How camest thou hither, tell me, and why?
The orchard walls are high and hard to climb,
And the place death, considering who thou art,
If any of my kinsmen find thee here.

**ROMEO:** Alack, there lies more danger in thine eyes
Than twenty of their swords! Look but sweet,
And I am protected from their anger.

**JULIET:** By whose directions foundest thou this place?

**ROMEO:** By love.

**JULIET:** O gentle Romeo,
If thou dost love, say it faithfully.

**ROMEO:** What shall I swear by?

**JULIET:** Do not swear at all. Although I joy in thee,
I have no joy of this love tonight.
It is too rash, too sudden.
Good night, good night! As sweet rest
Come to thy heart as that within my breast!

**ROMEO:** O, will thou leave me so unsatisfied?

**JULIET:** What satisfaction canst thou have tonight?

**ROMEO:** The exchange of thy love's faithful vow for mine.

**JULIET:** If that thy aim of love be honorable,
Thy purpose marriage, send me word tomorrow,
And all my fortunes at thy foot I'll lay
And follow thee my lord throughout the world.

**ROMEO:** My sweet!

**JULIET:** Good night, good night! Parting is such sweet sorrow
That I shall say good night till it be morrow.

---

**kinsmen,** male relatives
**alack,** used to express sorrow
**foundest,** did you find
**dost,** do

## ABOUT THE **PLAYWRIGHT**

**William Shakespeare** (1564–1616) was a poet, an actor, and a theater owner. Born in Stratford-on-Avon, England, he is regarded as one of the greatest writers in the English language. *Romeo and Juliet* is one of his most famous plays.

---

✔ **LITERARY CHECK**
*What words in this section foreshadow Romeo and Juliet's fate?*

---

**BEFORE YOU GO ON**

1 Why does Romeo say his name is hateful to him?

2 What are Romeo and Juliet planning to do?

**On Your Own**
Why do you think Juliet calls parting "sweet sorrow"?

# Review and Practice

## DRAMATIC READING

One of the best ways to understand and appreciate a play is to act it out. Work in five groups to act out the scenes in the play. Assign parts. Use the description of the scene to help you get an overview of what's going on. Read your parts aloud and stop to discuss the stage directions. Talk about what kind of person each character is. How should you portray the character? If you need more information, check the original play.

Evaluate your progress as you practice your scene. How can you improve your presentation? Can you add props, costumes, or music? Keep practicing until you feel comfortable with your scene. Act out your scenes, in order, with the rest of the class.

## COMPREHENSION

Workbook
Page 133

### Right There

1. What does Lord Capulet think of Romeo?

2. Who reveals Juliet's identity to Romeo? Who reveals Romeo's identity to Juliet?

### Think and Search

3. How do Romeo's and Juliet's identities affect their relationship?

4. How does Tybalt make the drama in this story more intense?

### Author and You

5. Shakespeare's plays show life in England during the late 1500s and early 1600s. What was life like then, judging from *Romeo and Juliet*?

6. *Romeo and Juliet* is a tragedy. Yet some people think it begins more like a comedy. What do you think? Explain.

### On Your Own

7. Romeo and Juliet fell deeply in love—do you feel happy for them or sorry for them?

8. In your opinion, if two people are in love, should it matter what anyone else thinks? Why or why not?

## DISCUSSION

Discuss in pairs or small groups.

1. In Shakespeare's time, parents decided who their children would marry. Do you think this practice was fair?

2. Juliet isn't even fifteen yet. Her father says she's too young for marriage and asks Paris to wait two years. What do you think? Is fourteen too young to be married?

3. Why do you think this play, written hundreds of years ago, is still so popular today?

**Q How do conflicts affect us?** Summarize the conflict that Romeo and Juliet have to deal with in this story. Do you think this kind of conflict occurs in families and communities today? Give examples.

**Listening TIP**

Listen carefully to what others have to say. If you strongly disagree, continue listening to the point being made. Wait until the person is finished before giving your opinion.

## RESPONSE TO LITERATURE

Workbook
Page 133

Sometimes Shakespeare's plays are performed in modern-day English with modern settings. Work in groups of four to rewrite Scene 3 on page 277 in your own words. Decide who will play Lady Capulet, Nurse, Juliet, and the Servant. Rehearse the scene together and then perform it for the class. Afterwards, discuss how your modern-day versions are similar and how they are different.

# Grammar and Writing

## Transforming Nouns into Adjectives

You can transform nouns into adjectives by adding suffixes. Suffixes are endings that are added to words to change the meaning. The suffix of a word establishes its part of speech.

Read the chart below to see how to form adjectives from nouns. Pay attention to spelling changes that occur when the suffix is added.

| Suffix | Nouns | Adjectives |
|--------|-------|------------|
| -ous | torture, fury | tortur**ous**, furi**ous** |
| -ful | beauty, hate, faith | beauti**ful**, hate**ful**, faith**ful** |
| -able | honor | honor**able** |
| -y | worth | worth**y** |
| -ly | coward | coward**ly** |

## Practice

**Workbook**
**Page 134**

Work with a partner. Copy the sentences below into your notebook. Change the nouns in the box to adjectives, and use them to complete the sentences. Check a dictionary if necessary.

| coward | fury | help | love | monster | truth |
|--------|------|------|------|---------|-------|

1. When Benvolio gave Romeo advice, he wanted to be _____.
2. Benvolio and Romeo were not _____ about their identities.
3. Tybalt was _____ that Romeo dared to come to the party.
4. Romeo thought Juliet was a _____ woman.
5. When Juliet learned that Romeo was a Montague, she called their love a _____ one.
6. Tybalt thought Benvolio was acting very _____ when he refused to fight.

## WRITING AN EXPOSITORY PARAGRAPH

### Write a News Article

At the end of this unit, you'll write an expository essay that expands one of this unit's four paragraphs. Now you'll write a newspaper gossip column, using the 5Ws to help you organize it. Use a chart to answer the following questions:

- **Who** was involved?
- **Where** did the event happen?
- **When** did the event happen?
- **What** happened?
- **Why** did it happen?

Who?

Where?

When?

What?

Why?

---

*Kate Munz*

*Romeo and Juliet, Up Close and Personal*

    *Today in Verona, the names on everyone's minds are Romeo Montague and Juliet Capulet. It all started last night when Benvolio convinced Romeo to go to the Capulet's masquerade ball. He was trying to help Romeo get over the lovely Rosaline. (Can you believe she broke up with him?) Anyway, things started to heat up when Tybalt recognized Romeo. Tybalt was furious! He became even angrier when his uncle told him to leave Romeo alone. Not long after that, Romeo and Juliet were spotted in a corner talking, dancing, and kissing! Sources say that Romeo was later seen talking to Juliet by her balcony, and he asked her to marry him! Looks like our boy has stolen the beautiful Juliet's heart. But how will this turn out? After all, he is a Montague and she is a Capulet—and their families are enemies. Read my next column to find out!*

**Practice**

Write your own gossip column about the event. Try to take a different viewpoint—one less favorable to Romeo, more favorable to the count, and include different details—focusing on the balcony scene, for example. Use a graphic organizer with the 5Ws to list your main points. Be sure to use adjectives correctly.

**Writing Checklist**

**VOICE:**
- ✔ My gossip column makes my readers want to read on to find out what happens.

**ORGANIZATION:**
- ✔ I included the 5Ws in a logical way.

285

# Prepare to Read

## What You Will Learn

**Reading**

- Vocabulary building: *Context, dictionary skills, word study*
- Reading strategy: *Restate main ideas*
- Text type: *Informational text (social studies)*

**Grammar, Usage, and Mechanics**

Showing opposition: adverb clauses beginning with *although, even though, even after*

**Writing**

Write a problem–and–solution paragraph

 **THE BIG QUESTION**

**How do conflicts affect us?** Feuds, like the one you read about in *Romeo and Juliet*, can sometimes be long and bitter. What are the long-term affects of a feud? Do you think the longer a feud continues, the harder it will be to end it? Why or why not? Discuss with a partner.

**BUILD BACKGROUND**

You're going to read a news article entitled **"Furious Feuds: Enemies by Association."** News articles focus on recent and past events. They often appear in magazines and newspapers and are intended to give meaning and depth to a complex issue. When you read a news article, you may read about events that took place in different areas of the world. Sometimes, it is presumed that the reader has some basic geographical and historical knowledge about where and when the events took place. Two of the stories in this news feature take place in India and Korea. Look for these countries on the map.

## VOCABULARY

### Learn Key Words

Read these sentences. Use the context to figure out the meaning of the **red** words. Use a dictionary to check your answers. Then write each word and its meaning in your notebook.

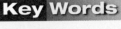

**Key Words**

ancestor
aristocratic
centuries
claim
descendants
rekindled

1. An **ancestor** of one family started a feud, which continued for many years.

2. Some **aristocratic** families feuded over the right to be kings and queens.

3. The feud began **centuries** ago, in the 1600s.

4. When Henry VII took **claim** to the throne, the House of Tudor finally was in power after years of fighting.

5. It was actually **descendants** of two families who, eight centuries later, kept one long-standing feud going.

6. Even after a period of peace between two groups, feuds can be **rekindled** because of an insult or disagreement.

**Practice**  Workbook Page 136

Work with a partner to answer these questions. Try to include the **red** word in your answer. Write the sentences in your notebook.

1. Why might it be important to know about an **ancestor**?

2. What do you know about **aristocratic** families in Europe's history?

3. Why do you think some feuds go on for **centuries**?

4. How do you think a **claim** to something might start a feud?

5. Why might **descendants** living years later start up a feud again?

6. What causes some feuds to be **rekindled**?

▲ Elizabeth of York and Henry VII

## Learn Academic Words

Study the **red** words and their meanings. You will find these words useful when talking and writing about informational texts. Write each word and its meaning in your notebook. After you read "Furious Feuds," try to use these words to respond to the text.

| | |
|---|---|
| **civil** = of or pertaining to citizens (civil wars are wars between citizens of the same country) | ➡ Americans fought Americans in a **civil** war that lasted five years. |
| **convinced** = made someone decide to do something | ➡ They wanted to fight, but the police **convinced** them to go home peacefully. |
| **despite** = in spite of something | ➡ The two tribes continued to fight, **despite** their agreement to stop. |
| **individuals** = particular people, considered separately from other people in the same group | ➡ The two **individuals** had never met, but they hated each other because their families had been feuding for years. |
| **tension** = the feeling that exists when people do not trust each other and may suddenly attack or start arguing | ➡ No one had started fighting yet, but you could feel the **tension** between the rival gangs. |

## Practice

**Workbook**
**Page 137**

Write the sentences in your notebook. Choose a **red** word from the box above to complete each sentence. Then take turns reading the sentences aloud with a partner.

1. The war raged on, _____ best efforts to stop it.

2. The _____ between the two clans was growing and made everyone feel nervous.

3. That country's own _____ wars prevented them from taking a united stand against their enemies.

4. A disagreement between just two _____ can rekindle a family feud.

5. She wanted to marry him, but her family _____ her not to.

▲ Tension in a family

288

## Word Study: Long Vowel Spelling Patterns

Each long vowel has several different spellings. When you read and write a word with a long vowel, you will need to remember the spelling pattern that is used. The chart below shows the different spelling patterns for many common long vowels.

| VCe | CVVC | CV(*e*) CV(*y*) | CVCC | igh (long *i*) |
|-----|------|-----------------|------|----------------|
| gave<br>tribe<br>wrote<br>fortune | claim (long *a*)<br>leader (long *e*)<br>between (long *e*)<br>believe (long *e*)<br>roots (long *u*)<br>feud (long *u*) | she (long *e*)<br>monkey (long *e*)<br>happy (long *e*)<br>by (long *i*)<br>pie (long *i*) | wild (long *i*)<br>both (long *o*) | fight |

**Practice**  Workbook Page 138

Work with a partner. Take turns reading aloud and spelling the words in the box below. After you spell the word, identify its long vowel sound.

| | | | | |
|---|---|---|---|---|
| authorities | die | knights | peace | throne |
| day | go | moon | queen | times |
| decide | grave | own | rose | try |

## READING STRATEGY    TAKE NOTES

Taking notes keeps you focused on what you're reading. It also helps you understand and remember new information. To take notes, follow these steps:

- Identify what your purpose is for reading the text.
- Read the text quickly and take notes as you read.
- Don't write incomplete sentences, for example: began around 1878
- Focus on what is important to you, not on the details.
- Review your notes. Go back and check facts if necessary.

As you read "Furious Feuds," think about the information you want to remember and take notes. Then review them to check they are correct.

 Workbook Page 139

**Set a purpose for reading** What starts a feud, or conflict, between groups of people? And why do some feuds last for such a long time?

# Furious Feuds
## Enemies by Association
### *Alfred Meyer*

▲ A marketplace in India

## Tribal Rivals

"You just wait," said a boy on the playground to another larger boy who was bullying him. "I'm sick of this. I'm going to get my big brother."

"Ha," replied the bully, "then I'll get *my* big brother."

Often, the big brother threats prove empty. But sometimes they don't. Also, sometimes more than close relatives are called in to take part on one side of a dispute.

In a small market store in India, not long ago, two young men nearly came to blows over which of them would get to buy the last remaining CD made by a popular musician. Neither man gave in as a crowd gathered, expecting a fight.

---

**came to blows**, started hitting each other

As it happened, each man belonged to a different local tribe, tribes that for forty years had feuded with each other, often resulting in bloodshed when conflicts arose between them. As the tension in the market rose, word spread.

First, the brothers of each of the young men dashed up and confronted one another. Members of each of the two tribes appeared next, eager to represent their tribe in this squabble. But then, just as serious violence seemed about to break out, the police arrived. The police captain quickly recognized the two tribal chiefs, and convinced them to order their tribe members to turn around and go home peacefully.

Although the feud between the two tribes may not have ended for good, at least on this day no fighting took place. Nor, when it comes to feuds in general, is forty years a very long time. Some feuds last for generations, and even centuries.

## A Grave Competition

One of the longest lasting feuds on record began centuries ago in Korea. It is also a strange one since it involves two individuals who never met each other and who actually lived more than 400 years apart. Instead, it is the descendants of twelfth-century General Yoon Gwam and seventeenth-century Prime Minister Shim Ji Won who started and kept the feud going. For like many Koreans, the descendants believe that the gravesite of an important ancestor must be as perfect as possible to assure good fortune. That is, a poor gravesite will displease the spirit of the ancestor, which will then bring about bankruptcies, illness, and all manner of calamity to anxious descendants. Over the years, the rivalry for a better gravesite between the Yoon and Shim clans resulted in the two gravesites being moved many times, always in the desire of creating a gravesite more spectacular than that of the rival's ancestor. The competing clans took into account the physical beauty of the landscape as well as the architectural splendor of the tombs themselves.

The rivalry also turned nasty, and sometimes violent, despite efforts by Korean authorities to calm matters. The clans simply wouldn't stop trying to outdo each other. Today, bad feelings still mark the relationship between the clans, even though a kind of peace treaty exists between them. Yet the elders of both clans strongly frown upon marriage between Yoons and Shims.

"Not even over my dead body!" says 77-year-old Yoon Bu Hyun, a leader of the Yoon clan. "You tell me," he says. "Would you marry your son to the daughter of your sworn enemy?"

---

**tribe**, a social group that shares a common ancestry and culture and who are typically ruled by a leader or council
**squabble**, disagreement
**generations**, average periods of time between parents and children

**calamity**, very bad, unexpected event
**clans**, large families
**frown upon**, disapprove of

### BEFORE YOU GO ON

1 What caused the tribal conflict?

2 What is the Yoon and Shim feud about?

**On Your Own**
Do you think most feuds are rational or emotional?

## Family Feud

In the United States, the best-known family feud began around 1878 between the Hatfields and McCoys. They lived near each other along the Kentucky-West Virginia border. It's hard to know exactly what happened, but one day a McCoy hog was found on Hatfield property, so the Hatfields claimed the hog was theirs. Not so, said the McCoys, adding that it was *their* property anyway. The disagreement ended up in a court of law. Based in large part on what Bill Staton, a relative of both families, had to say, the jury ruled in favor of the Hatfields. Shortly after, Staton was shot dead by two McCoy brothers.

The feud now simmered. What brought it to a boil was when a pretty young McCoy girl, Roseanna, fell in love with Johnse Hatfield. The couple did not marry, and Roseanna eventually moved back into the McCoy household. But when she decided to go with Johnse after all, the McCoys chose to act. They kidnapped Johnse, intending to do him harm. But Roseanna alerted the Hatfields, who sent out a rescue party and saved him.

The feud, however, grew worse. The fighting got so bad that the governors of West Virginia and Kentucky called out the National Guard to restore peace between the two families. Yet even after the feuding ended, Roseanna and Johnse stayed apart, although she still loved him. It must have saddened her to learn a few years later that Johnse ended up married oddly enough to one of her cousins, a McCoy. Roseanna died unmarried and, folks said, maybe of a broken heart shortly after her thirtieth birthday.

## Houses at War

If William Shakespeare had lived toward the end of the nineteenth century, he might well have written a play about "star-crossed lovers" called *Johnse and Roseanna*. He actually wrote *Romeo and Juliet*, a tragedy that unfolds against the background of a feud between two families, the Montagues and the Capulets. [See pages 274–281.] The story of this feud had been told and retold many times before Shakespeare turned it into a play in 1590. Indeed, the same story served as the basis for a popular musical play, *West Side Story*. In this version, Tony and Maria were based on Romeo and Juliet, and two rival street gangs—the Jets and the Sharks—were based on the Montagues and Capulets.

In his history plays Shakespeare wrote about conflicts that were greater in scale than most family feuds. That is, what started as feuds between aristocratic families in England over land and the right to become king or queen grew into a series of civil wars. This meant that families had to be powerful and rich enough to enlist knights and soldiers for an army. Then it could wage war against the army of a rival family.

---

**scale**, size, compared to what is normal
**knights**, men trained to fight for a king

Perhaps the best known of such conflicts is called "The Wars of the Roses," which took place from 1455 until 1487 just before Shakespeare's time. It involved two rival branches of the royal Plantagenet family—the Lancasters and the Yorks. Among the English nobility, family roots were key to power and influence in the country's affairs. Families themselves were referred to as Lines or Houses. The House of Lancaster used a red rose as its emblem, while the House of York used a white rose. Each House wanted nothing less than the throne of England itself.

Unfortunately for both Houses, the wars between them proved so costly that neither of them could successfully claim the throne. Instead, the House of Tudor made good its own claim as Henry VII became king.

Feuds start up—or are occasionally rekindled—for a variety of reasons such as an insult to a family, tribe, or gang member; a disagreement over who owns a farm animal; who should inherit a house; or who gets to rule over a group of people or an entire country.

---

**branches,** family groups who share the
   same ancestors
**emblem,** a picture, shape, or object
   that represents something

▲ A portrait of Queen Elizabeth I with Tudor rose

## ABOUT THE **AUTHOR**

**Alfred Meyer** is a writer and former magazine editor who has a special interest in science. He was born in Detroit, Michigan, and his first job was piloting a ferryboat across the St. Clair River. He later floated a raft most of the length of the Mississippi River. A graduate of Columbia University, he also studied wildlife biology at Cornell University. Meyer currently lives in Chatham, New York.

## BEFORE YOU GO ON

1 What did feuds between aristocratic families in England turn into?

2 What are four things that can start feuds?

**On Your Own**
What caused the conflicts in this feature story?

# Review and Practice

## COMPREHENSION

Workbook
Page 140

### Right There

1. What is the best-known family feud in the United States?
2. When did the Wars of the Roses take place?

### Think and Search

3. What was the basis of the conflict between the Yoons and the Shims and why is it such a strange one?
4. What makes the situation between Johnse Hatfield and Roseanna McCoy a modern-day *Romeo and Juliet*?

### Author and You

5. How do you think the author feels about feuds? Why?
6. Why do you think the author chose these feuds?

### On Your Own

7. What do you think turns a simple conflict into a feud? Why?
8. Do you know about any feuds between tribes, clans, or families? If so, how did they begin? What is the conflict about?

## IN YOUR OWN WORDS

Use the phrases and vocabulary below, as well as your own words, to discuss feuds with a partner.

| | | |
|---|---|---|
| Who can be involved in a feud? | ➡ | descendants, aristocratic, individuals |
| Why might feuds be caused? | ➡ | ancestors, individuals, claim |
| What can feuds lead to? | ➡ | civil wars, conflicts, violence |
| How can feuds be resolved? | ➡ | convinced, court of law, agreement, rekindled |

> 🔊 *Speaking* TIP
>
> Write important ideas on note cards. Review your notes before you begin speaking.

## DISCUSSION

Discuss in pairs or small groups.

1. What were the outcomes of the various feuds in "Furious Feuds: Enemies by Association"? If you were to choose one feud to show the pointlessness of feuds, which one would you choose? Why?

2. Why are the individuals or groups involved in feuds and conflicts "enemies by association"? If someone wanted to mediate in a feud, how might the person use this phrase to help the feuding parties?

**Q How do conflicts affect us?** When it comes to conflict, some people have the ability to "forgive and forget." Others stay angry for a long time. In the case of family feuds, family members often carry their anger from one generation to the next. Why do you think this is so? And what do you think has to happen in order for the feud to end?

## READ FOR FLUENCY

Reading with feeling helps make what you read more interesting. Work with a partner. Choose a paragraph from the reading. Read the paragraph. Ask each other how you felt after reading the paragraph. Did you feel happy or sad?

Take turns reading the paragraph aloud to each other with a tone of voice that represents how you felt when you read it the first time. Give each other feedback.

## EXTENSION

**Workbook**
**Page 140**

**Listening TIP**

Practice your interview before presenting it. Listen carefully to each other's questions and responses so your interview will sound natural.

Work with a partner. From the feuds you read about, choose one of the parties to interview: one of the young men from India, a Yoon or a Shim, Roseanna McCoy or Johnse Hatfield, a member of the House of York or Lancaster. Decide who will be the interviewer and the person who will be interviewed. List questions about the feud. Who was feuding and why? What did the conflict accomplish, if anything? What is a solution or a possible solution? Take turns presenting your interviews in front of the class.

# Grammar and Writing

## Showing Opposition: Adverb Clauses Beginning with *although*, *even though*, *even after*

An adverb clause is a kind of dependent clause. It gives information about what is going on in the main (independent) clause. For example, *Everyone admires her because she's a good student.* Here, the adverb clause (*because she's a good student*) explains the main clause (*Everyone admires her*).

Adverb clauses can also show opposition. When an adverb clause begins with a subordinating conjunction such as *although, even though,* or *even after*, it indicates that the idea in the main clause is unexpected. Read these examples.

| dependent clause | independent clause |
|---|---|

**Although** she still loved him, they stayed apart.

| independent clause | dependent clause |
|---|---|

There are still bad feelings between the clans **even though** a peace treaty exists.

| dependent clause | independent clause |
|---|---|

Yet **even after** the feuding ended, Roseanna and Johnse remained apart.

Notice that when you begin a sentence with an adverb clause, the clause is followed by a comma. When the independent clause comes first, there is no comma.

## Practice

**Workbook Page 141**

Work with a partner. Match each clause in the first column with the correct clause in the second column. Make sure that you use correct punctuation and that your sentences are logical. Write the sentences in your notebook.

| | |
|---|---|
| Civil war often breaks out | feuds are often started by individuals. |
| Although families can get involved | there may be tension between families. |
| Even after a feud is resolved | although the situation may seem hopeless. |
| Conflict resolution is possible | even though there is a peace treaty. |

### Write a Problem–and–Solution Paragraph

At the end of this unit, you'll write an expository essay that expands one of this unit's four paragraphs. Now you'll write a paragraph that clearly states a problem and offers a solution for it. Once you've stated the problem, you'll pose and answer a question.

   Read the student model below. Notice that the writer first defines the problem and gives examples. Then she poses a question. Finally, she presents a solution. She used a problem–and–solution graphic organizer to help organize her ideas.

| Problem |
|---|
| ↓ |
| Solution |

*Nola Smith*

*Family Feuds*

*Sometimes, families engage in long-standing feuds. For example, in Korea, a long and bitter family feud revolves around two people who lived 400 years apart from each other. In another example, members of two tribes in India are still fighting bitterly even though forty years have passed since the feud began. When so much time goes by, doesn't the feud begin to lose its meaning? Yet the fighting goes on. So what can be done to help resolve family feuds? A mediator can be called in to help. The mediator can begin by pointing out how feuds can be started or rekindled over very simple things. Then the mediator can give examples of how such feuds have resulted in violence, death, and even civil wars. Finally, the mediator can help families see how important it is to resolve small conflicts before they become feuds.*

**Practice**

Write a paragraph with a clearly stated problem and a solution. Be sure to pose a question. Use feuds from the reading or your own idea. Use a problem–and–solution graphic organizer to help you organize your ideas. Try to include phrases of opposition such as *although* and *despite.*

**Writing Checklist**

**ORGANIZATION:**
☑ My problem is stated clearly at the beginning.

**SENTENCE FLUENCY:**
☑ My sentences begin in different ways, using adverbs of opposition.

297

## What You Will Learn

**Reading**

■ Vocabulary building: *Literary terms, word study*

■ Reading strategy: *Make inferences*

■ Text type: *Literature (novel excerpt)*

**Grammar, Usage, and Mechanics**

Modals of advisability: *should, ought to, had better*; adverb clauses of condition: *if*

**Writing**

Support a position

### THE BIG QUESTION

**How do conflicts affect us?** When we are faced with a conflict, we can choose how to react to it. We can face the conflict alone, or we can ask for help. How does our reaction to conflict affect the outcome? How does it affect others who are involved? How do you know if you can handle a conflict alone, or if you need help to resolve it? Discuss with a partner.

### BUILD BACKGROUND

You're going to read an excerpt from the novel ***Romiette and Julio.*** Romiette Cappelle and Julio Montague are two teenagers whose relationship puts them in danger. They are targeted because Romiette, an African American, is dating Julio, who is Hispanic. While students at the school are aware of the Devildogs gang, other members of the Cincinnati, Ohio, community where they live are not. Even Romiette's father, a television newscaster, had concluded on his show that there was "no real evidence of gangs in our city"— until the incident involving his own daughter and Julio.

▲ Rival gangs in the movie *West Side Story* (1961), a modern version of *Romeo and Juliet*

## VOCABULARY

### Learn Literary Words

**Mood**, or atmosphere, is the feeling that a literary work or passage creates. Often, mood can be described in a single word, such as *lighthearted* or *fearful*. Read the excerpt below from *Romiette and Julio*. What mood is being created here? You might describe it as tense, desperate, or terrifying. Certain words help create this mood, such as *alone, struggling, fruitlessly, hoping*, and *clinging* (which means *holding onto something tightly*).

> Both Romiette and Julio could feel the electricity of the lightning bolt as the small boat was incinerated and crumpled. Her hand was wrenched from his, and he was alone struggling to find the surface. Julio reached for Romi in the darkness, but all was fire and acrid smoke and swirling water. He searched the area, fruitlessly grabbing broken pieces of wood from the boat, hoping that Romi was somehow clinging to one of them.

**Plot** is the sequence of events in a literary work. In most cases, a plot has characters and a main conflict. The excerpt you will be reading from *Romiette and Julio* covers three passages from the story. As you read, notice these elements of the plot: changes in setting, the way the conflict builds, the climax (the high point in the story), and the resolution (how the story ends).

**Practice**  **Workbook Page 143**

Review the scenes from *Romeo and Juliet* on pages 274–281. Copy the chart below into your notebook and complete it. Use what you know and then add to the chart for *Romiette and Julio*. Discuss similarities and differences in the plot and mood.

| Story or Drama Element | *Romeo and Juliet* | *Romiette and Julio* |
|---|---|---|
| Setting | | |
| Main characters | | |
| Conflict | | |
| Mood | | |

## Learn Academic Words

Study the **red** words and their meanings. You will find these words useful when talking and writing about literature. Write each word and its meaning in your notebook. After you read the excerpt from *Romiette and Julio,* try to use these words to respond to the text.

### Academic Words

apparently
chemical
exposure
identified
target
volunteers

| | | |
|---|---|---|
| **apparently** = almost certainly | ➡ | When Romiette and Julio weren't where they were supposed to be, their friends concluded that something had **apparently** gone very wrong. |
| **chemical** = relating to changes that happen when two substances combine | ➡ | When the fire broke out, a strong **chemical** smell filled the air. |
| **exposure** = the harmful effects of staying outside for a long time in extremely cold weather | ➡ | As the temperature dropped, rescuers thought the two teenagers might be suffering from **exposure**. |
| **identified** = be closely connected with an idea or group of people | ➡ | The five teenagers, who were **identified** as members of a gang, were arrested by the police. |
| **target** = an object, person, or place chosen to be attacked | ➡ | The Devildogs saw Julio as a **target** simply because he was Hispanic. |
| **volunteers** = people who offer to do something without reward or pay | ➡ | The victims of the disaster were thankful to the **volunteers** who helped with the relief effort. |

## Practice

**Workbook** Page 144

Work with a partner to answer these questions. Try to include the **red** word in your answer. Write the sentences in your notebook.

1. How does the title *Romiette and Julio* show that the book **apparently** is related to *Romeo and Juliet*?
2. Why do fires often create strong **chemical** odors?
3. How can people guard against the effects of **exposure**?
4. How can gang members be **identified**?
5. What can make a person the **target** of a gang?
6. Why are **volunteers** so important in relief efforts?

▲ Volunteers provide free food and water to the victims of Hurricane Katrina.

## Word Study: Prefixes *in-*, *im-*, *inter-*, *re-*, and *un-*

A prefix is a letter or group of letters that can be added to the beginning of a word to change its meaning. Learning the meaning of prefixes will help you read and understand more words. Here are some examples.

| Prefix | Meaning | Example Words |
|--------|---------|---------------|
| in-, im- | not | **in**appropriate, **im**proper |
| inter- | between | **in**terracial |
| re- | again | **re**assure |
| un- | not | **un**controllably, **un**tie |

**Practice**
Workbook Page 145

Work with a partner. Read the sentences below and replace the underlined words in each sentence with a word that has a prefix. Write the sentences in your notebook and include the meaning of the prefix. Use a dictionary if you to need to.

1. Julio is <u>not happy</u> with his friends.
2. Is Romiette <u>not able</u> to tell Julio how she feels?
3. The problem seems to be <u>not visible</u> to everyone in the story.
4. I thought it was <u>not polite</u> to interrupt the speaker.
5. Then he has to <u>read</u> everything <u>again</u>.

## READING STRATEGY    MAKE INFERENCES

When you read a text, it helps to make inferences about events that probably happened. You use your own knowledge to fill in the details of what you are reading.

- Malaka's warning
- What the Devildogs probably did
- Why the situation is especially difficult for Romiette
- How Romiette and Julio's friendship has been growing

Then when the scene shifts again to a TV newsroom, ask yourself:

- What has probably happened?

Workbook Page 146

**Set a purpose for reading** In this story, a gang has threatened Romiette and Julio. Rather than go to someone for help, they choose to deal with this conflict alone. What happens to them as a result?

*from*

# Romiette and Julio

## Sharon M. Draper

*When Julio Montague and his family move to Cincinnati, Ohio, to escape gang violence in Corpus Christi, Texas, they soon learn that gangs exist there, too. And when Julio starts spending a lot of time with Romiette— even helping her with her recurring nightmare about fire and water—the dangerous Devildogs see an opportunity to use Romiette and Julio's interracial relationship to make a statement. When Romiette and Julio come up with a plan to secretly videotape the Devildogs harassing them and to expose the gang, things go desperately wrong.*

### School Hallway at Lunchtime

"Malaka, you still didn't tell me what the Devildogs plan to do."

"I don't really know. I just know that you better stay away from places where you might be caught alone."

Romiette was incredulous. She gasped in surprise. "I can't believe this! Are you for real?"

Malaka was unruffled. "Real as a heart attack."

"What about Julio?"

"What about him?"

"Is he in any danger?"

"If he don't learn the rules, he might have to be taught a lesson."

"What rules? Who made up these rules? How can he follow laws when he doesn't know what they are?"

"The Devildogs don't want to hurt you, 'cause you're one of the sisters on the list. You always dressed like a sister, and hung with the sisters, so there was no problem. But now you're about to get cut off the list. And that's dangerous."

"The list? You're talking crazy." Romi was angry, irritated, and very late for lunch now.

---

**incredulous,** unable or unwilling to believe something

"I'm trying to get some basic stuff into your black head. And never forget—it is black," Malaka reminded Romi. "If you get cut off the list, you get no protection."

"I never asked for any protection from some gang! I don't want it or need it." Romi was so angry she wanted to cry, but she refused to give Malaka the satisfaction.

"Suit yourself. That boyfriend of yours ain't got a chance."

"What did he ever do to you? Or to anybody black?" Romi asked in disbelief.

"Nothing. We just don't need no foreigners around here mixing it up with the sisters."

"He's not foreign! He was born in this country just like you were!"

"Doesn't matter. We don't want him here."

"You're treating him just like the whites treated us! Don't you think that's a little stupid?" Romi asked, trying to appeal to Malaka's sense of reason.

"I don't make the rules. I just pass on the information. Gang rules. Gang laws. Things change."

"You sure have changed, Malaka," Romi said angrily. "You used to think for yourself."

"Now I got Mr. T to think for me, and take care of me. I like that better."

"You really like Terrell?"

"Yeah, he's got it together. He makes me feel strong and safe."

"Look, can't you see? That's how Julio makes me feel."

"You shoulda picked somebody black. Look, I've already said too much. Be careful. Something is going to go down, and soon. The Devildogs have to make a statement—make a showing to the school. There's too many white kids for them to try anything, but your Mexican is the perfect target."

\* \* \* \*

**BEFORE YOU GO ON**

1  What makes Romiette's boyfriend Julio the perfect target for the Devildogs?

2  Is Romiette in danger, too?

**On Your Own**
What can happen when people let others think for them?

## Nighttime on London Woods Lake

"What are we going to do, Julio?" Romi's voice jarred Julio back into reality. "I'm sure our parents are looking for us, and the police are too. They are, don't you think?" Romi asked, suddenly doubtful.

"Sure, they're looking," Julio said, trying to reassure her, "but do you think they'll find us? If we're on London Woods Lake, it's big, and it's dark, and it's getting ready to storm."

"They'll never find us in a storm," Romi said.

A bolt of lightning speared past them and landed with a flaming, steaming sizzle in a tree about ten feet up the shore.

Julio told her clearly, "We've got to get out of this boat, Romi."

"NO!" she screamed. "I'll drown!"

"I won't let you drown." Julio lowered himself into the freezing water. He gasped at the coldness of it. He held out his hand to her. "Take my hand. Hold on to me. I will not let you go."

"No, Julio, I'm terrified of water. I'll pull you down. I can't do it." She let go of his hand and sat shaking in the boat.

"Romi, the lightning is hitting trees on shore. It will hit this boat. I know it." In the flashes of lightning she could make out his face, pleading and full of concern not for himself but for her. "Come on, Romi. You'll be fine."

Trembling, she seized his hand and let him lead her over the side of the boat. "Please don't let me go," she said, trembling.

"I've got you. Relax. I won't let anything happen to you, do you hear me? I love you, Romiette."

"What did you say? The thunder, the noise, the water!"

"*Te amo*. I love you! You're not going to die."

With a crack that split the heavens, a huge bolt of fire was spit from the sky. It arced, twisted, and with vicious rage, the lightning stabbed the small wooden boat.

---

**jarred**, shocked (someone), especially by making an
   unpleasant noise
**vicious**, violent and dangerous, and likely to hurt someone

The air smelled of charred wood and the harsh chemical odor of fire between water and sky. Flames, which were quickly extinguished by the driving rain, rose from the gaping hole and tried to spread along the bottom of the boat. Both Romiette and Julio could feel the electricity of the lightning bolt as the small boat was incinerated and crumpled. Her hand was wrenched from his, and he was alone struggling to find the surface. Julio reached for Romi in the darkness, but all was fire and acrid smoke and swirling water. He searched the area, fruitlessly grabbing broken pieces of wood from the boat, hoping that Romi was somehow clinging to one of them. He shouted her name, went under again and again, but Romi was deep within the thing she feared the most—the dark, cold water.

Julio swam to the surface once more and breathed deeply. It was still raining in strong sheets of water, but the fury of the storm seemed to have subsided. He looked around frantically for Romiette, but he could see no sign of her. He knew she was terrified. This was her nightmare, her fear dream, and he was unable to help her. He plunged beneath the water but, except for the diminishing sound of the thunder as it retreated into the distance, he could hear nothing. He shouted her name, half praying, half pleading to the hidden stars to help him find her.

"Romiette! Romiette!" He dove under the water again, reaching for her, feeling for her, sensing her closeness. He knew he only had a short time to find her. He let himself drift to the bottom of the lake where the darkness of the water was total and complete. The only thing that led him was his heart, his knowledge that he would never leave that lake without her. His lungs were burning fire, about to explode, when he touched her arm. She was floating facedown, her hair caught on a jagged rock. He touched her face, gently freed her, and swam with her to the surface.

He reached the shore, half lifted, half dragged Romiette from the water, and laid her gently on the ground. He forgot about the pain in his arms and back and head. He forgot about how cold he was. His only thought was to make her breathe, to make her live. He tried to remember all the steps of CPR as he breathed into her mouth and compressed her chest. He couldn't tell if she was dead or just unconscious. She lay in the mud, unmoving, and Julio shouted curses to the stars.

---

incinerated, burned up
acrid, having a very strong and bad smell that burns your nose or throat
CPR, cardiopulmonary resuscitation; a set of actions that you do to help someone
    who has stopped breathing or whose heart has stopped beating
compressed, pressed something to make it smaller so that it takes up less space

**LITERARY CHECK**
*How is the plot building?*

**BEFORE YOU GO ON**

1 What kind of trouble are Romiette and Julio in?

2 What does Julio do to Romiette to try to save her?

**On Your Own**
What do you think will happen next?

305

The wind blew hard, much colder now that the rain had stopped, and Julio knew he could do no more. He shivered uncontrollably in the darkness and looked for shelter. He was dizzy, weak, and was starting to fade into unconsciousness himself. He picked up Romiette's cool, damp body and stumbled as far as he could into the woods. He tripped over a huge tree that had fallen many storms before, and almost dropped Romi as he landed in a hollow under it. He gently placed Romi on the spongy pine needles and leaves, then squeezed himself into the shallow hole next to her. He pulled Romiette as close to himself as he could. At least there was a bit of shelter from the wind, he thought vaguely. He tried to concentrate, but he was so tired, and the air was so cold. It was easy to rest for a bit. Julio shivered, hugged Romi closer to him, and faded into sleep.

* * * *

✔ **LITERARY CHECK**
*How is the **mood** changing? What one word would you use to describe it? Which story details did you use?*

## Six O'Clock Evening News

It was one minute to airtime. The red light on top of Camera One blinked. It was time.

Ladies and gentlemen—this is Cornell Cappelle. Standing next to me is my wife, Lady Brianna Cappelle, and on this side are Maria and Luis Montague, our new friends.

I would like to bring you up to date on the facts as we know them right now. First of all, I would like to thank everyone—the volunteers, the searchers, the organizers—for their help in finding my daughter, Romiette, and the Montagues' son, Julio.

From what we can gather, Romiette and Julio had been harassed at school by some young people who may or may not have been identified with a gang. They were stopped near London Woods, grabbed and placed in a car, then taken to the boathouse near London Woods Lake. From what we can tell, it was a means to frighten and intimidate our children, and it got out of hand.

Romiette and Julio were then tied up, put in the bottom of a small boat, and set afloat on London Woods Lake. On an ordinary day, that might not have been life-threatening, but you are all aware of the storm last night, and there is the fact that my daughter cannot swim.

Evidently, they were able to untie the ropes that held them, but they were adrift in the boat in a storm in the dark. Lightning finally struck the boat, and it was destroyed. They were forced to jump into those frigid waters, and Romiette almost drowned. Julio managed to drag her to safety, even after she had been overcome by the force of the water and the storm.

When they reached the shore, Julio, carrying the unconscious Romiette, apparently tripped and fell over some storm-fallen trees. Close to unconscious himself from the cold and exposure, he dragged her to safety in a hollow under some rocks and branches lodged under a huge fallen tree. The two of them huddled there the rest of the night—both of them drifting in and out of consciousness, Julio protecting Romiette with his body. That is how we found them—huddled together—barely conscious but, praise the Lord, very much alive.

They are both awake, alert, and hungry. Neither seems to have suffered any major injuries, although both will probably have headaches for a few days, and Romiette had quite a bit of water in her lungs.

Once again, let me thank our new friends, the Montagues, and our many other friends who helped in the rescue effort. It shows what a community can do when it cares about its young people. And, although I love Shakespeare, I sure am glad that this story of the Montagues and the Cappelles did not end as Shakespeare's tale did.

## Epilogue

*Malaka cooperated with the police and expressed regret about her involvement with the gang. The five Devildogs involved in the incident were apprehended and arrested.*

---

**apprehended**, caught by the police

### ABOUT THE **AUTHOR**

**Sharon M. Draper** is a long-time high school English teacher and writer who instructs other teachers in her master classes. She was named National Teacher of the Year in 1997. Her books for young adults include *Romiette and Julio,* as well as *Tears of a Tiger* and *Copper Sun.* She is also the author of the popular *Ziggy* series of books for children. The mother of four, Draper lives in Cincinnati, Ohio, with her husband, a high school science teacher, and Honey, a golden retriever.

**BEFORE YOU GO ON**

1 What condition were Romiette and Julio in when they were found?

2 How did the event affect the two families?

**On Your Own**
In your opinion, what could have prevented this incident from happening?

307

# Review and Practice

## READER'S THEATER

**Speaking** TIP

Decide how your character feels and should be acting. Use the appropriate body language and tone of voice for your character as you speak.

In a small group, act out this special TV news report about gangs.

**Cornell Cappelle:** Tonight we're speaking with three of the kids involved in last week's incident on London Woods Lake. A short time ago, I reported that TV Six had found no evidence of gangs in our city. Well, we were wrong. We should have been talking with our children. We might have prevented what happened last week. Malaka, you cooperated with the police to help find Romi and Julio, but you used to be a member of the Devildogs. How did you first get involved with them?

**Malaka:** [*nervous and clearing her throat*] Well, my mom and me—we weren't getting along. And then I met Terrell. He was tellin' me that I could be in the gang and be popular and all that. And it sounded real good. I never thought things would go as far as they did. [*starts crying*] Romi, I . . .

**Romi:** [*looks seriously at Malaka*] To be honest, I still don't feel safe around anyone who's been associated with that gang. I got over one nightmare—and now, I have another.

**Cornell:** [*nodding*] And now, Julio—you're the real hero.

**Julio:** [*thinking hard*] Yes and no. We never should have thought we could stand up to the gang alone. It was just too dangerous.

**Cornell:** All of us have learned from this. The school and community are doing all they can. I urge you to talk to your parents, your teachers, your counselors, and each other. Admitting we have a problem is the first step.

## COMPREHENSION

Workbook
Page 147

**Right There**

1. What warning does Malaka give Romiette about Julio?
2. What two factors make the situation on the lake life-threatening?

### Think and Search

3. How does Malaka's warning come true?
4. How does Julio find Romiette under the water?

### Author and You

5. Why do you think the author chose the particular title, setting, and conflict that she did?
6. Is the author's message a hopeful or despairing one? Why?

### On Your Own

7. How would you advise a friend who seems to be hanging around with the wrong people?
8. In your opinion, how big of a problem are gangs?

▲ **A TV reporter at a crime scene**

## DISCUSSION

Discuss in pairs or small groups.

1. Malaka and Romi used to be friends. What do you think happened? Why is it that some teenagers are attracted to gangs and bullies and others are not? Why do some teenagers want someone like Mr. T to do their thinking for them?
2. Can you always believe what you hear on TV? Cornell Cappelle admits that his station was clearly wrong about gangs in the community. What advice would you give to help reporters investigating problems with youth in a community? Why?

**Q How do conflicts affect us?** Romiette and Julio decide that they can handle the situation alone. They don't tell their parents about the conflict they're having with the gang. Do you think there are some things teenagers can't handle alone and need to ask adults for help with? Why?

*Listening* TIP

Listen to what others have to say. Their ideas may help you join in the discussion.

## RESPONSE TO LITERATURE

**Workbook**
Page 147

Write a letter to the editor expressing whether you think Malaka's punishment should be lesser than that given the five Devildogs. Use what you know of her role in the incident. How should authorities view her cooperation with the police? How should they view her silence at a time when she knew enough to help prevent the incident?

# Grammar and Writing

## GRAMMAR, USAGE, AND MECHANICS

### Modals of Advisability: *should, ought to, had better*; Adverb Clauses of Condition: *if*

Use *should* and *ought to* to give advice. *Should* and *ought to* have the same meaning. *Ought to* is usually not used in the negative. Use *shouldn't* instead.

> Teenagers **should/ought to** tell their parents if they're in trouble.
> Teenagers **shouldn't (should not)** associate with gang members.

Use *had better* and *had better not* to give a warning. They are stronger than *should*.

> You**'d better (had better)** stay away from deep water if you can't swim.
> You**'d better not (had better not)** try standing up to gang members alone.

Adverb clauses of condition, called *if* clauses, can also be used to give advice. *If* clauses are even stronger than *had better* and express a warning.

| Adverb Clause (*if* clause) | Result Clause |
|---|---|
| **If** he doesn't learn the rules, | he might have to be taught a lesson. |
| **If** you don't get out of the boat, | you might get hit by lightning. |

### Practice  **Workbook Page 148**

Work with a partner. At the lake, Romiette and Julio are fighting for their lives. Give them advice by completing each sentence starter. Write the sentences in your notebook. Take turns reading the sentences aloud.

1. You should . . .
2. You shouldn't . . .
3. You ought to . . .
4. You had better . . .
5. If you don't tell your parents about the gang, . . .

## WRITING AN EXPOSITORY PARAGRAPH

### Support a Position

At the end of this unit, you'll write an expository essay that expands one of this unit's four paragraphs. Now you'll write a paragraph that tells your position on something and how you support that position.

Read the student model below. Notice how the writer states her position and then gives reasons that support it. She used a word web to help organize her ideas.

*Karimah McCarthy*

**No Place for Gangs in Our Schools**

Some teenagers get pressured into being in a gang because they think it's cool. In my opinion, schools should take steps to discourage gangs. They ought to enforce policies that require student groups to be open to all students, allow each member a voice, and serve useful purposes. Gangs like the Devildogs do not meet these requirements. First of all, to be a member, you have to be a certain race. Second, gangs like the Devildogs serve no useful purpose. They do no good for the school community. In fact, such gangs can lead to major violence. Finally, people in gangs have no voice and must follow gang rules, no matter what. Malaka did not think for herself; she allowed her boyfriend Terrell to think for her. Gangs ought to be put to the test and not allowed in our schools for the reasons outlined here.

### Practice

**Workbook Page 149**

Write a paragraph that supports your position on something. It could be about one of the issues related to the events in *Romiette and Julio*. Here are some ideas: *Malaka should be punished; news channels should thoroughly investigate serious issues; teenagers should not take dangerous matters into their own hands; the Devildogs should be severely punished.* Organize your ideas in a word web. Be sure to correctly use modals of advice, such as *should*, *ought to*, and *had better*. Also use adverbs of condition in *if* statements when appropriate.

**Writing Checklist**

**VOICE:**
☑ My position about the topic is clear.

**ORGANIZATION:**
☑ I state standards and give reasons why something does or does not measure up.

## What You Will Learn

**Reading**

- Vocabulary building: *Context, dictionary skills, word study*

- Reading strategy: *Compare and contrast*

- Text type: *Informational text (social studies)*

**Grammar, Usage, and Mechanics**
Present real conditional

**Writing**
Write to compare and contrast

### ⓠ THE BIG QUESTION

**How do conflicts affect us?** Experiencing conflict can cause us to feel tense, confused, and, in some cases, depressed. But is the outcome of conflict always bad? Can something good ever come out of conflict? Discuss with a partner.

### BUILD BACKGROUND

The excerpt from ***Conflict Resolution: The Win-Win Situation*** is an informational text that gives tips and advice about how to solve problems and resolve conflicts. Many conflicts can be resolved, but sometimes they perpetuate, or go on and on. In some cases they even result in violence. Some schools have introduced their own ways of dealing with conflict:

- Conflict resolution programs with trained mediators
- School crime-watch programs
- Nonviolence rallies or events
- Anonymous hotlines
- Forums to brainstorm solutions to conflicts

▲ Sometimes, just talking can help solve a problem.

**Survey of High School Students about Behavior during One Year**

33 percent had been in a physical fight

12.5 percent had been in a physical fight on school property

4 percent had been hurt badly enough to need medical treatment

### Learn Key Words

Read these sentences. Use the context to figure out the meaning of the **red** words. Use a dictionary to check your answers. Then write each word and its meaning in your notebook.

1. He agreed not to drive at night. Once he made this **accommodation**, she let him use the car.

2. His **avoidance** didn't help the situation; ignoring his girlfriend's rudeness to his friend just made things worse.

3. If we **compromise**, we can end the argument. You must accept less than you want, and so must I.

4. When the conflict grew, he tried to **defuse** the tension by telling a joke.

5. They agreed to talk about it so they could **negotiate** a solution they'd both like.

6. We need a solution that **preserves** our relationship. We don't want to lose what we have.

| Key Words |
|---|
| accommodation |
| avoidance |
| compromise |
| defuse |
| negotiate |
| preserves |

### Practice  Workbook Page 150

Write the sentences in your notebook. Choose a **red** word from the box above to complete each sentence. Then take turns reading the sentences aloud with a partner.

1. A solution acceptable to both sides _____ friendships.

2. Counting to ten is one way to _____ a tense situation.

3. While the two friends did not get exactly what they wanted, their _____ ended the disagreement.

4. She didn't want to talk about the conflict, so she chose _____ and changed the subject.

5. I can't come to any meetings on Fridays. If you can make this _____ for me, I'll join the club.

6. The two people worked together to _____ a solution; they talked for an hour before they finally came to an agreement.

## Learn Academic Words

Study the **red** words and their meanings. You will find these words useful when talking and writing about informational texts. Write each word and its meaning in your notebook. After you read the excerpt from *Conflict Resolution: The Win-Win Situation*, try to use these words to respond to the text.

| | | |
|---|---|---|
| **clarifying** = making something easier to understand by explaining it in more detail | ➡ | By asking questions and **clarifying**, you can find out how someone really feels about a situation. |
| **issues** = subjects or problems that people discuss or debate | ➡ | Trust and respect are important **issues** when trying to resolve conflicts. |
| **principled** = having strong beliefs about what is morally right and wrong | ➡ | She is very **principled** and believes that lying is morally wrong. |
| **validate** = recognize or acknowledge | ➡ | When we **validate** someone's feelings, we make him or her feel accepted and understood. |

## Practice

**Workbook**
**Page 151**

Work with a partner to answer these questions. Try to include the **red** word in your answer. Write the sentences in your notebook.

1. Why is **clarifying** both sides of an argument important?

2. What are some **issues** people commonly disagree about?

3. In your opinion, does a **principled** person make a good friend? Why or why not?

4. Why is it important to **validate** someone's feelings?

Just being there is a way of
validating someone's feelings. ▶

314

# Word Study: Spelling the Long and Short *u* Sound

The long and short *u* sound are both spelled with the letter *u*. Look at the examples in the chart below. The short *u* sound can be spelled with other combinations of letters. Notice the different spelling combinations that can produce a long *u* sound.

| Spelling | Long vowels /ü/, /ū/ | Short vowel /u/ |
|---|---|---|
| u | f**u**rious, tr**u**ly, comm**u**nicate | **u**pset, r**u**t, **u**p, t**u**mbled, misj**u**dge, **u**s |
| ue | arg**ue**, iss**ue**s | |
| u-e | h**uge**, def**use** | |
| -ou | **you** | enc**ou**ragement |
| -ew | curf**ew**, n**ew**, f**ew**, Hebr**ew** | |

## Practice

**Workbook** Page 152

Work with a partner. Copy the chart above into your notebook. Read the words in the box below. Decide if the words have a long or short *u* sound based on their spelling. Add them to the appropriate column in the chart. Then write sentences in your notebook using the words in the chart. Practice the long and short *u* sounds by reading your sentences aloud.

| | | | | |
|---|---|---|---|---|
| blue | cube | Junc | run | stuck |
| continue | fun | renew | soup | tough |

---

## READING STRATEGY   COMPARE AND CONTRAST

One strategy that will help you understand *Conflict Resolution* is to compare and contrast. When you compare, you tell how things are alike. When you contrast, you tell how they are different.

A Venn diagram can help you organize your ideas. Use a Venn diagram like this one to compare and contrast two conflicting groups. The overlapping area is the type of resolution strategy used to resolve the conflict.

As you read, compare and contrast the various conflicts and the various strategies used to resolve them.

Resolution strategy

Conflict   Conflict

**Workbook** Page 153

**Set a purpose for reading** Think of a time you got into an argument with someone close to you. How did you feel after the argument? Did you resolve the conflict? What tips from the following reading could have helped you?

# *from* Conflict Resolution:
## The Win-Win Situation

### *Carolyn Casey*

### Getting to the Root of a Conflict

Often what people argue about is not really what they are upset about. A friend might blow up because her locker partner's books tumbled onto the floor when she opened the door. On a different day, she might have laughed at the mess. But because she did not get enough sleep the night before and has a huge test in an hour, the heap of books is no laughing matter. A student might get furious with his girlfriend for canceling their date. But he might actually be worried about being chosen for the basketball team and just be transferring that anxiety onto his girlfriend. It is impossible to solve a conflict without understanding the real reason for the problem.

Feeling caught in a rut is often a sign that people are paying too much attention to the wrong things, or not understanding what the fights are really about. For example,

battles between teens and their parents that seem to center on friends or curfews are often reflections of much deeper issues, such as privacy and trust.

It can be helpful to try to look at the situation from the other person's viewpoint. This is difficult to do in the heat of an argument, but it can be done a few hours or days later. Sometimes looking at a problem from someone else's perspective helps people understand the issues better. The issues may be completely different ones than those that were shouted about earlier.

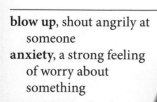

---

**blow up**, shout angrily at someone
**anxiety**, a strong feeling of worry about something

## Using an Ear instead of a Mouth: Why Listening Is an Essential Step

An old Hebrew saying is "The beginning of wisdom is silence." When working on conflict resolution, it is important to remember that no one will ever understand the opposite point of view until he or she stops talking and starts listening.

It is easy during an argument to be so busy stating one side of the conflict that no one stops to hear the other side. Sometimes, with careful listening, people discover there is more agreement than disagreement.

There are different ways to listen. Everyone has had the experience of talking to a parent or friend and realizing that person has his or her mind someplace else and is not really hearing what is being said. In our fast-paced society with televisions and radios competing for conversation, people often forget to stop and carefully listen to what is being said.

*Active listening* is a style of listening in which people are actually hearing and understanding what is being said. Linda Lantieri and Janet Patti, the authors of the conflict resolution book, *Waging Peace in Our Schools*, write, "Active listening is really listening with the heart. It helps us defuse anger and hostility and gain information." Sometimes people think listening is what happens when they take a breath and wait to make their next statement. But it is much more than that. Active listening—an essential communications tool—involves setting everything aside and truly paying attention to the person who is speaking. People who are active listeners are better able to understand the other person's feelings and learn his or her perspective. Active listening techniques include:

*Paraphrasing* Repeat the information you've just heard and reword it. It can feel artificial at first, but it is a good way to make sure you are hearing the right information. *Example:* "I am hearing you say that when I take the car without permission, you feel like I am not showing you respect."

*Clarifying* Get more understanding and information by asking some questions. *Example:* "What did you mean when you said that?" "When did this begin?" or "How did you feel about it?"

*Reflecting* Echo back the feelings you think someone has. This is similar to paraphrasing but focuses on someone's underlying feelings, not the words. *Example:* "You sound really sad about that." Be aware that at times we misjudge someone else's feelings, so this also can be the time for that person to correct us and say, "No, I'm not sad, I'm angry."

---

### Getting to the Root of an Argument

Make a list of what you are fighting about and look for patterns. The argument may start out over a clothing allowance, but the real issue is making purchases without needing to get a parent's permission.

Ask yourself if you are giving mixed messages. Are you telling your friends that you want to be included in their activities but are always rejecting their invitations? Are you telling your boyfriend you want to break up with him, but are still spending hours on the phone with him each night? Make sure you are giving out clear information.

---

**hostility,** unfriendly and angry feelings or behavior
**artificial,** not natural
**underlying,** very basic or important, but not easily noticed

### BEFORE YOU GO ON

1. Why is knowing the real reason for a conflict so important?

2. What makes reflecting different from paraphrasing?

**On Your Own**
Are you an active listener? Why?

*Encouraging* Get the person to continue talking. *Example:* "Go ahead and tell me about it. I want to hear what you have to say."

*Validating* Let the person know that his or her sharing information is appreciated. *Example:* "I know you are uncomfortable, but I'm glad you are telling me about this."

*Summarizing* Briefly recap what the other person said. *Example:* "So my understanding is that you still want to be friends if I stop gossiping about you."

## Learning a New Approach

Responses to conflict can be categorized into three basic groups: soft, hard, and principled. Most people use all three approaches at different times.

In both soft and hard responses, the arguing parties take positions or stands. They then negotiate these positions by trying either to avoid or to win a contest of wills. Soft and hard negotiations either bring about one-sided losses or demand one-sided gains. In principled responses, the parties use conflict resolution strategies to produce lasting "wise agreements" that address the interests of both, resolve conflicting interests fairly, and take into account how others will be affected by the agreement.

Sharon and Tami are ninth graders who have been best friends since kindergarten. They share everything: clothes, makeup, and secrets. Last weekend, Tami borrowed Sharon's favorite pair of jeans to wear rollerblading. When Tami fell off a curb, she tore a huge hole in the jeans. Sharon, who was going to wear the jeans on a date this weekend, is about to get the news. Look at the chart to see each type of response.

---

**contest of wills,** situation in which people with strong determination oppose each other
**take into account,** allow or plan for a certain possibility

Soft responses such as avoidance, accommodation, and compromise usually occur between people who are friends or who want to be pleasant to each other because they will continue to have contact in the future. While a soft response might work well in some situations, it can be a problem if it is a teen's only approach to conflict. Usually hard responses to conflict happen between people who are adversaries and whose goal is victory. On the sports field, this type of response can win an athletic event. But in relationships, it can cause big problems. Notice that by using a principled response, Tami and Sharon are able to find a solution that works and neither one is hiding her feelings. People who are problem solvers usually pick a principled response to conflict.

Using a principled response preserves relationships. If people work toward a principled response, they are likely to find more cooperation in places where they once found conflict. Why? This response does not create a winner and a loser. Instead people work together to find a solution.

---

**adversaries,** opponents

▲ **A principled response preserves relationships.**

Read Tami's apology and the possible responses Sharon could have.

**Tami:** I'm so sorry. I can't believe I ruined your favorite jeans. I don't know what to do.

### The Soft Conflict Resolution Response

**Sharon:** It's okay. I didn't really like them that much. I'm just glad you didn't get hurt.

**Tami:** Do you want me to pay for them or give you a pair of mine?

**Sharon:** No, it's fine. Really, it doesn't matter. I didn't want to wear them anymore, anyway.

### The Hard Conflict Resolution Response

**Sharon:** I can't believe you ruined them! You knew they were my favorite jeans. You always do this. You have to buy me an identical pair and I need them tonight.

**Tami:** But I won't have any money until I baby-sit on Saturday, and even then I don't know if I'll have enough. I can probably get you another pair in a week and you could borrow anything of mine until then.

**Sharon:** I don't want to wear your clothes. I want you to get me a new pair of jeans just like the ones you borrowed. How you come up with the money is your problem.

### The Principled Conflict Resolution Response

**Sharon:** I'm really disappointed that you tore them. I really like them and I wanted to wear them this weekend. Now I'm stuck.

**Tami:** I could lend you a pair of my jeans.

**Sharon:** That would help, but I think you should replace the pair you tore.

**Tami:** I wish I could, but I don't have enough money. It might take a couple of weeks to earn it.

**Sharon:** I do want you to replace the jeans and if it takes a few weeks, that's okay.

*Avoidance in an argument is a soft response.* ▶

## What Is Your Style?

☐ Do you always like to win arguments? Are you more concerned with winning an argument than with hearing the reasons for the other person's opinion? You are using a hard response.

☐ Do you constantly give in? Are you more concerned about not hurting anyone's feelings or inconveniencing anyone than you are about getting what you want? You are using a soft response.

☐ Are you able to slow down and listen to both sides of a disagreement? Are you able to tell people what you want and hear what they want? Do you look for a win-win solution? You are using a principled response.

Now, take a few minutes and, on a separate piece of paper, write down a short description of a conflict you had. Maybe it was with your parents, your sister or brother, or a friend.

- What was the argument about?
- What did you want? What did the other person want?
- Do you know why he/she wanted that?
- How did you resolve the conflict?
- How did you feel afterward?
- Was there a possible solution that could have worked for everyone?
- What might you do differently next time?

### BEFORE YOU GO ON

**1** What is a principled response to conflict resolution?

**2** What can make soft responses a real problem?

**On Your Own**
What is your conflict resolution style?

# Review and Practice

**COMPREHENSION**  **Workbook Page 154**

### Right There

1. What is active listening?
2. In what three ways can responses to conflict be categorized?

### Think and Search

3. Why is active listening important?
4. Why is a principled response better than a soft or hard response?

### Author and You

5. Why do you think the author says that most people use all three responses at different times? Does this mean that she recommends all three? Explain.

6. Do you think the author believes we should all learn what our style of resolving conflicts is? Why? Do you agree?

### On Your Own

7. How do you resolve conflicts? Are there any things you'd like to change about your approach? Why?

8. Do you think that the same techniques can be used to solve any conflict? Why or why not?

▲ Resolving a conflict

## IN YOUR OWN WORDS

Imagine you are having a disagreement with a friend or a parent. What techniques from *Conflict Resolution: The Win-Win Situation* could help you solve the problem? With a partner, take turns explaining the problem and the techniques you'd use. Take notes about what each other said. Did you include the same techniques? How many key points from the selection did each of you use?

*Speaking* **TIPS**

Be sure to explain your problem clearly and tell how you'd use the techniques.

Speak slowly and invite questions from your partner.

## DISCUSSION

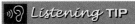 **Listening TIP**

Use one or two active listening techniques in your discussion.

Discuss in pairs or small groups.

1. How might active listening techniques—paraphrasing, clarifying, reflecting, encouraging, validating, or summarizing—have helped Romiette when Malaka confronted her? Would some of the techniques *not* have worked?

2. Which response to conflict would work best in a disagreement with a close friend? A parent or other adult? A classmate you don't know that well? Is a principled response always best to use?

3. Some people think teenagers are involved in more conflicts than other age groups. Do you think this is true? Explain.

**Q How do conflicts affect us?** Share a story about an argument you had with a friend. Did your friendship grow from the argument, or does one of you still have bad feelings about it? Is there anything you would do differently now? If so, what?

## READ FOR FLUENCY

When we read aloud to communicate meaning, we group words into phrases, pause or slow down to make important points, and emphasize important words. Pause for a short time when you reach a comma and for a longer time when you reach a period. Pay attention to rising and falling intonation at the end of sentences.

Work with a partner. Choose a paragraph from the reading. Discuss which words seem important for communicating meaning. Practice pronouncing difficult words. Give each other feedback.

## EXTENSION

 **Workbook Page 154**

Studies show that violence, vandalism, school absence, and suspensions are reduced when conflict resolution strategies are used in schools. Does your school have a conflict resolution program? If not, should it have one? Do research to find out the positive effects of making students aware of conflict resolution strategies. In small groups, write a short brochure that describes the benefits of conflict resolution programs in schools. Share with the class.

# Grammar and Writing

## Present Real Conditional

The present real conditional is used to express true, factual ideas. The *if* clause indicates the condition, and the result clause indicates what happens if the condition is met.

| *if* clause | result clause |
|---|---|
| **If** you **summarize** what people say, | it **proves** you're listening carefully. |

Use the simple present in the *if* clause and the result clause. If you aren't certain about the result, you can use a modal, such as *can*, *might*, or *must* in the result clause.

**If** a conflict **develops**, it **might not be** good to discuss it right away.
If I **stop** gossiping about you, **could** we **be** friends?
A soft response **can be** a problem **if** it **is** a teenager's only approach to conflict.

Remember: When you begin a conditional sentence with the *if* clause, use a comma before the result clause.

## Practice  Workbook Page 155

Work with a partner. Copy the sentence starters below into your notebook. Complete the *if* clauses with a result clause. Use a modal if you're unsure about the result.

1. If people feel caught in a rut, . . .

2. If people send mixed messages, . . .

3. If you use active listening techniques, . . .

4. If someone is a problem solver, . . .

5. If you avoid a problem, . . .

# WRITING AN EXPOSITORY PARAGRAPH

## Write to Compare and Contrast

At the end of this unit, you'll write an expository essay that expands one of this unit's four paragraphs. Now you'll write a paragraph that compares and contrasts the three different responses to conflict and shows that a principled response to conflict works best.

| Soft response | Hard response | Principled response |
|---|---|---|
| | | |
| | | |
| | | |

   Read the student model below. Notice how the writer first briefly describes a conflict and then shows the advantages of using a principled response as opposed to a soft or hard response. The writer used a three-column chart to help organize her ideas.

---

*Chelsea A. Hamlet*

### A Principled Response

   Michelle is angry. There are three more days until final exams, and her classmate Katherine is talking and whispering excessively—in the library, in study hall, and even in class when she can—preventing Michelle and others from concentrating and studying. Lately, Michelle has been under a lot of stress and needs total concentration. What can Michelle do? If she uses a soft response and tries to avoid Katherine, her tension will build. She pretends that everything is okay, but deep down inside she is annoyed and even takes out her stress on others. If she uses a hard response, she ends up feeling bad and accomplishes nothing. If Michelle uses a principled response, she can get the results she needs and preserve her relationship with her friend. She can do this by taking Katherine aside, explaining how she feels, and asking Katherine what they, together, can do about it.

---

## Practice  **Workbook Page 156**

Write a paragraph about a conflict that could be resolved using a principled response. Compare and contrast the three different ways the conflict could be resolved and what the outcome of each response would be. Use a three-column chart to organize your ideas. Be sure to present real conditionals correctly.

## Writing Checklist

**IDEAS:**

☑ My conflict is one that can be resolved in one of the three ways.

**SENTENCE FLUENCY:**

☑ My sentences begin in different ways.

323

# Link the Readings

## Critical Thinking

Look back at the readings in this unit. Think about what they have in common. They all tell about conflicts. Yet they do not all have the same purpose. The purpose of one reading might be to inform, while the purpose of another might be to entertain or persuade. In addition, the content of each reading relates to conflicts differently. Now copy the chart below into your notebook and complete it.

| Title of Reading | Purpose | Big Question Link |
|---|---|---|
| From *Romeo and Juliet* | *to entertain* | |
| "Furious Feuds: Enemies by Association" | | *about conflicts around the world and over the years* |
| From *Romiette and Julio* | | |
| From *Conflict Resolution: The Win-Win Situation* | | |

## Discussion

Discuss in pairs or small groups.

- What are some causes and effects of conflicts? Can all conflicts be resolved? Why or why not?

- Think about the readings. Is it possible to avoid conflicts? If so, what are some situations where conflicts could be avoided? How?

## Fluency Check

Work with a partner. Choose a paragraph from one of the readings. Take turns reading it for one minute. Count the total number of words you read. Practice saying the words you had trouble reading. Take turns reading the paragraph three more times. Did you read more words each time? Copy the chart below into your notebook and record your speeds.

| | 1st Speed | 2nd Speed | 3rd Speed | 4th Speed |
|---|---|---|---|---|
| Words Per Minute | | | | |

# Projects

Work in pairs or small groups. Choose one of these projects.

**1** Write a book review of *Romiette and Julio*, based on the excerpts you read. Explain why you do or do not recommend the book. In your review, compare and contrast the book to Shakespeare's *Romeo and Juliet*. Share your reviews in a student newspaper.

**2** Be a movie director. How will you make *Romiette and Julio* into a movie? Who will you cast in the roles? Where will you shoot the movie? What special effects and music will you use? Write stage directions for the three "scenes" you read. Talk about your ideas or present scenes to the class.

**3** Look through newspapers and magazines. Find pictures about different kinds of conflict. Create a collage and display it.

**4** Create a survey about teen conflict. Make a list of questions and have volunteers complete it. Be sure to use items that you can measure, like some yes-or-no questions. Add up the results and present them to the class.

# Further Reading

To find out more about the theme of this unit, choose from these reading suggestions.

**Ripley's Game**, Patricia Highsmith
In this Penguin Reader® adaptation, Tom Ripley seeks revenge for an insult he received at a party. How far will he go?

**The River Between Us**, Richard Peck
The year is 1861 and the Civil War is about to begin. Tilly Pruitt's brother, Noah, is eager to fight for the North. With her father long gone, Tilly, her sister, and their mother struggle to hold the family together.

**The White Heron and Other American Short Stories**,
Sarah Orne Jewett and Others
A hunter in search of a white heron is friendly to Sylvia. She knows where the heron's nest is, but she has to decide what is more important: protecting this beautiful bird or making a new friend.

# Put It All Together

## LISTENING & SPEAKING WORKSHOP

### TV Talk Show

With a group, you will present a TV talk show about conflicts. One person will be the talk show host. The other group members will be guests who share their stories or knowledge about conflicts and conflict resolution.

**1** **THINK ABOUT IT** Work in small groups. List some topics you could include in a TV talk show about conflicts. Look back at the readings in this unit for ideas. For example:

- Family feuds through the years
- What to do about teen gangs
- School and community resources for conflict resolution
- Top teen problems that can lead to conflict

Choose your host and decide which topic each guest will talk about. If you're the host, think of a name for yourself and your show. If you're a guest, give yourself a name and a role that shows your point of view on the topic. For example: *I'm Ben Garcia, a high school counselor* or *I'm Gabby Pinelli, a former gang member.*

**2** **GATHER AND ORGANIZE INFORMATION** Write down facts and details you already know about your topic. If you're the host, write down some questions you'd like to ask and share them with the group.

**Research** Do some research and take notes about your topic at the library or on the Internet. Find some examples that support your point of view. If you're the talk show host, compile a few interesting points about each topic and revise your list of questions.

**Order Your Notes** Make an outline showing the two or three main points you want to make on the show. List evidence and examples to support each point. If you're the host, decide how you will introduce your guests and in what order.

**Use Visuals** Think about how you should dress for the show. Wear a simple costume or bring an appropriate prop to help express your role.

**3** **PRACTICE AND PRESENT** As a group, practice your talk show. Keep your outline handy for reference, but try to speak naturally as you ask and answer questions. Place your chairs at an angle so that the host and guests can see each other and the audience. Be careful not to turn your face away from the audience when you speak. Ask a friend or family member to listen and give feedback. Keep practicing until you can present your show confidently, with smooth transitions between speakers.

**Deliver Your TV Talk Show** TV talk shows are informal and relaxed. Try to create that atmosphere during your presentation. Saying things you didn't rehearse ("ad-libbing") can help. Use gestures and facial expressions to help convey your role and your feelings about the topic.

**4** **EVALUATE THE PRESENTATION**
You can improve your skills as a speaker and a listener by evaluating each presentation you give and hear. Use this checklist to help you judge your group's TV talk show and the talk shows of other groups.

- ☑ Was the talk show clearly related to the unit theme of conflicts?
- ☑ Did the host ask interesting questions? Did the guests give appropriate answers?
- ☑ Did you understand each speaker's role and point of view?
- ☑ Could you hear and understand the speakers easily?
- ☑ What suggestions do you have for improving the talk show?

### Speaking TIPS

Use sentences like these to express disagreement politely:

- *I'm not sure I agree with that.*
- *That's a good point. However, . . .*

Present facts clearly. Help your listeners distinguish facts from opinions you have by using phrases like *In my opinion* and *I believe . . .*

### Listening TIPS

Think about the examples people give to support their points. Are these examples similar to or different from your own experiences?

When you participate in a talk show, listen carefully. If you don't understand a question or answer, ask the host or guest to repeat or explain it.

# WRITING WORKSHOP

## Expository Essay

You've already learned how to write a variety of expository paragraphs and some techniques to develop them. Like an expository paragraph, an expository essay gives information about a topic. An expository essay begins with an introductory paragraph that presents the writer's main idea. Three body paragraphs develop and support the main idea with details and examples. The writer ends with a concluding paragraph that restates the main idea or draws a conclusion. Some different ways to organize the information in an expository essay include using the 5Ws format of a news article, exploring cause and effect, evaluating something against a standard, or comparing and contrasting aspects of a topic.

Your assignment is to write a five-paragraph expository essay that expands one of the four paragraphs you previously wrote for this unit.

**1 PREWRITE** Choose the paragraph you want to expand. Then, use your notebook to list additional details you want to include when you expand your paragraph. Also, think about the voice you will use. Is your essay a lively gossip column? A serious look at the causes and effects of conflict? Your voice should both express your personality and also suit your topic.

**List and Organize Ideas and Details** After you choose your topic, use a graphic organizer to help you plan the information you want to include in your essay. A student named Kate used a question-and-answer outline to expand her gossip column about Romeo and Juliet. Here is her outline:

> I.  Q: Who am I focusing on?
>     A: Romeo and Juliet
> II. Q: Where did their romance start?
>     A: At Juliet's house
> III. Q: When did it start?
>     A: During the ball
> IV. Q: What am I focusing on?
>     A: Their romantic troubles
> V.  Q: Why are they having romantic troubles?
>     A: Feuding between the Capulets and the Montagues

**2 DRAFT** Use the model on page 331 and your graphic organizer to help you write a first draft. Develop the information in your essay by using one of the organization methods you learned about in this unit.

**3** **REVISE** Read over your draft. As you do so, ask yourself the questions in the writing checklist. Use the questions to help you revise your essay.

### SIX TRAITS OF WRITING CHECKLIST

☑ **IDEAS:** Do the details and examples I use support my main ideas?

☑ **ORGANIZATION:** Are details and examples presented in a logical order?

☑ **VOICE:** Do my tone and style suit my topic?

☑ **WORD CHOICE:** Do I use transition words to connect my main points?

☑ **SENTENCE FLUENCY:** Do I use a variety of sentence lengths and types?

☑ **CONVENTIONS:** Does my writing follow the rules of grammar, usage, and mechanics?

Here are the changes Kate plans to make when she revises her first draft:

---

Trouble Ahead for Romeo and Juliet!

Readers, have you heard what happened at the masquerade ball last night? Quite the drama! What was that crazy boy thinking, sneaking *young Romeo created* into a ball given by the Capulets, his family's worst ~~enemys~~ enemies, when he is a Montague!

My sources tell me that Romeo found out about the party only by chance. Luckily, lord Capulet was in a very good mood, or Romeo could have been killed on the spot after being discovered. I guess risking his life turned out to be worth it for our reckless Romeo, since He found the ~~beautyful~~ beautiful Juliet inside that ballroom. When he spotted Juliet, Lord Capulet's daughter, I hear it was love at first sight.

---

Juliet and Romeo went into a corner by themselves and started dancing and talking. I bet Romeo was charming his way into her heart. Sources say that after some time they kissed! How romantic! One of my readers who attended at the party last night informed me of the juicy details.

Unfortunately, this romance is surely destined for disaster! Juliets parents will never accept Romeo. Capulets hate Montagues, and Montagues hates Capulets. These two noble families have always feuded, In fact, the tension before the party was so terrible, that The Prince of the city had to threaten Lord Capulet and Lord Montague with death if they didn't make peace. The sad truth is that Romeo and Juliet will never be allowed to marry.

The only way I can see them being together is if they run away from this madness. If They had better not stay here. They will surely be caught and then either sentenced to death or forced to marry someone else. On the other hand, if they leave, they will never see their familys families again. Poor Romeo! Poor Juliet! Why can't their familys families get along? In my opinion, if people are nice to one another, they are more likely to be happy in life.

## 4 EDIT AND PROOFREAD  Workbook Page 157

Copy your revised draft onto a clean sheet of paper. Read it again. Correct any errors in grammar, word usage, mechanics, and spelling. Here are the additional changes Kate plans to make when she prepares her final draft.

Kate Munz

### Trouble Ahead for Romeo and Juliet!

Readers, have you heard what happened at the masquerade ball last night? Quite the drama young Romeo created! What was that crazy boy thinking, sneaking into a ball given by the Capulets, his family's worst enemies, when he is a Montague!

My sources tell me that Romeo found out about the party only by chance. Luckily, lord Capulet was in a very good mood, or Romeo could have been killed on the spot after being discovered. I guess risking his life turned out to be worth it for our reckless Romeo, since he found the beautiful Juliet inside that ballroom. When he spotted Juliet, Lord Capulet's daughter, I hear it was love at first sight.

One of my readers who attended the party last night informed me of the juicy details. Juliet and Romeo went into a corner by themselves and started dancing and talking. I bet Romeo was charming his way into her heart. Sources say that after some time they kissed! How romantic!

Unfortunately, this romance is surely destined for disaster! Juliets parents will never accept Romeo. Capulets hate Montagues, and Montagues hates Capulets. These two noble families have always feuded. In fact, the tension before the party was so terrible that the Prince of the city had to threaten Lord Capulet and Lord Montague with death if they didn't make peace. The sad truth is that Romeo and Juliet will never be allowed to marry.

The only way I can see them being together is if they run away from this madness. If they had stay here, they will surely be caught and then either sentenced to death or forced to marry someone else. On the other hand, if they leave, they will never see their families again. Poor Romeo! Poor Juliet! Why can't their families get along? In my opinion, if people are nice to one another, they are more likely to be happy in life.

**5** **PUBLISH** Prepare your final draft. Share your essay with your teacher and classmates.

Workbook
Page 158

# Fighting for Land

*P*eople have always fought one another throughout history. People fight over land, water, food, ideas, and sometimes things no one can explain. Of course, conflict is dramatic, which makes it a good subject for artists. From an artist's point of view, conflict creates opportunities for vivid colors and action or to make strong political statements.

### George Catlin, *Comanche Warriors, with White Flag, Receiving the Dragoons* (1834–35)

By 1830, most of the Native Americans on the East coast of the United States had been forced to move West by white settlers and the federal government. Artist George Catlin, eager to record the changing lifestyles of these tribes, set out on a 2,900-kilometer (1,800-mi.) journey through the West. He wanted to paint Native American culture before it disappeared. He eventually produced more than 2,000 paintings, hundreds of which are in the Smithsonian American Art Museum's collection.

In *Comanche Warriors, with White Flag, Receiving the Dragoons* (heavily armed troops), Catlin painted a meeting between U.S. soldiers and warriors from a Comanche village whose wigwams are in the background. The village seems trapped between the mountain range in the background and the U.S. soldiers in the foreground. The artist contrasts the open plains and the tall mountains with the size of the men, who seem small in comparison. The fact that two of the Native Americans on horseback carry white flags means that they want peace. But their small flags seem to get swallowed up in the larger image.

▲ George Catlin, *Comanche Warriors, with White Flag, Receiving the Dragoons,* 1834–35, oil, 24 x 29⅛ in., Smithsonian American Art Museum

▲ Jaune Quick-To-See Smith, *State Names*, 2000, mixed media,
48 × 72 in., Smithsonian American Art Museum

### Jaune Quick-To-See Smith, *State Names* (2000)

"We were the original owners of this country," says artist
Jaune Quick-To-See Smith, a Native American who lives
in New Mexico. "Our land was stolen from us by the Euro-
American invaders. I can't say strongly enough that my maps
are about stolen lands, our very heritage, our cultures, our
world view, our being."

The actual battles in the field may be over between Native
Americans and the U.S. military, but even today people feel
the impact of those conflicts. Smith uses her map of the
United States and part of Mexico to show a land already
lost to her people. The dripping blur of colors makes the
boundaries between the states less firm. She identifies only
states that have names based on Native-American words.
Kansas, for example, means "people of the south wind" in the
Sioux language.

Conflicts almost always cause damage. Fortunately, most
people resolve their differences with words rather
than weapons.

## Apply What You Learned

**1** Why do you think artist
George Catlin chose to
show the people fighting
over land in his painting as
very small figures against
the landscape?

**2** Why do you think Jaune
Quick-To-See Smith
identified only states that
had Native-American names
in her painting?

 **Big Question**
In what way does each of
these artworks address the
subject of fighting over land?
Explain your answer.

**Workbook**
Pages 159–160

333

# UNIT 6

## THE BIG Q QUESTION

# Do things really change?

This unit is about changing times. What was life like in the earliest times? In medieval times? How do some things change and yet remain the same? Reading about attitudes toward women, disease epidemics, and war and secrecy—through the years—helps us gain perspective on issues today.

### READING 1: Novel Excerpt and Short Story

- From *Catherine, Called Birdy* by Karen Cushman
- "The Dinner Party" by Mona Gardner

### READING 2: Science and Social Studies Articles

- From *Oh, Rats!: The Story of Rats and People* by Albert Marrin
- From *Outbreak: Plagues That Changed History* by Bryn Barnard

### READING 3: Myth

- From *Dateline: Troy* by Paul Fleischman

### READING 4: Social Studies Article

- From *Top Secret: A Handbook of Codes, Ciphers, and Secret Writing* by Paul B. Janeczko

## Listening and Speaking

At the end of this unit, you will give an **oral report** about a unit topic.

## Writing

At the end of this unit, you will write a **research report**. A research report analyzes information based on an in-depth study of a subject. It provides support from sources for its main premise.

### QuickWrite

Write about one way that things have changed in your lifetime.

Visit *LongmanKeystone.com*

# Prepare to Read

## What You Will Learn

**Reading**
- Vocabulary building: *Literary terms, word study*
- Reading strategy: *Ask questions (5Ws)*
- Text type: *Literature (novel excerpt, short story)*

**Grammar, Usage, and Mechanics**
Adjective clauses: relative pronouns as subjects and objects

**Writing**
Write an introductory paragraph

 **THE BIG QUESTION**

**Do things really change?** In the United States today, women own and run businesses. They are active in politics. However, it was not so long ago that women could not own land or vote. They rarely worked outside the home. How does our culture view women today? What challenges do women still face?

▲ Women marching for suffrage in 1912.

**BUILD BACKGROUND**

***Catherine, Called Birdy*** is a novel written in the form of a diary. It takes the reader to medieval England in the year 1290. It tells about the thoughts and events in the life of a girl named Catherine. Catherine's father wants her to marry a rich man. It was a tradition at that time for fathers to choose their daughters' husbands. But Catherine is unwilling to do as her father wishes.

**"The Dinner Party"** takes place in India during the early 1900s. An army colonel at the party is explaining that men have greater self-control than women. He claims that women scream and panic in a crisis, while men stay calm.

### Learn Literary Words

When authors write stories, they choose a narrator and a point of view to relate the events to the reader. You're going to read an excerpt from a fictional diary written from the **first-person point of view**. You'll find out everything, including the events, from the main character Catherine's perspective. Notice the use of the first person in this entry:

> If I had to be born a lady, why not a *rich* lady, so someone else could do the work and I could lie on a silken bed and listen to a beautiful minstrel sing while my servants hemmed?

In the short story "The Dinner Party," the events are told from the **third-person point of view**. The reader sees the characters and events of a dinner party mostly through the eyes of one of the characters—the American scientist. Notice the use of the third person:

> The American scientist does not join in the argument, but sits watching the faces of the other guests. As he looks, he sees a strange expression come over the face of the hostess.

**Practice**  **Workbook Page 161**

Work with a partner. Rewrite the two passages above from different points of view.

**Literary Words**

first-person point of view
third-person point of view

▲ Christine de Pisan, a medieval writer

## Learn Academic Words

Study the **red** words and their meanings. You will find these words useful when talking and writing about literature. Write each word and its meaning in your notebook. After you read the excerpt from *Catherine, Called Birdy* and "The Dinner Party," try to use these words to respond to the text.

consented
economics
reaction
status
tradition

| | | |
|---|---|---|
| **consented** = agreed | ➡ | She **consented** to marry the man her parents had chosen, but she didn't love him. |
| **economics** = relating to the development and management of wealth | ➡ | Money and **economics** were the main reasons that fathers wanted to find rich husbands for their daughters. |
| **reaction** = something you feel or do because of what has happened or been said to you | ➡ | Even though she was frightened, she showed no **reaction** and looked calm. |
| **status** = your social or professional rank or position, in relation to other people | ➡ | If a daughter married someone of higher **status**, her parents' own importance increased. |
| **tradition** = something that people have done for a long time and continue to do | ➡ | It was against **tradition**, but she didn't care and refused to marry a man she didn't love. |

**Practice**  **Workbook** Page 162

Write the sentences in your notebook. Choose a **red** word from the box above to complete each sentence. Then take turns reading the sentences aloud with a partner.

1. While he expected her to be overjoyed about the news, she showed no _____, not even a smile.

2. A long time ago, it was a _____ for girls to learn how to cook and sew.

3. A family's _____ could be measured by how many knights the family had.

4. In medieval England, most girls _____ to do whatever their parents expected of them.

5. The _____ of a family's household determined how many knights the family could support.

338

## Word Study: Silent Letters

The letter combinations *wr*, *kn*, *gn*, and *mb* each stand for one sound when they are at the beginning or end of a word or syllable. We say that one letter is "silent." Since many words in English have these combinations, it's a good idea to learn them and the sounds they stand for in words.

| Words with Silent Letter | Letter Combination | Sound | Which Letter Is Silent? |
|---|---|---|---|
| **wr**ite | wr | /r/ | w |
| **kn**ight | kn | /n/ | k |
| ali**gn** | gn | /n/ | g |
| co**mb** | mb | /m/ | b |

▲ A knight

**Practice**  Workbook Page 163

Work with a partner. Take turns reading aloud and spelling the words in the box below. Then copy the words into your notebook and underline the letters *wr*, *kn*, *gn*, or *mb*. Circle the letter combinations in which one letter is silent (some are not silent).

| | | | | |
|---|---|---|---|---|
| acknowledge | December | foreign | ignorant | remember |
| climb | dowry | grumble | know | writing |

**READING STRATEGY**  ASK QUESTIONS (5Ws)

As you read, check your comprehension, or understanding, by asking questions. You can easily form your own questions by remembering the 5Ws: *who*, *where*, *when*, *what*, and *why*.

- Who is the text about?
- Where do the events take place?
- When do the events take place?
- What happens in the text?
- Why does the event happen?

 Workbook Page 164

**LITERATURE**

**NOVEL AND
SHORT STORY**

**Set a purpose for reading** The women in these two readings challenge their culture's view of women. As you read, think about how women were viewed in society. How has that view changed over time?

# from
# Catherine, Called Birdy

## Karen Cushman

*It isn't easy being a young woman in England in the year 1290. Teenage Catherine's father is determined to marry her off to the richest suitor. But Catherine has other ideas. In this excerpt, she scares away another suitor, "Poor Fire Eyes."*

### Author's Note

The England of 1290 is a foreign country. Medieval people live in a place we can never go, made up of what they value, how they think, and what they believe is true and important and possible. The difference begins with how people saw themselves. Everyone had a particular place in a community. Girls were mostly trained for marriage. Marriage among the noble classes was not a matter of love but economics. Marriages were arranged to increase land, gain allies, or pay back debts. Women were essentially property, used to further a family's alliances, wealth, or status.

# 19th Day of September

My mother and I have made a bargain. I may forgo spinning as long as I write this account for Edward.

What follows will be my book—the book of Catherine, called Little Bird or Birdy Begun this 19th day of September in the year of Our Lord 1290, the fourteenth year of my life. The writing I learned of my brother Edward, but the words are my own.

Picked off twenty-nine fleas today.

# 21st Day of September

Something is astir. I can feel my father's eyes following me about the hall, regarding me as he would a new warhorse or a bull bought for breeding. I am surprised that he has not asked to examine my hooves.

This morning: "Exactly how old are you, daughter?"

This forenoon: "Have you all your teeth?"

"Is your breath sweet or foul?"

"Are you a good eater?"

"What color is your hair when it is clean?"

Before supper: "How are your sewing and your bowels and conversation?"

What is brewing here?

✔ **LITERARY CHECK**
*How does **first-person point of view** help you understand what Catherine thinks of her life?*

# 22nd Day of September

If I had to be born a lady, why not a *rich* lady, so someone else could do the work and I could lie on a silken bed and listen to a beautiful minstrel sing while my servants hemmed? Instead I am the daughter of a country knight with but ten servants, seventy villagers, no minstrel, and acres of unhemmed linen. It grumbles my guts.

Morwenna says it is the altar cloth for me. Corpus bones!

# 24th Day of September

The stars and my family align to make my life black and miserable. My mother seeks to make me a fine lady—dumb, docile, and accomplished. My brother Edward thinks even girls should not be ignorant, so he taught me to read holy books and to write. Now my father, the toad, conspires to sell me like a cheese to some lack-wit seeking a wife.

---

**astir**, happening or going on
**minstrel**, singer or musician in the Middle Ages
**hemmed**, sewed
**grumbles my guts**, upsets me
**altar cloth**, time to get married
**corpus bones**, over my dead body
**docile**, quiet and easy to control
**lack-wit**, someone who's not very smart

**BEFORE YOU GO ON**

**1** What were girls trained for in medieval times?

**2** Why is Catherine's father asking her these questions?

💡**On Your Own**
What's your impression of Catherine so far?

## 15th Day of December

I was seated at dinner this day with another clodpole in search of a wife. This one was friendly and good-tempered, and had all his teeth and hair. Our talk at dinner went like this:

"Do you enjoy riding, Lady Catherine?"

"Mmph."

"Could we perhaps ride together while I am here?"

"Pfgh."

"I understand you read Latin. I admire learned women when they are also beautiful."

"Urgh."

"Mayhap you could show me about the manor after dinner."

"Grmph."

So it went until I conceived my plan, after realizing that the only thing my father would want more than a rich son-in-law is not to part with one of his pennies or acres or bushels of onions. So I grew quite lively and talkative, bubbling with praise for our chests of treasure and untold acres and countless tenants and hoards of silver and for the modesty that prompted my father to hide his wealth and appear as a mere country knight. My suitor's eyes, which had already rested kindly on me, caught fire, and he fairly flew over the rushes to talk with my father in the solar.

The storm I expected was not long in coming. Poor Fire Eyes tumbled down the stairs from the solar, hands over his head, and rolled across the hall floor to the door and out while my father bellowed above, "Dowry! Manors! Treasure! You want me to pay you to take the girl? Dowry? I'll give you her dowry!"

And as the comely young man ran across the yard on his way to the stable and freedom, a brimming chamber pot came flying from the solar window and landed on his head. Farewell, suitor. Benedicite.

---

**clodpole**, stupid person
**mayhap**, perhaps
**manor**, a large house with a large area of land around it
**acres**, land
**bushels**, containers
**rushes**, certain plants that grow on wet land
**solar**, sunroom
**dowry**, money or property that the wife's family gives to the husband
**benedicite**, bless you

## ABOUT THE **AUTHOR**

**Karen Cushman** was born in Chicago, Illinois. Her first novel, *Catherine, Called Birdy*, was a Newbery Honor Book. Fascinated by the lives of ordinary people in history, Cushman bases her work on extensive library research. Cushman and her husband live on Vashon Island, Washington.

**BEFORE YOU GO ON**

1. How does Catherine mislead her suitor?

2. What does the suitor ask her father to give him?

**On Your Own**
Who do you feel more sorry for—Catherine or her suitor?

343

# The Dinner Party

*Mona Gardner*

The country is India. A large dinner party is being given in an up-country station by a colonial officer and his wife. The guests are army officers and government attachés and their wives, and an American naturalist.

At one side of the long table a spirited discussion springs up between a young girl and a colonel. The girl insists women have long outgrown the jumping-on-a-chair-at-the-sight-of-a-mouse era, that they are not as fluttery as their grandmothers. The colonel says they are, explaining that women haven't the actual nerve control of men. The other men at the table agree with him.

"A woman's unfailing reaction in any crisis," the colonel says, "is to scream. And while a man may feel like it, yet he has that ounce more of control than a woman has. And that last ounce is what counts!"

The American scientist does not join in the argument, but sits watching the faces of the other guests. As he looks, he sees a strange expression come over the face of the hostess. She is staring straight ahead, the muscles of her face contracting slightly. With a small gesture she summons the native boy standing behind her chair. She whispers to him. The boy's eyes widen: he turns quickly and leaves the room. No one else sees this, nor the boy when he puts a bowl of milk on the verandah outside the glass doors.

---

**colonial**, related to a colony, which is land that is controlled by a more powerful country (in this case, the British Empire)
**attachés**, staff officials who represent their government in a foreign country
**spirited**, energetic
**fluttery**, nervous and excited
**contracting**, pulling together

The American comes to with a start. In India, milk in a bowl means only one thing. It is bait for a snake. He realizes there is a cobra in the room.

He looks up at the rafters—the likeliest place—and sees they are bare. Three corners of the room, which he can see by shifting only slightly, are empty. In the fourth corner a group of servants stand, waiting until the next course can be served. The American realizes there is only one place left—under the table.

His first impulse is to jump back and warn the others. But he knows the commotion will frighten the cobra and it will strike. He speaks quickly, the quality of his voice so arresting that it sobers everyone.

"I want to know just what control everyone at this table has. I will count three hundred—that's five minutes—and not one of you is to move a single muscle. The persons who move will forfeit 50 rupees. Now! Ready!"

The twenty people sit like stone images while he counts. He is saying ". . . two-hundred and eighty . . ." when, out of the corner of his eye, he sees the cobra emerge and make for the bowl of milk. Four or five screams ring out as he jumps to slam shut the verandah doors.

"You certainly were right, Colonel!" the host says. "A man has just shown us an example of real control."

"Just a minute," the American says, turning to his hostess, "there's one thing I'd like to know. Mrs. Wynnes, how did you know that cobra was in the room?"

A faint smile lights up the woman's face as she replies: "Because it was lying across my foot."

---

**bait**, food used for attracting an animal so you can catch it
**cobra**, a poisonous snake
**rafters**, sloping pieces of wood in a roof
**arresting**, attracting and holding the attention
**rupees**, Indian money

## ABOUT THE **AUTHOR**

**Mona Gardner** (1900–1981) was born in Seattle, Washington, and traveled widely. She spent long periods in Hong Kong, South Africa, and California. Many of her novels, travel books, and short stories take place in Asia. "The Dinner Party," Gardner's best known story, takes place in India at a time when the country was a British colony.

✔ **LITERARY CHECK**

*Why is **third-person point of view** an effective way to relate the events of this story?*

**BEFORE YOU GO ON**

**1** What are the colonel and the girl arguing about?

**2** What does the American scientist realize?

**On Your Own**
Were you surprised by the ending? Why or why not?

## READER'S THEATER

Act out this scene in groups of three.

**Birdy:** My father may act modest, but he has many acres of land and chests of silver. He is much richer than he says.

**Suitor:** Oh, really? In that case, I must go talk to your father now. [*Father enters.*] You have a lovely daughter, sir. I should like to discuss a marriage arrangement.

**Father:** Ah, wonderful. You're quite pleased with my daughter, then?

**Suitor:** Oh yes, sir.

**Father:** She's got a good set of teeth. And her hair is quite a nice color.

**Suitor:** I am impressed that such a beautiful girl can read *and* write.

**Father:** That was her brother's doing, to be honest. I don't see much use for it personally. She *is* good at spinning. But let's talk about more important matters—matters of economics.

**Suitor:** Of course! I want to consider the girl's dowry before I agree. I should think one trunk of silver and some linen should be sufficient.

**Father:** Dowry? Silver? This is all you'll get from me!! OUT!! OUT!! [*Suitor runs away as the father throws a chamber pot at him.*]

**Birdy:** [*waving good-bye, laughing*] So long! Good-bye!

## COMPREHENSION
**Workbook Page 165**

### Right There

1. In what year did Birdy write her diary?
2. How does the American get everyone to hold still, but not panic?

### Think and Search

3. Why is Birdy's diary account funny?
4. How did Mrs. Wynnes prove the colonel wrong?

Speaking TIP

Knowing your character's motivation will help you speak your lines effectively. Remember: Birdy wants to discourage the suitor; the suitor wants to marry a girl with a nice dowry; the father wants Birdy to marry a rich man.

### Author and You

**5.** Why do you think the author of *Catherine, Called Birdy* describes the England of 1290 as "a foreign country" and "a place we can never go"?

**6.** After reading "The Dinner Party," how would you describe the author's view of women? Why?

### On Your Own

**7.** From what you know about different periods in history, when was the best period for women to live in? When was the worst? Why?

**8.** How would you advise potential suitors for Catherine? Why?

## DISCUSSION

Discuss in pairs or small groups.

**1.** What different viewpoints about women are presented in these readings?

**2.** How do the attitudes toward women in the two different periods help you better appreciate the struggle for women's rights? In what ways?

**3.** Which selection—the novel excerpt or the short story—do you think is more effective in showing attitudes toward women? Why?

**Q Do things really change?** How are Catherine and the hostess in "The Dinner Party" viewed by the men of their time? Are attitudes toward women the same today in any way?

»)) **Listening TIP**

Try to understand what others are talking about. Ask questions if you're not sure.

## RESPONSE TO LITERATURE

**Workbook**
**Page 165**

Imagine you are Catherine's suitor—Poor Fire Eyes. With a partner, discuss your experience at Birdy's. What did you think of Catherine? Her father? Write a diary entry from Poor Fire Eye's point of view. Use some of the expressions Catherine did like "Corpus bones!" and "grumbles my guts." Share your diary entry with the class.

# Grammar and Writing

## Adjective Clauses: Relative Pronouns as Subjects and Objects

Remember that an adjective clause describes a noun and that a relative pronoun begins an adjective clause. The relative pronouns *who*, *whom*, and *that* are used to describe people; *that* is used to describe things. Relative pronouns can be subjects or objects in adjective clauses. Look at the examples below.

| Relative Pronoun as Subject of Clause |
|---|
| Anyone **who moves** will forfeit 50 rupees. |
| [*Who* is the subject of the clause. The clause describes "anyone."] |
| The snake **that is under the table** is sitting on her foot. |
| [*That* is the subject of the clause. The clause describes "the snake."] |

| Relative Pronoun as Object of Clause |
|---|
| He's the suitor **whom I met**. |
| [*Whom* is the object of the clause. The clause describes "the suitor."] |
| She couldn't see the cobra **that she felt on her foot**. |
| [*That* is the object of the clause. The clause describes "the cobra."] |

## Practice

Work with a partner. Copy the following sentences into your notebook. Complete each sentence with the correct relative pronoun. Circle the noun that the relative pronoun describes. Then decide if the relative pronoun is the subject or object of the clause.

1. She is the woman _____ offended the colonel.
2. The suitor _____ I love has asked me to marry him.
3. This is the story _____ she told in her diary.
4. We know the man _____ is coming to dinner.
5. We found the diary _____ she kept.
6. The American scientist _____ came to dinner sat watching the guests.

348

# WRITING A PARAGRAPH FOR A RESEARCH REPORT

## Write an Introductory Paragraph

At the end of this unit you'll write a research report. Here you'll learn how to begin one. Your first step will be to come up with questions that you'd like to answer in your report. Then you'll use an inverted pyramid graphic organizer to help narrow your topic and decide on the controlling idea or premise (what you would like to say about your topic). Your introductory paragraph should include your controlling idea as well as an interesting fact, quote, or example that engages the reader. You'll begin by framing questions you'd like to answer in your report.

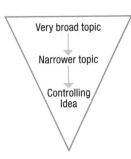

Very broad topic

Narrower topic

Controlling Idea

The writer of the model paragraph below began with the question: *How has society changed since the thirteenth century?* He then narrowed his topic to: *How have marriage practices changed since the thirteenth century?* Notice how the writer begins his paragraph with a controlling idea.

*Michael Ruiz*

### Marriage Then and Now

Marriage practices have changed a lot since medieval England. In medieval times, fathers chose who their daughters would marry. Birdy, a character in the novel Catherine, Called Birdy, faced this situation. Although Birdy didn't like the suitors that her father chose for her, most likely, her father would have decided whom she would marry in the end. Yet, if this story had taken place today in the United States, Birdy's father wouldn't have been so involved with the person that his daughter married. Birdy would have found someone that she liked, not someone that her father chose. Marriage practices today show that attitudes toward women's freedoms have come a long way since medieval times.

**Writing Checklist**

**ORGANIZATION:**
☑ I clearly stated my controlling idea in my introductory paragraph.

**IDEAS:**
☑ I used details that support my main idea.

## Practice

**Workbook Page 167**

Think of a question about something that has changed over time, such as attitudes toward child labor or women in the workplace, etc. Use an inverted pyramid graphic organizer to help you narrow your question. Then research your topic and write an introductory paragraph. Be sure to use adjective clauses correctly.

## What You Will Learn

**Reading**

■ Vocabulary building: *Context, dictionary skills, word study*

■ Reading strategy: *Analyze different kinds of text*

■ Text type: *Informational text (science/social studies)*

**Grammar, Usage, and Mechanics**
*Verb tense in reported speech*

**Writing**
Include quotations and citations

---

### 🔍 THE BIG QUESTION

**Do things really change?** Have you ever read about the Black Death or the bubonic plague? Plague is an infectious disease—it spreads from person to person. The Black Death struck Europe in the 1340s, killing millions of people worldwide. How do you think major outbreaks of disease, like the bubonic plague, change society?

### BUILD BACKGROUND

You're going to read two informational texts about the bubonic plague, ***Oh, Rats!: The Story of Rats and People*** and ***Outbreak: Plagues that Changed History***. The plague began in southwestern Asia. The disease was a bacteria that was spread by rats and fleas. Rats traveled on ships and across land, so the plague spread quickly to Europe. Look at the map that shows where and when the plague spread.

The plague spread along the sea and land trade routes to Europe. ▶

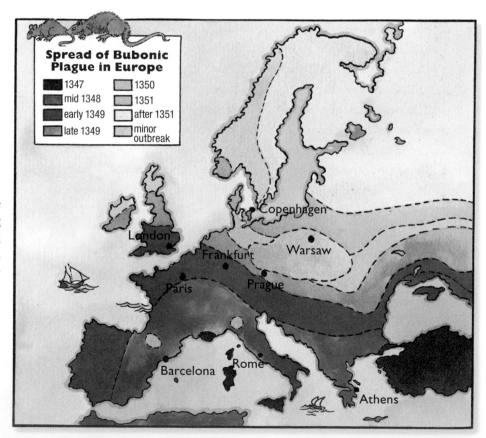

**Spread of Bubonic Plague in Europe**

- 1347
- mid 1348
- early 1349
- late 1349
- 1350
- 1351
- after 1351
- minor outbreak

Copenhagen
London
Frankfurt
Warsaw
Paris
Prague
Barcelona
Rome
Athens

## VOCABULARY

### Learn Key Words

Read these sentences. Use the context to figure out the meaning of the **red** words. Use a dictionary to check your answers. Then write each word and its meaning in your notebook.

1. During the **epidemic**, the disease spread rapidly through the country.

2. The illness increased the **fragility** of the eighty-year-old man, and his condition worsened each day.

3. The young girl had a **host** of symptoms from the virus, including headache, fever, chills, and sore throat.

4. The officials warned that younger people might not be **immune** to the virus. They could easily become ill.

5. The **society** of the time was greatly hurt by the widespread disease, and the economy suffered throughout Europe.

6. Epidemics progress in **stages**, with few affected at first, and then eventually hundreds, and then, if unchecked, thousands of people.

**Key Words**

epidemic
fragility
host
immune
society
stages

**Practice**  **Workbook Page 168**

Work with a partner to complete these sentences using the sentence starters. Include the **red** word in your sentence. Then write the sentence in your notebook.

1. The **epidemic** spread so quickly that . . .

2. The first signs of her growing **fragility** included . . .

3. The plague resulted in a **host** of . . .

4. It turned out that they were not **immune** to the disease and . . .

5. In my opinion, present-day **society** has a more positive view about . . .

6. In the early **stages** of disease . . .

◀ The plague of 1630, England

## Learn Academic Words

Study the **red** words and their meanings. You will find these words useful when talking and writing about informational texts. Write each word and its meaning in your notebook. After you read the excerpts from *Oh, Rats!: The Story of Rats and People* and *Outbreak: Plagues That Changed History*, try to use these words to respond to the text.

| | | |
|---|---|---|
| **consumers** = those who buy or use goods and services | ➡ | **Consumers** need to shop wisely and look at labels. |
| **eliminate** = get rid of something completely | ➡ | Since rats carry disease, it's important to **eliminate** them in populated areas. |
| **expose** = put someone in a situation or place that could be harmful or dangerous | ➡ | When people have an infectious disease, they have to be careful not to **expose** others to it. |
| **predominant** = more powerful, common, or noticeable than others | ➡ | The **predominant** theory of the researchers was that mosquitoes spread the disease. |
| **regions** = fairly large areas of a state, country, etc., usually without exact limits | ➡ | The virus spread from the more remote **regions** as traders came back to the cities and towns. |
| **structure** = the way in which relationships between people or groups are organized in a society | ➡ | The **structure** of the land-owning European society crumbled as the plague killed millions of people. |

## Practice

**Workbook**
**Page 169**

Write the sentences in your notebook. Choose a **red** word from the box above to complete each sentence. Then take turns reading the sentences aloud with a partner.

1. Plague spread across all _____ of the known world.
2. The _____ view of scientists is that bird flu is a concern.
3. People should not _____ themselves to diseased birds.
4. The first step in an epidemic should be to _____ the cause.
5. The _____ of society today allows people more opportunities.
6. As responsible _____ , people need to read food labels and know what they are eating to avoid any reactions.

## Word Study: Word Roots

Several words in the selections you will read include Greek and Latin word roots. Learning these word roots will help you read and understand many other words that contain them. Here are some examples:

| Word Root | Meaning | Example Words |
|-----------|---------|---------------|
| micro | small | **micro**organism |
| scope | to see | micro**scope** |
| bio | life | anti**bio**tics |
| vis | to see | **vis**ible |
| epi | upon, over, or attached to | **epi**demic |
| dem | people | epi**dem**ic |

▲ A microscope

**Practice** 

Workbook Page 170

Work with a partner. Choose four example words from the chart above and try to guess the meaning. Use a dictionary if necessary. Use each word in a sentence and then write the sentences in your notebook.

## READING STRATEGY    ANALYZE DIFFERENT KINDS OF TEXTS

When you research a topic, you need to be selective about the sources you use. Sources vary in terms of content, reliability, and focus. Once you have chosen your topic and found your sources, it helps to analyze them to make sure they are appropriate for your research. Scan the source, including the table of contents, headings, and photos and illustrations, to see if it provides the information you need. Also, look at a wide variety of sources. If you are researching a science topic, for example, your sources might include websites, textbooks, magazines, and newspapers.

   You will read two informational texts about the plague. One is a science article and the other is a social studies text. Both texts provide useful information about the plague and include both scientific information and historical context. As you read, be aware of the kind of information each author is providing.

Workbook Page 171

**Set a purpose for reading** As you read the two selections, look for ways in which people's actions caused plague to spread. Over the years, have scientific discoveries and advances changed the way we deal with disease?

# *from* Oh, Rats!

## The Story of Rats and People    *Albert Marrin*

Rats are disease carriers. Scientists nicknamed them "germ elevators," for they bring up microorganisms, or minute life-forms, from streams of sewage that flow beneath the earth's surface. Microscopic bacteria and viruses live in their bodies. Larger creatures such as fleas, lice, ticks, and mites live in their fur. Because of this, rats carry and spread a host of diseases.

An old children's song tells of the worst disease carried by rats.

> *Ring around the rosy,*
> *Pockets full of posies.*
> *Ashes, ashes,*
> *All fall down.*

The song deals with a disease called plague. From 1348 to 1352, it was the scourge of the known world. When plague struck, many people died. One never knew who would sicken and die next. Even staying at home, behind locked doors, could not keep you safe. To calm their fears, children sang while playing funeral.

The song describes the course of infection. One of plague's earliest signs

▲ Monks infected with the plague

is a round red rash, "ring around the rosy." As victims sickened, friends filled their pockets with posies, sweet-smelling flowers to mask the foul odor they gave off. Before dying—falling down—victims often had fits of violent sneezing, a sound children imitated as "ashes, ashes."

Buboes are another sign of plague. Sick people develop buboes, or swollen glands, in the neck and armpits. Thus, the disease is also called bubonic plague. "Black Death" is yet another name for it. That is because, in its last stages, victims develop large purple or black spots on their skin.

Whatever we choose to call it, the disease is caused by bacteria called *Yersinia pestis*. This is Latin for "Yersin's plague," named for Dr. Alexandre Yersin, the French scientist who discovered it in 1894, during an epidemic in the Chinese city of Hong Kong. *Yersinia pestis* is a bacillus belonging to a family of bacteria shaped like thin rods. Visible only under a microscope, a single plague bacillus is 1/10,000th of an inch in length. Thousands of them could fit into the period at the end of this sentence. Like all bacteria, it reproduces by dividing into two identical individuals. Each new bacterium then divides again and again. In this way, a single plague germ can become billions inside a victim's body.

At first, *Yersinia pestis* lived in the bodies of wild rodents in China, including rats. A type of flea, the rat flea, lives in rat fur. A giant compared to a plague bacterium, this insect is smaller than a lowercase *o* on this page. Yet it is a mighty creature. Although wingless, it can jump two hundred times higher than its body length. If you could do that, you could easily leap over a sixty-story building.

Fleas feed on mammal blood, which they draw out with a sharp, stiff sucking tube that resembles a mosquito sucker or an injection needle. A single rat can have hundreds of rat fleas. If a rat is carrying the plague bacillus in its blood, fleas will take it in with their sucking tubes. If they bite other mammals, they will pass on the bacillus in turn.

---

**mammal**, humans and other animals that are warm-blooded and drink mother's milk

Swiss-born French bacteriologist Alexandre Yersin, one of the discoverers of the bubonic plague bacillus ▼

Bubonic plague bacillus ▼

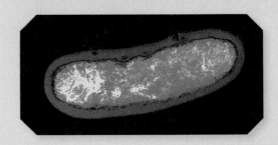

## BEFORE YOU GO ON

**1** What is the earliest sign of plague?

**2** What causes plague?

💡**On Your Own**
Children sang to help them with their fears about the plague. Do you ever sing when you're scared?

When poisons given off by the bacillus start killing an infected rat, its body temperature drops. This tells the resident fleas to move on. The first sign of a coming outbreak of plague is hundreds of dying rats staggering out of their burrows. If fleas cannot find another rat, they go after other mammals. If people are nearby, they will bite them. Eventually, the bacillus kills the fleas, too.

History's worst outbreak of plague began in China around the year 1333. Called "the Destroying Angel," it killed 13 million people in China and another 25 million in the rest of Asia. After that, it moved westward across the Russian plains in the bodies of fleas and rats that joined the camel caravans.

By 1347, it had reached the Russian port of Kaffa on the Black Sea. A war was going on. To get Kaffa to surrender, the attackers used catapults to hurl dead plague victims over its walls into the city. In other words, they used plague as a "weapon of mass destruction." The tactic worked—only too well. Plague killed most of Kaffa's population, and much of the attacking army besides. It also infected rats aboard Italian ships that had come there to trade for silks and spices.

Before long, infected rats with infected fleas came ashore in Italian seaports. From there, the plague traveled with them in wagons along the roads. It went from town to town, even to distant farming villages, reaching almost every corner of Europe.

Right now, you know more about plague than the most educated person in those days. Nobody knew about bacteria because nobody had ever seen any before the invention of the microscope three centuries later. Ignorant of the cause of plague, or how it spread, people tried to save themselves. It never occurred to anyone that rats and the fleas that lived on their fur could be responsible for the sickness.

Doctors who visited the sick wore special costumes. These consisted of a gown that went from their shoulders to their feet and a hood with a long "beak"

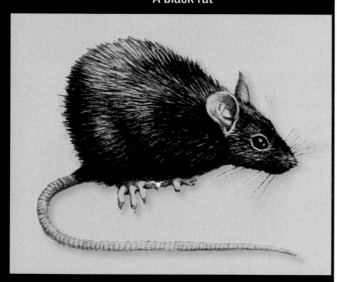

A black rat

A micrograph of a rat flea

---

**plains,** prairie areas
**caravans,** groups of people who travel together over a long distance
**tactic,** plan of action
**ignorant,** unaware; not knowing

# Rat-Borne Diseases

Rats carry eighteen diseases that affect people. The most serious are:
- rat-bite fever, marked by high temperature, rashes, and heart damage, especially in children.
- Lassa fever, a high fever often leading to death.
- typhus, marked by splitting headache, high fever, sometimes leading to death.
- polio, also called infantile paralysis.
- meningitis, a swelling of the area around the brain. It can cause brain damage or even death.
- trichinosis, caused by tiny worms that hook onto human intestines to steal food.

◀ Doctors wore costumes like this to try to protect themselves.

to carry spices thought to protect against plague. Yet doctors died as fast as their patients.

By 1351, the plague had run its course. "The Great Dying," as it was called, left about 25 million dead. That is, one in three Europeans. In the centuries that followed, it often returned. Plague died out in Europe around 1732 for reasons scientists still do not completely understand. The last serious outbreak struck Asia in the 1890s, taking 10 million lives.

From time to time, there are still small outbreaks of plague in Asia. In the United States, hospitals treat a few infected individuals each year, mostly those who have been near infected rodents in the wild. Although we must always be vigilant about a serious epidemic, the chances of its happening are slight.

Plague research has taken great strides in the last century. Nowadays, scientists know the disease's cause and how it spreads. That knowledge has enabled them to develop vaccines to make people immune to the disease and antibiotics to treat it. Everywhere, governments and health workers have sought to eliminate rats and the conditions in which they thrive.

---

**vigilant**, very aware
**slight**, small in amount
**strides**, improvements

## ABOUT THE **AUTHOR**

**Albert Marrin** is a former professor of history at Yeshiva University and has produced many history-based nonfiction books for young readers. Born in New York City, he spent his childhood in Baltimore, Maryland. He began his career as an educator as a junior high school social studies teacher. Marrin and his wife live in Riverdale, New York.

## BEFORE YOU GO ON

**1** By the end of the plague in Europe in 1351, how many people had died?

**2** When and where was the last serious outbreak of plague?

**On Your Own**
How have changing times made it unlikely that plague will be an epidemic today?

357

# Outbreak

## Plagues That Changed History    *Bryn Barnard*

Great epidemics, like wars, natural disasters, and other catastrophes, can expose the fragility of human society. Given enough stress, what seems the most solid and immobile social system can shatter. Such was the case in fourteenth-century Europe, a frozen society built on vast inequality and limited social mobility. For nearly a thousand years, Europeans were held in the rigid, unyielding grip of two interconnected forces: the feudal aristocracy and the Catholic Church. A third group, the knights, enforced their will. These power centers controlled all the wealth, owned all the land, determined all the laws, and were gatekeepers of all knowledge. They ruled over a body of ill-paid, ill-housed, illiterate peasant serfs, who did the work. Compared to competing regions like the inquisitive and inventive realm of golden age Islam or the continent-spanning empire of the Mongols, Europe was a Podunk backwater.

▲ A woodcut of the
Great Plague of 1665

The arrival in 1346 of a new disease changed this situation. Arcing across Europe from the Mediterranean to Scandinavia, the epidemic caused victims to become feverish and grow painful black welts that exuded a nauseating stench. Half who were sickened by the illness died. Europeans called it the Great Mortality, the Pestilence, and the Pest. We call it the Black Death. In four years, it destroyed a third of Europe's population. Afterward, nothing in Europe was quite the same. The entire

---

**feudal aristocracy**, highest social class in a system that existed in the Middle Ages
**inquisitive**, interested in a lot of different things
**realm of golden age Islam**, explosion of science and culture
**Mongols**, members of nomadic tribes of Mongolia
**Podunk backwater**, a situation regarded as stagnant and backward
**exuded**, gave off steadily

structure of European society became porous, more mobile. With fewer workers, wages went up. With fewer consumers, prices went down. In both the countryside and the cities, a rising middle class was able to accumulate, at bargain prices, the land, businesses, and wealth the dead had left behind. This economic revolution in turn sparked other changes: in law (to make sense of the new order), in the arts (to reflect on the horror and to show off the new money), and in trade (to accumulate even more).

In the Church, the catastrophe smashed an ossified orthodoxy, leading to questions, inventions, heresy, wars, and ultimately a world with not one Christianity but many. Finally, in the world of the nobility, the social, economic, and political crises caused by the Black Death were blows from which the ruling classes never fully recovered. Bit by bit, their power seeped away to others, never to return.

What was the Black Death? The most common explanation for the epidemic is bubonic plague, a disease passed to people by rodents. Historically, plague had been confined to populations of rats in isolated mountain regions, one in South Asia and the other in East Africa. When human activities like war and trade disturbed these ancient reservoirs, the plague escaped its natural confines. The devastating Justinian's Plague that hit the Mediterranean in 542 C.E. was likely bubonic, imported by Roman soldiers returning from Ethiopia. The Roman Empire never recovered, and European power shifted north; a century later, Islam became the predominant civilization of the eastern Mediterranean. The World Health Organization calls this the first plague pandemic. The Black Death was the beginning of the second. In all, the second pandemic lasted over three hundred years. Plague returned several times in the 1500s, struck London in the Great Plague of 1664–66, and finally sputtered out in the 1750s.

---

**ossified orthodoxy**, rigid adherence to traditional religious practices
**heresy**, a belief that disagrees with the official principles of a particular religion
**reservoirs**, large amounts of something that have not been used
**confines**, limits or borders

## ABOUT THE **AUTHOR**

**Bryn Barnard** is a graphic artist and a writer. He was raised in southern California; his experiences as an exchange student in Malaysia led him to the University of California, Berkeley, where he studied studio art and Asian culture. Barnard currently lives with his wife in Friday Harbor, Washington, and maintains his connections with Southeast Asia.

**BEFORE YOU GO ON**

1 What three changes happened in Europe as a result of the "economic revolution"?

2 What was Justinian's Plague?

**On Your Own**
Can you interpret any of the phrases in the illustration on page 358?

# Review and Practice

## COMPREHENSION  Workbook Page 172

### Right There

1. When did history's worst outbreak of plague begin?
2. What two forces controlled Europe before plague hit?

### Think and Search

3. Why wasn't plague eliminated when it began?
4. How did plague spread?

### Author and You

5. What different information do the authors include? How are the authors' purposes different?
6. According to the authors, how did plague affect Europe and European society? Which author takes a stronger position? Explain.

### On Your Own

7. Do you think there could be a serious epidemic in your lifetime? Why or why not?
8. If a serious epidemic did break out, how do you think it would affect society? Explain.

▲ A weekly death census

## IN YOUR OWN WORDS

Work with a partner. Copy these questions into your notebook:
- What is plague?
- Who did it affect?
- Where did it begin and spread to?
- Why did it spread?
- When did it begin and end?
- How did it affect society?

Answer the questions individually. Then, compare your answers with your partner's answers. Create a summary by deciding together which details are the most important. Present your summaries to another pair of students.

> **Speaking TIP**
>
> Practice giving your summaries to each other before presenting to another pair. Give each other suggestions for improving the summaries.

## DISCUSSION

Discuss in pairs or small groups.

1. After reading these two selections, why do you think it's important to do everything possible to prevent serious epidemics?

2. Which selection helped you understand the plague and its consequences better? Why? Which one did you enjoy reading more? Why?

**Q Do things really change?** Which diseases do you think are the biggest threats to humans today? Is society better able to cope with outbreaks than it was in the past?

## READ FOR FLUENCY

It is often easier to read a text if you understand the difficult words and phrases. Work with a partner. Choose a paragraph from the reading. Identify the words and phrases you do not know or have trouble pronouncing. Look up the difficult words in a dictionary.

Take turns pronouncing the words and phrases with your partner. If necessary, ask your teacher to model the correct pronunciation. Then take turns reading the paragraph aloud. Give each other feedback on your reading.

## EXTENSION  Workbook Page 172

Many countries in Asia, Africa, and Latin America require or recommend that travelers get vaccinated before they visit. Vaccines are medicines or injections that protect a person against disease. Choose three countries that you'd like to visit one day. Go to the website of the Centers for Disease Control and Prevention (CDC) and find out what vaccinations are recommended or required before traveling there. You may also find this information in an almanac or other library resource. Put your notes into a chart and share it with the class.

# Grammar and Writing

## Verb Tense in Reported Speech

In reported speech, there is a reporting verb in the main clause, such as *said*, *asked*, or *told*, followed by a noun clause. If the reporting verb is in the past, the verb in the noun clause may change to the past.

| Quoted speech | Reported speech |
|---|---|
| Tania said, "I **have to** study." | She said that she **had to** study. |

If the statement in the quoted speech is a general truth, the verb in the noun clause often remains in the present. This is true even if the reporting verb is in the past.

| Quoted speech | Reported speech |
|---|---|
| Marrin *claims*, "Rats **are** disease carriers." | Marrin *claims* that rats **are** disease carriers. |
| The article *reported*, "Rats **carry** diseases." | The article *reported* that rats **carry** diseases. |

Writers use a variety of reporting verbs to describe what others say. Commonly used verbs include:

| comment | declare | explain | indicate | mention | point out | report | state |
|---|---|---|---|---|---|---|---|

> The author **states** that Great epidemics can expose the fragility of human society.
> Health workers **declared** that rats must be eliminated.
> Scientists **have explained** that rats bring up microorganisms from streams of sewage.

## Practice  Workbook Page 173

Work with a partner. Change the quoted speech below to reported speech. Use an appropriate reporting verb. Be sure to keep the reporting verb in the same tense. Write the sentences in your notebook.

1. Marrin says, "Microscopic bacteria and viruses live in rats' bodies."

2. The article says, "The song deals with a disease called plague."

3. The author says, "Buboes are another sign of plague."

4. Scientists said, "The disease is caused by bacteria."

5. Barnard said, "The Black Death is passed to people by rodents."

# WRITING A PARAGRAPH FOR A RESEARCH REPORT

## Include Quotations and Citations

Using quotations in your research report can add richness and depth to your writing. Whenever you quote someone, it's important to give credit to your source. You should include an "in-text citation" (the author or title of the piece, and the page number, if known). The citation should be keyed to an alphabetized "Works Consulted List." There the reader can get more information about your source. There are many ways to cite sources. See pages 459–460 for some common methods.

This model paragraph, taken from an essay on Avian Flu, includes a quotation, an in-text citation, and the source. The writer used a main-idea-and-details web to organize her ideas.

> Chelsea A. Hamlet
>
> ### Avian Flu
>
> Avian Flu, also known as bird flu, is a disease transmitted by contact with live, infected birds, such as chickens and turkeys. The CDC reports that the disease is spread through an infected bird's "saliva, nasal secretions, and feces." ("Key Facts") The disease was first discovered in Italy more than 100 years ago in 1878. Back then, it was referred to as the "Fowl Plague." The current strain of bird flu is also known as H5N1, which stands for its molecular structure. The CDC has reported that in rare cases, this disease is being transmitted from person to person. Cases of Avian Flu in the United States are rare.
>
> ### Works Consulted List
>
> "Key Facts About Avian Influenza." Centers for Disease Control and Prevention. 7 May 2007. 24 Sept. 2009 <http:www.cdc.gov/flu/avian/gen-info/facts.htm>.

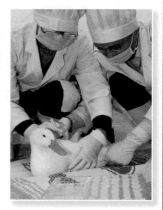

## Practice

**Workbook Page 174**

Write a paragraph about a disease that became an epidemic, such as cholera, polio, or tuberculosis. Do research and decide on the main point you want to make. Then write your main idea and supporting details in a word web. Include at least one quotation and be sure to cite your source. Use correct punctuation in your quotes.

### Writing Checklist

**VOICE:**
- [x] I thought through my research and came up with a main point that I stated in my own words.

**ORGANIZATION:**
- [x] I supported my main idea with facts and citations.

## What You Will Learn

**Reading**

■ Vocabulary building: *Literary terms, dictionary skills, word study*

■ Reading strategy: *Make generalizations*

■ Text type: *Literature (myth)*

**Grammar, Usage, and Mechanics**

Passive voice: overview of verb tenses

**Writing**

Include paraphrases and citations

 **THE BIG QUESTION**

**Do things really change?** There have been many wars throughout history, from ancient times to the present. What ancient wars do you know about? Think about modern wars, and compare them to ancient wars. In what ways have wars changed over time?

**BUILD BACKGROUND**

You're going to read an excerpt from **Dateline: Troy**, a retelling of the myth of the Trojan War. For many years, people believed the city of Troy itself was fictional, that it never existed. However, archaeologists discovered ruins of the ancient city of Troy in 1868, in what is now Turkey.

In *Dateline: Troy*, the author talks about how war and other aspects of civilization have changed over the years, yet remain the same. Pay attention to the images you see on the following pages. As you read, ask yourself what similarities the images suggest between ancient and modern times.

A map of the ancient world ▶

▼ Troy today

364

## VOCABULARY

### Learn Literary Words

The **theme** of a literary work is its central idea or message. Longer works often have a number of major themes. For example, *The Illiad*, an epic poem about the story of the Trojan War by the ancient Greek writer Homer, calls out the themes of duty, honor, and bravery. Read what the Trojan warrior Hector says to his family before leaving for battle:

| Literary Words |
| --- |
| theme |
| mood |

> "But I would die of shame . . . if I would shrink from battle now, a coward. I've learned it all too well. To stand up bravely, always to fight in the front ranks of Trojan soldiers, winning my father great glory, glory for myself."

**Mood**, or atmosphere, is the feeling that a literary work creates. Read the passage below from *Dateline: Troy* and consider what kind of mood it creates.

▲ Troy burning

> The Greeks set sail, savoring the sight of Troy's smoking ruins. They had no notion that they were viewing their own future, that the suffering and death they'd dealt the Trojans would now rebound upon themselves.

What is the mood of this passage? It could be described as *foreboding*—the sense that something bad is coming in the future. In literature, the author's choice of words contributes to the mood. What words in this passage contribute to the mood of foreboding?

**Practice**  Workbook Page 175

Look at the illustrations and photos on pages 368–373. How do they help you understand the theme and the mood of this reading? Discuss with a partner. Keep in mind that the mood of a work may change as the action builds.

## Learn Academic Words

Study the **red** words and their meanings. You will find these words useful when talking and writing about literature. Write each word and its meaning in your notebook. After you read the excerpt from *Dateline: Troy*, try to use these words to respond to the text.

**Academic Words**

approached
committed
ethical
ignored
notion
rigid

| | | |
|---|---|---|
| **approached** = moved closer | ➡ | As the Trojans **approached** the Greek camp, they were surprised to see no soldiers. |
| **committed** = did something wrong or illegal | ➡ | The goddess was upset about the violent acts that were **committed** in her temple. |
| **ethical** = morally good and correct | ➡ | Many people believe that war is not **ethical**, since people are killed or wounded in them. |
| **ignored** = didn't pay any attention | ➡ | The Trojans wanted to believe that the horse was a gift, and **ignored** warnings about it. |
| **notion** = an idea, belief, or opinion about something, especially one that you think is wrong | ➡ | The **notion** that they could meet the same fate as the Trojans never occurred to the Greek warriors. |
| **rigid** = stiff and not moving or bending | ➡ | Inside of the horse, the Greeks remained very still and **rigid** so no one would suspect they were there. |

## Practice

**Workbook Page 176**

Work with a partner to rewrite the sentences. Use the **red** word in each new sentence. Write the sentences in your notebook.

1. The Trojans were very cautious as they came up to the horse. (**approached**)
2. When humans did acts that displeased the gods, the gods got revenge. (**committed**)
3. Is it possible to find something morally good about war? (**ethical**)
4. The Trojans made a mistake when they didn't pay attention to the warnings about the horse. (**ignored**)
5. The Greek's idea that victory over the Trojans would bring them lasting peace was untrue. (**notion**)
6. The soldiers remained stiff while standing at attention in front of their leader. (**rigid**)

▲ The Trojan horse

366

## Word Study: Homographs

A homograph is a word that is spelled the same as another word but has a different meaning, origin, part of speech, or pronunciation. You can figure out the meaning of a homograph by the part of speech. Is the word a noun or verb? Look for context clues. Do any of the other words in the sentence give you a hint?

Look at the examples of homographs in the sentences below.

> The Greeks **level** the walls of Troy.
>
> > **lev•el** (*verb*) to knock down or completely destroy
>
> Few soldiers could fight at the **level** of the Greeks.
>
> > **lev•el** (*noun*) a particular standard of skill or ability in a subject, sport, etc.

**Practice**  Workbook Page 177

Work with a partner. Find the words in the box below in the myth *Dateline: Troy*. Use context to figure out the meaning and part of speech of the words. Use a dictionary to find a homograph for each word. Then use each word in a sentence and write the sentences in your notebook. Try to find other homographs in the reading.

| | | | | |
|---|---|---|---|---|
| crowd | down | pass | smell | waves |
| deep | drove | rose | still | wind |

## READING STRATEGY — MAKE GENERALIZATIONS

When you read a text, it helps to make generalizations about what you read. As you read *Dateline: Troy*, ask yourself how the account of the Trojan War shows differences from, and similarities to, war today. As you read, write down the stages and other main aspects of the Trojan War, such as the cause, the length of the war, the strategies used, the distrust, the damage and destruction, the battle or slaughter, and the aftermath. Look at the illustrations of the ancient war and photos of more recent war times, and make some generalizations about war—then and now.

 Workbook Page 178

**Set a purpose for reading** In reading about the Trojan War, what similarities and differences do you see between ancient civilization and modern times?

# Dateline: Troy
*Paul Fleischman*

When Paris (son of Priam and Hecuba of Troy) is asked by Zeus to choose the fairest among three women—Zeus's wife, Hera; his daughter, Athena; or the goddess of love, Aphrodite—Paris chooses Aphrodite because she promises him the love of the most beautiful woman in the world—Queen Helen of Sparta. At the time, neither Paris nor anyone else imagines that this choice will ultimately cause years of war, suffering, and death between the Trojans and the Greeks. We enter the story near the end of the war. The Greek warriors are just outside of Priam's city, Troy.

| The Greeks |
| --- |
| **Agamemnon**, warrior and high king |
| **Diomedes**, warrior and king of Argos |
| **Epeius**, carpenter |
| **Idomeneus**, warrior and king of Crete |
| **Neoptolemus**, son of warrior Achilles |
| **Odysseus**, warrior and king of Ithaca |
| **Sinon**, soldier |

| The Trojans |
| --- |
| **Cassandra**, Paris's sister, a prophetess doomed by the god Apollo never to be believed |
| **Hecuba**, queen of Troy |
| **Laocoön**, priest |
| **Priam**, king of Troy |

| The Gods |
| --- |
| **Athena**, goddess of wisdom and battle      **Zeus**, king of the gods |

Priam's city remained untaken. Would the war never end? Then Odysseus saw that deceit might accomplish what spears had not. His ruse held great risk but was the Greeks' only hope. Agamemnon, desperate, approved it.

---

**deceit**, secretive, dishonest behavior
**ruse**, trick

Odysseus met with the carpenter Epeius. Gradually, an enormous horse, wooden and hollow, rose above the Greek camp. On one flank was carved an inscription dedicating the image to Athena and asking in return for a safe voyage home. On the other flank was a hidden trap door. When the horse was finally finished, Odysseus and twenty others climbed up a rope ladder and through the door. Epeius locked it from within. The men listened raptly. There came the sound of the camp burning, as Odysseus had planned. Then they made out the shouts of their comrades launching the fleet and sailing off. Only a soldier named Sinon remained, hiding nearby, as Odysseus ordered.

It was black within the horse's belly. The men dared not speak. Slowly, night passed. At last, two shafts of sunlight entered through the air holes built into the horse's ears. Then a voice was heard. Another answered, both in the Trojan tongue. Rigid with attention, the Greeks waited. Silently, they prayed to the gods.

---

**flank**, between the ribs and the hip
**raptly**, carefully

**BEFORE YOU GO ON**

**1** What was on each flank of the horse?

**2** What time of day was it when the Greeks heard the Trojans talking outside of the horse?

**On Your Own**
What do you think will happen next? Why?

369

The Trojan scouts who approached the Greek camp were dumbfounded. The smoldering huts were deserted. The fleet was gone. All that remained was the horse towering before them. The war was over! They flew back to Troy.

The great gates opened. Jubilant Trojans streamed out to see the Greeks' camp and strange offering. Many of them scented deception. "Burn it!" came the shout. "Cut it open with axes!" Priam, however, fearing to harm a gift to Athena, who'd opposed him for so long, believed that the horse should be hauled into Troy.

"The belly holds armed men!" shrieked Cassandra.

"Beware!" cried Laocoön, a priest. "It's a sham!" He flung a spear into the horse's side, nearly splitting open the wood. Just then, the Greek soldier Sinon appeared. Reciting the tale Odysseus had devised to get the horse brought into Troy, he explained that the horse had been built so tall to keep the Trojans from drawing it through their gates. If it were brought in, Sinon said, Calchas had warned that the Trojans would one day lay waste to Greece. Odysseus smiled to hear the crowd clamoring to drag the horse into Troy.

---

**dumbfounded**, very surprised
**deserted**, empty and quiet
**jubilant**, extremely happy
**sham**, fake

"Lies!" roared Laocoön. Then, of a sudden, two giant sea serpents left the waves and glided across the sand straight toward him. Coiling about him while the throng watched in awe, they crushed him to death and killed him as well as his two sons who'd come to his aid. Here was an undeniable sign that Athena's offering must be respected. On rollers, the horse was pulled to Troy's gates, where the lintel had to be removed to allow it to pass into the city. The crowd trailed it to Athena's temple and there laid armloads of flowers about it.

That night, while all Troy feasted and danced, the Greeks in the horse trembled with terror, still dreading they might be discovered. Odysseus had to strangle one man and hold his sword at Epeius' ribs to keep the frantic carpenter quiet. Slowly, the sounds of celebrating faded. After a long silence, there came footsteps.

"It's Sinon," a voice called softly. "Come down."

The trap door opened. Warily, the Greeks climbed down. All was still. Worn out with revelry, the Trojans were sleeping deep as the dead.

Odysseus quickly dispersed his men. The sleeping sentries' throats were cut. The gates were opened. A beacon was lit as a signal to Agamemnon, who'd not sailed for Greece but hidden the fleet behind the island of Tenedos. The ships landed. The army raced into Troy, and the slaughter began. Awake and asleep, young and old, the Trojans were butchered by the pitiless Grecks. It was not a battle, but a massacre.

---

**throng**, large number of people
**lintel**, piece of stone or wood across the top of an opening in a door or gate
**warily**, in a careful and worried way
**revelry**, noisy dancing, eating, drinking
**dispersed**, scattered in different directions
**sentries'**, guards'
**pitiless**, showing no mercy

**BEFORE YOU GO ON**

1 What did the Trojans say about the horse?

2 What did the Trojans do with the horse?

**On Your Own**
Who do you think was right about the horse? Why?

371

Queen Hecuba awoke smelling smoke. "Troy burns!" she cried. Priam saw that it was true. They fled to Zeus' altar for protection. But Achilles' bloodthirsty son, Neoptolemus, found them and hacked off Priam's head.

For three days the killing and looting continued. The streets were heaped with the dying and the dead.

The plunder and women were divided up. Then building by building, the city was burned. Last, the Greeks leveled the walls that had kept them at bay for so long. When they left, the hill on which Troy had been built held nothing that rose above a man's knee.

Gorged with booty, the Greeks set sail, savoring the sight of Troy's smoking ruins. They had no notion that they were viewing their own future, that the suffering and death they'd dealt the Trojans would now rebound upon themselves.

✔ **LITERARY CHECK**

*Knowing that the Greeks suffer greatly later, how do these passages help you understand the author's **theme** of the senselessness of war?*

**plunder**, stolen things
**gorged**, filled
**booty**, valuable things
**savoring**, enjoying

That night, the wind began to shriek. Athena, furious at the violence committed in her temple during Troy's sack, let loose her rage in a tremendous storm. Scores of ships sank or were splintered on rocks. Floating bodies choked inlets and washed up in hundreds on beaches. Odysseus struggled to return home still longer, losing all his men along the way. When at last he reached Ithaca, he found his palace filled with his wife's lovers. Repelled, he sailed off. When he returned ten years later, his own son didn't recognize him—and taking Odysseus for a pirate, drove a stingray spear through his heart.

King Diomedes reached his palace to find that his wife had taken a new husband. King Idomeneus' wife had done the same, only to be murdered by the man she'd made king. Both Diomedes and Idomeneus were banished from their homelands.

Agamemnon's wife, seeing her husband approach with Cassandra, took her to be his new queen. Prophetic Cassandra refused to step into the palace, shouting out: "I smell blood!" Agamemnon ignored her, strode inside, and at once was felled by a broadsword. His vengeful wife then slew Cassandra. After ten years of fighting, both lay in their own lifeblood, Greek king and Trojan princess. Who could tell the victor from the vanquished?

---

**sack**, destruction
**inlets**, narrow areas of water
**repelled**, disgusted
**banished**, driven away
**prophetic**, able to predict the future
**vanquished**, defeated

## ABOUT THE **AUTHOR**

**Paul Fleischman** writes primarily for a young audience. He has produced picture books, novels, short stories, poetry, and nonfiction books. A graduate of the University of New Mexico and a Newbery Medal winner, he is also a musician. He plays the accordion, the banjo, and the bagpipes. Fleischman lives with his wife in Aromas, California.

### BEFORE YOU GO ON

1 What happened to Troy?

2 Why was the goddess Athena angry at the Greeks?

**On Your Own**
What parallel do you see between the two images on page 372?

# Review and Practice

Act out this scene between Priam, Sinon, and a soldier.

[*A group of Trojans approaches the horse and looks at the inscription.*]

**Priam:** What does it say?

**Soldier:** It's a prayer to Athena for a safe journey home. I think they've given up. We've won! The war is over. [*The crowd cheers.*]

**Priam:** What should we do with the horse?

**Soldier:** Light it on fire! Break it apart!

**Priam:** Aren't you afraid of Athena? What would she do if we destroyed it? Maybe we should haul it into Troy.

[*Sinon enters.*]

**Sinon:** You can't bring it into the city. It's too tall. It won't fit through your gates.

**Priam:** What do you mean?

**Sinon:** Calchas warned Agamemnon not to build it. He said that if you brought it into Troy, the Trojans would conquer Greece. So, it was built so that you couldn't get it in.

**Priam:** Haul it to the city now! We'll take the lintel down if we have to.

**Soldier:** Victory over Greece will be ours!

  Workbook Page 179

**Right There**

1. How many men were inside of the horse and for how long?
2. What were the other Greeks doing to carry out Odysseus's plan?

**Think and Search**

3. Was Odysseus's plan successful? Explain.
4. What is meant by: "Who could tell the victor from the vanquished?"

### Author and You

5. If the author had ended the story after the sacking of Troy, what would you have thought of the Greeks? Why do you think he went on to explain what happened to the Greeks next?

6. How do you think the author feels about war? Explain.

### On Your Own

7. In your opinion, was there anything about the Trojan War that justified it? Why or why not?

8. Do you think most wars could be prevented? How?

## DISCUSSION

Discuss in pairs or small groups.

1. Myths often reflect beliefs. What did this retelling reveal about the beliefs of ancient Greeks?

2. From what you read, was any character a "war hero"? Explain.

**Q Do things really change?** How has war changed over the years? What aspects of war remain the same? Give examples.

▲ "Fighting in the Trojan War," relief frieze, c. 525 B.C.E.

## RESPONSE TO LITERATURE

**Workbook Page 179**

In small groups, write a different ending to the Trojan War. What if the Trojans had discovered the Greeks were inside the horse? What might they have done? Could the large-scale loss of lives have been prevented? Practice reading your new ending. Then take turns reading it to the rest of the class.

**»)) Listening TIP**

Listen to the versions of other groups to see how they are different from what your group came up with.

# Grammar and Writing

## Passive Voice: Overview of Verb Tenses

Writers use both the active voice and the passive voice. The active voice is used when the focus is on the performer, the person or thing doing the action. The passive voice is used when the focus is on the receiver of the action. Remember that the *by*-phrase may be omitted if the performer of the action is unknown or is not as important as the receiver of the action.

The passive voice can be used with any verb tense. All forms of the passive contain a form of the verb *be* + the past participle.

| Verb Tense | Active Voice | Passive Voice |
|---|---|---|
| Simple present | A broadsword **fells** Agamemnon. | Agamemnon **is felled** by a broadsword. |
| Simple past | The Greeks **surprised** the Trojans. | The Trojans **were surprised** by the Greeks. |
| Present perfect | The Greeks **haven't finished** the horse yet. | The horse **hasn't been finished** yet. |
| Past perfect | The soldiers **had not taken** the city. | The city **had not been taken**. |
| Simple future | We **will win** the war! | The war **will be won**! |

**Practice**  Workbook Page 180

Work with a partner. In your notebook, rewrite the active-voice sentences below in the passive voice. Decide whether or not the *by*-phrase should be used. Be sure to use the correct verb tense.

1. The Greeks opened the trap door.
2. They will fight the battle to the death.
3. They have divided up the plunder.
4. We study Greek mythology in school.
5. The soldiers had carved an inscription on the horse.
6. Odysseus will give the orders

# WRITING A PARAGRAPH FOR A RESEARCH REPORT

## Include Paraphrases and Citations

You have learned how to include quotations in your writing. Now you will learn about paraphrasing, or putting someone else's ideas into your own words. Paraphrasing adds credibility to your writing, especially when your source is an authority on your topic.

In this model paragraph, the writer highlights paraphrased text by providing an in-text citation. Notice how he gives reasons and explanations to support his premise. He used a question-and-answer graphic organizer to help him focus on his topic.

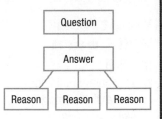

*Jack Kefauver*

### The Battle of Troy—Myth or Reality?

Many historians believe Troy was a real city. In fact, we may know exactly where it was. For the past two decades, a team of scientists, headed by Manfred Korfmann, has been studying the archaeological remains of a site in northwestern Turkey. On this site, scientists have found traces of a heavily fortified city surrounded by an enormous ditch. Many skeletons and sling bullets have been found there, as well as evidence of a devastating fire. Most people in the scientific community agree this is indeed the site of the ancient city of Troy. Is it possible that one of the wars fought at this site was the same war described in the myth of the Trojan War? There is no evidence that contradicts this possibility (Korfmann). In other words, this ancient myth may actually be a reality.

### Works Consulted List

Korfmann, Manfred. "Was there a Trojan war?" *Archaeology.* May/June 2004. 26 Nov 2009 <http://www.archaeology.org/0405/etc/troy.html>.

## Practice

**Workbook Page 181**

Write a paragraph about a person or place that people aren't sure existed. You could write about a place like the lost city of Atlantis, or a folk hero like John Henry, Mulan, or Robin Hood. Research your topic. Use a question-and-answer graphic organizer to help you focus on your topic. Paraphrase a fact or idea from your source, and include an in-text citation and bibliographic entry for it.

## Writing Checklist

**CONVENTIONS:**
☑ I used the passive voice correctly.

**ORGANIZATION:**
☑ I gave reasons to support my premise.

377

## What You Will Learn

**Reading**

■ Vocabulary building:
  *Context, dictionary skills, word study*

■ Reading strategy:
  *Identify main ideas*

■ Text type:
  *Informational text (social studies)*

**Grammar, Usage, and Mechanics**
Adverb clauses of time:
*since (then), when, once, after*

**Writing**
Support the main idea

### THE BIG QUESTION

**Do things really change?** Has the need for sending secret messages changed? Is it just as important today as it was in the past? Explain.

### BUILD BACKGROUND

You're going to read an excerpt from **Top Secret: A Handbook of Codes, Ciphers, and Secret Writing,** an informational text about codes and secret writing. A cipher is a secret system of writing. Morse code is an example of a cipher because each letter is represented by a single set of dots and dashes. It was used in World War II by signaling with flashes of light to transmit messages secretly so the enemy would not understand.

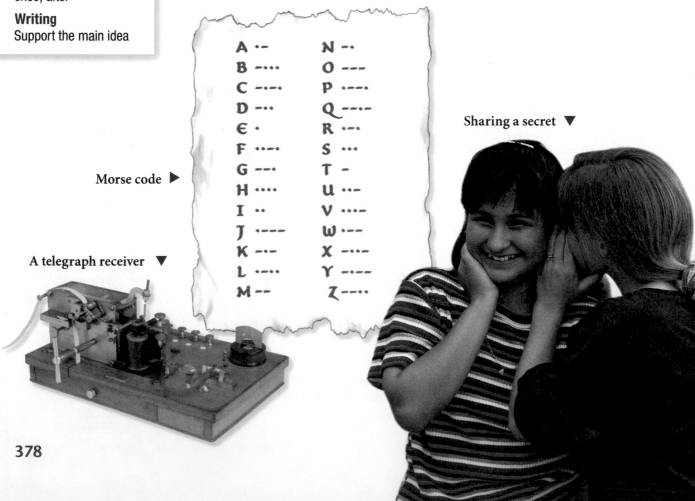

Sharing a secret ▼

Morse code ▶

| | | | |
|---|---|---|---|
| A | ·– | N | –· |
| B | –··· | O | ––– |
| C | –·–· | P | ·––· |
| D | –·· | Q | ––·– |
| E | · | R | ·–· |
| F | ··–· | S | ··· |
| G | ––· | T | – |
| H | ···· | U | ··– |
| I | ·· | V | ···– |
| J | ·––– | W | ·–– |
| K | –·– | X | –··– |
| L | ·–·· | Y | –·–– |
| M | –– | Z | ––·· |

A telegraph receiver ▼

### Learn Key Words

Read these sentences. Use the context to figure out the meaning of the **red** words. Use a dictionary to check your answers. Then write each word and its meaning in your notebook.

1. Detectives can take many years to catch **devious** criminals because they are so clever at evading the law.

2. Some methods of sending secret messages were not as **humane** as others. One individual branded a secret message on his servant's head!

3. The enemy **intercepted** the letter by removing it from the mailbox before the general got his mail.

4. Apple juice, lemon juice, and other **organic** substances can be used as invisible inks.

5. During a war, both sides may use **spies** to secretly discover information about the enemy.

6. The army circled the enemy. This **tactic** worked well, because it cut off the enemy's supplies.

**Practice**  Workbook Page 182

Write the sentences in your notebook. Choose a **red** word from the box above to complete each sentence. Then take turns reading the sentences aloud with a partner.

1. Keep a schedule of your homework assignments. This _____ will help you keep you organized.

2. Animals should always be given _____ treatment. They should never be abused or neglected.

3. Our secret plans were _____ by the enemy. Now everyone knows what we had planned to do!

4. The _____ criminal avoided being caught by the detective by wearing a disguise.

5. _____ fruits and vegetables are healthy because they don't have any chemicals on them.

6. In some cases, governments use _____ to gather secret information.

▲ A detective at work after dark

379

## Learn Academic Words

Study the **red** words and their meanings. You will find these words useful when talking and writing about informational texts. Write each word and its meaning in your notebook. After you read the excerpt from *Top Secret*, try to use these words to respond to the text.

| | | |
|---|---|---|
| **code** = a system of words, letters, or signs that are used instead of ordinary writing to keep something secret | ➡ | The spies made up a **code** and used it to send each other secret messages. |
| **equipment** = the tools or machines that you need for a particular activity | ➡ | A paintbrush, lemon juice, and a sheet of paper are examples of some **equipment** you'll need to write an invisible message. |
| **instructions** = information or advice that tells you how to do something | ➡ | The informational text gives **instructions** on how to read messages written with invisible ink. |
| **intelligence** = information about the secret activities of others | ➡ | The military tries to gather **intelligence** about weapons that other countries might be developing. |
| **strategic** = having a military, business, or political purpose | ➡ | Having a **strategic** plan about the timing of the battles helped give them an advantage. |
| **traced** = studied or described the history, development, or origin of something | ➡ | The use of spies and spy tactics can be **traced** back to ancient times. |

## Practice

**Workbook Page 183**

Work with a partner to complete these sentences using the sentence starters. Include the **red** word in your sentence. Then write the sentence in your notebook.

1. It was impossible . . . (**code**)
2. A hammer, nails, and wood are examples of some . . . (**equipment**)
3. According to . . . (**instructions**)
4. The government needs . . . (**intelligence**)
5. When you play . . . (**strategic**)
6. Their ancestors can be . . . (**traced**)

## Word Study: Soft *c* and Soft *g*

The letter *c* can stand for the soft sound /s/ or the hard sound /k/. The word *conceal* contains both of these sound-spellings—the first *c* has the sound /k/, and the second *c* has the sound /s/. The letter *c* has the soft sound /s/ when followed by *e*, *i*, or *y*.

Similarly, the letter *g* can stand for the soft sound /j/ or the hard sound /g/. The word *gigantic* contains both of these sound-spellings—the first *g* has the sound /j/, and the second *g* has the sound /g/. The letter *g* has the soft sound /j/ when followed by *e*, *i*, or *y*.

| Soft *c* | Soft *g* |
|----------|----------|
| **ce**ntury | **ge**neral |
| **ci**pher | **gi**ant |
| **cy**cle | **gy**m |

**Practice**
Workbook Page 184

Work with a partner. Look at the words in the box below. Write the words that have a soft *c* or soft *g* in your notebook. Check your work in a dictionary.

| advantage | citrus | gallows | message | ragged |
|-----------|--------|---------|---------|--------|
| bandage | civil | Greek | pig | record |
| cigars | comfort | grim | race | secret |
| circle | escape | mercy | rage | strategy |

## READING STRATEGY  IDENTIFY MAIN IDEAS

When you read an informational text, use these steps to help you identify the main ideas:

- Read the first paragraph. Ask, *What is this selection mainly about?* Write a main idea sentence in your own words.

- Find the headings and list them. Ask, *What is each section mainly about?* Skim for a few key words and jot them down.

- Read each section and list the main idea of each. Did you use any of the key words that you listed before?

- After you read, work with a partner to summarize the selection, using your list of main ideas. Did you and your partner choose the same main ideas?

Workbook Page 185

**Set a purpose for reading** How have the methods of sending secret messages and spying changed over the years? How have they stayed the same?

*from*

# Top Secret

## A Handbook of Codes, Ciphers, and Secret Writing

*Paul B. Janeczko*

As long as people have had secrets, they have developed many ingenious and devious ways of keeping secrets from one another. The ancient Greeks had a word for it: steganography. This term comes from the words *stegano*, meaning "covered," and *graphein*, meaning "to write." Concealment tactics fall into two categories: physically hiding a message in some way and concealing the secret message within another message.

### Early Concealment Techniques

Concealment started with the ancient Greeks. In battles between the two powerful city-states of Athens and Sparta,

both sides were always looking for the strategic advantage in battle. Part of that advantage came through good intelligence. But good intelligence doesn't do you much good if you cannot send it and receive it without your enemy finding out your plans should your message be intercepted. So, as they say, necessity was the mother of invention, and several concealment tactics were born.

Herodotus, the ancient Greek historian who became known as the Father of History, tells of one general, Histaiaeus, who used his servants as messengers, but not in the sense of simply carrying a secret message in the usual manner. The general shaved the head of a servant and tattooed the message on his skull. When the servant's hair grew in, he was sent on his way, the message safely concealed beneath a healthy head of hair.

---

**ingenious**, clever
**concealment**, carefully hiding things
**branded**, burned a mark onto skin

Another master that Herodotus described wasn't nearly as kind to his servants when he wanted to send sensitive military information to his generals. He found a servant who complained of poor eyesight and promised him a solution to his problem. He shaved the slave's head, then branded a message on his scalp! When the hair grew in, the master told the servant that his eyesight would be better when he had his head shaved at a camp some miles away.

Another general, Demaratus, who was exiled in Persia, used more humane methods of concealment. He carved a message in a plank of wood, then covered the message with wax. When the wax was melted, the message was revealed.

The Romans had a few concealment tricks of their own. Tacitus, the Roman historian, told of battlefield generals who would dress the wound of an injured soldier with a bandage that contained a secret message. Another trick they used was sewing a message into the sole of a sandal and sending its owner on his way, bearing the secret.

---

**branded**, burned a mark onto skin
**exiled**, forced to leave one's country

▲ An ancient Greek general tattoos a secret message onto the bald head of his servant.

A Roman soldier sews a secret message into the sole of his sandal. ▼

**BEFORE YOU GO ON**

**1** When did concealment techniques start being used?

**2** What were some early concealment techniques?

**On Your Own** Which technique surprised you the most?

383

## The Cipher That Saved a Life

In the seventeenth century, during England's Civil War, the Puritans captured Sir John Trevanion, a Royalist, and were holding him in a castle in Colchester, a city not too far from London. More than likely, Trevanion was beginning to sweat because he knew that two of his comrades had already made the long walk to the gallows.

Things indeed looked grim for Sir John, when he received a message from a friend.

Sir John's jailers didn't know who R.T. was—indeed, his identity is lost to history—but they found nothing suspicious in the letter and delivered it to the prisoner. Sir John, however, took immediate relief in the message because he knew a secret message was concealed within the letters of this letter. If you circle the third letter after each punctuation mark—the system agreed upon by Sir John and his friends—you will find the message that pleased the prisoner so much: PANEL AT EAST END OF CHAPEL SLIDES.

Just as no one questioned the letter Sir John received, no one questioned his request to spend time in quiet prayer in the chapel. After an hour, his jailer finally entered the chapel to check on the prisoner. Sir John was long gone through the secret escape panel.

---

**gallows,** structure used for killing criminals by hanging them from a rope

**grim,** very serious

Worthie Sir John:

Hope, that ye beste comfort of ye afflicted, cannot much, I fear me, help you now. That I would say to you, is this only: if ever I may be able to requite that I do owe you, stand not upon asking me. 'Tis not much I can do: but what I can do, bee ye verie sure I wille. I knowe that, if dethe comes, if ordinary men fear it, it frights not you, accounting it for a high honour, to have such a rewarde of your loyalty. Pray yet that you may be spared this soe bitter, cup. I fear not that you will grudge any sufferings; only if bie submissions you can turn them away, 'tis the part of a wise man. Tell me, an if you can, to do for you anythinge that you wolde have done. The general goes back on Wednesday. Restinge your servant to command. R.T.

▲ A message to Sir John

Cipher sheets hidden in a walnut shell ▶

## Tales of Concealment

During World War II, invisible ink was one of the methods of concealment used by spies. As you might suspect, some of their other methods were quite ingenious. During World War II, intelligence agencies had to be on alert at all times for letters and phone messages that may have included concealed messages. There is evidence of one secret agent who disguised her message as knitting instructions! Another spy, who was watching U.S. Navy activity, cabled his numbers disguised as an order for cigars from a tobacco retailer. He was successful with his concealment until a savvy U.S. agent realized that he was ordering an extraordinary number of cigars. When agents confronted him, he quickly admitted his treachery.

---

**savvy**, knowledgeable
**treachery**, actions that are not loyal to someone who trusts you

## Invisible Inks

Just like many other code and cipher techniques and systems, the use of invisible inks can be traced to ancient times. There are records that the Greeks and the Romans used invisible inks from plants and nuts. For example, Pliny the Elder, a Roman naturalist, used the "milk" of the thithymallus plant as an invisible ink. Since then, of course, invisible inks have become more sophisticated, though not nearly as popular as during the Middle Ages and the Renaissance. Nevertheless, they have played a part in times of war.

There are two kinds of invisible inks. Some chemicals can be used as invisible inks, but they can be dangerous to use. These chemicals become invisible when they dry. Then they are "developed" with another chemical. This developing chemical is called a reagent. It could be something like iodine vapor or ammonia fumes. The other kind of invisible ink is organic, something easily obtained in nature. Believe it or not, onion juice and vinegar both make good invisible inks. These organic inks are developed by heat.

---

**naturalist**, someone who studies plants or animals

◀ A Kryha cipher machine

**BEFORE YOU GO ON**

1 Do you need to understand the letter to Sir John to get its message?

2 What unusual concealment techniques were used in World War II?

💡**On Your Own**
Which concealment technique seems more reliable to you? Why?

385

# Making Your Own Invisible Inks

First of all, you will need some equipment. To write with your ink, you can use a quill (made by cutting the tip off of a feather), toothpicks, or a small brush, the kind you use for model painting or watercolors. While it takes some practice to write with a paintbrush, it does make a good "pen" for invisible ink. It will not leave indentations in the paper, a sure giveaway of your invisible secret. You might want to gather a few small jars to keep your ink in. Baby food jars or 35mm film canisters work well. You will want a fibrous paper, like school composition paper. Glossy paper won't absorb the ink. All of this equipment can be stored in your field kit.

Once you have your equipment, you can start working on your inks. Here are a few liquids that make good invisible inks:

apple juice

citrus juice (lemon, orange)

onion juice (It might take a few tears to mash enough
onion to get some ink, but it works well!)

vinegar

sugar or honey

salt or Epsom salts or baking soda.

You will need to experiment, particularly with the inks that require you to dissolve something in water. The juice inks may need to be diluted a bit if you can see their color on the paper.

There are other invisible inks. Cola drinks (not diet drinks because it is the sugar that makes the ink work) make good invisible inks. You'll need to dilute them so the brown color doesn't show your message.

When you write your message with one of these inks, it will become invisible once dry. To develop the ink, you need to put direct heat on the message. You can use a hair dryer, a small heater, an iron on a low setting, or a light bulb, about 150 watts or so. **Be careful when you use heat to develop your message.** You can get burned by any of these heat sources. If you use a light bulb or a heater, keep your message five or six inches away from the heat. Just give the heat time to work. If you iron your message, check constantly to make sure it isn't getting too hot.

Here are a couple of other invisible ink tricks: You can use milk as an invisible ink. Instead of developing it with heat, rub some ashes across it. The message will appear. Have you ever noticed when you press down very hard with a pencil or pen, you leave indentations in the next sheet of paper? Well, that could be a sort of invisible message. I would send the sheet that is two or three sheets beneath the one you wrote on. The indentations won't be as obvious. To "develop" such a message, rub the side of a pencil point across the message. You can also shine a light on the paper. Slant the light and you should be able to see the message. A message written with starch will be invisible in daylight or electric light. However, it will become visible when placed under fluorescent light or ultraviolet light. You might need to see if a science teacher can help you find an ultraviolet light at school.

Use your invisible inks in a way that works best for you. One of the drawbacks of invisible ink is that you cannot send a lot of information. Why? You need to find a way to hide all that information. In other words, if you are writing two pages of spy intelligence, you cannot simply send two blank pages. That will immediately draw close examination should it fall into unfriendly hands. Some spies wrote their invisible ink messages between the lines of a real letter. Others wrote the secret messages on the other side of the real letter. You could also put a dot of invisible ink over each letter in a newspaper article. When taken in order, the letters will spell out your message.

---

**fluorescent light**, very bright light from a gas-filled tube
**ultraviolet light**, beyond the purple end of the range of colors that people can see

## ABOUT THE **AUTHOR**

**Paul B. Janeczko** was a high school teacher. He now writes and compiles poems, anthologies, and nonfiction work for teenagers. He divides his time between writing and traveling to schools as a visiting poet. Janeczko lives in Maine with his family.

## BEFORE YOU GO ON

1 Why is it hard to send a lot of information when using invisible ink?

2 What did some spies do to avoid this problem?

**On Your Own**
In what situation would you like to use invisible ink?

387

# Review and Practice

## COMPREHENSION  Workbook Page 186

### Right There

1. What are the two categories of concealment tactics?

2. What system did Sir John use to read the secret message in the cipher?

### Think and Search

3. What were some concealment tactics used by the ancient Greeks and Romans? Why were some better than others?

4. What kind of equipment and techniques are used to read messages that are written in invisible ink?

### Author and You

5. The author points out in his introduction to the book that he "always enjoyed a good puzzle" and that he's a "fan of spy novels and movies." How are his interests evident in the excerpt from *Top Secret*?

6. The reading suggests that sending information secretly is a strategic advantage, that is, useful, to the people involved. Do you think this is true? Why or why not?

### On Your Own

7. Is spying and secrecy an interesting topic to you? Why or why not?

8. What kinds of secrets need to be kept in times of war? Explain.

## IN YOUR OWN WORDS

Copy the chart below into your notebook. List each technique from the reading in the correct category. With a partner, use your charts to summarize the selection.

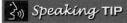 *Speaking* TIP

Use your chart to help you organize what you're going to say in your summary.

| Concealment Tactics | |
|---|---|
| **Physically Hiding a Message in Some Way** | **Concealing the Secret Message within Another Message** |
| | |

Listening TIP

Listen carefully
to reasons and
explanations others give
to see if you agree.

## DISCUSSION

Discuss in pairs or small groups.

1. When Sir John received the cipher, were his worries over? What
   might have gone wrong? Explain.

2. Why do you think invisible inks were more popular in the Middle
   Ages and the Renaissance than they are today? Is the use of
   invisible inks foolproof? What concerns would you have if you were
   relying on them to get an important message to someone in a
   crisis situation?

**Q** **Do things really change?** How do you think secret messages will
be sent in the future? What changes can you predict?

## READ FOR FLUENCY

When we read aloud to communicate meaning, we group words
into phrases, pause or slow down to make important points, and
emphasize important words. Pause for a short time when you reach a
comma and for a longer time when you reach a period. Pay attention
to rising and falling intonation at the end of sentences.

Work with a partner. Choose a paragraph from the reading. Discuss
which words seem important for communicating meaning. Practice
pronouncing difficult words. Take turns reading the paragraph aloud
and give each other feedback.

## EXTENSION

Workbook
Page 186

Find out about other concealment techniques, such as a Cardano
grille, a word grille, a dumbbell cipher, a dot cipher, a Caesar cipher,
or a St. Cyr slide. You can find information about these in the book
*Top Secret*, in reference books, or online. In small groups, choose
one concealment technique and write a secret message. Follow
these steps:

- Decide what you want to say in the message and create it.
- Write instructions for decoding and revealing your message.
- Give your instructions to another group and send the group
  your secret message.
- Could the group figure out your secret message?

# Grammar and Writing

## Adverb Clauses of Time: *since (then), when, once, after*

Adverb clauses of time tell when something happened. Use them to describe the relationship between two events. Look at the examples below from the informational text *Top Secret*.

*Since* + the main clause is used to talk about something that began at a specific point in the past and continues into the present. Use the expression *since then* to refer back to the specific point in time. The present perfect is often used in the main clause.

> Pliny the Elder, a Roman naturalist, used the "milk" of the thithymallus plant as an invisible ink. **Since then**, invisible inks have become more sophisticated.
>
> [*Since then* means any time after Pliny the Elder used the plant as an invisible ink.]

*When, once,* and *after* + the main clause show that one event happens, and then another event happens soon after it. The adverb clause of time expresses the first event. The main clause expresses the second event.

| The First Event | The Second Event |
|---|---|
| **When** you write a message with one of these inks, | it will become invisible when dry. |
| **Once** you have your equipment, | you can start working on your inks. |
| **After** an hour (went by), | his jailer finally entered the chapel. |

## Practice

Workbook
Page 187

Rewrite the sentences below in your notebook by joining each pair of sentences together. Be sure to use the adverb in parentheses to form an adverb clause of time. Then compare with a partner's sentences.

1. Agents confronted the spy. He admitted to treason. (when)

2. His head was shaved. A message was tattooed on his skull. (after)

3. You decide on your code. You can write your message. (once)

4. Intelligence agencies began using computers after World War II. Computers have been used to break codes. (since then)

## WRITING A PARAGRAPH FOR A RESEARCH REPORT

### Support the Main Idea

When writing a research report, it's important to support your main idea with facts and details. Once you state your main idea, expand on it in the clearest way you can, giving examples and explanations to support your premise.

The writer of the paragraph below supported his main idea with simple facts and details. Notice how he ends his paragraph with a restatement of his main idea.

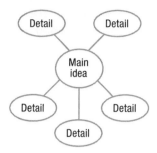

*Will Trigg*

**The Navajo Language in World War II**

When the United States needed a secret code during World War II, military intelligence decided to base it on the Native American Navajo language. This proved to be a perfect choice. The Navajo language is a very complex unwritten language. It is a language with no symbols and is spoken only on Navajo lands in the southwestern United States. Therefore, it was only understood by Navajos. During warwtime, Navajos would quickly encode, transmit, and decode brief messages. Here's how it worked. About 450 military terms (with no corresponding words for them in Navajo) were each assigned a Navajo word. Once a Navajo code talker memorized the code, he was sent to a marine unit. There he would receive and transmit messages in code about such things as tactics, troop movements, and orders. Throughout the war, the Navajo code was very successful because of its effectiveness in relaying sensitive information in a language that could not be understood by the enemy.

**Practice**

Workbook
Page 188

Write a paragraph about a concealment technique used in the past or present. Choose one method, such as invisible inks, ciphers, or codes used on the Internet today. Do research and develop a main idea that you can support with simple facts and details. List your ideas in a main-idea web. Include adverb clauses of time and be sure to use them correctly.

**Writing Checklist**

**WORD CHOICE:**
☑ I used words and details that add interest for my reader.

**ORGANIZATION:**
☑ I supported my main idea with simple facts and details.

# Link the Readings

## Critical Thinking

Look back at the readings in this unit. Think about what they have in common. They all tell about how things change or don't change. Yet they do not all have the same purpose. The purpose of one reading might be to inform, while the purpose of another might be to entertain or persuade. In addition, the content of each reading relates to how things change or don't change differently. Now copy the chart below into your notebook and complete it.

| Title of Reading | Purpose | Big Question Link |
|---|---|---|
| From *Catherine, Called Birdy* "The Dinner Party" | *to entertain* | |
| From *Oh, Rats!* From *Outbreak* | | |
| From *Dateline: Troy* | | |
| From *Top Secret: A Handbook of Codes, Ciphers, and Secret Writing* | | *It explains how secret codes have been used since ancient Greece.* |

## Discussion

Discuss in pairs or small groups.

- Which readings broadened your understanding of how things change and how things stay the same? How?

- **Do things really change?** What conclusions can you draw about how times, society, civilizations, attitudes, and ideas have changed through the years? How have they stayed the same?

## Fluency Check

Work with a partner. Choose a paragraph from one of the readings. Take turns reading it for one minute. Count the total number of words you read. Practice saying the words you had trouble reading. Take turns reading the paragraph three more times. Did you read more words each time? Copy the chart below into your notebook and record your speeds.

| | 1st Speed | 2nd Speed | 3rd Speed | 4th Speed |
|---|---|---|---|---|
| Words Per Minute | | | | |

# Projects

Work in pairs or small groups. Choose one of these projects.

**1** Go back in time to the days of the plague in medieval Europe. Do an on-the-scene interview with different people—a victim, a doctor, a nobleman, a peasant. How many people has the plague affected? Where is it spreading? What can people do? Comment on how the plague is affecting society.

**2** In small groups, invent your own cipher or secret code. For ideas, look back at the selection, in the book *Top Secret*, or in other sources. Take turns challenging other groups to try to break the code and discover your message.

**3** Choose either the diary or the short story, each of which reveal attitudes toward women. Act it out as a play. Make a list of characters and character descriptions. Decide how each should speak their lines. Put on your play for the class.

# Further Reading

To find out more about the theme of this unit, choose from these reading suggestions.

**American Life**, Vicky Shipton
This Penguin Reader® original covers the changing aspects of contemporary American life, including culture and sports.

**Crazy Horse**, Larry McMurtry
McMurtry draws a sensitive portrait of the great Sioux warrior who led his people in a resistance against white settlers. Sensing that the "Plains Indians ... stood in the way of progress," Crazy Horse was a reluctant participant at the Battle of the Little Bighorn.

**A Jetback Sunrise: Poems about War and Conflict,** Jan Marks
This poetry collection reflects the timeless nature of courage and horror during wartime. It is full of raw emotion that paints a vivid picture of war and conflict. The selection ranges from poems written before World War I to poems written today, and shows that wars may change but the way they affect us doesn't.

# Put It All Together

## LISTENING & SPEAKING WORKSHOP

### Oral Report

You will give an oral report related to the theme of changing times.

**1** **THINK ABOUT IT** Review the reading selections from this unit. With a partner, discuss how each reading reflects the idea of the way things change and the way they stay the same. Then work together to make a list of related topics. For example:

- Attitudes toward women
- Epidemics and their effects
- Ethics of war
- Spying and surveillance

**2** **GATHER AND ORGANIZE INFORMATION** Choose a topic from the list you made with your partner. Write down some facts and details you already know about the topic. Decide on the main points you want to make. Be sure your main points relate to the theme of the way things change and the way they stay the same. Consider your audience and think about ways you can make your oral report interesting to your listeners.

**Research** Use the library or Internet to do research on your topic. Look for evidence and examples that support your main points. Take notes on what you find. Write down the sources of the information.

**Order Your Notes** Make an outline that lists your main points, along with important facts, examples, and details to support them. Be prepared to tell where you got your information. Copy the parts of your outline onto numbered note cards if you wish.

**Use Visuals** Find pictures, diagrams, graphs, or other visuals that emphasize and help explain your main points. Make sure the visuals are big enough for the audience to see easily.

▲ A high school student giving a presentation

**3 PRACTICE AND PRESENT** Practice giving your oral report, referring to your outline or note cards to make sure you remember all the important ideas and facts. Be sure to give your sources by including phrases such as, *According to . . . .* Keep practicing until you can speak smoothly and confidently, glancing just occasionally at your notes. Try looking in a mirror as you speak, to check that you are facing your listeners instead of looking down at your notes.

**Deliver Your Oral Report** Although this is a formal presentation, you should appear relaxed and comfortable. Pause at the beginning and at certain points during your report. Speak in a clear but natural voice, and remember to use any visuals you've prepared.

**4 EVALUATE THE PRESENTATION**
You can improve your skills as a speaker and a listener by evaluating each presentation you give and hear. Use this checklist to help you judge your oral report and the reports of your classmates.

☑ Were the speaker's main points clear and related to the unit topic?

☑ Did the speaker support the main points with facts, examples, and details?

☑ Was the report interesting to you and the rest of the audience?

☑ Could you hear and understand the speaker easily?

☑ What suggestions do you have for improving the oral report?

 *Speaking* **TIPS**

Use appropriate body language when you deliver your main ideas. You can emphasize the main ideas by speaking louder, slowing down, or repeating them.

Connect with your audience by making eye contact with as many people as possible.

 *Listening* **TIPS**

Focus on the speaker's main points. If you have a question, write it down so you can ask it later. Don't let it distract you from listening to the rest of the presentation.

Listen for the speaker's sources. Do you think his or her information is reliable?

# WRITING WORKSHOP

## Research Report

You've learned how to write a variety of paragraphs for a research report. Now you'll put together what you've learned to write a research report. Research reports include information gathered from different sources. A good research report helps readers form an overall picture of a topic. In an introductory paragraph, the writer states the report's controlling idea or premise. Each body paragraph focuses on a main point that develops the premise. Clearly organized examples, explanations, details, and facts support the main points. The writer ends with a strong concluding paragraph that restates the premise in a new way. The report includes an accurate, complete list of citations identifying sources.

Your assignment for this workshop is to write a five-paragraph research report about an idea, issue, or event related to change in society. Use the following steps and models to help you.

**1 PREWRITE** Select a topic that interests you. Create a K-W-L-H chart that tells what you want to learn about your topic before writing. Do research on the topic. Possible sources include books about your topic, newspapers, magazines, encyclopedias, and websites. Take notes on note cards and list sources.

**List and Organize Ideas and Details** Use an outline to organize your ideas. A student named Michael decided to write about changes in marriage from medieval times to the present. Here is the outline he prepared.

> I. Introduction
>     A. Arranged marriage in medieval times
>     B. Choice in marriage for women today
> II. Economic Reasons for Medieval Marriage
>     A. Obligations of husband
>     B. Dowries
> III. Social Class and Medieval Marriage
>     A. Wealthy aristocrats
>     B. Servants, farmers, others
> IV. Love and Medieval Marriage
>     A. Love not important
>     B. Could develop after marriage
> V. Conclusion
>     A. Importance of love now
>     B. Greatest change in marriage
>     C. Future of marriage?

**2** **DRAFT** Use the model on pages 402–403 and your outline to help you write a draft of your research report. Remember to begin with an introduction that states your premise. Be sure to use your own words when you write your report. If you use exact words from a source, punctuate the quotation correctly. List all your sources at the end of your report.

**Citing Sources** Look at the style, punctuation, and order of the information in each of the following sources. Use these examples as models.

---

**Book**
Stanchak, John. Civil War. New York: Dorling Kindersley, 2000.

**Magazine article**
Kirn, Walter. "Lewis and Clark: The Journey That Changed America Forever." Time 8 July 2002: 36–41.

**Internet website**
Smith, Gene. "The Structure of the Milky Way." Gene Smith's Astronomy Tutorial. 28 April 1999. Center for Astrophysics & Space Sciences, University of California, San Diego. 20 July 2009 <http://casswww.ucsd.edu/public/tutorial/MW.html>.

**Encyclopedia article**
Siple, Paul A. "Antarctica." World Book Encyclopedia. 1991 ed.

---

**3** **REVISE** Read over your draft. As you do so, ask yourself the questions in the writing checklist. Use the questions to help you revise your report.

---

### SIX TRAITS OF WRITING CHECKLIST

☑ **IDEAS:** Does my first paragraph clearly state my controlling idea or premise?

☑ **ORGANIZATION:** Do my main points develop and support my premise?

☑ **VOICE:** Does my tone suit my purpose and audience?

☑ **WORD CHOICE:** Do I appropriately use words relevant to my topic?

☑ **SENTENCE FLUENCY:** Do I use transitional phrases to connect sentences and paragraphs?

☑ **CONVENTIONS:** Does my writing follow the rules of grammar, usage, and mechanics?

---

Here are the changes Michael plans to make when he revises his first draft:

## How Marriage Has Changed

The institution of marriage has changed greatly from medieval times to the present. During the middle ages, which lasted from about the fifth to the fourteenth century, a woman basically had no power to choose the man she married. Today, in the United States, women have more rights in all aspects of life, including the right to choose whether to marry or not, as well as whom to marry (Coontz 42).

In the middle ages, marriages generally were arranged by a woman's father. Marriage was viewed largely from an economic perspective, rather than from a romantic one. The husband was obligated to take care of his wife and to provide for her financially also. In exchange, The wife's family had to give a dowry, or a gift of money or goods, to the grooms family.

A bride and groom usually came from the same social class and very rarely did a rich person marry a poor one. When the children of two wealthy knights or merchants married, they not only joined hands in marriage, they also united the wealth and power of their two families. When the children of two farmers or servants married they joined hands in the hard work of surviving and raising a family. Whether a woman was spinning cloth, washing laundry, cooking, or cleaning, the work was difficult and exausting. ~~There were no~~ *Since then,* modern machines such as washing

machines and vacuum cleaners ~~to make~~ *have made* life easier (Clulow 18).

In the middle ages, a good reason for marriage ~~was not love~~ *love was not considered.* "For most

of history, it was inconceivable that people would choose their mates on *writes the scholar Stephanie Coontz,*

the basis of something as fragile and irrational as love." Nevertheless,

love of course sometimes developed in the years after a couple married,

but that usually depended on how well the spouses got along.

By the 1900s in the United States and Europe, *however,* love was probably

considered the most important reason for marriage (Hogan 153).

This is perhaps the major change to take place in the institution of

marriage between medieval times and now It is a change that has had

a great impact on the lives of both men and women. Who knows what

marriage will be like in the future?

**Works Consulted List**

Clulow, Christopher, ed. <u>Rethinking Marriage: Public and Private Perspectives</u>.
London: Karnac Books, 1993.

Coontz, Stephanie. <u>Marriage, a History: From Obedience to Intimacy, or How
Love Conquered Marriage</u>. New York: Viking Penguin, 2005.

Hogan, Margaret Monahan. <u>Marriage as a Relationship: Real and Rational</u>.
Milwaukee: Marquette University Press, 2002.

## 4 EDIT AND PROOFREAD  Workbook Page 189

Copy your revised draft onto a clean sheet of paper. Read it again. Correct any errors in grammar, word usage, mechanics, and spelling. Here are the additional changes Michael plans to make when he prepares his final draft.

Michael Ruiz

### How Marriage Has Changed

The institution of marriage has changed greatly from medieval times to the present. During the middle ages, which lasted from about the fifth to the fourteenth century, a woman basically had no power to choose the man she married. Marriages generally were arranged by a woman's father. Today, in the United States, women have more rights in all aspects of life, including the right to choose whether to marry or not, as well as whom to marry (Coontz 42).

In the middle ages, marriage was viewed largely from an economic perspective, rather than from a romantic one. The husband was obligated to take care of his wife and to provide for her financially, also. In exchange, the wife's family had to give a dowry, or a gift of money or goods, to the groom's family.

A bride and groom usually came from the same social class, and very rarely did a rich person marry a poor one. When the children of two wealthy knights or merchants married, they not only joined hands in marriage, they also united the wealth and power of their two families. When the children of two farmers or servants married, they joined hands in the hard work of surviving and raising a family. Whether a woman was spinning cloth, washing laundry, cooking, or cleaning, the work was difficult and exhausting. Since then, modern machines such as washing machines and vacuum cleaners have made life easier (Clulow 18).

In the middle ages, love was not considered a good reason for marriage. "For most of history," writes the scholar Stephanie Coontz, "it was inconceivable that people would choose their mates on the basis of something as fragile and irrational as love." Nevertheless, love of course sometimes developed in the years after a couple married, but that usually depended on how well the spouses got along.

By the 1900s in the United States and Europe, however, love was probably considered the most important reason for marriage (Hogan 153). This is perhaps the major change to take place in the institution of marriage between medieval times and now. It is a change that has had a great impact on the lives of both men and women. Who knows what marriage will be like in the future?

**Works Consulted List**

Clulow, Christopher, ed. <u>Rethinking Marriage: Public and Private Perspectives</u>. London: Karnac Books, 1993.

Coontz, Stephanie. <u>Marriage, a History: From Obedience to Intimacy, or How Love Conquered Marriage</u>. New York: Viking Penguin, 2005.

Hogan, Margaret Monahan. <u>Marriage as a Relationship: Real and Rational</u>. Milwaukee: Marquette University Press, 2002.

**5 PUBLISH** Prepare your final draft. Share your research report with your teacher and classmates.

Workbook
Page 190

# Old Becomes New

*Most grandmothers today who grew up in the 1930s and 1940s in the United States learned to sew their own clothes. Few children know how to do that now, because most people buy their clothes from a store. Yet those same grandmothers may not understand computers very well, while most young people use them easily. Artists often use new technology in their art. But some artists prefer old-fashioned ways of doing things. They might want to teach themselves a skill, like carving or metalwork, that was once commonly practiced but is no longer popular or needed.*

## Richard Mawdsley, *Feast Bracelet* (1974)

Richard Mawdsley used delicate tools to craft this silver, jade, and pearl bracelet, which recreates a fancy meal. The miniature table holds plates, silverware, bottles, fruit, and even a pie with a piece missing. Two jade balls on either end represent globe lights over the spectacular presentation.

Few artists today know how to work with silver in such detail. Mawdsley had to study the techniques of master gold- and silversmiths from hundreds of years ago to create this artwork. Although one could wear Mawdsley's bracelet, it was made only to be admired.

▲ Richard Mawdsley, *Feast Bracelet*, 1974, fabricated silver, jade, and pearls, 3¾ x 2¾ x 4½ in., Smithsonian American Art Museum

402

## Wendell Castle, *Ghost Clock* (1985)

Wendell Castle's *Ghost Clock* looks like a tall standing clock covered with a white cloth tied tight with a rope. But Castle tricks the viewer, because this is actually one piece of laminated mahogany wood. He carved the drapes of the cloth with great detail. Then he bleached it white so it would stand out against the dark stained "clock" underneath. The clock has no mechanical parts and cannot tell time. It is silent and still.

Castle made this clock as part of a series of thirteen clocks. You know that a clock face has only numbers. As the thirteenth clock, this sculpture represents the end of time, where there is no more room for change or anything new.

Technology continues to bring about dramatic changes in our everyday lives. Sometimes it's hard to keep up. But Castle uses his clock sculpture to show that in the end everything eventually comes to a full stop.

▲ Wendell Castle, *Ghost Clock*, 1985, mahogany, 86¼ x 24½ x 15 in., Smithsonian American Art Museum

### Apply What You Learned

**1** How do Mawdsley and Castle each explore the ideas of something old becoming something new in their artworks?

**2** Why do you think Wendell Castle chose a standing "grandfather" clock to illustrate his idea of something old?

**Big Question**
If you were to create an artwork that deals with something old or new, what would it look like?

Workbook
Pages 191–192

403

# Interpreting the Inventories
## Unit 2, Reading 2

As you read these interpretations and suggestions, keep in mind that labels can limit you. These inventories are meant to help you understand yourself better, not to label you. No one is one way all of the time.

### Learning Styles (page 90)
Look back at the number of the description you checked.

☑ If you checked 1, you might learn best by brainstorming, speaking, working in teams, gathering information, and listening.

☑ If you checked 2, you might learn best by analyzing, classifying, theorizing, organizing, observing, testing theories, and listening.

☑ If you checked 3, you might learn best by manipulating, experimenting, doing hands-on activities, tinkering, setting goals, and making lists.

☑ If you checked 4, you might learn best by leading, collaborating, influencing, adapting, taking risks, and modifying.

### Character Traits (page 91)
Make a list of the character traits you'd like to have or strengthen (anything you checked in the second column). Decide which trait to work on first.

### Interests (page 92)
In all four lists, the same letter represents the same category. Here are the categories:

a = music, art
b = writing
c = entertainment
d = computers, technology
e = animals (care or research)
f = public service (medicine, counseling, job service, etc.)
g = teaching
h = child care
i = environment, the outdoors, forestry, farming
j = mechanical, technical, electrical, engineering
k = cooking
l = business (starting one or being involved in one)
m = law enforcement
n = athletics
o = building, construction

Look back at how you scored this inventory. Your first choices (anything you marked with a 1) indicate your strongest areas of interest.

### Relationships (page 93)
For once, a low score is good! If you scored below 30, you probably have good relationships with other people. If you scored 31–40, you might want to work on developing better relationships with some of the people in your life. If you scored 41–60, you could meet with a favorite teacher, a school counselor or social worker, or another adult you trust and ask for help in developing better relationships.

There are no right or wrong responses to this inventory. Everyone learns differently.

# Contents

## Handbooks and Resources

# Study Skills and Language Learning

## HOW TO LEARN LANGUAGE

Learning a language takes time, but, just like learning to swim, it can be fun. Whether you're learning English for the first time or adding to your knowledge of English by learning academic or content-area words, you're giving yourself a better chance of success in your studies and in your everyday life.

Learning any language is a skill that requires you to be active. You listen, speak, read, and write when you learn a language. Here are some tips that will help you learn English more actively and efficiently.

### Listening

1. Set a purpose for listening. Think about what you hope to learn from today's class. Listen for these things as your teacher and classmates speak.

2. Listen actively. You can think faster than others can speak. This is useful because it allows you to anticipate what will be said next. Take notes as you listen. Write down only what is most important, and keep your notes short.

3. If you find something difficult to understand, listen more carefully. Do not give up and stop listening. Write down questions to ask afterward.

4. The more you listen, the faster you will learn. Use the radio, television, and Internet to practice your listening skills.

### Speaking

1. Pay attention to sentence structure as you speak. Are you saying the words in the correct order?

2. Think about what you are saying. Don't worry about speaking fast. It's more important to communicate what you mean.

3. Practice speaking as much as you can, both in class and in your free time. Consider reading aloud to improve your pronunciation. If possible, record yourself speaking.

4. Do not be afraid of making mistakes. Everyone makes mistakes!

## Reading

1. Read every day. Read as many different things as possible: Books, magazines, newspapers, and websites will all help you improve your comprehension and increase your vocabulary.

2. Try to understand what you are reading as a whole, rather than focusing on individual words. If you find a word you do not know, see if you can figure out its meaning from the context of the sentence before you look it up in a dictionary. Make a list of new vocabulary words and review it regularly.

3. Read texts more than once. Often your comprehension of a passage will improve if you read it twice or three times.

4. Try reading literature, poems, and plays aloud. This will help you understand them. It will also give you practice pronouncing new words.

## Writing

1. Write something every day to improve your writing fluency. You can write about anything that interests you. Consider keeping a diary or a journal so that you can monitor your progress as time passes.

2. Plan your writing before you begin. Use graphic organizers to help you organize your ideas.

3. Be aware of sentence structure and grammar. Always write a first draft. Then go back and check for errors before you write your final version.

## HOW TO BUILD VOCABULARY

### 1. Improving Your Vocabulary
**Listening and Speaking**

The most common ways to increase your vocabulary are listening, reading, and taking part in conversations. One of the most important skills in language learning is listening. Listen for new words when talking with others, joining in discussions, listening to the radio or audio books, or watching television.

You can find out the meanings of the words by asking, listening for clues, and looking up the words in a dictionary. Don't be embarrassed about asking what a word means. It shows that you are listening and that you want to learn. Whenever you can, use the new words you learn in conversation.

### Reading Aloud

Listening to texts read aloud is another good way to build your vocabulary. There are many audio books available, and most libraries have a collection of them. When you listen to an audio book, you hear how new words are pronounced and how they are used. If you have a printed copy of the book, read along as you listen so that you can both see and hear new words.

### Reading Often

Usually, people use a larger variety of words when they write than when they speak. The more you read, the more new words you'll find. When you see new words over and over again, they will become familiar to you and you'll begin to use them. Read from different sources—books, newspapers, magazines, Internet websites—in order to find a wide variety of words.

### 2. Figuring Out What a Word Means
**Using Context Clues**

When you come across a new word, you may not always need to use a dictionary. You might be able to figure out its meaning using the context, or the words in the sentence or paragraph in which you found it. Sometimes the surrounding words contain clues to tell you what the new word means.

Here are some tips for using context clues:
- Read the sentence, leaving out the word you don't know.
- Find clues in the sentence to figure out the new word's meaning.
- Read the sentence again, but replace the word you don't know with another possible meaning.
- Check your possible meaning by looking up the word in the dictionary. Write the word and its definition in your vocabulary notebook.

## 3. Practicing Your New Words

To make a word part of your vocabulary, study its definition, use it in your writing and speaking, and review it to make sure that you really understand its meaning.

Use one or more of these ways to remember the meanings of new words.

### Keep a Vocabulary Notebook

Keep a notebook for vocabulary words. Divide your pages into three columns: the new words; hint words that help you remember their meanings; and their definitions. Test yourself by covering either the second or third column.

| Word | Hint | Definition |
|------|------|------------|
| zoology | zoo | study of animals |
| fortunate | fortune | lucky |
| quizzical | quiz | questioning |

### Make Flashcards

On the front of an index card, write a word you want to remember. On the back, write the meaning. You can also write a sentence that uses the word in context. Test yourself by flipping through the cards. Enter any hard words in your vocabulary notebook. As you learn the meanings, remove these cards and add new ones.

### Say the Word Aloud

A useful strategy for building vocabulary is to say the new word aloud. Do not worry that there is no one to say the word to. Just say the word loud and clear several times. This will make you feel more confident and help you to use the word in conversation.

### Record Yourself

Record your vocabulary words. Leave a ten-second space after each word, and then say the meaning and a sentence using the word. Play the recording. Fill in the blank space with the meaning and a sentence. Replay the recording until you memorize the word.

## The Dictionary

When you look up a word in the dictionary, you find the word and information about it. The word and the information about it are called a dictionary entry. Each entry tells you the word's spelling, pronunciation, part of speech, and meaning. Many English words have more than one meaning. Some words, such as *handle*, can be both a noun and a verb. For such words, the meanings, or definitions, are numbered. Sometimes example sentences are given in italics to help you understand how the word is used.

Here is part of a dictionary page with its important features labeled.

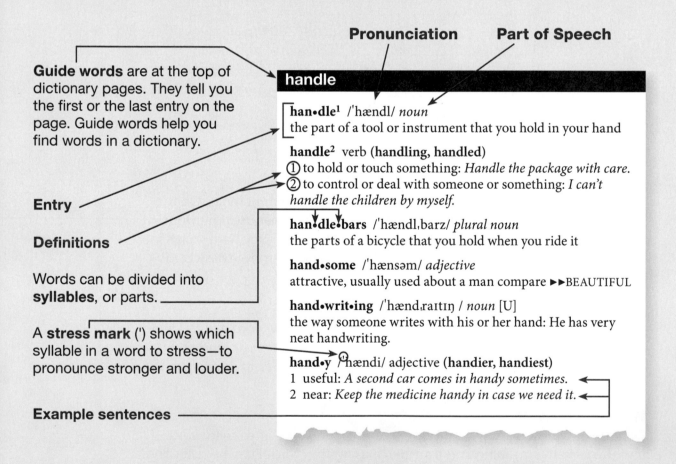

**Pronunciation**  **Part of Speech**

**Guide words** are at the top of dictionary pages. They tell you the first or the last entry on the page. Guide words help you find words in a dictionary.

**Entry**

**Definitions**

Words can be divided into **syllables**, or parts.

A **stress mark** (') shows which syllable in a word to stress—to pronounce stronger and louder.

**Example sentences**

### handle

**han•dle¹** /ˈhændl/ *noun*
the part of a tool or instrument that you hold in your hand

**handle²** verb (**handling, handled**)
① to hold or touch something: *Handle the package with care.*
② to control or deal with someone or something: *I can't handle the children by myself.*

**han•dle•bars** /ˈhændlˌbarz/ *plural noun*
the parts of a bicycle that you hold when you ride it

**hand•some** /ˈhænsəm/ *adjective*
attractive, usually used about a man compare ▶▶BEAUTIFUL

**hand•writ•ing** /ˈhændˌraɪtɪŋ / *noun* [U]
the way someone writes with his or her hand: He has very neat handwriting.

**hand•y** /ˈhændi/ adjective (**handier, handiest**)
1 useful: *A second car comes in handy sometimes.*
2 near: *Keep the medicine handy in case we need it.*

410

## The Thesaurus

A thesaurus is a kind of dictionary. It is a specialized dictionary that lists synonyms, or words with similar meanings, for words. You can use a print thesaurus (a book) or an online thesaurus on the Internet.

A thesaurus is a useful writing tool because it can help you avoid repeating the same word. It can also help you choose more precise words. Using a thesaurus regularly can help build your vocabulary by increasing the number of words you know that are related by an idea or concept.

In a thesaurus, words may either be arranged alphabetically or be grouped by theme. When the arrangement is by theme, you first have to look up the word in the index to find out in which grouping its synonyms will appear. When the thesaurus is arranged alphabetically, you simply look up the word as you would in a dictionary.

The entry below is from a thesaurus that is arranged alphabetically.

**sad** *adjective* Tending to cause sadness or low spirits : blue, cheerless, depressed, depressing, dismal, dispiriting, downcast, gloomy, heartbreaking, joyless, melancholy, miserable, poignant, sorrowful, unhappy. See **happy** (antonym) in Index.
—See also **depressed, sorrowful**.

Choose synonyms carefully. You can see from the thesaurus entry above that there are many synonyms for the word *sad*. However, not all of these words may be the ones you want to use. For example, *depressed* can mean that you have an illness called depression, but it can also mean that you feel sad. If you are not sure what a word means, look it up in a dictionary to check that it is in fact the word you want to use.

## HOW TO TAKE TESTS

In this section, you will learn some ways to improve your test-taking skills.

### 1. Taking Tests

Objective tests are tests in which each question has only one correct answer. To prepare for these tests, you should study the material that the test covers.

#### Preview the Test

1. Write your name on each sheet of paper you will hand in.
2. Look over the test to get an idea of the kinds of questions being asked.
3. Find out whether you lose points for incorrect answers. If you do, do not guess at answers.
4. Decide how much time you need to spend on each section of the test.
5. Use the time well. Give the most time to questions that are hardest or worth the most points.

#### Answer the Questions

1. Answer the easy questions first. Put a check next to harder questions and come back to them later.
2. If permitted, use scratch paper to write down your ideas.
3. Read each question at least twice before answering.
4. Answer all questions on the test (unless guessing can cost you points).
5. Do not change your first answer without a good reason.

#### Proofread Your Answers

1. Check that you followed the directions completely.
2. Reread questions and answers. Make sure you answered all the questions.

### 2. Answering Different Kinds of Questions

This section tells you about different kinds of test questions and gives you specific strategies for answering them.

#### True or False Questions

True-or-false questions ask you to decide whether or not a statement is true.

1. If a statement seems true, make sure that it is *all* true.
2. Pay special attention to the word *not*. It often changes the meaning of a statement entirely.
3. Pay attention to words that have a general meaning, such as *all, always, never, no, none,* and *only*. They often make a statement false.
4. Pay attention to words that qualify, such as *generally, much, many, most, often, sometimes,* and *usually*. They often make a statement true.

412

## Multiple-Choice Questions

This kind of question asks you to choose from four or five possible answers.

1. Try to answer the question before reading the choices. If your answer is one of the choices, choose that answer.
2. Eliminate answers you know are wrong. Cross them out if you are allowed to write on the test paper.

## Matching Questions

Matching questions ask you to match items in one group with items in another group.

1. Count each group to see whether any items will be left over.
2. Read all the items before you start matching.
3. Match the items you know first, and then match the others. If you can write on the paper, cross out items as you use them.

## Fill-In Questions

A fill-in question asks you to give an answer in your own words.

1. Read the question or exercise carefully.
2. If you are completing a sentence, look for clues in the sentence that might help you figure out the answer. If the word *an* is right before the missing word, this means that the missing word begins with a vowel sound.

## Short-Answer Questions

Short-answer questions ask you to write one or more sentences in which you give certain information.

1. Scan the question for key words, such as *explain*, *compare*, and *identify*.
2. When you answer the question, give only the information asked for.
3. Answer the question as clearly as possible.

## Essay Questions

On many tests, you will have to write one or more essays. Sometimes you are given a choice of questions that you can answer.

1. Look for key words in the question or questions to find out exactly what information you should give.
2. Take a few minutes to think about facts, examples, and other types of information you can put in your essay.
3. Spend most of your time writing your essay so that it is well planned.
4. Leave time at the end of the test to proofread and correct your work.

## STUDY SKILLS AND LEARNING STRATEGIES

### 1. Understanding the Parts of a Book
#### The Title Page
Every book has a **title page** that states the title, author, and publisher.

#### The Table of Contents and Headings
Many books have a **table of contents**. The table of contents can be found in the front of the book. It lists the chapters or units in the book. Beside each chapter or unit is the number of the page on which it begins. A **heading** at the top of the first page of each section tells you what that section is about.

#### The Glossary
While you read, you can look up unfamiliar words in the **glossary** at the back of the book. It lists words alphabetically and gives definitions.

#### The Index
To find out whether a book includes particular information, use the **index** at the back of the book. It is an alphabetical listing of names, places, and subjects in the book. Page numbers are listed beside each item.

#### The Bibliography
The **bibliography** is at the end of a nonfiction book or article. It tells you the other books or sources where an author got information to write the book. The sources are listed alphabetically by author. The bibliography is also a good way to find more articles or information about the same subject.

### 2. Using the Library
#### The Card Catalog
To find a book in a library, use the **card catalog**—an alphabetical list of authors, subjects, and titles. Each book has a **call number**, which tells you where to find a book on the shelf. Author cards, title cards, and subject cards all give information about a book. Use the **author card** when you want to find a book by an author but do not know the title. The **title card** is useful if you know the title of a book but not the author. When you want to find a book about a particular subject, use the **subject card**.

#### The Online Library Catalog
The **online library catalog** is a fast way to find a book using a computer. Books can be looked up by author, subject, or title. The online catalog will give you information on the book, as well as its call number.

## 3. Learning Strategies

| Strategy | Description and Examples |
|---|---|
| **Organizational Planning** | Setting a learning goal; planning how to carry out a project, write a story, or solve a problem |
| **Predicting** | Using parts of a text (such as illustrations or titles) or a real-life situation and your own knowledge to anticipate what will occur next |
| **Self-Management** | Seeking or arranging the conditions that help you learn |
| **Using Your Knowledge and Experience** | Using knowledge and experience to learn something new, brainstorm, make associations, or write or tell what you know |
| **Monitoring Comprehension** | Being aware of how well a task is going, how well you understand what you are hearing or reading, or how well you are conveying ideas |
| **Using/Making Rules** | Applying a rule (phonics, decoding, grammar, linguistic, mathematical, scientific, and so on) to understand a text or complete a task; figuring out rules or patterns from examples |
| **Taking Notes** | Writing down key information in verbal, graphic, or numerical form, often as concept maps, word webs, timelines, or other graphic organizers |
| **Visualizing** | Creating mental pictures and using them to understand and appreciate descriptive writing |
| **Cooperation** | Working with classmates to complete a task or project, demonstrate a process or product, share knowledge, solve problems, give and receive feedback, and develop social skills |
| **Making Inferences** | Using the context of a text and your own knowledge to guess meanings of unfamiliar words or ideas |
| **Substitution** | Using a synonym or paraphrase when you want to express an idea and do not know the word(s) |
| **Using Resources** | Using reference materials (books, dictionaries, encyclopedias, videos, computer programs, the Internet) to find information or complete a task |
| **Classification** | Grouping words, ideas, objects, or numbers according to their attributes; constructing graphic organizers to show classifications |
| **Asking Questions** | Negotiating meaning by asking for clarification, confirmation, rephrasing, or examples |
| **Summarizing** | Making a summary of something you listened to or read; retelling a text in your own words |
| **Self-evaluation** | After completing a task, judging how well you did, whether you reached your goal, and how effective your problem-solving procedures were. |

# Grammar Handbook

In English there are eight **parts of speech**: nouns, pronouns, adjectives, verbs, adverbs, prepositions, conjunctions, and interjections.

**Nouns**

**Nouns** name people, places, or things. There are two kinds of nouns: **common nouns** and **proper nouns**.

A **common noun** is a general person, place, or thing.

| | | |
|---|---|---|
| person | thing | place |

The **student** brings a **notebook** to **class**.

A **proper noun** is a specific person, place, or thing. Proper nouns start with a capital letter.

| | | |
|---|---|---|
| person | place | thing |

**Joseph** went to **Paris** and saw the **Eiffel Tower.**

A noun that is made up of two words is called a **compound noun**. A compound noun can be one word or two words. Some compound nouns have hyphens.

One word: **newspaper, bathroom**
Two words: **vice president, pet shop**
Hyphens: **sister-in-law, grown-up**

**Articles** identify nouns. *A*, *an*, and *the* are articles.

*A* and *an* are called **indefinite articles**. Use the article *a* or *an* to talk about one general person, place, or thing.

Use *an* before a word that begins with a vowel sound.

I have **an** idea.

Use *a* before a word that begins with a consonant sound.

> May I borrow **a** pen?

*The* is called a **definite article**. Use *the* to talk about one or more specific people, places, or things.

> Please bring me **the** box from your room.
> **The** books are in my backpack.

## Pronouns

**Pronouns** are words that take the place of nouns or proper nouns. In this example, the pronoun *she* replaces, or refers to, the proper noun *Angela*.

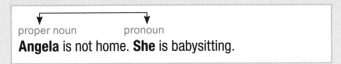

> proper noun    pronoun
> **Angela** is not home. **She** is babysitting.

Pronouns can be subjects or objects. They can be singular or plural.

|  | Subject Pronouns | Object Pronouns |
|---|---|---|
| **Singular** | I, you, he, she, it | me, you, him, her, it |
| **Plural** | we, you, they | us, you, them |

A **subject pronoun** replaces a noun or proper noun that is the subject of a sentence. A **subject** is who or what a sentence is about. In these sentences, *He* replaces *Daniel*.

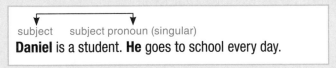

> subject    subject pronoun (singular)
> **Daniel** is a student. **He** goes to school every day.

In these sentences, *We* replaces *Heather* and *I*.

> —subject—    subject pronoun (singular)
> **Heather** and **I** like this movie. **We** think it's great.

417

An **object pronoun** replaces a noun or proper noun that is the object of a verb. A verb tells the action in a sentence. An **object** receives the action of a verb.

In these sentences the verb is *gave*. *Him* replaces *Ed*, which is the object of the verb.

object        object pronoun (singular)

Lauren gave **Ed** the notes. Lauren gave **him** the notes.

An object pronoun can also replace a noun or proper noun that is the **object of a preposition**. Prepositions are words like *for, to,* or *with*. In these sentences, the preposition is *with*. *Them* replaces *José* and *Yolanda*, which is the object of the preposition.

object of a preposition        object pronoun (plural)

I went to the mall with **José and Yolanda**. I went to the mall with **them**.

Pronouns can also be possessive. A **possessive pronoun** replaces a noun or proper noun. It shows who owns something.

| | Possessive Pronouns |
|---|---|
| **Singular** | mine, yours, hers, his |
| **Plural** | ours, yours, theirs |

In these sentences, *hers* replaces the words *Kyoko's coat*. It shows that Kyoko owns the coat.

It is **Kyoko's coat**. It is **hers**.

## Adjectives

**Adjectives** describe nouns. An adjective usually comes before the noun it describes.

| | | |
|---|---|---|
| **tall** grass | **big** truck | **two** kittens |

An adjective can also come *after* the noun it describes.

The bag is **heavy**. The books are **new**.

Do not add -*s* to adjectives that describe plural nouns.

| | | |
|---|---|---|
| the **red** houses | the **funny** jokes | the **smart** teachers |

## Verbs

**Verbs** express an action or a state of being.

subject   verb                subject   verb
Jackie **walks** to school. The school **is** near her house.

An **action verb** tells what someone or something does or did. You cannot always see the action of an action verb.

| Verbs That Tell Actions You Can See | | Verbs That Tell Actions You Cannot See | |
|---|---|---|---|
| dance | swim | know | sense |
| play | talk | remember | name |
| sit | write | think | understand |

A **linking verb** shows no action. It links the subject with another word that describes the subject.

| Linking Verbs | | |
|---|---|---|
| look | is | appear |
| smell | are | seem |
| sound | am | become |
| taste | were | |
| feel | | |

In this sentence, the adjective *tired* tells something about the subject, *dog*. *Seems* is the linking verb.

Our dog **seems** tired.

In this sentence, the noun *friend* tells something about the subject, *brother*. *Is* is the linking verb.

Your brother **is** my friend.

A **helping verb** comes before the main verb. It adds to the main verb's meaning. Helping verbs can be forms of the verbs *be*, *do*, or *have*.

| | Helping Verbs |
|---|---|
| **Forms of *be*** | am, was, is, were, are |
| **Forms of *do*** | do, did, does |
| **Forms of *have*** | have, had, has |
| **Other helping verbs** | can, must, could, have (to), should, may, will, would |

In this sentence, *am* is the helping verb; *walking* is the action verb.

helping action
 verb     verb
I **am walking** to my science class.

In this sentence, *has* is the helping verb; *completed* is the action verb.

 helping    action
  verb       verb
He **has completed** his essay.

In questions, the subject comes between a helping verb and a main verb.

  person
**Did** Liang **give** you the CD?

## Adverbs

**Adverbs** describe the action of verbs. They tell *how* an action happens. Adverbs answer the question *Where? When? How? How much?* or *How often?*

Many adverbs end in *-ly*.

| easily | slowly | carefully |
|---|---|---|

Some adverbs do not end in *-ly*.

| seldom | fast | very |
|---|---|---|

In this sentence, the adverb *everywhere* modifies the verb *looked*. It answers the question *Where?*

     verb     adverb
Nicole looked **everywhere** for her cell phone.

In this sentence, the adverb *quickly* modifies the verb *walked*. It answers the question *How?*

    verb     adverb
They walked home **quickly**.

Adverbs also modify adjectives. They answer the question *How much?* or *How little?*

In this sentence, the adjective *dangerous* modifies the noun *road*. The adverb *very* modifies the adjective *dangerous*.

    adverb adjective  noun
This is a **very** dangerous road.

Adverbs can also modify other adverbs. In this sentence, the adverb *fast* modifies the verb *runs*. The adverb *quite* modifies the adverb *fast*.

    verb adverb adverb
John runs **quite** fast.

## Prepositions

**Prepositions** can show time, place, and direction.

| Time | Place | Direction |
|------|-------|-----------|
| after | above | across |
| before | below | down |
| during | in | into |
| since | near | to |
| until | under | up |

In this sentence, the preposition *above* shows where the bird flew. It shows place.

> preposition
> A bird flew **above** my head.

In this sentence, the preposition *across* shows direction.

> preposition
> The children walked **across** the street.

A **prepositional phrase** starts with a preposition and ends with a noun or pronoun.

In this sentence, the preposition is *near* and the noun is *school.*

> prepositional phrase
> The library is **near the new school**.

## Conjunctions

A **conjunction** joins words, groups of words, and whole sentences.

| Conjunctions | | | |
|------|------|------|------|
| and | for | or | yet |
| but | nor | so | |

In this sentence, the conjunction *and* joins two proper nouns: *Jonah* and *Teresa*.

> noun      noun
> Jonah **and** Teresa are in school.

In this sentence, the conjunction *or* joins two prepositional phrases: *to the movies* and *to the mall*.

> prepositional    prepositional
> ┌─ phrase ─┐   ┌ phrase ┐
> They want to go to the movies **or** to the mall.

In this sentence, the conjunction *and* joins two independent clauses: *Amanda baked the cookies*, and *Eric made the lemonade*.

> ┌── independent clause──┐    ┌──independent clause ─┐
> Amanda baked the cookies, **and** Eric made the lemonade.

## Interjections

**Interjections** are words or phrases that express emotion.

Interjections that express strong emotion are followed by an exclamation point.

> **Wow!** Did you see that catch?
> **Hey!** Watch out for that ball.

Interjections that express mild emotion are followed by a comma.

> **Gee,** I'm sorry that your team lost.
> **Oh,** it's okay. We'll do better next time.

## CLAUSES

**Clauses** are groups of words with a subject and a verb. Some clauses form complete sentences; they tell a complete thought. Others do not.

This clause is a complete sentence. Clauses that form complete sentences are called **independent clauses**.

> subject  verb
> The dog's **tail wagged**.

This clause is not a complete sentence. Clauses that don't form complete sentences are called **dependent clauses**.

> subject  verb
> when the **boy patted** him.

Independent clauses can be combined with dependent clauses to form a sentence.

In this sentence, *The dog's tail wagged* is an independent clause. *When the boy patted him* is a dependent clause.

> ⌐independent clause⌐⌐independent clause⌐
> The dog's tail wagged when the boy patted him.

## SENTENCES

**Sentences** have a subject and a verb, and tell a complete thought. A sentence always begins with a capital letter. It always ends with a period, question mark, or exclamation point.

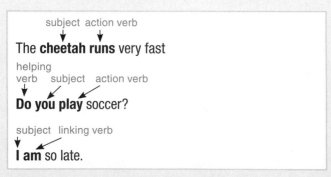

424

## Simple Sentences and Compound Sentences

Some sentences are called simple sentences. Others are called compound sentences. A **simple sentence** has one independent clause. Here is an example.

> ┌──── independent clause ────┐
> The dog barked at the mail carrier.

**Compound sentences** are made up of two or more simple sentences, or independent clauses. They are joined together by a **conjunction** such as *and* or *but*.

> ┌──── independent clause ────┐ ┌──── independent clause ────┐
> The band has a lead singer, **but** they need a drummer.

## Sentence Types

Sentences have different purposes. There are four types of sentences: declarative, interrogative, imperative, and exclamatory.

**Declarative sentences** are statements. They end with a period.

> We are going to the beach on Saturday.

**Interrogative sentences** are questions. They end with a question mark.

> Will you come with us?

**Imperative sentences** are commands. They usually end with a period. If the command is strong, the sentence may end with an exclamation point.

> Put on your life jacket. Now jump into the water!

**Exclamatory sentences** express strong feeling. They end with an exclamation point.

> I swam all the way from the boat to the shore!

## End Marks

**End marks** come at the end of sentences. There are three kinds of end marks: periods, question marks, and exclamation points.

Use a **period** to end a statement (declarative sentence).

| |
|---|
| The spacecraft *Magellan* took pictures of Jupiter. |

Use a **period** to end a command or request (imperative sentence) that isn't strong enough to need an exclamation point.

| |
|---|
| Please change the channel. |

Use a **question mark** to end a sentence that asks a question (interrogative sentence).

| |
|---|
| Where does Mrs. Suarez live? |

Use an **exclamation point** to end a sentence that expresses strong feeling (exclamatory sentence).

| |
|---|
| That was a great party!<br>Look at that huge house! |

Use an **exclamation point** to end an imperative sentence that gives an urgent command.

| |
|---|
| Get away from the edge of the pool! |

**Periods** are also used after initials and many abbreviations.

Use a **period** after a person's initial or abbreviated title.

| | | |
|---|---|---|
| Ms. Susan Vargas | Mrs. Fiske | J. D. Salinger |
| Gov. Lise Crawford | Mr. Vargas | Dr. Sapirstein |

Use a **period** after the abbreviation of streets, roads, and so on.

| | | | |
|---|---|---|---|
| Avenue | Ave. | Road | Rd. |
| Highway | Hwy. | Street | St. |

Use a **period** after the abbreviation of many units of measurement. Abbreviations for metric measurements do *not* use periods.

| | | | |
|---|---|---|---|
| inch | in. | centimeter | cm |
| foot | ft. | meter | m |
| pound | lb. | kilogram | kg |
| gallon | gal. | liter | l |

## Commas

**Commas** separate, or set off, parts of a sentence of phrase.

Use a comma to separate two independent clauses linked by a conjunction. In this sentence, the comma goes before the conjunction *but*.

> ┌— independent clause —┐      ┌—independent clause —┐
> We went to the museum, **but** it is not open on Mondays.

Use commas to separate the parts in a series. A series is a group of three or more words, phrases, or very brief clauses.

| Commas in Series | |
|---|---|
| **To separate words** | Lucio's bike is red, white, and silver. |
| **To separate phrases** | Today, he rode all over the lawn, down the sidewalk, and up the hill. |
| **To separate clauses** | Lucio washed the bike, his dad washed the car, and his mom washed the dog. |

Use a comma to set off an introductory word, phrase, or clause.

| Commas with Introductory Words | |
|---|---|
| **To separate words** | Yes, Stacy likes to go swimming. |
| **To set off a phrase** | In a month, she may join the swim team again. |
| **To set off a clause** | If she joins the swim team, I'll miss her at softball practice. |

Use commas to set off an interrupting word, phrase, or clause.

| | Commas with Interrupting Words |
|---|---|
| **To set off a word** | We left, finally, to get some fresh air. |
| **To set off a phrase** | Carol's dog, a brown pug, shakes when he gets scared. |
| **To set off a clause** | The assignment, I'm sorry to say, was too hard for me. |

Use a comma to set off a speaker's quoted words in a sentence.

Jeanne asked, "Where is that book I just had?"
"I just saw it," said Billy, "on the kitchen counter."

In a direct address, one speaker talks directly to another. Use commas to set off the name of the person being addressed.

Thank you, Dee, for helping to put away the dishes.
Phil, why are you late again?

Use a comma between the day and the year.

My cousin was born on September 9, 2003.

If the date appears in the middle of a sentence, use a comma before and after the year.

Daria's mother was born on June 8, 1969, in New Jersey.

Use a comma between a city and a state and between a city and a nation.

My father grew up in Bakersfield, California.
We are traveling to Acapulco, Mexico.

If the names appear in the middle of a sentence, use a comma before *and* after the state or nation.

My friend Carl went to Mumbai, India, last year.

Use a comma after the greeting in a friendly letter. Use a comma after the closing in both a friendly letter and formal letter. Do this in e-mail letters, too.

Dear Margaret,          Sincerely,          Yours truly,

## Semicolons and Colons

**Semicolons** can connect two independent clauses. Use them when the clauses are closely related in meaning or structure.

The team won again; it was their ninth victory.
Ana usually studies right after school; Rita prefers to study in the evening.

**Colons** introduce a list of items or important information.

Use a colon after an independent clause to introduce a list of items. (The clause often includes the words *the following, these, those,* or *this.*)

The following animals live in Costa Rica: monkeys, lemurs, toucans, and jaguars.

Use a colon to introduce important information. If the information is in an independent clause, use a capital letter to begin the first word after the colon.

There is one main rule: Do not talk to anyone during the test.
You must remember this: Stay away from the train tracks!

Use a colon to separate hours and minutes when writing the time.

1:30                7:45                11:08

## Quotation Marks

**Quotation Marks** set off direct quotations, dialogue, and some titles. A **direct quotation** is the exact words that somebody said, wrote, or thought.

Commas and periods *always* go inside quotation marks. If a question mark or exclamation point is part of the quotation, it is also placed *inside* the quotation marks.

> "Can you please get ready?" Mom asked.
> My sister shouted, "Look out for that bee!"

If a question mark or exclamation point is *not* part of the quotation, it goes *outside* the quotation marks. In these cases there is no punctuation before the end quotation marks.

> Did you say, "I can't do this"?

Conversation between two or more people is called **dialogue**. Use quotation marks to set off spoken words in dialogue.

> "What a great ride!" Pam said. "Let's go on it again."
> Julio shook his head and said, "No way. I'm feeling sick."

Use quotation marks around the titles of short works of writing or other art forms. The following kinds of titles take quotation marks:

| | |
|---|---|
| **Chapters** | "The Railroad in the West" |
| **Short Stories** | "The Perfect Cat" |
| **Articles** | "California in the 1920s" |
| **Songs** | "This Land Is Your Land" |
| **Single TV episodes** | "Charlie's New Idea" |
| **Short poems** | "The Bat" |

Titles of all other written work and artwork are underlined or set in italic type. These include books, magazines, newspapers, plays, movies, TV series, and paintings.

## Apostrophes

Apostrophes can be used with singular and plural nouns to show ownership or possession. To form the possessive, follow these rules:

For singular nouns: Add an apostrophe and an *s*.

| Maria's eyes | hamster's cage | the sun's warmth |

For singular nouns that end in *s*: Add an apostrophe and an *s* to these nouns, too.

| her boss's office | Carlos's piano | the grass's length |

For plural nouns that do not end in *s*: Add an apostrophe and an *s*.

| women's clothes | men's shoes | children's books |

For plural nouns that end in *s*: Add an apostrophe.

| teachers' lounge | dogs' leashes | kids' playground |

Apostrophes are also used in **contractions**. A contraction is a shortened form of two words that have been combined. The apostrophe shows where a letter or letters have been taken away.

I will
**I'll** be home in one hour.
do not
We **don't** have any milk.

## Capitalization

There are five main reasons to use capital letters:

1. To begin a sentence and in a direct quotation
2. To write the word *I*
3. To write a proper noun (the name of a specific person, place, or thing)
4. To write a person's title
5. To write the title of a work (artwork, written work, magazine, newspaper, musical composition, organization)

Use a capital letter to begin the first word in a sentence.

Cows eat grass. They also eat hay.

Use a capital letter for the first word of a direct quotation. Use the capital letter even if the quotation is in the middle of a sentence.

Carlos said, "We need more lettuce for the sandwiches."

Use a capital letter for the word *I*.

How will I ever learn all these things? I guess I will learn them little by little.

Use a capital letter for a proper noun: the name of a specific person, place, or thing. Capitalize the important words in names.

Robert E. Lee       Morocco          Tuesday        Tropic of Cancer

## Capital Letters in Place Names

| | |
|---|---|
| **Streets** | Interstate 95, Center Street, Atwood Avenue |
| **City Sections** | Greenwich Village, Shaker Heights, East Side |
| **Cities and Towns** | Rome, Chicago, Fresno |
| **States** | California, North Dakota, Maryland |
| **Regions** | Pacific Northwest, Great Plains, Eastern Europe |
| **Nations** | China, Dominican Republic, Italy |
| **Continents** | North America, Africa, Asia |
| **Mountains** | Mount Shasta, Andes Mountains, Rocky Mountains |
| **Deserts** | Mojave Desert, Sahara Desert, Gobi Desert |
| **Islands** | Fiji Islands, Capri, Virgin Islands |
| **Rivers** | Amazon River, Nile River, Mississippi River |
| **Lakes** | Lake Superior, Great Bear Lake, Lake Tahoe |
| **Bays** | San Francisco Bay, Hudson Bay, Galveston Bay |
| **Seas** | Mediterranean Sea, Sea of Japan |
| **Oceans** | Pacific Ocean, Atlantic Ocean, Indian Ocean |

| Capital Letters for Specific Things | |
|---|---|
| **Historical Periods, Events** | Renaissance, Battle of Bull Run |
| **Historical Texts** | Constitution, Bill of Rights |
| **Days and Months** | Monday, October |
| **Holidays** | Thanksgiving, Labor Day |
| **Organizations, Schools** | Greenpeace, Central High School |
| **Government Bodies** | Congress, State Department |
| **Political Parties** | Republican Party, Democratic Party |
| **Ethnic Groups** | Chinese, Latinos |
| **Languages, Nationalities** | Spanish, Canadian |
| **Buildings** | Empire State Building, City Hall |
| **Monuments** | Lincoln Memorial, Washington Monument |
| **Religions** | Hinduism, Christianity, Judaism, Islam |
| **Special Events** | Boston Marathon, Ohio State Fair |

Use a capital letter for a person's title if the title comes before the name. In the second sentence below, a capital letter is not needed because the title does not come before a name.

I heard **S**enator Clinton's speech about jobs. The **s**enator may come to our school.

Use a capital letter for the first and last word and all other important words in titles of books, newspapers, magazines, short stories, plays, movies, songs, paintings, and sculptures.

Lucy wants to read <u>The Lord of the Rings</u>.
The newspaper my father reads is <u>The New York Times</u>.
Did you like the painting called <u>Work in the Fields</u>?
This poem is called "The Birch Tree."

# Reading Handbook

People often think of reading as a passive activity—that you don't have to do much, you just have to take in words—but that is not true. Good readers are active readers.

Reading comprehension involves these skills:

1. Understanding what you are reading.
2. Being part of what you are reading, or engaging with the text.
3. Evaluating what you are reading.
4. Making connections between what you are reading and what you already know.
5. Thinking about your response to what you have read.

## Understanding What You Are Reading

One of the first steps is to recognize letters and words. Remember that it does not matter if you do not recognize all the words. You can figure out their meanings later. Try to figure out the meaning of unfamiliar words from the context of the sentence or paragraph. If you cannot figure out the meaning of a word, look it up in a dictionary. Next, you activate the meaning of words as you read them. That is what you are doing now. If you find parts of a text difficult, stop and read them a second time.

## Engaging with the Text

Good readers use many different skills and strategies to help them understand and enjoy the text they are reading. When you read, think of it as a conversation between you and the writer. The writer wants to tell you something, and you want to understand his or her message.

Practice using these tips every time you read.

- Predict what will happen next in a story. Use clues you find in the text.
- Ask yourself questions about the main idea or message of the text.
- Monitor your understanding. Stop reading from time to time and think about what you have learned so far.

### Evaluating What You Are Reading

The next step is to think about what you are reading. First, think about the author's purpose for writing. What type of text are you reading? If it is an informational text, the author wants to give you information about a subject, for example, about science, social science, or math. If you are reading literature, the author's purpose is probably to entertain you.

When you have decided what the author's purpose is for writing the text, think about what you have learned. Use these questions to help you:

- Is the information useful?
- Have you changed your mind about the subject?
- Did you enjoy the story, poem, or play?

### Making Connections

Now connect the events or ideas in a text to your own knowledge or experience. Think about how your knowledge of a subject or your experience of the world can help you understand a text better.

- If the text has sections with headings, notice what these are. Do they give you clues about the main ideas in the text?
- Read the first paragraph. What is the main idea?
- Now read the paragraphs that follow. Make a note of the main ideas.
- Review your notes. How are the ideas connected?

### Thinking About Your Response to What You Have Read

You read for a reason, so it is a good idea to think about how the text has helped you. Ask yourself these questions after you read:

- What information have I learned? Can I use it in my other classes?
- How can I connect my own experience or knowledge to the text?
- Did I enjoy reading the text? Why or why not?
- Did I learn any new vocabulary? What was it? How can I use it in conversation or in writing?

## WHAT ARE READING STRATEGIES?

Reading strategies are specific things readers do to help them understand texts. Reading is like a conversation between an author and a reader. Authors make decisions about how to effectively communicate through a piece of writing. Readers use specific strategies to help them understand what authors are trying to communicate. Ten of the most common reading strategies are Previewing, Predicting, Skimming, Scanning, Comparing and Contrasting, Identifying Problems and Solutions, Recognizing Cause and Effect, Distinguishing Fact From Opinion, Identifying Main Idea and Details, and Identifying an Author's Purpose.

## HOW TO IMPROVE READING FLUENCY

### 1. What Is Reading Fluency?

Reading fluency is the ability to read smoothly and expressively with clear understanding. Fluent readers are better able to understand and enjoy what they read. Use the strategies that follow to build your fluency in these four key areas: accuracy and rate, phrasing, intonation, expression.

### 2. How to Improve Accuracy and Rate

Accuracy is the correctness of your reading. Rate is the speed of your reading.
- Use correct pronunciation.
- Emphasize correct syllables.
- Recognize most words.

### 3. How to Read with Proper Rate

- Match your reading speed to what you are reading. For example, if you are reading a mystery story, read slightly faster. If you are reading a science textbook, read slightly slower.
- Recognize and use punctuation.

### 4. Test Your Accuracy and Rate

- Choose a text you are familiar with, and practice reading it multiple times.
- Keep a dictionary with you while you read, and look up words you do not recognize.
- Use a watch or clock to time yourself while you read a passage.
- Ask a friend or family member to read a passage for you, so you know what it should sound like.

### 5. How to Improve Intonation

Intonation is the rise and fall in the pitch of your voice as you read aloud. Pitch means the highness or lowness of the sound. Follow these steps:
- Change the sound of your voice to match what you are reading.
- Make your voice flow or sound smooth while you read.
- Make sure you are pronouncing words correctly.
- Raise the pitch of your voice for words that should be stressed, or emphasized.
- Use proper rhythm and meter.
- Use visual clues.

| Visual Clue and Meaning | Example | How to Read It |
| --- | --- | --- |
| Italics: draw attention to a word to show special importance | He is *serious*. | Emphasize "serious." |
| Dash: shows a quick break in a sentence | He is—serious. | Pause before saying "serious." |
| Exclamation point: can represent energy, excitement, or anger | He is serious! | Make your voice louder at the end of the sentence. |
| All capital letters: can represent strong emphasis, or yelling | HE IS SERIOUS. | Emphasize the whole sentence. |
| Boldfacing: draws attention to a word to show importance | He is **serious**. | Emphasize "serious." |
| Question mark: shows curiosity or confusion | Is he serious? | Raise the pitch of your voice slightly at the end of the sentence. |

## 6. How to Improve Phrasing

Phrasing is how you group words together. Follow these steps:

- Use correct rhythm and meter by not reading too fast or too slow.
- Pause for key words within the text.
- Make sure your sentences have proper flow and meter, so they sound smooth instead of choppy.
- Make sure you sound like you are reading a sentence instead of a list.
- Use punctuation to tell you when to stop, pause, or emphasize.

## 7. How to Improve Expression

Expression in reading is how you express feeling. Follow these steps:

- Match the sound of your voice to what you are reading. For example, read louder and faster to show strong feeling. Read slowly and more quietly to show sadness or seriousness.
- Match the sound of your voice to the genre. For example, read a fun, fictional story using a fun, friendly voice. Read an informative, nonfiction article using an even tone and a more serious voice.
- Avoid speaking in monotone, or using only one tone in your voice.
- Pause for emphasis and exaggerate letter sounds to match the mood or theme of what you are reading.

# Viewing and Representing

## Viewing

Viewing is something you do every day. Much of what you read and watch includes visuals that help you understand information. These visuals can be maps, charts, diagrams, graphs, photographs, illustrations, and so on. They can inform you, explain a topic or an idea, entertain you, or persuade you.

Websites use visuals, too. It is important for you to be able to view visuals critically in order to evaluate what you are seeing or reading.

## Representing

Representing is creating a visual to convey an idea. It is important for you to be able to create and use visuals in your own written work and presentations. You can use graphic organizers, diagrams, charts, posters, and artwork to illustrate and explain your ideas. Following are some examples of visuals.

## HOW TO READ MAPS AND DIAGRAMS

### Maps

Maps help us learn more about our world. They show the location of places such as countries, states, and cities. Some maps show where mountains, rivers, and lakes are located.

Many maps have helpful features. For example, a **compass rose** shows which way is north. A **scale** shows how miles or kilometers are represented on the map. A **key** shows what different colors or symbols represent.

◀ Three trails on which cowboys drove cattle north from Texas

**438**

## Diagrams

Diagrams are drawings or plans used to explain things or show how things work. They are often used in social studies and science books. Some diagrams show pictures of how objects look on the outside or on the inside. Others show the different steps in a process.

This diagram shows what a kernel of corn looks like on the inside.

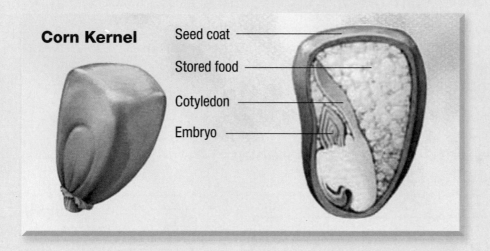

**Corn Kernel**

Seed coat

Stored food

Cotyledon

Embryo

A **flowchart** is a diagram that uses shapes and arrows to show a step-by-step process. The flowchart below shows the steps involved in baking chicken fingers. Each arrow points to the next step.

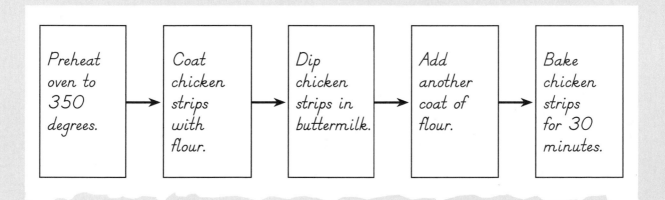

Preheat oven to 350 degrees. → Coat chicken strips with flour. → Dip chicken strips in buttermilk. → Add another coat of flour. → Bake chicken strips for 30 minutes.

Graphs organize and explain information. They show how two or more kinds of information are related, or how they are alike. Graphs are often used in math, science, and social studies books. Three common kinds of graphs are **line graphs**, **bar graphs**, and **circle graphs**.

### Line Graphs

A line graph shows how information changes over a period of time. This line graph explains how, over a period of about 100 years, the Native-American population of Central Mexico decreased by more than 20 million people. Can you find the population in the year 1540? What was it in 1580?

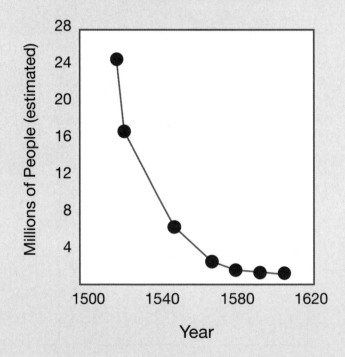

## Native-American Population of Central Mexico

## Bar Graphs

We use bar graphs to compare information. For example, this bar graph compares the populations of the thirteen United States in 1790. It shows that, in 1790, Virginia had over ten times as many people as Delaware.

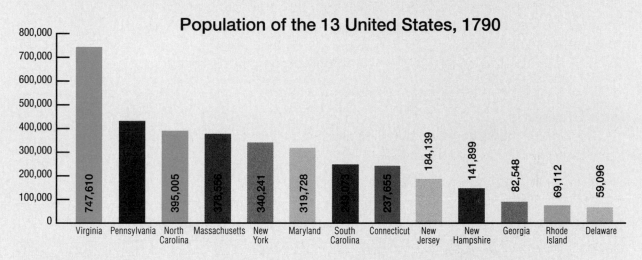

Population of the 13 United States, 1790

## Circle Graphs

A circle graph is sometimes called a pie chart because it looks like a pie cut into slices. Circle graphs are used to show how different parts of a whole thing compare to one another. In a circle graph, all the "slices" add up to 100 percent. This circle graph shows that only 29 percent of the earth's surface is covered by land. It also shows that the continent of Asia takes up 30 percent of the earth's land.

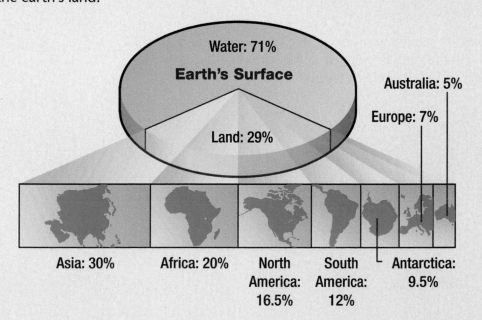

## HOW TO USE GRAPHIC ORGANIZERS

A graphic organizer is a diagram that helps you organize information and show relationships among ideas. Because the information is organized visually, a graphic organizer tells you—in a quick snapshot—how ideas are related. Before you make a graphic organizer, think about the information you want to organize. How are the ideas or details related? Choose a format that will show those relationships clearly.

**Venn diagrams** and **word webs** are commonly used graphic organizers. Here is an example of each.

### Venn Diagrams

A Venn diagram shows how two thing are alike and different. The diagram below compares oranges and bananas.

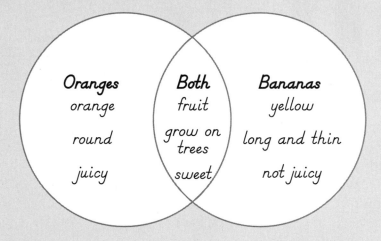

### Word Webs

A word web is often used to help a writer describe something. The word web below lists five sensory details that describe popcorn.

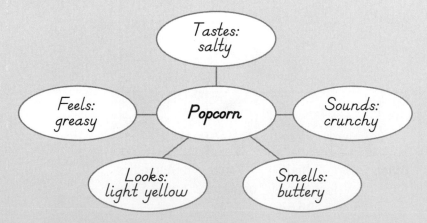

# Writing Handbook

## Narration

When writers tell a story, they use narration. There are many kinds of narration. Most include characters, a setting, and a sequence of events. Here are some types of narration.

A **short story** is a short, creative narrative. Most short stories have one or more characters, a setting, and a plot. A few types of short stories are realistic stories, fantasy stories, science-fiction stories, and adventure stories.

**Autobiographical writing** is a factual story of a writer's own life, told by the writer, usually in the first-person point of view. An autobiography may tell about the person's whole life or only a part of it.

**Biographical writing** is a factual story of a person's life told by another person. Most biographies are written about famous or admirable people.

## Description

Description, or descriptive writing, is writing that gives the reader a mental picture of whatever is being described. To do this, writers choose their words carefully. They use figurative language and include vivid sensory details.

## Persuasion

Writers use persuasion to try to persuade people to think or act in a certain way. Forms of persuasive writing include advertisements, essays, letters, editorials, speeches, and public-service announcements.

## Exposition

Exposition, or expository writing, is writing that gives information or explains something. The information that writers include in expository writing is factual. Here are some types of expository writing.

A **compare-and-contrast essay** analyzes the similarities and differences between or among things.

A **cause-and-effect essay** explains causes or effects of an event. For example, a writer might examine several causes of a single effect or several effects of a single cause.

Writers use a **problem-and-solution essay** to describe a problem and offer one or more solutions to it.

A **how-to essay** explains how to do or make something. The process is broken down into steps, which are explained in order.

A **summary** is a brief statement that gives the main ideas of an event or a piece of writing. One way to write a summary is to read a text and then reread each paragraph or section. Next put the text aside and write the main ideas in your own words in a sentence or two.

## Research Writing

Writers often use research to gather information about topics, including people, places, and things. Good research writing does not simply repeat information. It guides the readers through a topic, showing them why each fact matters and creating a complete picture of the topic. Here are some types of research writing.

**Research report** A research report presents information gathered from reference books, interviews, or other sources.

**Biographical report** A biographical report includes dates, details, and main events in a person's life. It can also include information about the time in which the person lived.

**Multimedia report** A multimedia report presents information through a variety of media, including text, slides, photographs, prerecorded music and sound effects, and digital imaging.

## Responses to Literature

A **literary essay** is one type of response to literature. In a literary essay, a writer discusses and interprets what is important in a book, short story, essay, article, or poem.

**Literary criticism** is another type of response to literature. Literary criticism is the result of a careful examination of one or more literary works. The writer makes a judgment by looking carefully and critically at various important elements in the work.

A book **critique** gives readers a summary of a book, encouraging the reader either to read it or to avoid reading it. A movie critique gives readers a summary of a movie, tells if the writer enjoyed the movie, and then explains the reasons why or why not.

A **comparison of works** compares the features of two or more works.

## Creative Writing

Creative writing blends imagination, ideas, and emotions, and allows the writer to present a unique view of the world. Poems, plays, short stories, dramas, and even some cartoons are examples of creative writing.

## Practical and Technical Documents

**Practical writing** is fact-based writing that people do in the workplace or in their day-to-day lives. A business letter, memo, school form, job application, and a letter of inquiry are a few examples of practical writing.

**Technical documents** are fact-based documents that identify a sequence of activities needed to design a system, operate machinery, follow a procedure, or explain the rules of an organization. You read technical writing every time you read a manual or a set of instructions.

In the following descriptions, you'll find tips for tackling several types of practical and technical writing.

**Business letters** are formal letters that follow one of several specific formats.

**News releases**, also called press releases, announce factual information about upcoming events. A writer might send a news release to a local newspaper, local radio station, TV station, or other media that will publicize the information.

**Guidelines** give information about how people should act or how to do something.

**Process explanations** are step-by-step explanations of how to do something. The explanation should be clear and specific and can include diagrams or other illustrations. Below is an example.

## KEYSTONE
### CD-ROM

**Usage Instructions**
1. Insert the *Keystone* CD-ROM into your CD drive.
2. Open "My Computer."
3. Double-click on your CD-ROM disk drive.
4. Click on the *Keystone* icon. This will launch the program.

## THE WRITING PROCESS

The **writing process** is a series of steps that can help you write effectively.

### Step 1: Prewrite

During **prewriting**, you collect topic ideas, choose a topic, plan your writing, and gather information.

A good way to get ideas for a topic is to **brainstorm**. Brainstorming means writing a list of all the topic ideas you can think of.

Look at your list of topic ideas. Choose the one that is the most interesting to you. This is your **topic**, the subject you will write about.

Plan your writing by following these steps:
- First, decide on the type of writing that works best with your topic. For example, you may want to write a description, a story, or an essay.
- The type of writing is called the **form** of writing.
- Then think about your **audience**. Identifying your audience will help you decide whether to write formally or informally.
- Finally, decide what your reason for writing is. This is your **purpose**. Is your purpose to inform your audience? To entertain them?

How you gather information depends on what you are writing. For example, for a report, you need to do research. For a description, you might list your ideas in a graphic organizer. A student named Becca listed her ideas for a description of her week at art camp in the graphic organizer below.

## Step 2: Draft

In this step, you start writing. Don't worry too much about spelling and punctuation. Just put your ideas into sentences.

Here is the first paragraph that Becca wrote for her first draft.

I saw an art contest advertised in the newspaper last spring. I entered my best drawing. I have always loved art. The prize was a week at an art camp in June with 9 other kids. I was very happy when I won.

## Step 3: Revise

Now it's time to revise, or make changes. Ask yourself these questions:
- Are my ideas presented in the order that makes the most sense?
- Does my draft have a beginning, a middle, and an end?
- Does each paragraph have a main idea and supporting details?

If you answered *no* to any of these questions, you need to revise. Revising can mean changing the order of paragraphs or sentences. It can mean changing general words for specific words. It can mean correcting errors.

Once you decide what to change, you can mark the corrections on your draft using editing marks. Here's how Becca marked up her first paragraph.

When I saw an art contest advertised in the newspaper last spring, I entered my best drawing. I have always loved art. The prize was a week at an art camp in June with nine other kids. I was very excited happy when I won.

## Step 4: Edit

In this step, you make a second draft that includes the changes you marked on your first draft. You can also add details you may have thought of since writing your first draft. Now you're ready to **proofread**, or check your work for errors and make final corrections.

Here's Becca's first draft after she finished proofreading.

My Week at Art Camp

I have always loved art. When I saw an art contest advertised in the newspaper last spring, I entered my best drawing. The prize was a week at an art camp in June with nine other students. I was very excited when I won.

The camp was located at the Everson museum of art. On the first day, we looked at paintings by different artists. My favorite was by a painter named Monet. He painted colorful land scapes of boats and gardens. On the second day, we began our own paintings. I choose to paint a picture of the duck pond on the campus. I worked hard on my painting because we were going to have an art show of all our work at the end of the week.

I learned alot about painting at camp. I especially liked learning to use watercolors. For example, I found out that you can make interesting designs by sprinkling salt on a wet watercolor painting.

I had a great time at art camp. The show at the end of the week was a big success, and I made some new friends. I hope to go again next year.

## Step 5: Publish

Prepare a final copy of your writing to **publish**, or share with your audience. Here are some publishing tips.

- Photocopy and hand out your work to your classmates.
- Attach it to an email and send it to friends.
- Send it to a school newspaper or magazine for possible publication.

Here is the final version of Becca's paper.

---

### My Week at Art Camp

I have always loved art. When I saw an art contest advertised in the newspaper last spring, I entered my best drawing. The prize was a week at an art camp in June with nine other students. I was very excited when I won.

The camp was located at the Everson Museum of Art. On the first day, we looked at paintings by different artists. My favorite was by a painter named Monet. He painted colorful landscapes of boats and gardens. On the second day, we began our own paintings. I chose to paint a picture of the duck pond on the campus. I worked hard on my painting because we were going to have an art show of all our work at the end of the week.

I learned a lot about painting at camp. I especially liked learning to use watercolors. For example, I found out that you can make interesting designs by sprinkling salt on a wet watercolor painting.

I had a great time at art camp. The show at the end of the week was a big success, and I made some new friends. I hope to go again next year.

---

Once you have shared your work with others, you may want to keep it in a **portfolio,** a folder or envelope with your other writing. Each time you write something, add it to your portfolio. Compare recent work with earlier work. See how your writing is improving.

## RUBRICS FOR WRITING

### What Is a Rubric?

A **rubric** is a tool, often in the form of a chart or a grid, that helps you assess your work. Rubrics are helpful for writing and speaking assignments.

To help you or others assess your work, a rubric offers several specific criteria to be applied to your work. Then the rubric helps you indicate your range of success or failure according to those specific criteria. Rubrics are often used to evaluate writing for standardized tests.

Using a rubric will save you time, focus your learning, and improve your work. When you know the rubric beforehand, you can keep the specific criteria for the writing in your mind as you write. As you evaluate the essay before giving it to your teacher, you can focus on the specific criteria that your teacher wants you to master—or on areas that you know present challenges for you. Instead of searching through your work randomly for any way to improve or correct it, you will have a clear and helpful focus.

### How Are Rubrics Structured?

Rubrics can be structured in several different ways:

1. Your teacher may assign a rubric for a specific assignment.
2. Your teacher may direct you to a rubric in your textbook.
3. Your teacher and your class may structure a rubric for a particular assignment together.
4. You and your classmates may structure a rubric together.
5. You can create your own rubric with your own specific criteria.

### How Will a Rubric Help Me?

A rubric will help you assess your work on a scale. Scales vary from rubric to rubric but usually range from 6 to 1, 5 to 1, or 4 to 1, with 6, 5, or 4 being the highest score and 1 being the lowest. If someone else is using the rubric to assess your work, the rubric will give your evaluator a clear range within which to place your work. If you are using the rubric yourself, it will help you improve your work.

### What Are the Types of Rubrics?

A **holistic rubric** has general criteria that can apply to a variety of assignments. An **analytic rubric** is specific to a particular assignment. The criteria for evaluation address the specific issues important in that assignment. The following pages show examples of both types of rubrics.

## Holistic Rubrics

**Holistic rubrics** such as this one are sometimes used to assess writing assignments on standardized tests. Notice that the criteria for evaluation are focus, organization, support, and use of conventions.

| Points | Criteria |
|---|---|
| **6 Points** | • The writing is focused and shows fresh insight into the writing task.<br>• The writing is marked by a sense of completeness and coherence and is organized with a logical progression of ideas.<br>• A main idea is fully developed, and support is specific and substantial.<br>• A mature command of the language is evident.<br>• Sentence structure is varied, and writing is free of fragments.<br>• Virtually no errors in writing conventions appear. |
| **5 Points** | • The writing is focused on the task.<br>• The writing is organized and has a logical progression of ideas, though there may be occasional lapses.<br>• A main idea is well developed and supported with relevant detail.<br>• Sentence structure is varied, and the writing is free of fragments.<br>• Writing conventions are followed correctly. |
| **4 Points** | • The writing is focused on the task, but unrelated material may intrude.<br>• Clear organizational pattern is present, though lapses occur.<br>• A main idea is adequately supported, but development may be uneven.<br>• Sentence structure is generally fragment free but shows little variation.<br>• Writing conventions are generally followed correctly. |
| **3 Points** | • Writing is focused on the task, but unrelated material intrudes.<br>• Organization is evident, but writing may lack a logical progression of ideas.<br>• Support for the main idea is present but is sometimes illogical.<br>• Sentence structure is free of fragments, but there is almost no variation.<br>• The work demonstrates a knowledge of conventions, with misspellings. |
| **2 Points** | • The writing is related to the task but generally lacks focus.<br>• There is little evidence of an organizational pattern.<br>• Support for the main idea is generally inadequate, illogical, or absent.<br>• Sentence structure is unvaried, and serious errors may occur.<br>• Errors in writing conventions and spellings are frequent. |
| **1 Point** | • The writing may have little connection to the task.<br>• There has been little attempt at organization or development.<br>• The paper seems fragmented, with no clear main idea.<br>• Sentence structure is unvaried, and serious errors appear.<br>• Poor diction and poor command of the language obscure meaning.<br>• Errors in writing conventions and spelling are frequent. |
| **Unscorable** | • The response is unrelated to the task or is simply a rewording of the prompt.<br>• The response has been copied from a published work.<br>• The student did not write a response.<br>• The response is illegible.<br>• The words in the response are arranged with no meaning.<br>• There is an insufficient amount of writing to score. |

## Analytic Rubrics

This analytic rubric is an example of a rubric to assess a persuasive essay. It will help you assess presentation, position, evidence, and arguments.

| Presentation | Position | Evidence | Arguments |
|---|---|---|---|
| **6 Points** Essay clearly and effectively addresses an issue with more than one side. | Essay clearly states a supportable position on the issue. | All evidence is logically organized, well presented, and supports the position. | All reader concerns and counterarguments are effectively addressed. |
| **5 Points** Most of essay addresses an issue that has more than one side. | Essay clearly states a position on the issue. | Most evidence is logically organized, well presented, and supports the position. | Most reader concerns and counterarguments are effectively addressed. |
| **4 Points** Essay adequately addresses issue that has more than one side. | Essay adequately states a position on the issue. | Many parts of evidence support the position; some evidence is out of order. | Many reader concerns and counterarguments are adequately addressed. |
| **3 Points** Essay addresses issue with two sides but does not present second side clearly. | Essay states a position on the issue, but the position is difficult to support. | Some evidence supports the position, but some evidence is out of order. | Some reader concerns and counterarguments are addressed. |
| **2 Points** Essay addresses issue with two sides but does not present second side. | Essay states a position on the issue, but the position is not supportable. | Not much evidence supports the position, and what is included is out of order. | A few reader concerns and counterarguments are addressed. |
| **1 Point** Essay does not address issue with more than one side. | Essay does not state a position on the issue. | No evidence supports the position. | No reader concerns or counterarguments are addressed. |

## WRITING LETTERS

### Friendly Letters

A friendly letter is less formal than a business letter. It is a letter to a friend, a family member, or anyone with whom the writer wants to communicate in a personal, friendly way. Most friendly letters are made up of five parts: the **date**, the **greeting** (or salutation), the **body**, the **closing**, and the **signature**. The greeting is followed by a comma, and the paragraphs in the body are indented.

The purpose of a friendly letter is usually to share personal news and feelings, to send or to answer an invitation, or to express thanks.

In this letter, Maité tells her friend Julio about her new home.

**Greeting**          **Date**

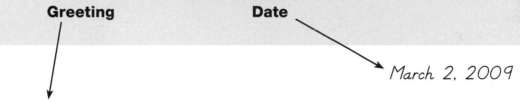

March 2, 2009

Dear Julio,

I was so happy to receive your letter today. I am feeling much better. My mom and I finally finished decorating my room. We painted the walls green and the ceiling pink. At first, my mom was nervous to paint the ceiling something other than white, but I knew it would look good. Now that my bedroom is finished, Manhattan is starting to feel more like home.

Over the weekend I went to the Museum of Natural History. The whale exhibit made me think of back home and how you and I would spend hours at the beach. I am starting to adjust to city life, but I miss the smell of salt in the air and collecting sea glass on the shore.

My parents said I can spend the summer with my grandparents at their beach house. They said I could invite you for a couple of weeks. We'll go swimming every day. I can't wait!

**Body**

Your friend,    ← **Closing**

Maité    ← **Signature**

453

## Business Letters

Business letters follow one of several formats. In **block format**, each part of the letter begins at the left margin. A double space is used between paragraphs. In **modified block format**, some parts of the letter are indented to the center of the page. No matter which format is used, all letters in business format have a date, an inside address, a greeting (or salutation), a body, a closing, and a signature. These parts are shown on the model business letter below, formatted in block style.

---

June 11, 2009 ⟵————————— **Date**

Edward Sykes, Vice President
Animal Rights Group ⟵————————— **Inside Address**
154 Denver Street
Syosset, NY 11791

Dear Mr. Sykes: ⟵————————— **Greeting**

Many students at Bellevue High School would like to learn about animal rights for a project we're starting next fall. We've read about your program on your website and would like to know more about your activities.

Would you send us some information about your organization? We're specifically interested in learning what we as students can do to help protect animals. About 75 students have expressed interest so far—I think we'll have the people power to make the project a success and have an impact.

⟵————— **Body**

Please help us get started. Thank you for your time and consideration.

Sincerely, ⟵————— **Closing**

*Pedro Rodriguez* ⟵————— **Signature**

Pedro Rodriguez

---

The **inside address** shows where the letter will be sent. The **greeting** is punctuated with a colon. The **body** of the letter states the writer's purpose. The **closing** "Sincerely" is common, but "Yours truly" or "Respectfully yours" are also acceptable. The writer types his or her name and writes a **signature**.

Forms are preprinted documents with spaces for the user to enter specific information. Some include directions; others assume that users will follow the labels and common conventions. Two common forms in the workplace are fax cover sheets and applications. When you fill out forms, it is important to do the following:

- Fill them out accurately and completely.
- Write neatly in blue or black ink.
- Include only information that is asked for on the form.

Forms usually have limited space in which to write. Because space is limited, you can use standard symbols and abbreviations, such as *$10/hr* to mean "10 dollars per hour."

# FAX COVER SHEET

**To:** *Mr. Robert Thompson*    **From:** *Laura Rivas*

**Fax:** *(001) 921-9833*    **Pages:** *2 (including cover sheet)*

**Date:** *12/04/09*

**Re:** *Job Application*

**Message:**

*Dear Mr. Thompson:*

*Thank you for meeting with me today about the sales associate position at Story Land Bookshop. The following page is my completed application form.*

*Sincerely,*

*Laura Rivas*

# Filling in an Application for Employment

## Story Land Bookshop

**PRE-EMPLOYMENT QUESTIONNAIRE**
EQUAL OPPORTUNITY EMPLOYER
*Date:* 12/04/2009

### PERSONAL INFORMATION

**Name (last name first)**
Rivas, Laura

**Social Security No.**
145-53-6211

| **Present Address** | **City** | **State** | **Zip Code** |
|---|---|---|---|
| 351 Middleton Road | Osborne | TX | 78357 |

| **Permanent Address** | **City** | **State** | **Zip Code** |
|---|---|---|---|
| Same | | | |

**Phone No.**
(001) 661-1567

**Referred by**
Josh Logan

### EMPLOYMENT DESIRED

| **Position** | **Start Date** | **Salary Desired** |
|---|---|---|
| Sales associate | immediately | $10/hr. |

Are you presently employed? ☐ Yes ☑ No
May we contact your former employer? ☑ Yes ☐ No
Were you ever employed by this company? ☐ Yes ☑ No

### EDUCATION

| **Name and Location of School** | **Yrs Attended** | **Did you graduate?** |
|---|---|---|
| Osborne High School, Osborne TX | 3 | Expect to graduate 2010 |

### FORMER EMPLOYERS

| **Name and Address of Employer** | **Salary** | **Position** |
|---|---|---|
| Blue River Summer Camp 127 Horse Lane Millwood, TX 78721 | $195 per week | Junior camp counselor |

| **Date Month and Year** | **Reason for Leaving** |
|---|---|
| 6/20/09 to 9/20/09 | Summer ended |

## CONDUCTING RESEARCH

### Reference Skills

There is a wide range of print and electronic references you can use to find many different kinds of information.

### Encyclopedias

Encyclopedias contain facts on a great many subjects. They provide basic information to help you start researching a topic. Use encyclopedias for basic facts, background information, and suggestions for additional research.

### Periodicals

Periodicals are magazines and journals. Once you've used a periodical index to identify the articles you want to read, ask a librarian to help you locate the periodicals. Often, past issues of magazines are stored electronically on microfilm, a database, or CD-ROMs. The librarian can help you use these resources. Use the table of contents, the titles, and other magazine features to help you find information.

### Biographical References

These books provide brief life histories of famous people in many different fields. Biographical references may offer short entries similar to those in dictionaries or longer articles more like those in encyclopedias. Most contain an index to help you locate entries.

### Nonfiction Books

Nonfiction books about your topic can also be useful reference tools. Use titles, tables of contents, prefaces, chapter headings, glossaries, indexes, and appendixes to locate the information you need.

### Almanacs

Almanacs are published annually. They contain facts and statistics about many subjects, including government, world history, geography, entertainment, business, and sports. To find a subject in a printed almanac, refer to the index in the front or back. In an electronic almanac, you can usually find information by typing a subject or key word.

### Electronic Databases

Available on CD-ROMs or on-line, electronic databases provide quick access to a wealth of information on a topic. Using a search feature, you can easily access any type of data, piece together related information, or look at the information in a different way.

## PROOFREADING

All forms of writing—from a letter to a friend to a research paper—are more effective when they are error-free. Once you are satisfied with the content of your writing, polish the grammar, usage, and mechanics.

Challenge yourself to learn and apply the skills of proofreading to everything you write. Review your writing carefully to find and correct all errors. Here are the broad categories that should direct your proofreading:

☑ **CHECK YOUR SPELLING:** Use a dictionary or an electronic spelling checker to check any spelling of which you are unsure.

☑ **CHECK YOUR GRAMMAR AND USAGE:** Use a writing handbook to correct problems in grammar or usage.

☑ **REVIEW CAPITALIZATION AND PUNCTUATION:** Review your draft to be sure you've begun each sentence with a capital letter and used proper end punctuation.

☑ **CHECK THE FACTS:** When your writing includes facts gathered from outside sources, confirm the accuracy of your work. Consult reference materials. Check names, dates, and statistics.

| Editing Marks | | |
|---|---|---|
| **To:** | **Use This Mark:** | **Example:** |
| add something | ∧ | We ate rice, bean, and corn. |
| delete something | ℰ | We ate rice, beans, and corns. |
| start a new paragraph | ¶ | ¶ We ate rice, beans, and corn. |
| add a comma | ⌄ | We ate rice, beans and corn. |
| add a period | ⊙ | We ate rice, beans, and corn⊙ |
| switch letters or words | ∼ | We ate rice, baens, and corn. |
| change to a capital letter | ≡ | we ate rice, beans, and corn. |
| change to a lowercase letter | ⧸ | WE ate rice, beans, and corn. |

## CITING SOURCES

### Proofreading and Preparing Manuscript

Before preparing a final copy, proofread your manuscript.

- Choose a standard, easy-to-read font.
- Type or print on one side of unlined 8 1/2" x 11" paper.
- Set the margins for the side, top, and bottom of your paper at approximately one inch. Most word-processing programs have a default setting that is appropriate.
- Double-space the document.
- Indent the first line of each paragraph.
- Number the pages in the upper right corner.

Follow your teacher's directions for formatting formal research papers. Most papers will have the following features: Title page, Table of Contents or Outline, Works Consulted List.

### Crediting Sources

When you credit a source, you acknowledge where you found your information and you give your readers the details necessary for locating the source themselves. Within the body of the paper, you provide a short citation, a footnote number linked to a footnote, or an endnote number linked to an endnote reference. These brief references show the page numbers on which you found the information. Prepare a reference list at the end of the paper to provide full bibliographic information on your sources. These are two common types of reference lists:

A **bibliography** provides a listing of all the resources you consulted during your research. A **works consulted list** lists the works you have referenced in your paper.

The chart on the next page shows the Modern Language Association format for crediting sources. This is the most common format for papers written in the content areas in middle school and high school. Unless instructed otherwise by your teacher, use this format for crediting sources.

# MLA Style for Listing Sources

| | |
|---|---|
| Book with one author | Pyles, Thomas. *The Origins and Development of the English Language*. 2nd ed. New York: Harcourt Brace Jovanovich, Inc., 1971. |
| Book with two or three authors | McCrum, Robert, William Cran, and Robert MacNeil. *The Story of English*. New York: Penguin Books, 1987. |
| Book with an editor | Truth, Sojourner. *Narrative of Sojourner Truth*. Ed. Margaret Washington. New York: Vintage Books, 1993. |
| Book with more than three authors or editors | Donald, Robert B., et al. *Writing Clear Essays*. Upper Saddle River, NJ: Prentice Hall, Inc., 1996. |
| Single work from an anthology | Hawthorne, Nathaniel. "Young Goodman Brown." *Literature: An Introduction to Reading and Writing*. Ed. Edgar V. Roberts and Henry E. Jacobs. Upper Saddle River, NJ: Prentice-Hall, Inc., 1998. 376–385. [Indicate pages for the entire selection.] |
| Introduction in a published edition | Washington, Margaret. Introduction. *Narrative of Sojourner Truth*. By Sojourner Truth. New York: Vintage Books, 1993, pp. v–xi. |
| Signed article in a weekly magazine | Wallace, Charles. "A Vodacious Deal." *Time* 14 Feb. 2000: 63. |
| Signed article in a monthly magazine | Gustaitis, Joseph. "The Sticky History of Chewing Gum." *American History* Oct. 1998: 30–38. |
| Unsigned editorial or story | "Selective Silence." Editorial. *Wall Street Journal* 11 Feb. 2000: A14. [If the editorial or story is signed, begin with the author's name.] |
| Signed pamphlet or brochure | [Treat the pamphlet as though it were a book.] |
| Pamphlet with no author, publisher, or date | *Are You at Risk of Heart Attack?* n.p. n.d. [n.p. n.d. indicates that there is no known publisher or date.] |
| Filmstrips, slide programs, videocassettes, DVDs, and other audiovisual media | *The Diary of Anne Frank*. Dir. George Stevens. Perf. Millie Perkins, Shelly Winters, Joseph Schildkraut, Lou Jacobi, and Richard Beymer. Twentieth Century Fox, 1959. |
| Radio or television program transcript<br>Internet | "Nobel for Literature." Narr. Rick Karr. *All Things Considered*. National Public Radio. WNYC, New York. 10 Oct. 2002. Transcript.<br>*National Association of Chewing Gum Manufacturers*. 19 Dec. 1999 <http://www.nacgm.org/consumer/funfacts.html> [Indicate the date you accessed the information. Content and addresses at websites change frequently.] |
| Newspaper | Thurow, Roger. "South Africans Who Fought for Sanctions Now Scrap for Investors." *Wall Street Journal* 11 Feb. 2000: A1+ [For a multipage article, write only the first page number on which it appears, followed by a plus sign.] |
| Personal interview<br>CD (with multiple publishers) | Smith, Jane. Personal interview. 10 Feb. 2000.<br>Simms, James, ed. *Romeo and Juliet*. By William Shakespeare. CD-ROM. Oxford: Attica Cybernetics Ltd.; London: BBC Education; London: HarperCollins Publishers, 1995. |
| Signed article from an encyclopedia | Askeland, Donald R. "Welding." *World Book Encyclopedia*. 1991 ed. |

# Technology Handbook

**WHAT IS TECHNOLOGY?**

Technology is a combination of resources that can help you do research, find information, and write. Good sources for research include the Internet and your local library. The library contains databases where you can find many forms of print and non-print resources, including audio and video recordings.

## The Internet

The Internet is an international network, or connection, of computers that share information with each other. It is a popular source for research and finding information for academic, professional, and personal reasons. The World Wide Web is a part of the Internet that allows you to find, read, and organize information. Using the Web is a fast way to get the most current information about many topics.

Words or phrases can be typed into the "search" section of a search engine, and websites that contain those words will be listed for you to explore. You can then search a website for the information you need.

## Information Media

Media is all the organizations, such as television, radio, and newspapers that provide news and information for the public. Knowing the characteristics of various kinds of media will help you to spot them during your research. The following chart describes several forms of information media.

| Types of Information Media | |
|---|---|
| **Television News Program** | • Covers current news events<br>• Gives information objectively |
| **Documentary** | • Focuses on one topic of social interest<br>• Sometimes expresses controversial opinions |
| **Television Newsmagazine** | • Covers a variety of topics<br>• Entertains and informs |
| **Commercial** | • Presents products, people, or ideas<br>• Persuades people to buy or take action |

## Other Sources of Information

There are many other reliable print and non-print sources of information to use in your research. For example: magazines, newspapers, professional or academic journal articles, experts, political speeches, press conferences.

Most of the information from these sources is also available on the Internet. Try to evaluate the information you find from various media sources. Be careful to choose the most reliable sources for this information.

# HOW TO USE THE INTERNET FOR RESEARCH

## Keyword Search

Before you begin a search, narrow your subject to a keyword or a group of **keywords**. These are your search terms, and they should be as specific as possible. For example, if you are looking for information about your favorite musical group, you might use the band's name as a keyword. You might locate such information as band member biographies, the group's history, fan reviews of concerts, and hundreds of sites with related names containing information that is irrelevant to your search. Depending on your research needs, you might need to narrow your search.

## How to Narrow Your Search

If you have a large group of keywords and still don't know which ones to use, write out a list of all the words you are considering. Then, delete the words that are least important to your search, and highlight those that are most important.

**Use search connectors to fine-tune your search:**

**AND:** narrows a search by retrieving documents that include both terms.
For example: *trumpets AND jazz*

**OR:** broadens a search by retrieving documents including any of the terms.
For example: *jazz OR music*

**NOT:** narrows a search by excluding documents containing certain words.
For example: *trumpets NOT drums*

## Good Search Tips

1. Search engines can be case-sensitive. If your first try at searching fails, check your search terms for misspellings and search again.
2. Use the most important keyword first, followed by the less important ones.
3. Do not open the link to every single page in your results list. Search engines show pages in order of how close it is to your keyword. The most useful pages will be located at the top of the list.
4. Some search engines provide helpful tips for narrowing your search.

## Respecting Copyrighted Material

The Internet is growing everyday. Sometimes you are not allowed to access or reprint material you find on the Internet. For some text, photographs, music, and fine art, you must first get permission from the author or copyright owner. Also, be careful not to plagiarize while writing and researching. Plagiarism is presenting someone else's words, ideas or work as your own. If the idea or words are not yours, be sure to give credit by citing the source in your work.

## HOW TO EVALUATE THE QUALITY OF INFORMATION

Since the media presents large amounts of information, it is important to learn how to analyze this information critically. Analyzing critically means you can evaluate the information for content, quality, and importance.

### How to Evaluate Information from Various Media

Sometimes the media tries to make you think a certain way instead of giving all the facts. These techniques will help you figure out if you can rely on information from the media.

- ☑ Ask yourself if you can trust the source, or if the information you find shows any bias. Is the information being given in a one-sided way?
- ☑ Discuss the information you find from different media with your classmates or teachers to figure out its reliability.
- ☑ Sort out facts from opinions. Make sure that any opinions given are backed up with facts. A fact is a statement that can be proved true. An opinion is a viewpoint that cannot be proved true.
- ☑ Be aware of any loaded language or images. Loaded language and images are emotional words and visuals used to persuade you.
- ☑ Check surprising or questionable information in other sources. Are there instances of faulty reasoning? Is the information adequately supported?
- ☑ Be aware of the kind of media you are watching. If it's a program, is it a documentary? A commercial? What is its purpose? Is it correct?
- ☑ Read the entire article or watch the whole program before reaching a conclusion. Then develop your own views on the issues, people, and information presented.

## How to Evaluate Information from the Internet

There is so much information available on the Internet that it can be hard to understand. It is important to be sure that the information you use as support or evidence is reliable and can be trusted. Use the following checklist to decide if a Web page you are reading is reliable and a credible source.

- ☑ The information is from a well-known and trusted website. For example, websites that end in **.edu** are part of an educational institution and usually can be trusted. Other cues for reliable websites are sites that end in **.org** for "organization" or **.gov** for "government." Sites with a **.com** ending are either owned by businesses or individuals.

- ☑ The people who write or are quoted on the website are experts, not just everyday people telling their ideas or opinions.

- ☑ The website gives facts, not just opinions.

- ☑ The website is free of grammatical and spelling errors. This is often a hint that the site was carefully made and will not have factual mistakes.

- ☑ The website is not trying to sell a product or persuade people. It is simply trying to give correct information.

- ☑ If you are not sure about using a website as a source, ask your teacher for advice. Once you become more aware of the different sites, you will become better at knowing which sources to trust.

## HOW TO USE TECHNOLOGY IN WRITING

### Personal Computers

A personal computer can be an excellent writing tool. It enables a writer to create, change, and save documents. The cut, copy, and paste features are especially useful when writing and revising.

### Organizing Information

Create a system to organize the research information you find from various forms of media, such as newspapers, books, and the Internet.

Using a computer and printer can help you in the writing process. You can change your drafts, see your changes clearly, and keep copies of all your work. Also, consider keeping an electronic portfolio. This way you can store and organize copies of your writing in several subject areas. You can review the works you have completed and see your improvement as a writer.

It is easy to organize electronic files on a computer. The desktop is the main screen, and holds folders that the user names. For example, a folder labeled "Writing Projects September" might contain all of the writing you do during that month. This will help you find your work quickly.

As you use your portfolio, you might think of better ways to organize it. You might find you have several drafts of a paper you wrote, and want to create a separate folder for these. Every month, take time to clean up your files.

### Computer Tips

1. Rename each of your revised drafts using the SAVE AS function. For example, if your first file is "essay," name the first revision "essay2" and the next one "essay3."
2. If you share your computer with others, label a folder with your name and keep your files separate by putting them there.
3. Always back up your portfolio on a server or a CD.

Personal computer ▶

465

# Glossary

**access** the right to enter a place, use something, or see something

**accommodation** way of solving a problem between two people or groups so that both are satisfied

**accustomed** be used to something and accept it as normal

**achieve** to succeed in doing something, especially by working hard

**activist** a person who performs some kind of action in an effort to gain social or political change

**adapt** to change your behavior or ideas because of a new situation you are in

**adaptable** able to adjust

**adaptation** something that is changed to be used in a new or different way

**adequate** enough

**adult** a grown-up person

**advocate** someone who publicly supports someone or something

**affect** to do something that produces a change in someone or something

**allegory** a story, poem, painting, etc., in which the events and characters represent good and bad qualities

**alliteration** the use of the same sound in the beginning of several words, to make a special effect, especially in poetry

**analytical** able to use logic

**analyze** examine something in detail in order to understand it

**ancestor** someone in your family who lived a long time before you were born

**apathy** feeling of not being interested in something or not caring about life

**apparently** almost certainly

**approach** move closer to someone or something

**approached** moved close

**aristocratic** having the highest social class

**assonance** the repetition of vowel sounds

**assumed** took control, power, or a particular position

**attitude** the way you think or feel about something or someone

**authorized** given permission to do something

**avoidance** staying away from a person, place, or thing

**behavior** the things that a person or animal does, or the way in which they do them

**biometric** relating to machines that can be used to measure things such as people's eyes or fingerprints

**blog** a website that is made up of information about a particular subject, in which the newest information is always at the top of the page

**bred** kept animals or plants in order to develop new animals or plants

**captivity** the state of being a prisoner, or being kept in a small space

**categories** groups of people or things that are like one another in some way

**centuries** periods of a hundred years

**challenge** something that tests one's skills or ability

**championed** publicly fought for and defended an aim or idea

**character motivation** why a character in a book, play, or movie does something

**character traits** special qualities or features that someone or something has that make that person or thing different from others

**character** a person who takes part in the action of a story

**characterization** a particular description of someone or something in a story

**chemical** relating to changes that happen when two substances combine

**circumstances** the facts or conditions that affect a situation, action, event, etc.

**civil** of or pertaining to citizens (civil wars are wars between citizens of the same country)

**claim** an act of officially saying that you have a right to receive or own something

**clarifying** making something easier to understand by explaining it in more detail

**code** a system of words, letters, or signs that are used instead of ordinary writing to keep something secret

**committed** did something

**communicate** exchange information

**communication** the process of expressing thoughts and feelings or sharing information

**community** a group of people who live in the same town or area

**compromise** an agreement that is achieved after everyone involved accepts less than what he or she wanted at first

**concept** an idea or thought

**conclude** reach a decision based in facts or logic

**conduct** allow electricity or heat to travel along or through

**conflict** disagreement between people, groups, or countries, or with yourself

**Congress** a group of people chosen or elected to make the laws in a country

**consented** agreed

**constitutional** officially allowed or restricted by a government's set of rules

**construct** build something large such as a building, bridge, or sculpture

**construction** the process or method of building something large, such as a house or road

**consumers** those who buy or use goods and services

**contacted** got in touch with, wrote, or telephoned someone

**convinced** made someone decide to do something

**culture** the beliefs, customs, and way of life of a particular society

**cycle** related events that happen again and again in the same order

**data bank** a large amount of data stored in a computer system

**definitely** certainly, and without any doubt

**defuse** improve a difficult situation by making someone less angry

**descendents** people who are related to a person who lived a long time ago

**despite** in spite of something

**devious** using tricks or lies to get what you want

**diagnosis** the name of an illness a person has or what is wrong with something

**dialogue** a conversation in a book, play, or movie

**distinctive** different from other people or things and easy to recognize

**drama** a play that is about a serious topic or theme

**economics** the development and management of wealth

467

**elections** a process by which people decide who will represent them in government

**empathy** the ability to understand someone else's feelings and problems

**emphasis** special importance

**encounter** see or meet someone or something without planning to

**engaged** became involved in an activity

**entitled** gave someone the right to have or do something

**environment** the situations, things, and people that affect the way in which people live

**epidemic** an illness that spreads quickly to a lot of people

**equalized** made two or more things equal in size, value, etc.

**equipment** the tools, machines, etc., that you need for a particular activity

**establishment** an institution, especially a business, store, or hotel

**estimate** judge an approximate value, amount, cost, etc.

**ethical** morally good and correct

**evidence** words or facts that prove something

**expose** put someone in a situation, place, etc., that could be harmful or dangerous

**exposure** the harmful effects of staying outside for a long time in extremely cold weather

**expressed** said or did something to let people know what you think or feel

**external** on the outside

**factors** things that cause or influence a situation

**figurative language** writing that the reader isn't supposed to take literally

**first-person point of view** a way of telling a story in which the writer uses one character's perspective and the pronoun *I*

**flashback** part of a movie, play, book, etc., that shows something that happened earlier

**foreshadowing** a hint or clue in a story about what will happen later on

**fragility** weak and likely to become worse

**function** purpose; action that a thing performs

**generations** groups of people born around the same time

**genetic** relating to genes—the parts of a cell in a living thing that control how it develops

**host** a large number of things

**humane** treating people or animals in a way that is kind, not cruel

**hyperbole** a way of describing something by saying that it is much bigger, smaller, heavier, etc., than it really is

**identical** exactly the same

**identification** official documents that show who you are

**identified** be closely connected with an idea or group of people

**identities** the qualities that make people recognizable

**identity** who someone is, or what something is

**ignore** not pay attention to someone or something

**image** the opinion that people have about someone or something

**imagery** the use of words, pictures, or phrases to describe ideas or actions in poems, books, movies, etc.

**immune** not able to be affected by a disease or illness

individual  one person separate from others

individuals  particular people, considered separately from other people in the same group

influence  the power to affect the way someone or something behaves, thinks, or develops

injure  hurt a person or animal

injuries  physical harm or damages caused by an accident or attack

instructions  information or advice that tells you how to do something

intelligence  information about the secret activities of other governments; groups of people who gather this

intensified  increased in strength, size, or amount

interact  talk to other people and work together with them

intercepted  stopped someone or caught something that was going from one place to another

internal  inside something such as your body

interpret  to put the words spoken in one language into the words of another language

inventory  a list of all the things in a place

invisible  not able to be seen

irony  the part of a situation that is unusual or amusing because something strange happens, or the opposite of what is expected happens

issue  a subject or problem that people think is important

issues  subjects or problems that people discuss or debate

labor  work, especially that using a lot of physical effort

laser  a very strong and narrow beam of light used in some machines or in medical operations

logical  able to use reason

maneuver  to move or turn skillfully, or to move or turn something skillfully

manipulate  to make someone do what you want them to do by deceiving or influencing him or her

maximize  increase something as much as possible

methods  planned ways of doing something

moderation  control of your behavior so you keep your actions, feelings, habits, etc., within reasonable or sensible limits

mood  the feeling a literary work creates

moral  a lesson about what is right and wrong that you learn from a story or an event

narrator  the speaker or character who tells a story

negotiate  discuss something in order to reach an agreement

nerve  a very small part of your body that controls your movements and carries messages to and from your brain

neurons  small cells in the brain that send and receive messages

notion  an idea, belief, or opinion about something, especially one that you think is wrong

occupying  filling a particular amount of space

occur  happen; take place

offense  something that is wrong; a crime

official  approved by someone in authority

organ  a part of an animal or plant that has a special purpose organic grown without using dangerous chemicals

outcome final result

perception the way you understand something and your beliefs about what it is like

period length of time

persisted continued to exist or happen

perspective a way of thinking about something

petition a piece of paper signed by a lot of people and sent to someone in authority to ask for something or to complain about something

physical relating to someone's body

plot the story of a book, movie, or play

point of view the perspective from which a story is written

policy a way of doing things that has been officially agreed upon and chosen by a political party, business, or organization

precisely exactly

predict foretell

predominant more powerful, common, or noticeable than others

preserves keeps something from being harmed or damaged

presumption something that you think must be true

previous happening or existing before a particular event, time, or thing

prey an animal that is hunted and eaten by another animal

principle a moral rule or set of ideas that makes you behave in a particular way

principled having strong beliefs about what is morally right and wrong

privilege a special advantage given only to one person or group

process a series of actions

project a carefully planned piece of work

protest to say strongly that you do not agree with something

protested said strongly that you do not agree with something

publication a book, magazine, etc.

public awareness common knowledge about a social or political issue

react change in response to a message or stimulus

reaction something you feel or do because of what has happened or been said about you

reconstruct construct or enact again

regions fairly large areas of a state, country, etc., usually without exact limits

rekindled made someone have a particular feeling, thought, etc., again

relationship the way in which people behave toward each other

relay to send a message from one person, thing, or place to another person, thing, or place

repetition the act of saying or doing something again

required must be done because of a rule or law

respond react or answer

response an answer

restricted controlled or limited

reveal say or show something that was secret or hidden

rhyme a word that ends in the same sound as another

rhythm regular repeated pattern of sounds in music or speech

rigid stiff and not moving or bending

schedule plan; a list of times and events

setting the time and place of a story's action

society a large group of people who live together and share the same laws, religions, ways of doing things, etc.

spies people whose job is to watch other people secretly in order to discover facts or information about them

stage directions instructions that tell the actors what they should do and how they should do it

stages particular times or states in a long process

stationary not moving; still

status your social or professional rank or position in relation to other people

strategic having a military, business, or political purpose

stressful making you worry a lot

stressors things that cause stress

structure the way in which relationships between people or groups are organized in a society

surviving continuing to stay alive or exist

suspense a feeling of not knowing what is going to happen next

symbol picture, person, or object that represents something else

symptoms signs of something, especially a disease

system a group of things that work together for a particular purpose

systematic organized carefully and done thoroughly

tactics skillfully planned actions used for achieving something

target an object, person, or place chosen to be attacked

technologies equipment such as computers, lasers, etc.

technology the use of scientific or industrial methods

tension the feeling that exists when people do not trust each other and may suddenly attack or start arguing

theme the main idea or subject in a book, movie, speech, etc.

third-person point of view a way of telling a story in which the writer writes about the characters by using their names or using *he*, *she*, or *they* instead of *I*

threshold the level at which something begins to happen or have an effect on something

tolerant having the ability to accept something, even though you do not like it

tone the writer's attitude toward his or her audience and subject

traced studied or described the history, development, or origin of something

tradition something that people have done for a long time and continue to do

turbulent experiencing a lot of sudden changes and often wars or violence

unique different from all others

vacated left a seat, room, etc., so that someone else can use it

validate recognize or acknowledge

violating disobeying or doing something against a law, rule, agreement, etc.

virtually almost completely

visible able to be seen

visualize form a picture of someone or something in your mind

volunteers people who offer to do something without reward or pay

# Index of Skills

473

# Index of Authors, Titles, Art, and Artists

# Acknowledgments

**UNIT 1**

Excerpt from *Criss Cross* by Lynne Rae Perkins. Copyright © 2005, HarperCollins Publishers.

"Oranges" from *New and Selected Poems* by Gary Soto. Copyright © 1995 by Gary Soto. Used with permission of Chronicle Books, LLC, San Francisco, CA.

"Managing Stress." Excerpt from *Stress and Depression* by Sarah Lennard-Brown. Copyright © 2001 by Steck-Vaughn Company. Reprinted by permission of Harcourt Education.

Excerpt from *The Phantom Tollbooth* by Norton Juster. Copyright © 1961 and renewed 1989 by Norton Juster. Reprinted by permission of Random House Children's Books, a Division of Random House, Inc., Warner Bros. Entertainment Inc., and HarperCollins Publishers Ltd.

"Grandma Ling" by Amy Ling. Reprinted by permission of Gelston Hinds, Jr.

Excerpt from "Your Brain and Nervous System" from *Teens' Health*. Reprinted with permission from The Nemours Foundation.

**UNIT 2**

Excerpt from *Finding Miracles* and excerpt from "A Conversation with Julia Alvarez" by Julia Alvarez. Copyright © 2004 by Julia Alvarez. Published by Dell Laurel Leaf in 2006 and originally in hardcover by Alfred A. Knopf. Reprinted by permission of Susan Bergholz Literary Services, New York, NY, and Lamy, NM. All rights reserved.

Excerpt from *What Do You Stand For? For Teens: A Guide to Building Character* by Barbara A. Lewis. Copyright © 2005. Used with permission from Free Spirit Publishing Inc., Minneapolis, MN. All rights reserved.

Excerpt from "An Interview with An Na" from *A Step from Heaven* by An Na, published by Penguin Putnam Inc., 2002. Interview reprinted by permission of Penguin Group.

Excerpt from *A Step from Heaven* by An Na. Copyright © 2001 by An Na. Reprinted by permission of Boyds Mills Press.

"Learning English/Aprender el Inglés" by Luis Alberto Ambroggio from *Cool Salsa: Bilingual Poems on Growing Up Latino in the United States*, edited by Lori M. Carlson, Ballantine Publishing Group, 1994. Reprinted by permission of Luis Alberto Ambroggio.

Excerpt from *Crime Scene: How Investigators Use Science to Track Down the Bad Guys* by Vivien Bowers. Copyright © 1997, 2006 by Vivien Bowers. Used by permission of Maple Tree Press, Inc.

**UNIT 3**

Excerpt from *going going* by Naomi Shihab Nye. Copyright © 2005 by Naomi Shihab Nye. Used by permission of HarperCollins Publishers.

Excerpt from "Claudette Colman" from *Freedom Walkers: The Story of the Montgomery Bus Boycott* by Russell Freedman. Copyright © 2006 by Russell Freedman. All rights reserved. Reprinted by permission of Holiday House, Inc., NY.

"The Ravine" by Graham Salisbury from *On the Edge, Stories at the Brink*, edited by Lois Duncan. Copyright © 2000 by Graham Salisbury. Reprinted by permission of The Flannery Literary Agency.

"Speak Your Mind: How to Get a Voice In Government and Make Yourself Heard" by Charlotte Steinecke, and "Voice Box" by Emily Cutler from *New Moon®: The Magazine for Girls and Their Dreams*, September/October 2006. Copyright © New Moon® Publishing, Duluth, MN. Reprinted with permission.

**UNIT 4**

"The Great Circle" by Hehaka Sapa from *In a Sacred Manner I Live*, edited by Neil Philip. Copyright © 2001. Reprinted from *Black Elk Speaks: Being The Life Story of a Holy Man of the Oglala Sioux* by John G. Neihardt by permission of the University of Nebraska Press. Copyright © 1932, 1959, 1972 by John G. Neihardt. Copyright © 1961 by the John G. Neihardt Trust. Copyright © 2000 by the University of Nebraska Press.

Excerpt from *Touching Spirit Bear* by Ben Mikaelsen. Copyright © 2001 by Ben Mikaelsen. Used by permission of HarperColllins Publishers.

"Take a Chance." Excerpt from *Go Figure!* by Johnny Ball. Copyright © 2005, Dorling Kindersley.

"A Survival Mini-Manual" from *Time for Kids Almanac, 2006*. Copyright © 2006 by Time for Kids. Reprinted by permission.

"John Henry" from *American Tall Tales* by Adrien Stoutenburg. Copyright © 1966, 1968 by Adrien Stoutenburg. First appeared in *American Tall Tales*, published by Viking. Used by permission of Viking Penguin, a Division of Penguin Young Readers Group, a Member of Penguin Group (U.S.A.) Inc., 345 Hudson Street, New York, NY 10014 and Curtis Brown, Ltd. All rights reserved.

Lyrics to "John Henry" by Pete Seeger, Folkways Music Publications. Public domain.

Excerpt from *Franklin Delano Roosevelt: The New Deal President* by Brenda Haugen, Compass Point Books.

"Eleanor Roosevelt." Excerpt from *Madam President: The Extraordinary, True (and Evolving) Story of Women in Politics* by Catherine Thimmesh. Copyright © 2004 by Catherine Thimmesh. Reprinted by permission of Houghton Mifflin Company. All rights reserved.

## UNIT 5

Excerpt from *Romeo and Juliet* by William Shakespeare, adapted by Diana Stewart. Published by Raintree Publishers Inc., Milwaukee, WI, 1980.

"Furious Feuds: Enemies by Association" by Alfred Meyer. Copyright © Pearson Longman, 10 Bank Street, White Plains, NY 10606.

Excerpt from *Romiette and Julio* by Sharon M. Draper. Copyright © 1999 by Sharon M. Draper. Reprinted with the permission of Atheneum Books for Young Readers, an Imprint of Simon & Schuster Children's Publishing Division.

Excerpt from *Conflict Resolution: The Win-Win Situation* by Carolyn Casey. Copyright © 2001 by Carolyn Casey. Published by Enslow Publishers, Inc., Berkeley Heights, NJ. All rights reserved.

## UNIT 6

Excerpts from *Catherine, Called Birdy* by Karen Cushman. Copyright © 1994 by Karen Cushman. Reprinted by permission of Clarion Books, an Imprint of Houghton Mifflin Company. All rights reserved.

"The Dinner Party" by Mona Gardner. Copyright © 1942, 1970 by Saturday Review. Reprinted by permission.

Excerpt from *Oh, Rats! The Story of Rats and People* by Albert Marrin. Copyright © 2006 by Albert Marrin. Used by permission of Dutton Children's Books, a Division of Penguin Young Readers Group, a Member of Penguin Group (U.S.A.) Inc., 345 Hudson Street, New York, NY. 10014 and Wendy Schmalz Agency. All rights reserved.

Excerpt from *Outbreak: Plagues that Changed History* by Bryn Barnard. Copyright © 2005 by Bryn Barnard. Used by permission of Crown Publishers, an Imprint of Random House Children's Books, a Division of Random House, Inc.

Excerpt from *Dateline: Troy*. Copyright © 1996, 2006 by Paul Fleischman. Reproduced by permission of the publisher Candlewick Press, Inc., Cambridge, MA, and the author.

Excerpt from *Top Secret: A Handbook of Codes, Ciphers, and Secret Writing*. Copyright © 2004 by Paul B. Janeczko. Reproduced by permission of the publisher Candlewick Press, Inc., Cambridge, MA.

# Credits

Images; 311 right, Charles Gullung/Zefa/CORBIS; 312, bottom, Image 100/CORBIS; 314 bottom, Thinkstock/CORBIS; 316 bottom, Richard Hutchings/PhotoEdit; 318 bottom, David Young-Wolff/PhotoEdit; 319 bottom, SW Productions/Photodisc/Getty Images; 320 right, Ariel Skelley/CORBIS; 322 bottom, Nick North/CORBIS; 323 right, H. Schmid/Zefa/CORBIS.

UNIT 6: 334–335 background, Purestock/Getty Images; 334 top-left, Courtesy of the Library of Congress; 334 top-center, Bob Daemmrich/PhotoEdit; 334 top-right, Dagli Orti/The Art Archive; 334 bottom, John Rush/Stock Illustration Source/Getty Images; 335 top, © Bob Daemmrich/The Image Works; 335 center, Topical Press Agency/Hulton Archive/Getty Images; 335 bottom, Jeffrey Hamilton/Digital Vision/Getty Images; 336 right, Courtesy of the Library of Congress; 337 right, © The British Library/Dorling Kindersley; 339 right, De Agostini Editore Picture Library/Getty Images; 343 bottom, Fred Mertz/Clarion Books, Cover from An American Plague: The True and Terrifying Story of the Yellow Fever Epidemic of 1793 by Jim Murphy. Jacket illustration copyright © 2003 by Leslie Evans. Reprinted by permission of Clarion Books, an imprint of Houghton Mifflin Company; 349 right, Archivo Iconografico, S.A./Bettmann/CORBIS; 351, bottom, North Wind Picture Archives; 353 right, Bob Daemmrich/PhotoEdit; 354–359 background, Richard Kaylin/Stone Allstock/Getty Images; 354 right, AKG Images/British Library; 355 top, SPL/Photo Researchers, Inc.; 355 bottom, A B Dowsett/ Legacy Corporate Digital Archive/Photo Researchers, Inc.; 356 top, Malcolm McGregor/Dorling Kindersley; 356 bottom, Kent Wood/Photo Researchers, Inc.; 357 bottom, Penguin Group US, Penguin; 358 right, The Granger Collection, New York; 359 bottom, Photo of Bryn Barnard courtesy of the author; 360 right, Nicole Duplaix/Peter Arnold, Inc.; 363 right, China Photos/Getty Images; 364 bottom, Danita Delimont Photography/Ancient Art & Architecture; 365 right, Archivo Iconografico, S.A/CORBIS; 366 right, Bettmann/CORBIS; 369 top-right, Hulton Archive Photos/Getty Images; 370 upper-left, CORBIS; 372 upper-right, Bettmann/CORBIS; 373 bottom, Brittany Duncan/Candlewick Press; 375 right, Dagli Orti/The Art Archive; 377 right, Shutterstock; 378 left, Clive Streeter/Dorling Kindersley/Courtesy of The Science Museum, London; 378 right, © Bob Daemmrich/The Image Works; 379 bottom, Mel Lindstrom/Mira; 381 right, C Squared Studios/Photodisc/Getty Images.; 382–387, background, Harnett/Hanzon/Photodisc/Getty Images; 382–387 Hulton Archive Photos/Getty Images; 384 top, Dave King/Dorling Kindersley; 384 bottom, Dorling Kindersley/Courtesy of the H Keith Melton Collection; 385 bottom, Dorling Kindersley/Courtesy of the H Keith Melton Collection; 377 bottom, Brittany Duncan/Candlewick Press; 391 right, Bettmann/CORBIS; 394 bottom, Charles Gupton/CORBIS.

# Smithsonian American Art Museum
# List of Artworks

## UNIT 1 Bridging the Distance
**Page 68**
Philip Evergood
*Dowager in a Wheelchair* (detail)
1952
oil on fiberboard
47⅞ x 36 in.
Smithsonian American Art Museum, Gift of the Sara Roby Foundation

**Page 69**
Yuriko Yamaguchi
*Reach Out #3*
1989
wood
34 x 72½ x 3 in.
Smithsonian American Art Museum, Gift of Anthony T. Podesta
© Smithsonian American Art Museum

## UNIT 2 Exploring Mixed Identity in America
**Page 134**
Maria Castagliola
*A Matter of Trust*
1994
paper on fiberglass screen with cotton thread
72 x 72 x ⅛ in.
Smithsonian American Art Museum, Gift of the artist
© 1994 Maria Castagliola

**Page 135**
Pepón Osorio
*El Chandelier*
1988
chandelier with plastic toys and other objects
60⅞ x 42 in. diam.
Smithsonian American Art Museum, Museum purchase through the Smithsonian Latino
Initiatives Pool and the Smithsonian Institution Collections Acquisition Program
© 1988 Pepón Osorio

## UNIT 3 Battling Inequality
**Page 200**
William H. Johnson
*Three Great Abolitionists: A. Lincoln, F. Douglass, J. Brown*
about 1945
oil on paperboard
37⅜ x 34¼ in.
Smithsonian American Art Museum, Gift of the Harmon Foundation

**Page 201**
Miriam Schapiro and Sherry Brody
*Dollhouse*
1972
mixed media
79¾ x 82 x 8½ in.
Smithsonian American Art Museum, Museum purchase through the Gene Davis Memorial Fund
© Smithsonian American Art Museum

## UNIT 4 Beating the Odds
**Page 266**
Carmen Lomas Garza
*Lotería-Tabla Llena*
1972
Hand-colored etching and aquatint on paper
16¾ x 21 in.
Smithsonian American Art Museum, Gift of Tomas Ybarra-Frausto

**Page 267**
Eric Hilton
*Storm*
1996
kiln-formed crystal ground and granite
9½ x 8 x 8 in.
Smithsonian American Art Museum, Gift of the James Renwick Alliance
on the occasion of the 25th anniversary of the Renwick Gallery
© Smithsonian American Art Museum

## UNIT 5 Fighting for Land
**Page 332**
George Catlin
*Comanche Warriors, with White Flag, Receiving the Dragoons*
1834–35
oil on canvas
24 x 29⅛ in.
Smithsonian American Art Museum, Gift of Mrs. Joseph Harrison Jr.

**Page 333**
Jaune Quick-To-See Smith
*State Names*
2000
oil, collage, and mixed media on canvas
48 x 72 in.
Smithsonian American Art Museum, Gift of Elizabeth Ann Dugan and museum purchase
© 2000 Jaune Quick-To-See Smith

**484**

**UNIT 6 Old Becomes New**
**Page 402**
Richard Mawdsley
*Feast Bracelet*
1974
fabricated sterling silver, jade, and pearls
3¾ x 2¾ x 4½ in.
Smithsonian American Art Museum, Gift of the James Renwick Alliance in honor of Lloyd E. Herman, director, emeritus, Renwick Gallery

**Page 403**
Wendell Castle
*Ghost Clock*
1985
Honduras mahogany
86¼ x 24½ x 15 in.
Smithsonian American Art Museum, Museum purchase through the Smithsonian Institution Collections Acquisition Program
© 1985 Wendell Castle